fushigi yûgi™

The Mysterious Play
VOL. 15: GUARDIAN

Story & Art By
YUU WATASE

FUSHIGI YÛGI
THE MYSTERIOUS PLAY
VOL. 15: GUARDIAN
SHÔJO EDITION

STORY AND ART BY YUU WATASE

Editor's Note: At the author's request, the spelling of Ms. Watase's first name has been changed from "Yû," as it has appeared on previous VIZ publications, to "Yuu."

English Adaptation/William Flanagan
Touch-up & Lettering/Bill Spicer
Touch-up Assistance/Walden Wong
Design/Hidemi Sahara
Editor/Frances E. Wall

Managing Editor/Annette Roman
Director of Production/Noboru Watanabe
Vice President of Publishing/Alvin Lu
Sr. Director of Acquisitions/Rika Inouye
Vice President of Sales & Marketing/Liza Coppola
Publisher/Hyoe Narita

Printed in Canada

Published by VIZ, LLC
P.O. Box 77010
San Francisco, CA 94107

Shôjo Edition
10 9 8 7 6 5 4 3 2 1
First printing, June 2005

www.viz.com

store.viz.com

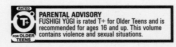

CONTENTS

STORY THUS FAR

In the winter of her third year of middle school, Miaka was whisked away into the pages of a mysterious old book called *The Universe of the Four Gods* and began a dual existence as an ordinary schoolgirl in modern Japan and a priestess of the god Suzaku in a fictional version of ancient China. Miaka fell in love with Tamahome, one of the Celestial Warriors of Suzaku responsible for the protection of the priestess. Miaka's best friend Yui was also sucked into the world of the book and became the priestess of Seiryu, the bitter enemy of Suzaku and Miaka. After clashing repeatedly with the corrupt and vengeful Seiryu Celestial Warriors, Miaka summoned Suzaku and vanquished her enemies, reconciled with Yui, and saved the earth from destruction. In the end, Suzaku granted Miaka one impossible wish: for Tamahome to be reborn as a human in the real world so that the two lovers would never again be separated.

Miaka enters Yotsubadai High School and plans to settle into a normal life with her beloved Tamahome, who is now named Taka Sukunami and working as an underpaid waiter! But the voice of Suzaku begins to invade Miaka's thoughts, and he gives Miaka a new mission: She must re-enter *The Universe of the Four Gods* and find seven special stones that contain Taka's memories from his former life as Tamahome...or her soulmate could disappear forever! After explaining this new task, Suzaku takes up residence in Miaka's watch, and with the help of the reunited Seven Celestial Warriors of Suzaku, Miaka and Taka are able to recover two of the stones. But a strange monster keeps terrorizing Miaka and Taka, and when the creature's master, a demon-god named Tenkô, appears, he declares himself a "Celestial Enemy" and says he will stop at nothing to thwart their quest and destroy the Suzaku Warriors! And Shi-Hang Lian, the dashing new exchange student at Yotsubadai High, has a sinister air about him....

The Universe of the Four Gods is based on ancient Chinese legend, but Japanese pronunciation of Chinese names differs slightly from their Chinese equivalents. Here is a short glossary of the Japanese pronunciation of the Chinese names in this graphic novel:

CHINESE	JAPANESE	PERSON OR PLACE	MEANING
Shi-Hang Lian	Shigyo Ren	Transfer student	Worship-Journey Collect
Tai Yi-Jun	Taiitsukun	An Oracle	Preeminent Person
Daichi-san	Daikyokuzan	A Mountain	Greatest Mountain
Hong-Nan	Konan	Southern Kingdom	Crimson South
Qu-Dong	Kutô	Eastern Kingdom	Gathered East
Feng-Qi	Hôki	Empress	Phoenix Beauty
Mang-Chen	Bôshin	Crown Prince	Spreading Dawn
Yang	Yô	A Monster	Illness
Po-Leiwu	Hakuraibu	A Technique	Body Puppet Dance
Lian-Fang	Renhô	A Yang monster	Retreat Virtue
Lai Lai	Nyan Nyan	Helper(s)	Daughter (x2)
Diedu	Kodoku	A Potion	Seduction Poison

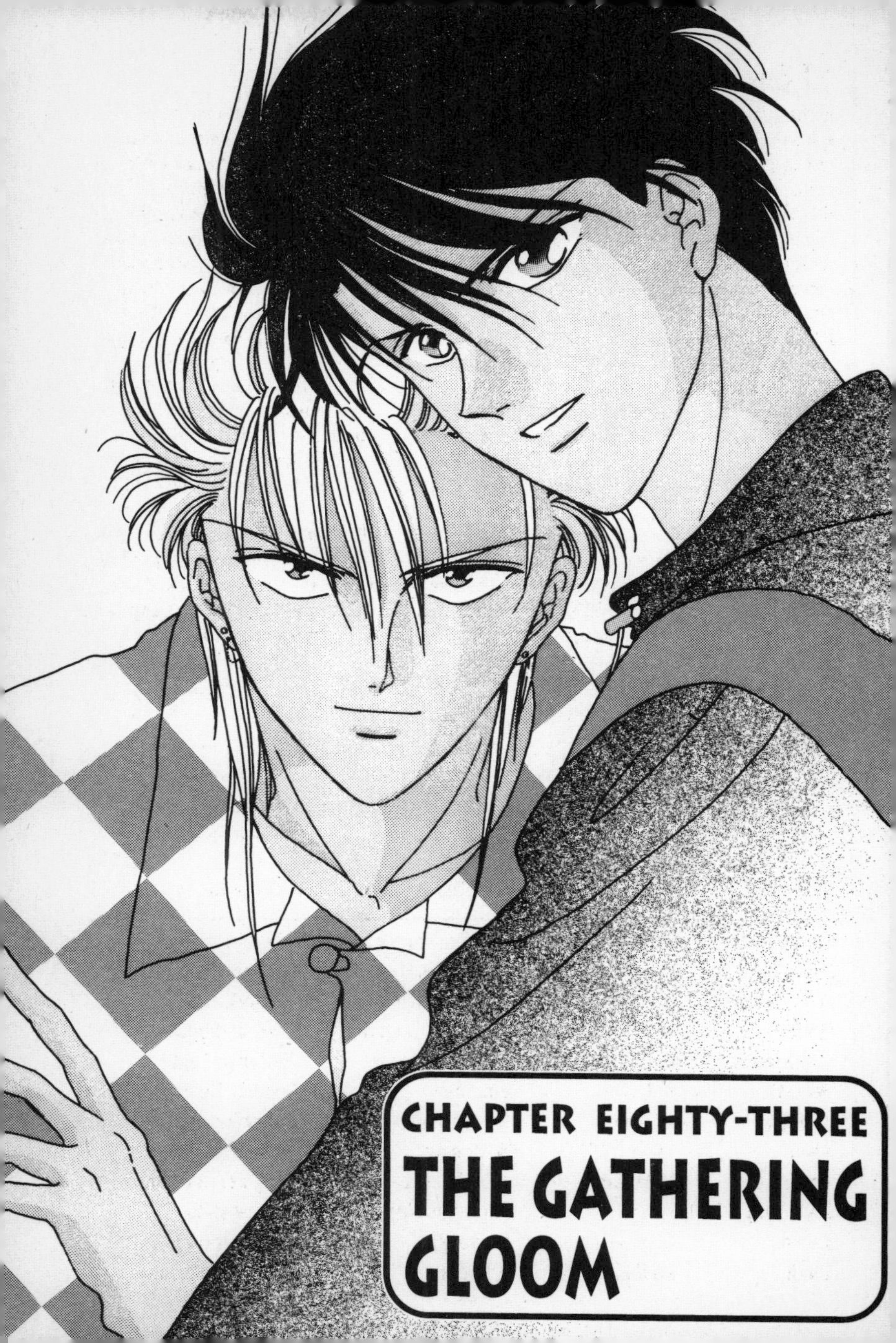

CHAPTER EIGHTY-THREE
THE GATHERING GLOOM

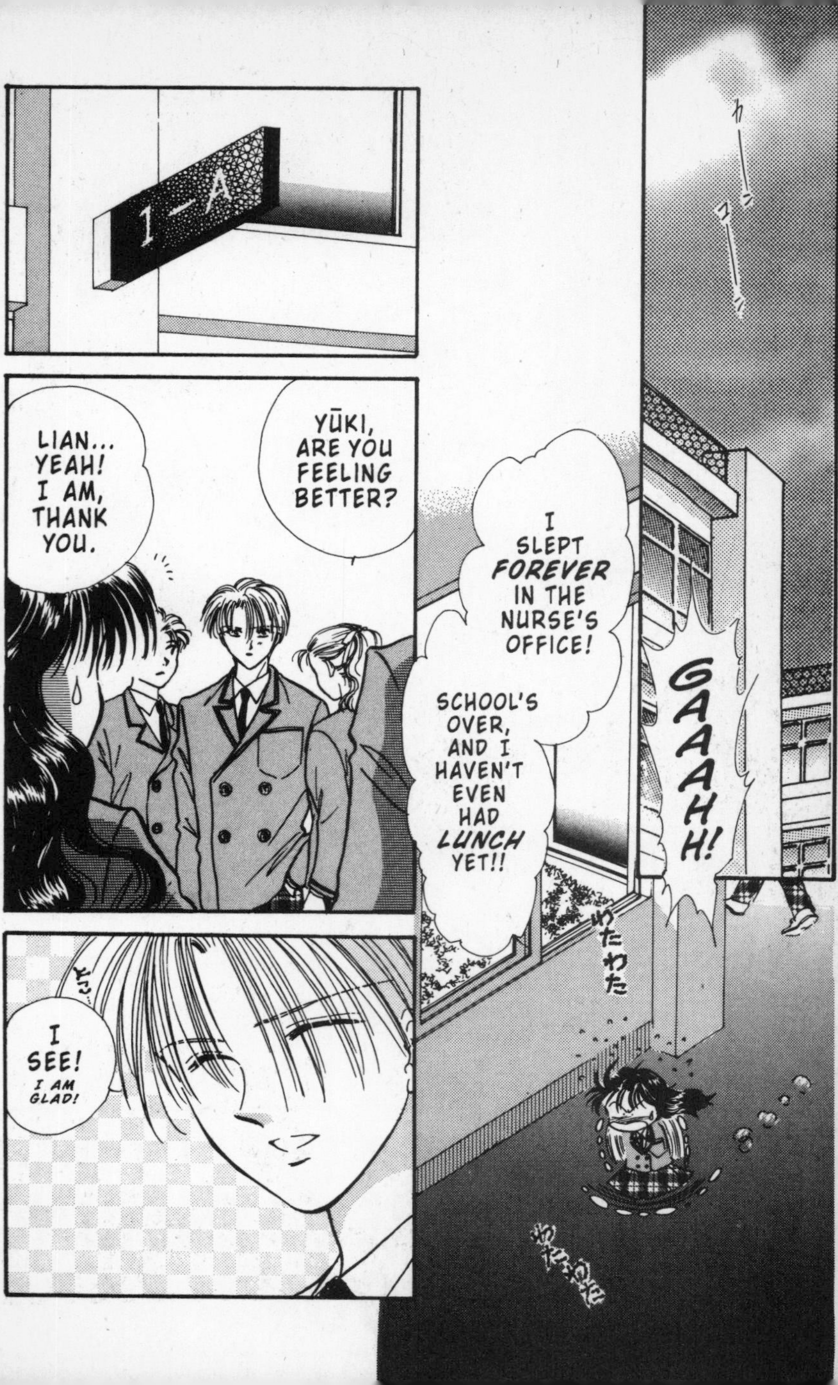
I SLEPT FOREVER IN THE NURSE'S OFFICE!
SCHOOL'S OVER, AND I HAVEN'T EVEN HAD LUNCH YET!!
GAAAH!
わたわた
1–A
YŪKI, ARE YOU FEELING BETTER?
LIAN... YEAH! I AM, THANK YOU.
I SEE! I AM GLAD!

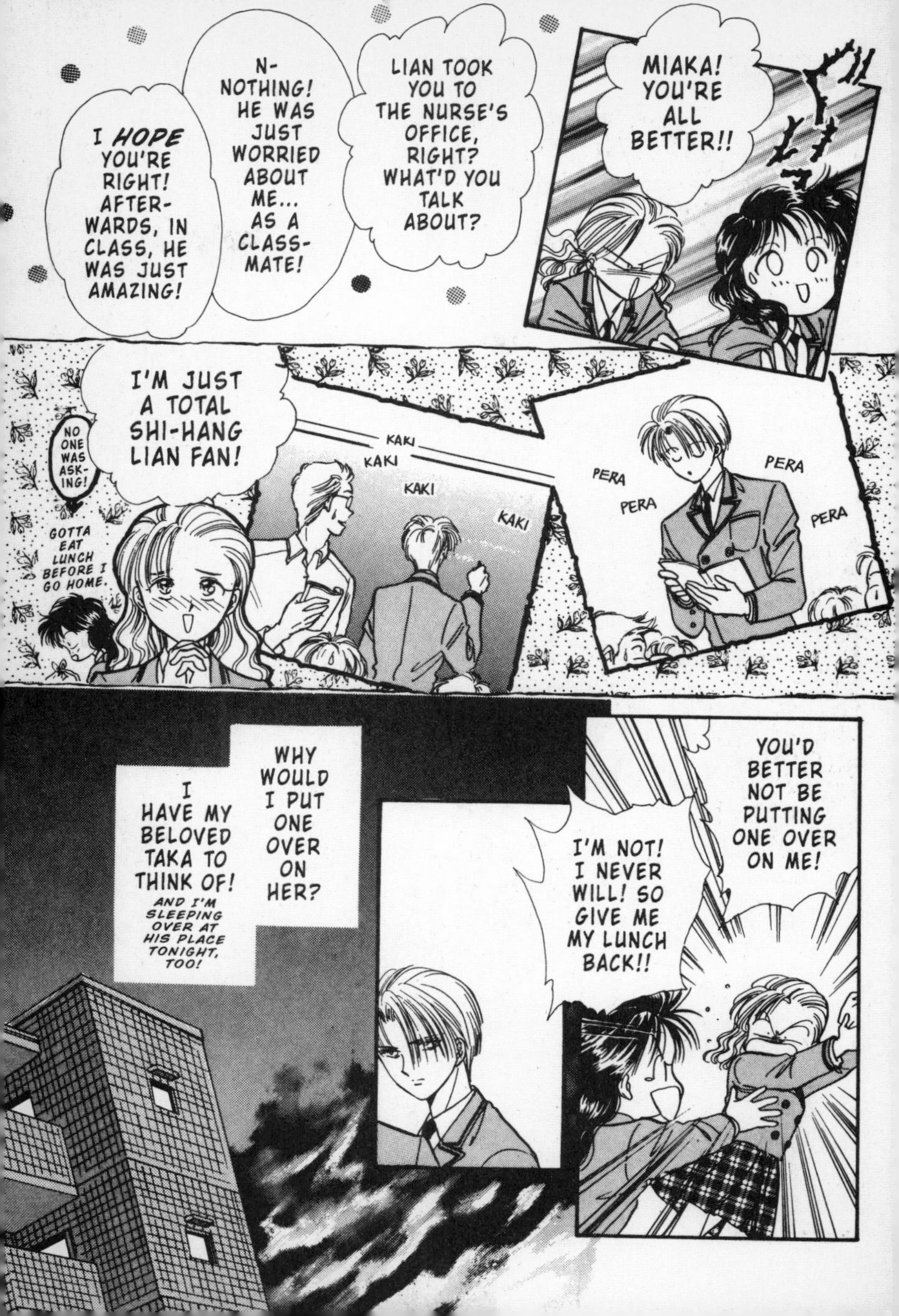
MIAKA! YOU'RE ALL BETTER!!
LIAN TOOK YOU TO THE NURSE'S OFFICE, RIGHT? WHAT'D YOU TALK ABOUT?
N-NOTHING! HE WAS JUST WORRIED ABOUT ME... AS A CLASSMATE!
I *HOPE* YOU'RE RIGHT! AFTER-WARDS, IN CLASS, HE WAS JUST AMAZING!
PERA
PERA
PERA
PERA
KAKI
KAKI
KAKI
KAKI
I'M JUST A TOTAL SHI-HANG LIAN FAN!
NO ONE WAS ASKING!
GOTTA EAT LUNCH BEFORE I GO HOME.
YOU'D BETTER NOT BE PUTTING ONE OVER ON ME!
I'M NOT! I NEVER WILL! SO GIVE ME MY LUNCH BACK!!
WHY WOULD I PUT ONE OVER ON HER?
I HAVE MY BELOVED TAKA TO THINK OF!
AND I'M SLEEPING OVER AT HIS PLACE TONIGHT, TOO!

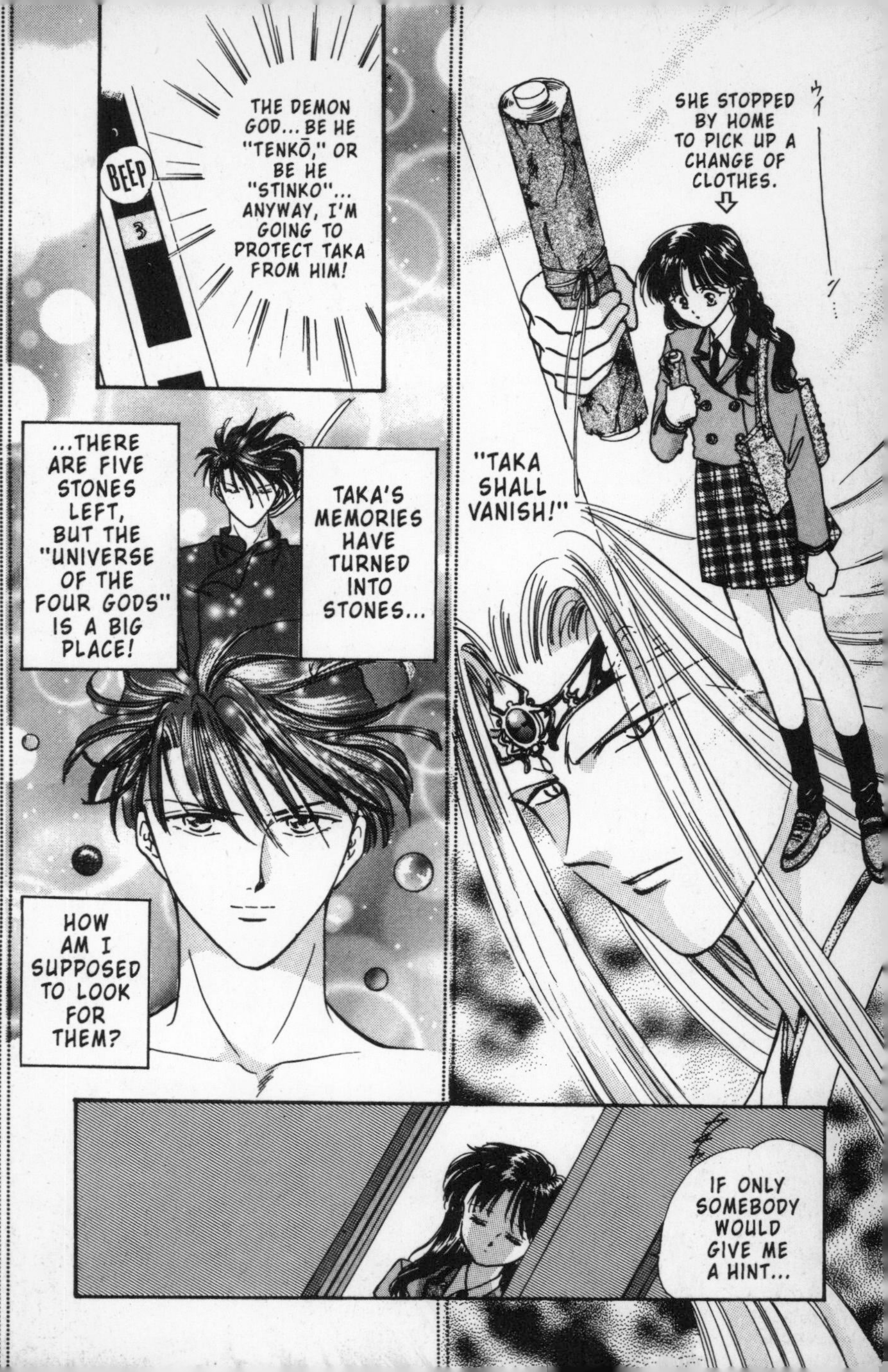
SHE STOPPED BY HOME TO PICK UP A CHANGE OF CLOTHES.
"TAKA SHALL VANISH!"
BEEP
THE DEMON GOD... BE HE "TENKŌ," OR BE HE "STINKO"... ANYWAY, I'M GOING TO PROTECT TAKA FROM HIM!
TAKA'S MEMORIES HAVE TURNED INTO STONES...
...THERE ARE FIVE STONES LEFT, BUT THE "UNIVERSE OF THE FOUR GODS" IS A BIG PLACE!
HOW AM I SUPPOSED TO LOOK FOR THEM?
IF ONLY SOMEBODY WOULD GIVE ME A HINT...

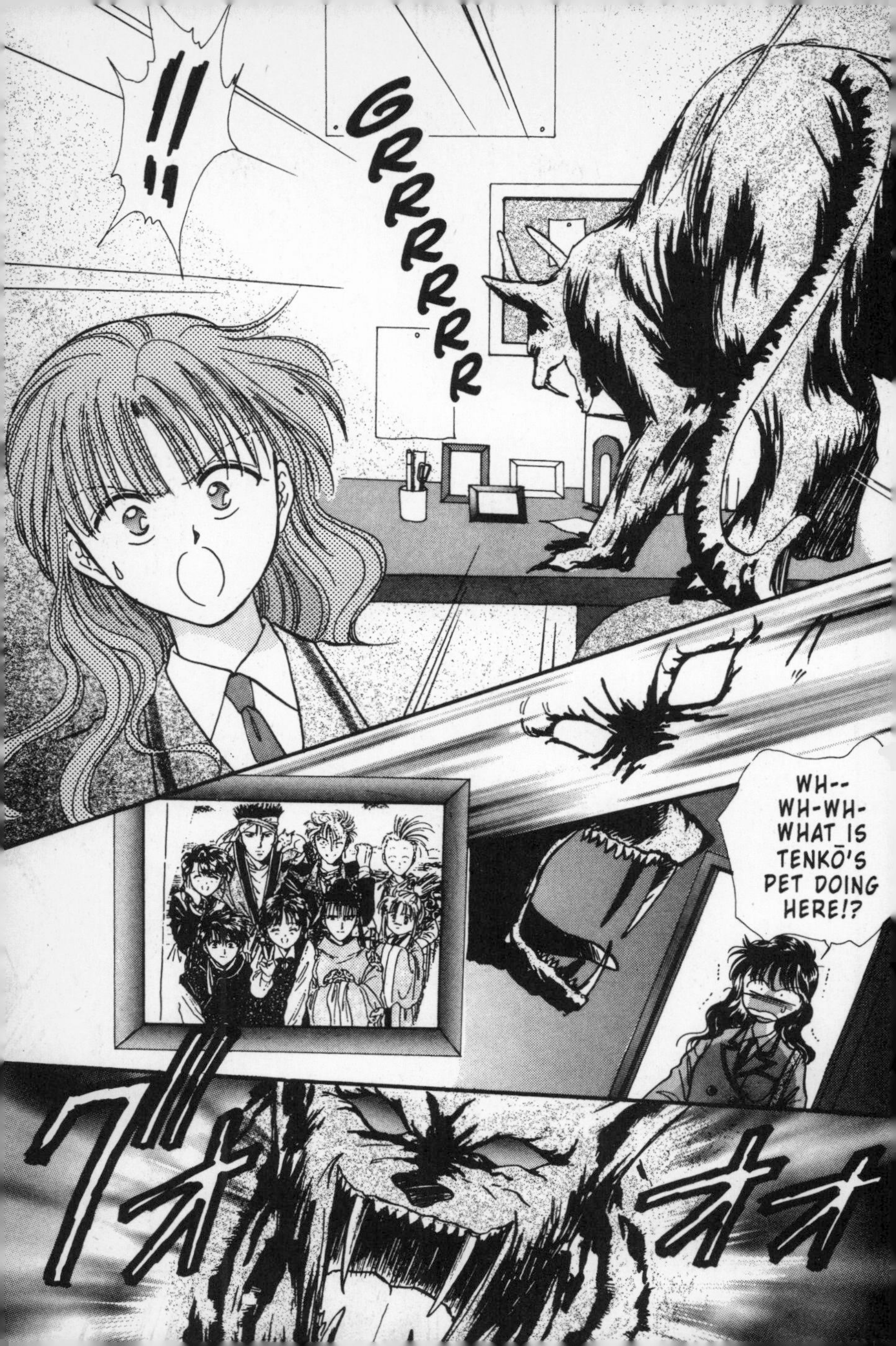
GRRRRRRR
!!
WH-- WH-WH- WHAT IS TENKŌ'S PET DOING HERE!?
ワオオオ

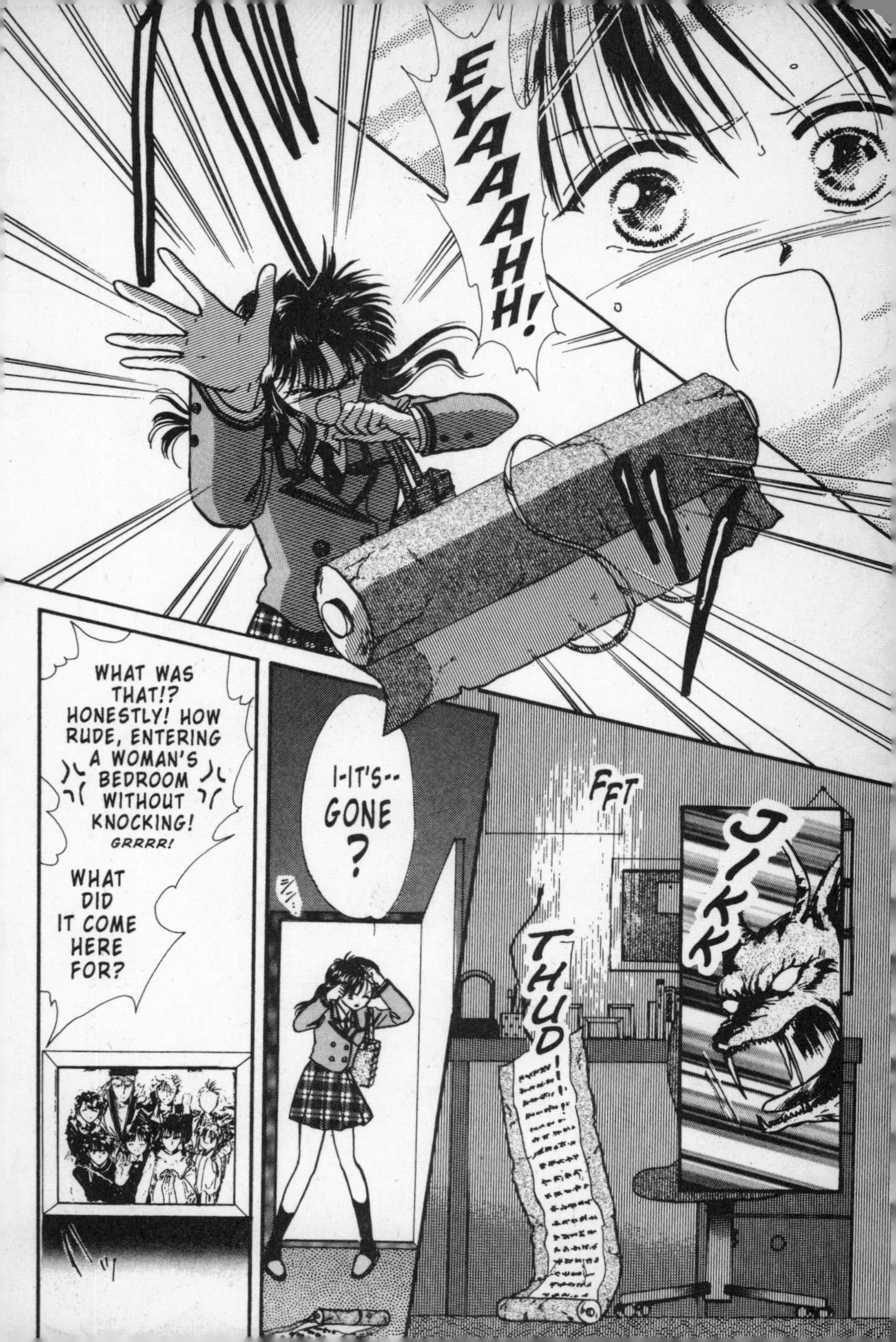
EYAAAHH!
FFT
JIKK
THUD!
I-IT'S-- GONE ?
WHAT WAS THAT!? HONESTLY! HOW RUDE, ENTERING A WOMAN'S BEDROOM WITHOUT KNOCKING! GRRRR!
WHAT DID IT COME HERE FOR?

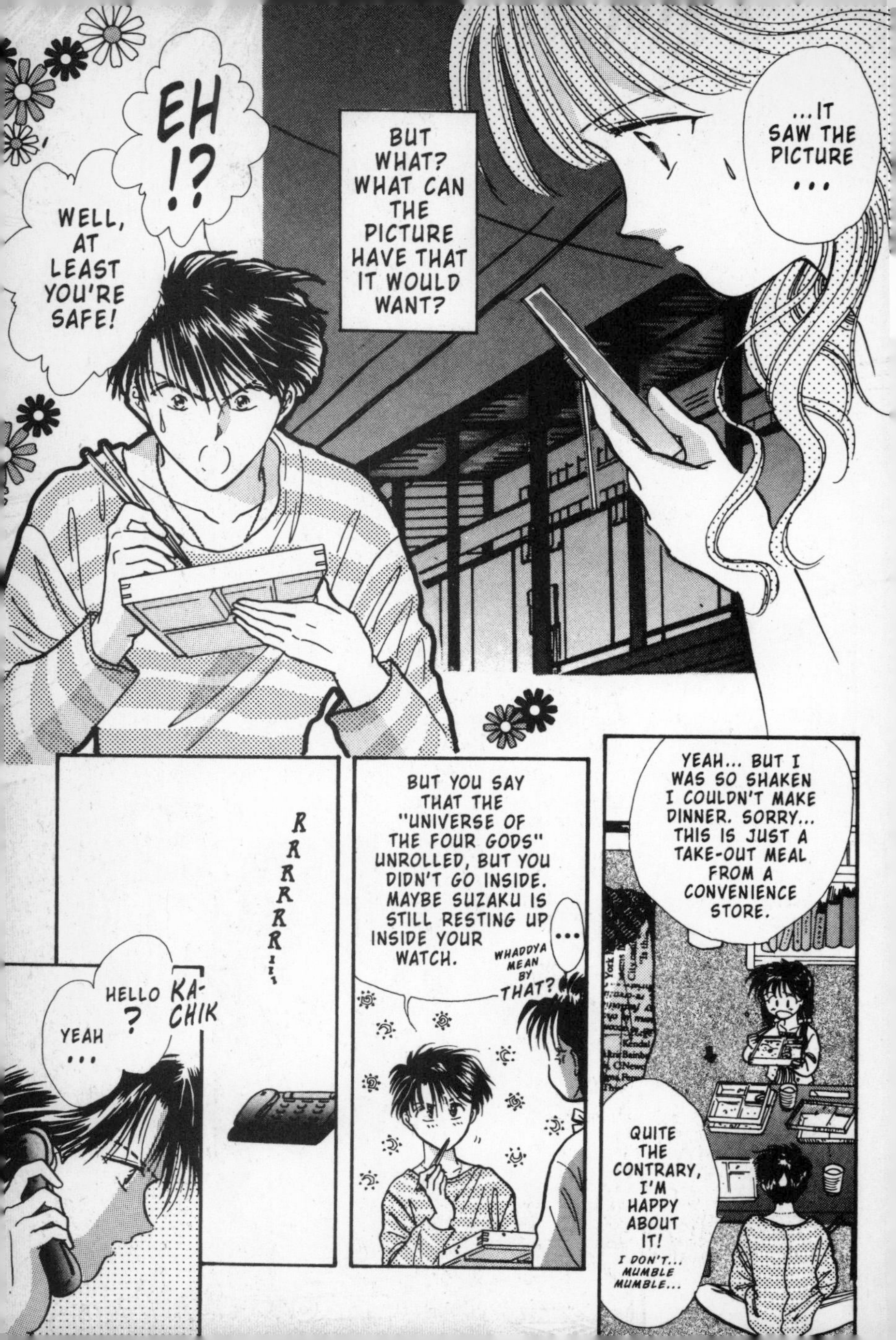
...IT SAW THE PICTURE...
BUT WHAT? WHAT CAN THE PICTURE HAVE THAT IT WOULD WANT?
EH!?
WELL, AT LEAST YOU'RE SAFE!
YEAH... BUT I WAS SO SHAKEN I COULDN'T MAKE DINNER. SORRY... THIS IS JUST A TAKE-OUT MEAL FROM A CONVENIENCE STORE.
QUITE THE CONTRARY, I'M HAPPY ABOUT IT!
I DON'T... MUMBLE MUMBLE...
BUT YOU SAY THAT THE "UNIVERSE OF THE FOUR GODS" UNROLLED, BUT YOU DIDN'T GO INSIDE. MAYBE SUZAKU IS STILL RESTING UP INSIDE YOUR WATCH.
...
WHADDYA MEAN BY THAT?
RRRRR
KA-CHIK
HELLO?
YEAH...

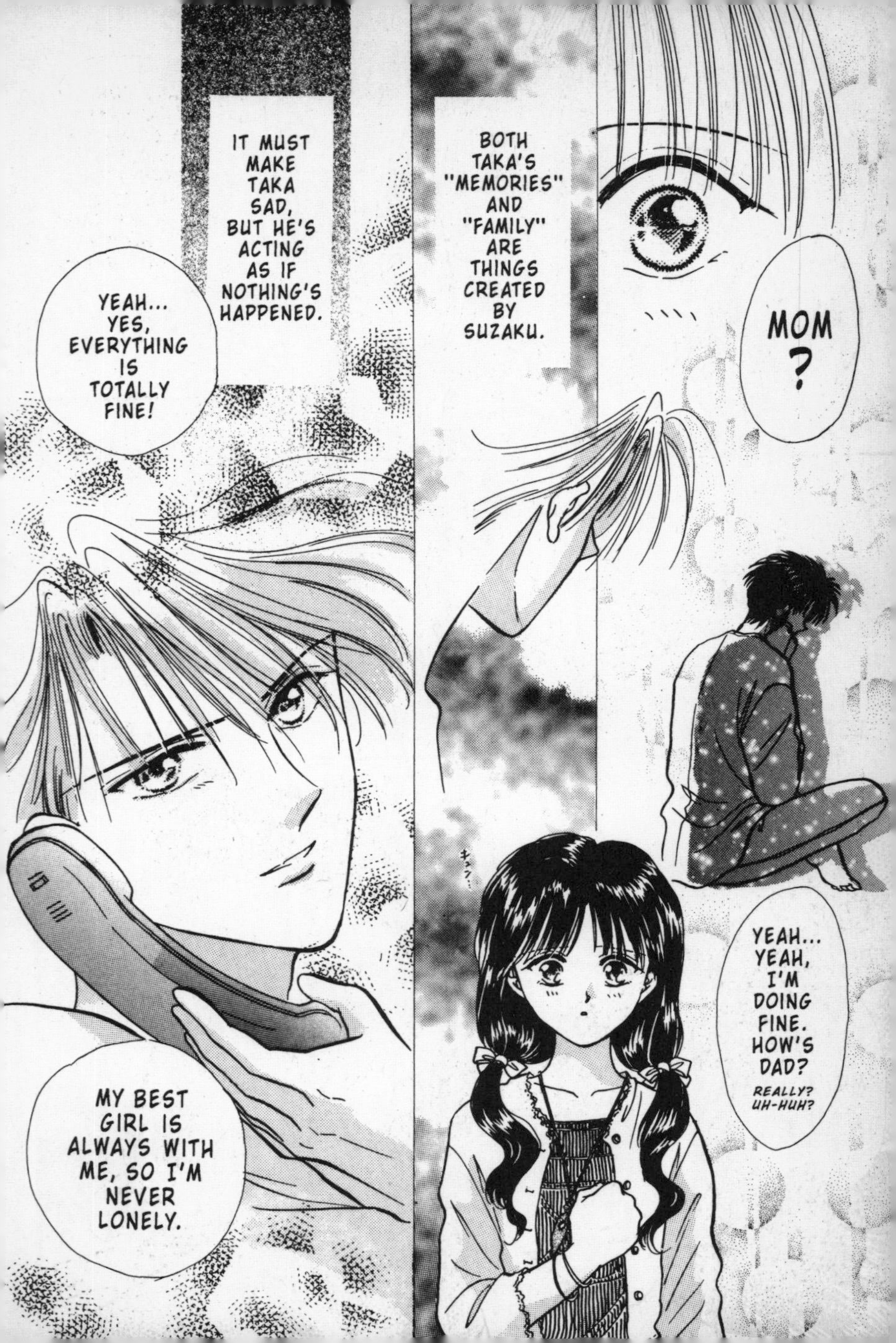
MOM ?
BOTH TAKA'S "MEMORIES" AND "FAMILY" ARE THINGS CREATED BY SUZAKU.
YEAH... YEAH, I'M DOING FINE. HOW'S DAD?
REALLY? UH-HUH?
IT MUST MAKE TAKA SAD, BUT HE'S ACTING AS IF NOTHING'S HAPPENED.
YEAH... YES, EVERYTHING IS TOTALLY FINE!
MY BEST GIRL IS ALWAYS WITH ME, SO I'M NEVER LONELY.

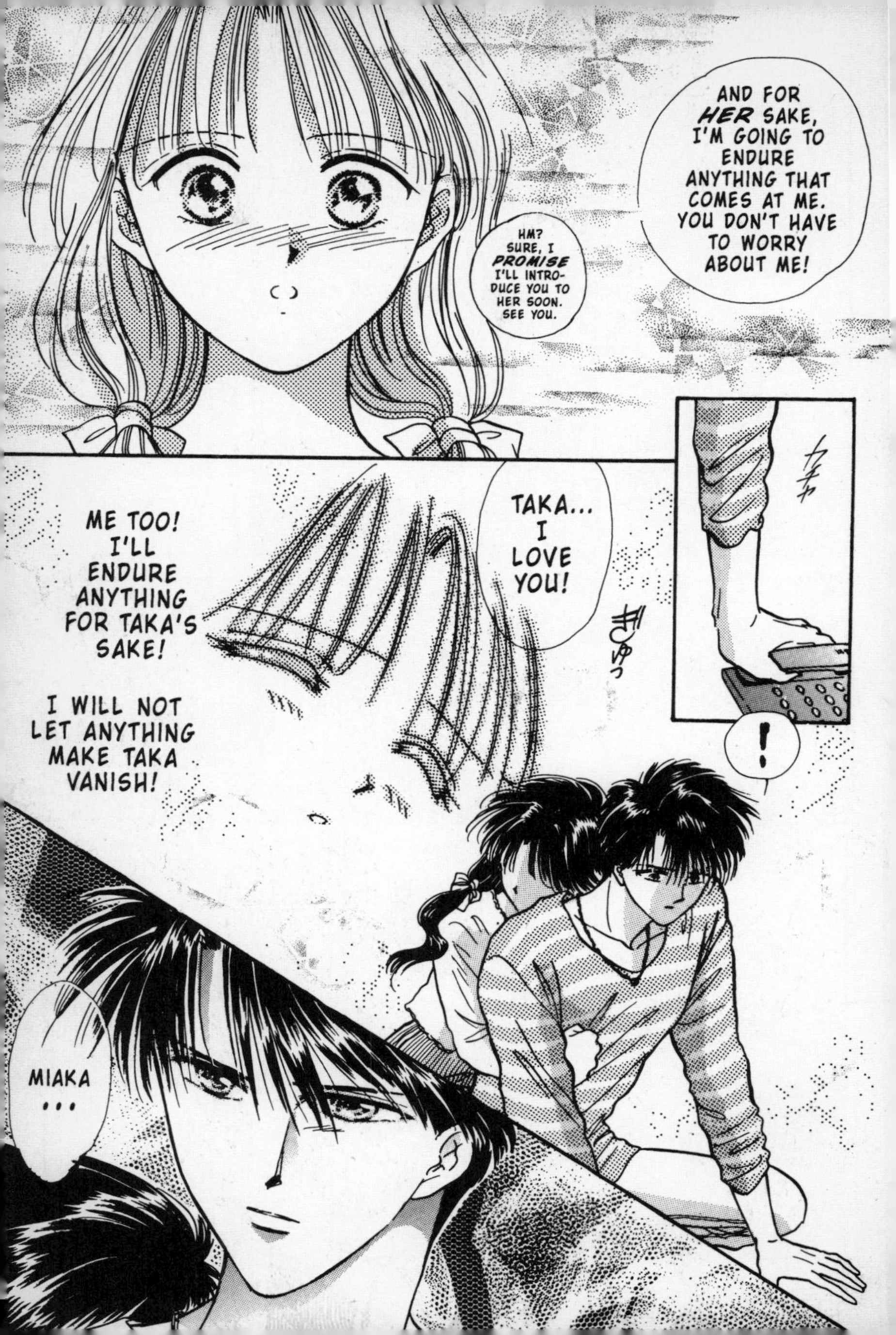

AND FOR HER SAKE, I'M GOING TO ENDURE ANYTHING THAT COMES AT ME. YOU DON'T HAVE TO WORRY ABOUT ME!
HM? SURE, I PROMISE I'LL INTRO-DUCE YOU TO HER SOON. SEE YOU.
カチャ
TAKA... I LOVE YOU!
ぎゅっ
!
ME TOO! I'LL ENDURE ANYTHING FOR TAKA'S SAKE!
I WILL NOT LET ANYTHING MAKE TAKA VANISH!
MIAKA ...

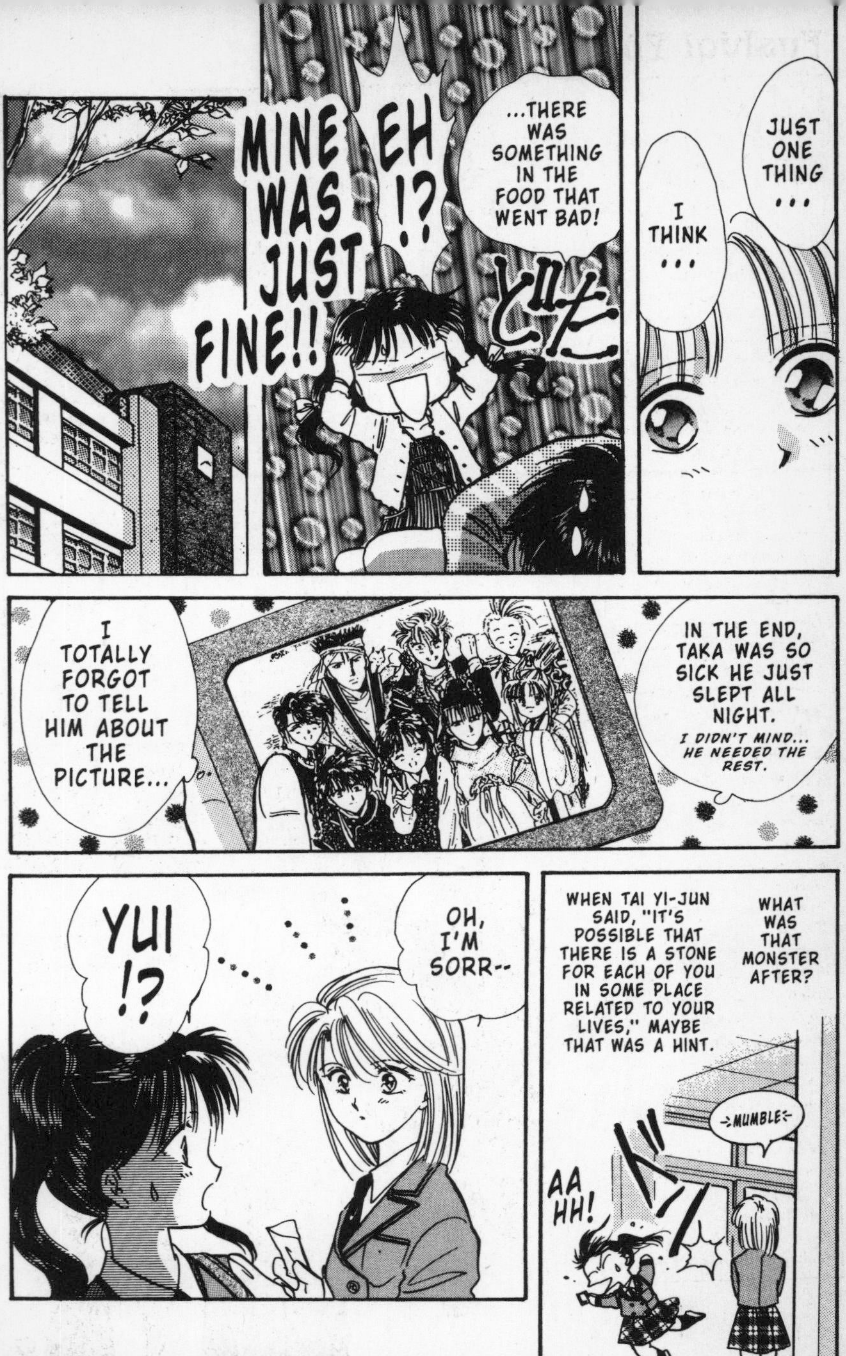
JUST ONE THING...
I THINK...
...THERE WAS SOMETHING IN THE FOOD THAT WENT BAD!
EH!?
MINE WAS JUST FINE!!
IN THE END, TAKA WAS SO SICK HE JUST SLEPT ALL NIGHT.
I DIDN'T MIND... HE NEEDED THE REST.
I TOTALLY FORGOT TO TELL HIM ABOUT THE PICTURE...
WHAT WAS THAT MONSTER AFTER?
WHEN TAI YI-JUN SAID, "IT'S POSSIBLE THAT THERE IS A STONE FOR EACH OF YOU IN SOME PLACE RELATED TO YOUR LIVES," MAYBE THAT WAS A HINT.
MUMBLE
AAHH!
OH, I'M SORR--
.....
YUI!?

Hi! Nice to see you! I'm Watase! And here it is!! Volume 15! I'm so tired, my head is spinning! This Summer ('95) was wonderful! It was filled with events!
First, there was a signing in Shinjuku on July 31. Thank you everyone! I was so nervous that even when people shouted my name at me (like an army of guy fans did), I didn't look up at people's faces as much as I should have. But I was surprised at all the people who lined up in the summer heat in the stairwell of a shop to buy character merchandise. It must have been awful for you! *From floor 8 to floor 3, huh?* I was also shocked by how many people showed up to get tickets! *About 2000?* Tokyo sure has a lot of people! There were only tickets for 100 people! Thanks for the interest, everyone! Also, at the signing that started at 2:00 p.m. (there were two signings, with the first at noon), there were people doing cosplay of Miaka, Yui, and Tamahome. I was so surprised! They had the school uniforms exactly right! Miaka had hair in buns and Yui had short hair.
For those who don't know, cosplay (costume play) is where real people make costumes and makeup in order to match the look of their favorite characters. It's like they become the characters, and it's really attention-getting!
That was a weird sentence, wasn't it?
Oh, yeah! My assistant went to Natsu-Komi!
For those who don't know Natsu-Komi (the Summer Comic Market): It's a place for fans of manga, games, etc. to sell or buy dōjinshi. Dōjinshi are manga parodies (and the like) that are drawn and made into books by fans to be sold at the Komiketto Comic Market. They're pretty famous.
And now that I've explained it, I've run out of space to talk about it! Watase, you're too considerate of your audience! ☺ This has nothing to do with anything, but a friend took me to Komiketto in '94.

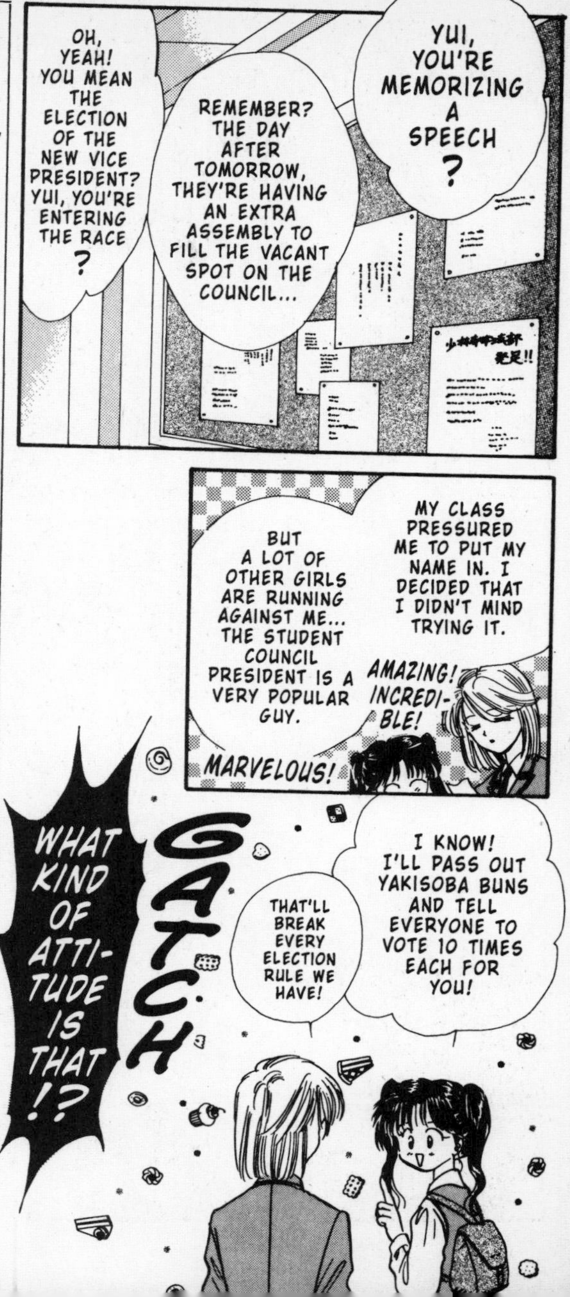
YUI, YOU'RE MEMORIZING A SPEECH?
REMEMBER? THE DAY AFTER TOMORROW, THEY'RE HAVING AN EXTRA ASSEMBLY TO FILL THE VACANT SPOT ON THE COUNCIL...
OH, YEAH! YOU MEAN THE ELECTION OF THE NEW VICE PRESIDENT? YUI, YOU'RE ENTERING THE RACE?
MY CLASS PRESSURED ME TO PUT MY NAME IN. I DECIDED THAT I DIDN'T MIND TRYING IT.
BUT A LOT OF OTHER GIRLS ARE RUNNING AGAINST ME... THE STUDENT COUNCIL PRESIDENT IS A VERY POPULAR GUY.
AMAZING! INCREDI-BLE!
MARVELOUS!
I KNOW! I'LL PASS OUT YAKISOBA BUNS AND TELL EVERYONE TO VOTE 10 TIMES EACH FOR YOU!
THAT'LL BREAK EVERY ELECTION RULE WE HAVE!
GATCH
WHAT KIND OF ATTI-TUDE IS THAT!?

So what??

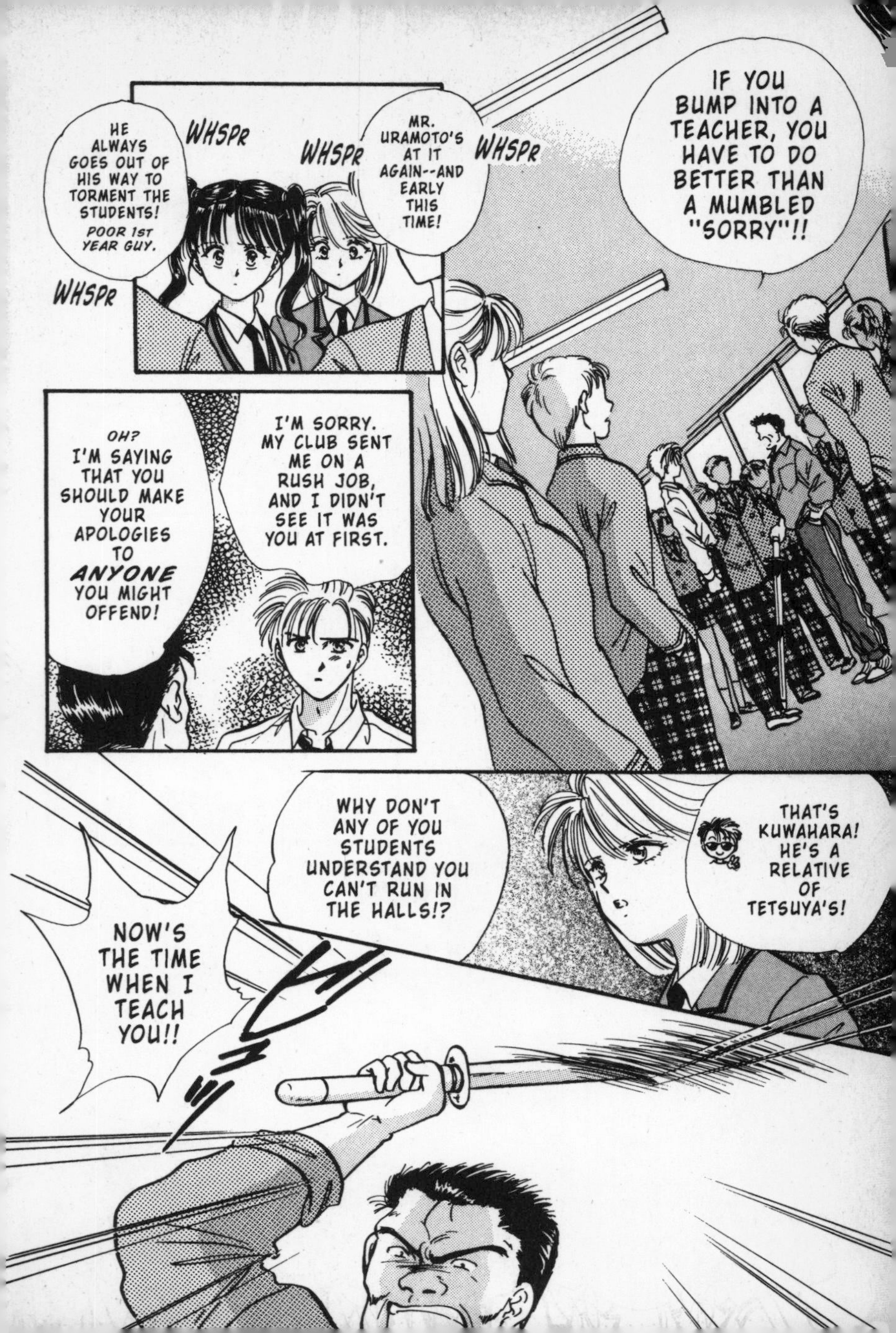
IF YOU BUMP INTO A TEACHER, YOU HAVE TO DO BETTER THAN A MUMBLED "SORRY"!!
WHSPR
MR. URAMOTO'S AT IT AGAIN--AND EARLY THIS TIME!
WHSPR
WHSPR
HE ALWAYS GOES OUT OF HIS WAY TO TORMENT THE STUDENTS!
POOR 1ST YEAR GUY.
WHSPR
I'M SORRY. MY CLUB SENT ME ON A RUSH JOB, AND I DIDN'T SEE IT WAS YOU AT FIRST.
OH? I'M SAYING THAT YOU SHOULD MAKE YOUR APOLOGIES TO ANYONE YOU MIGHT OFFEND!
THAT'S KUWAHARA! HE'S A RELATIVE OF TETSUYA'S!
WHY DON'T ANY OF YOU STUDENTS UNDERSTAND YOU CAN'T RUN IN THE HALLS!?
NOW'S THE TIME WHEN I TEACH YOU!!

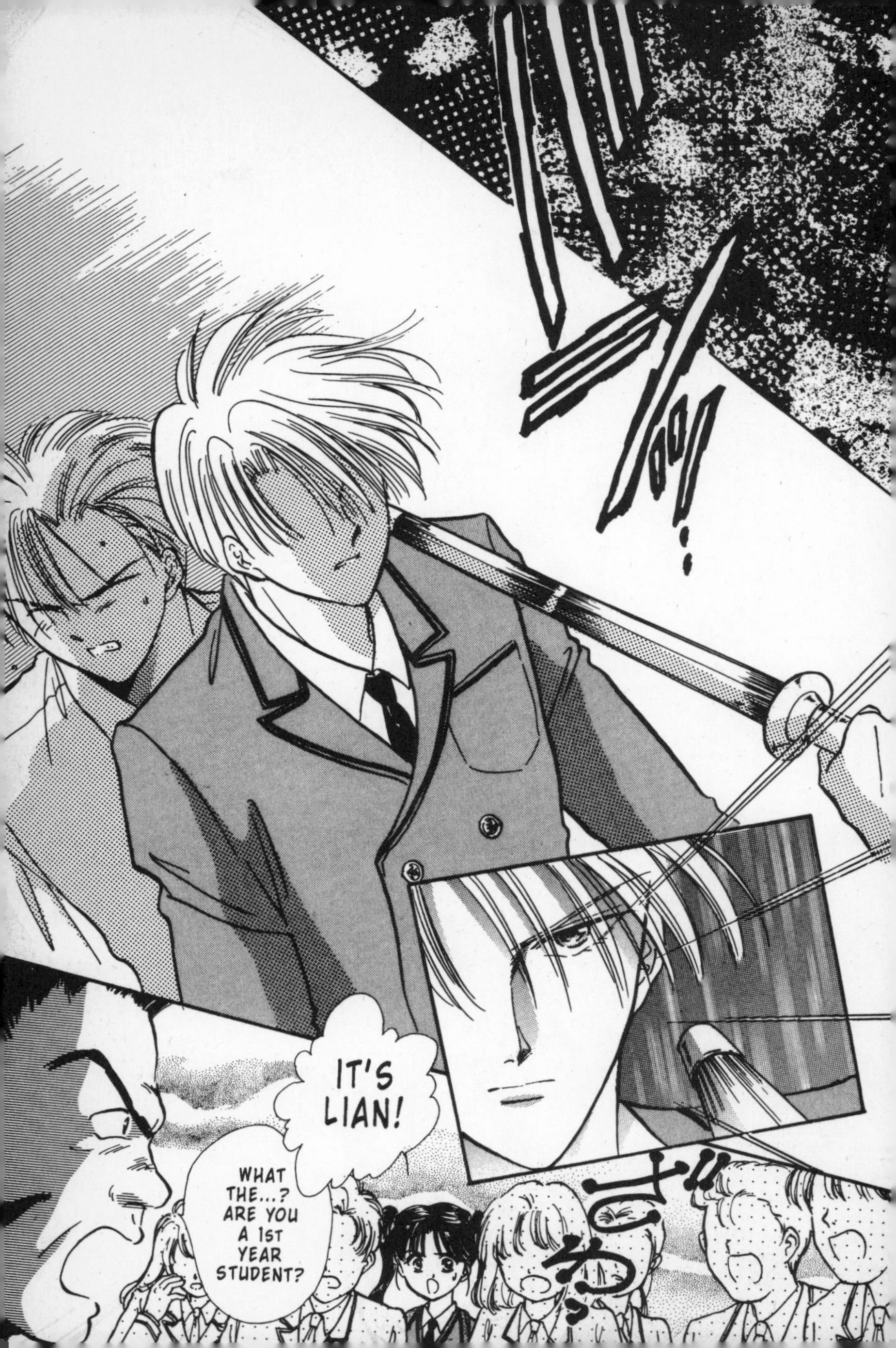
IT'S LIAN!
WHAT THE...? ARE YOU A 1ST YEAR STUDENT?

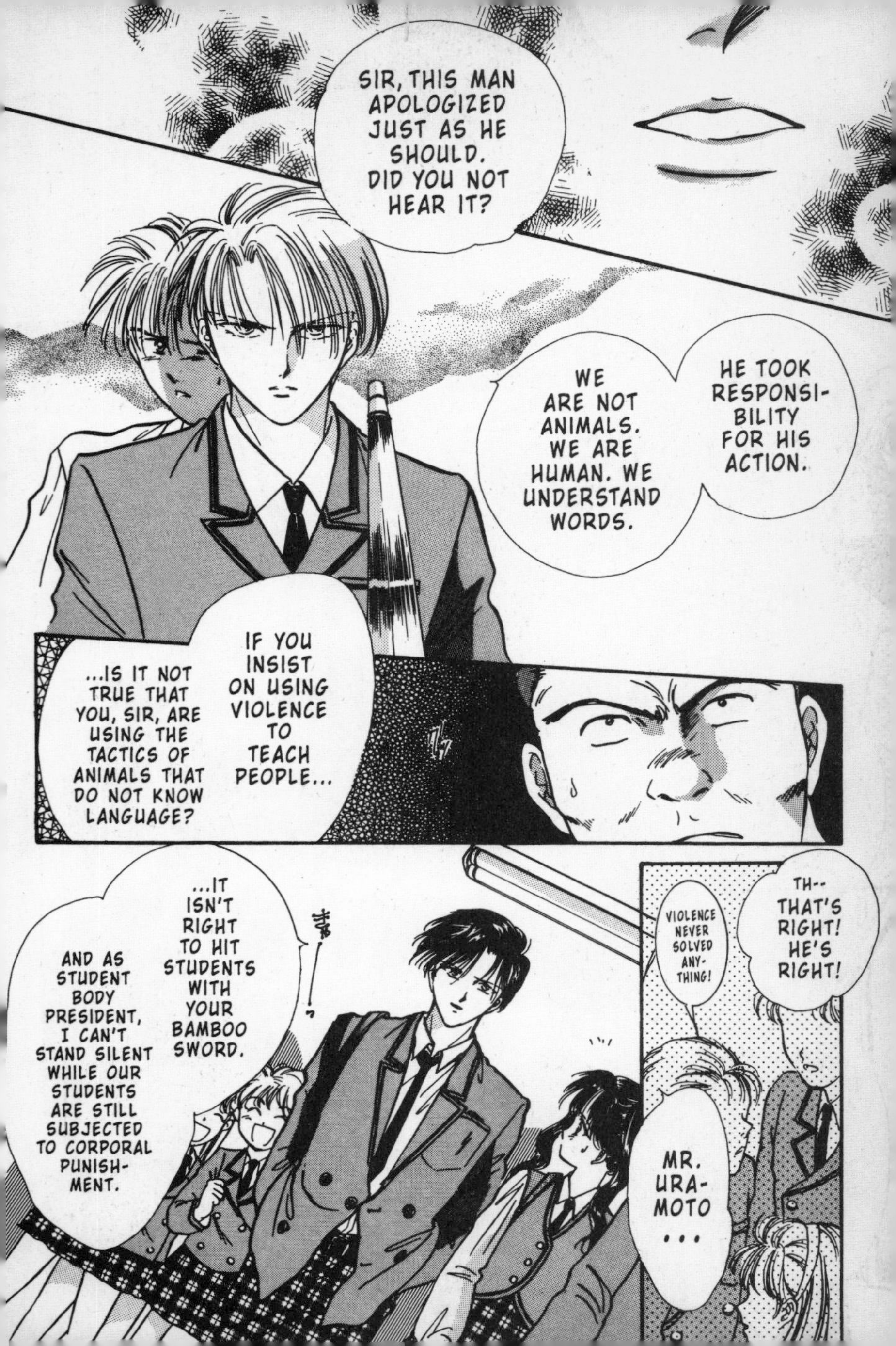

SIR, THIS MAN APOLOGIZED JUST AS HE SHOULD. DID YOU NOT HEAR IT?
HE TOOK RESPONSIBILITY FOR HIS ACTION.
WE ARE NOT ANIMALS. WE ARE HUMAN. WE UNDERSTAND WORDS.
IF YOU INSIST ON USING VIOLENCE TO TEACH PEOPLE...
...IS IT NOT TRUE THAT YOU, SIR, ARE USING THE TACTICS OF ANIMALS THAT DO NOT KNOW LANGUAGE?
TH-- THAT'S RIGHT! HE'S RIGHT!
VIOLENCE NEVER SOLVED ANYTHING!
MR. URAMOTO...
...IT ISN'T RIGHT TO HIT STUDENTS WITH YOUR BAMBOO SWORD.
AND AS STUDENT BODY PRESIDENT, I CAN'T STAND SILENT WHILE OUR STUDENTS ARE STILL SUBJECTED TO CORPORAL PUNISHMENT.

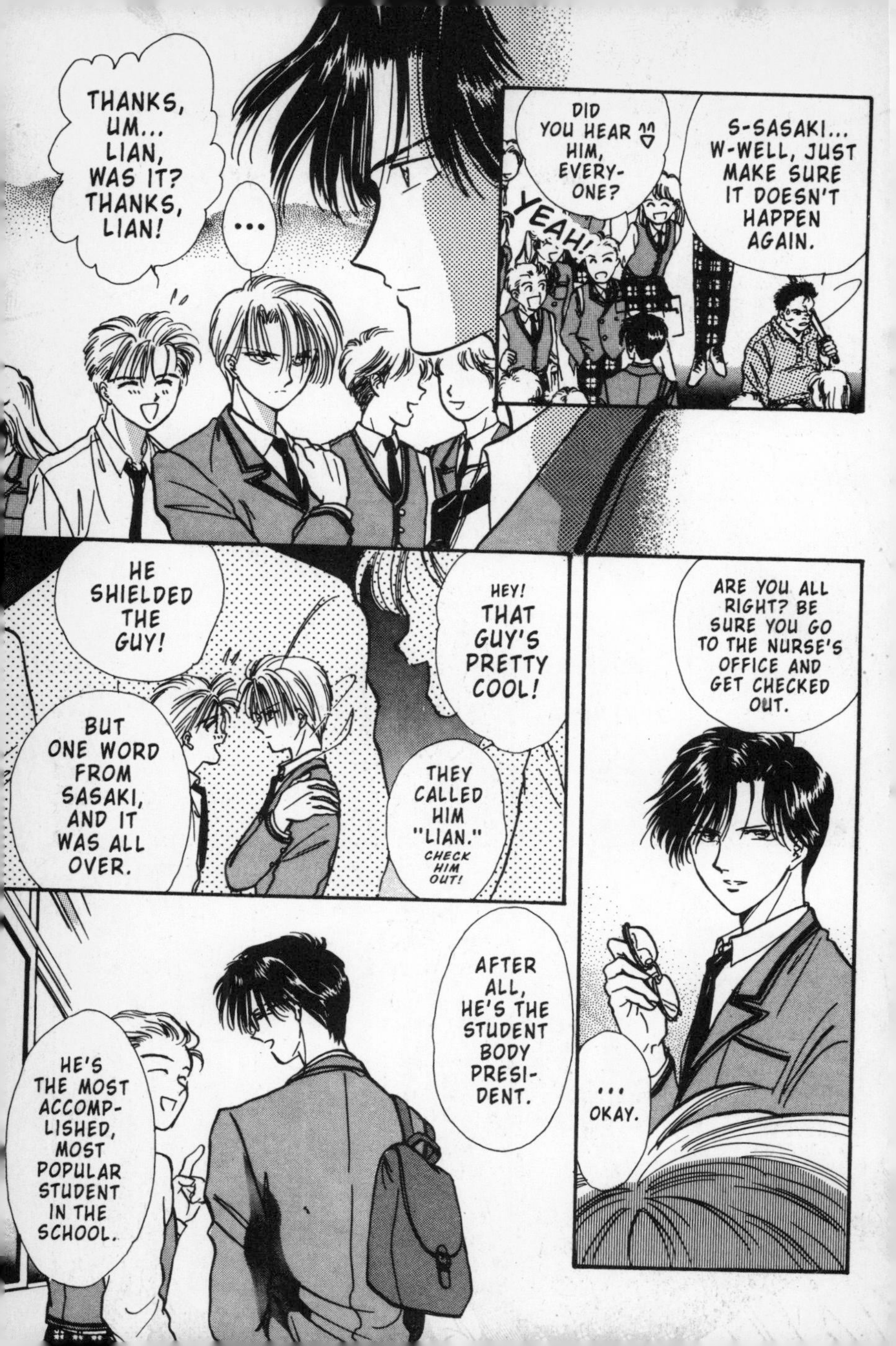
S-SASAKI... W-WELL, JUST MAKE SURE IT DOESN'T HAPPEN AGAIN.
DID YOU HEAR HIM, EVERYONE?
YEAH!
THANKS, UM... LIAN, WAS IT? THANKS, LIAN!
...
ARE YOU ALL RIGHT? BE SURE YOU GO TO THE NURSE'S OFFICE AND GET CHECKED OUT.
... OKAY.
HEY! THAT GUY'S PRETTY COOL!
HE SHIELDED THE GUY!
THEY CALLED HIM "LIAN." CHECK HIM OUT!
BUT ONE WORD FROM SASAKI, AND IT WAS ALL OVER.
AFTER ALL, HE'S THE STUDENT BODY PRESIDENT.
HE'S THE MOST ACCOMPLISHED, MOST POPULAR STUDENT IN THE SCHOOL.

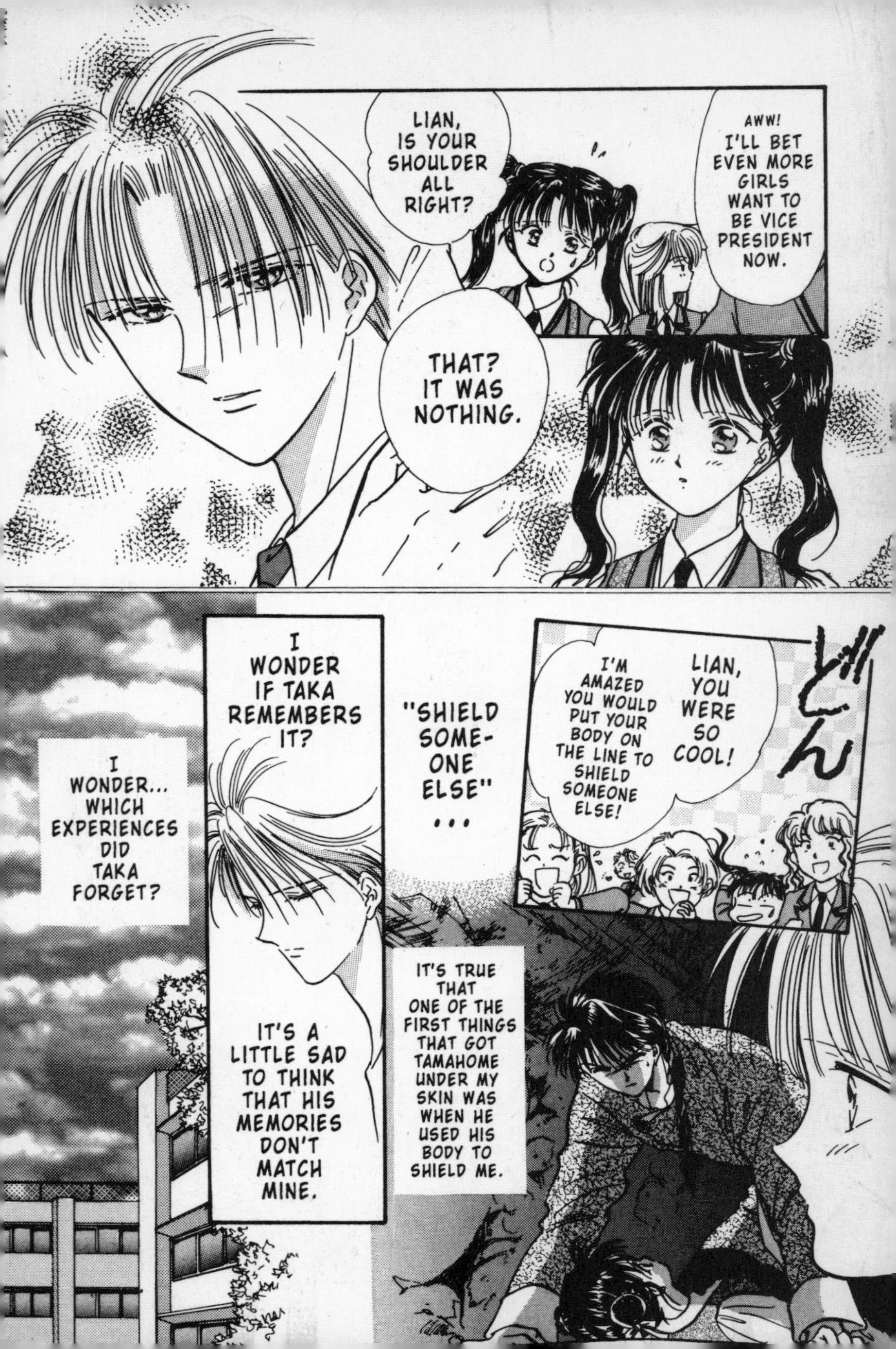
AWW! I'LL BET EVEN MORE GIRLS WANT TO BE VICE PRESIDENT NOW.
LIAN, IS YOUR SHOULDER ALL RIGHT?
THAT? IT WAS NOTHING.
LIAN, YOU WERE SO COOL!
I'M AMAZED YOU WOULD PUT YOUR BODY ON THE LINE TO SHIELD SOMEONE ELSE!
どん
IT'S TRUE THAT ONE OF THE FIRST THINGS THAT GOT TAMAHOME UNDER MY SKIN WAS WHEN HE USED HIS BODY TO SHIELD ME.
"SHIELD SOME-ONE ELSE"...
I WONDER IF TAKA REMEMBERS IT?
IT'S A LITTLE SAD TO THINK THAT HIS MEMORIES DON'T MATCH MINE.
I WONDER... WHICH EXPERIENCES DID TAKA FORGET?

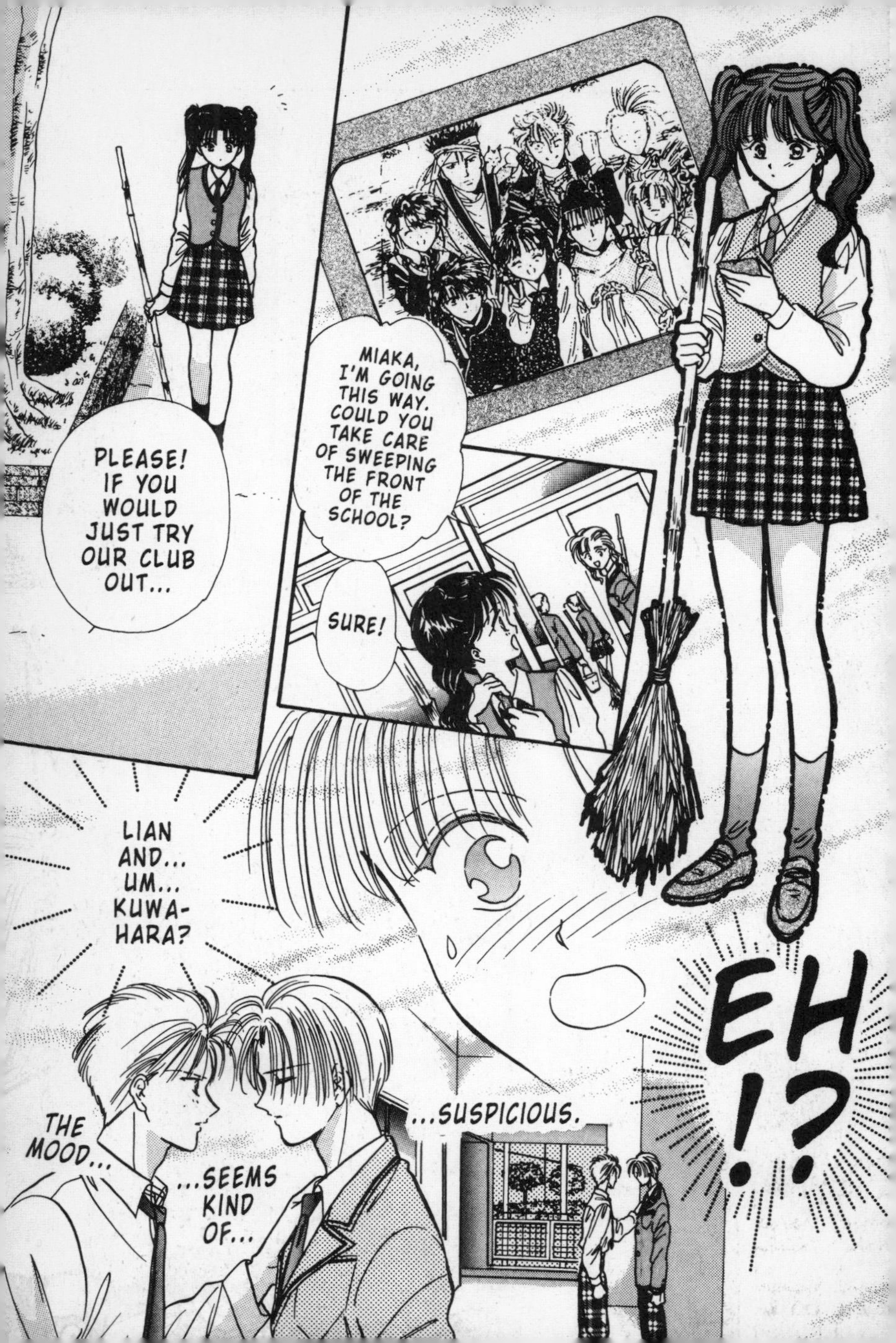
MIAKA, I'M GOING THIS WAY. COULD YOU TAKE CARE OF SWEEPING THE FRONT OF THE SCHOOL?
SURE!
PLEASE! IF YOU WOULD JUST TRY OUR CLUB OUT...
EH!?
LIAN AND... UM... KUWAHARA?
THE MOOD...
...SEEMS KIND OF...
...SUSPICIOUS.

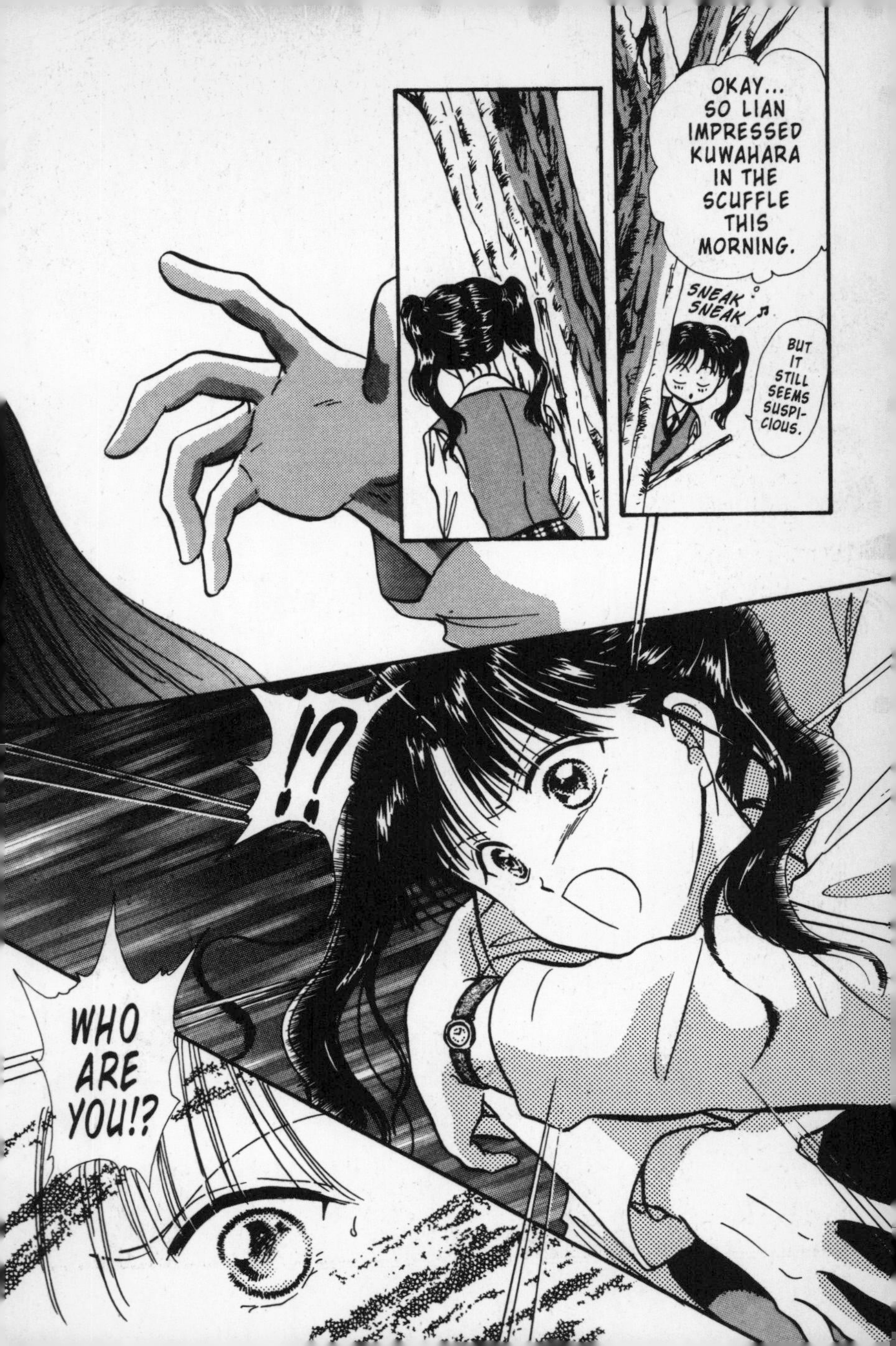
OKAY... SO LIAN IMPRESSED KUWAHARA IN THE SCUFFLE THIS MORNING.
SNEAK SNEAK
BUT IT STILL SEEMS SUSPICIOUS.
!?
WHO ARE YOU!?

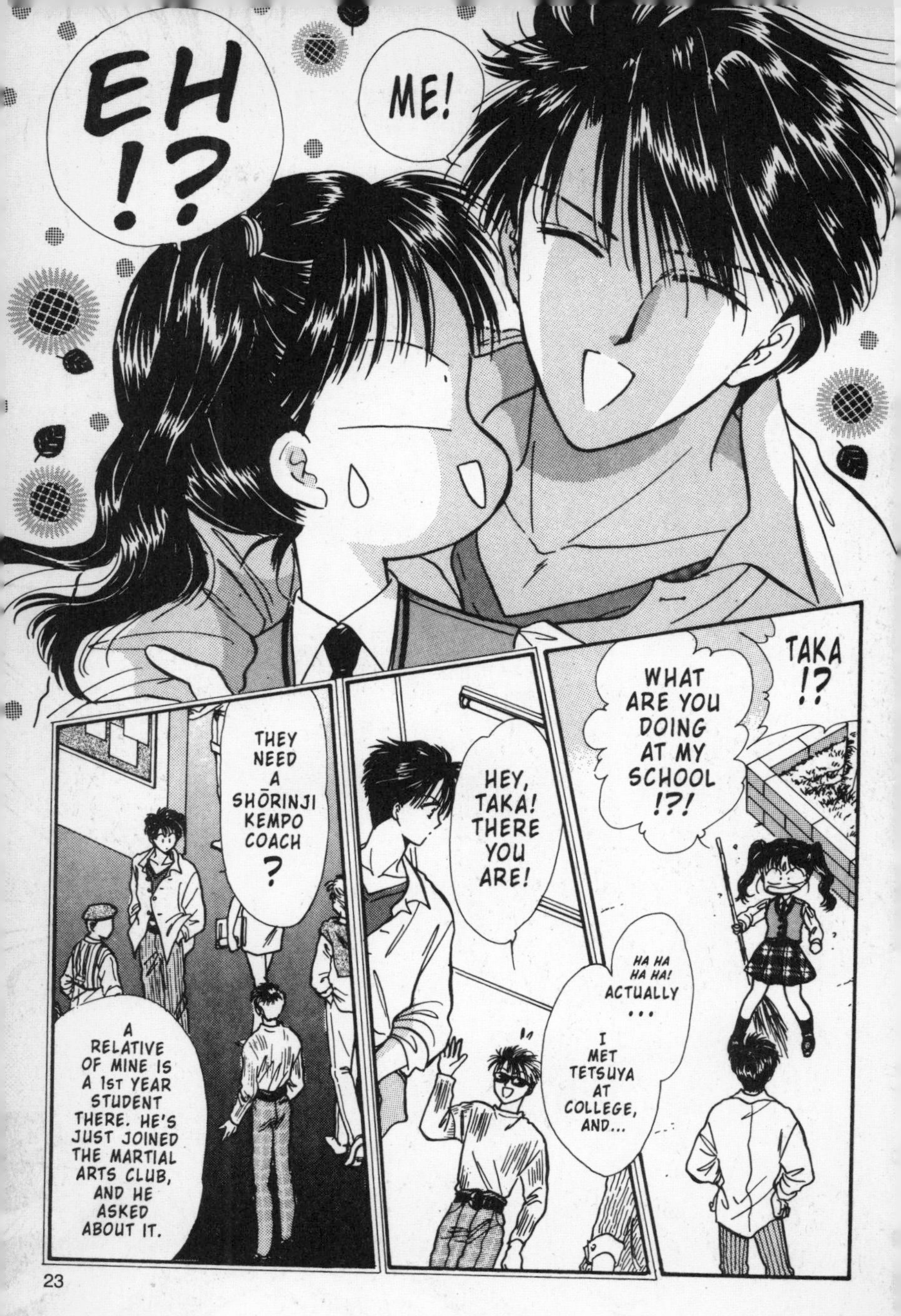
ME!
EH !?
TAKA !?
WHAT ARE YOU DOING AT MY SCHOOL !?!
HEY, TAKA! THERE YOU ARE!
HA HA HA HA! ACTUALLY ...
I MET TETSUYA AT COLLEGE, AND...
THEY NEED A SHŌRINJI KEMPO COACH ?
A RELATIVE OF MINE IS A 1ST YEAR STUDENT THERE. HE'S JUST JOINED THE MARTIAL ARTS CLUB, AND HE ASKED ABOUT IT.

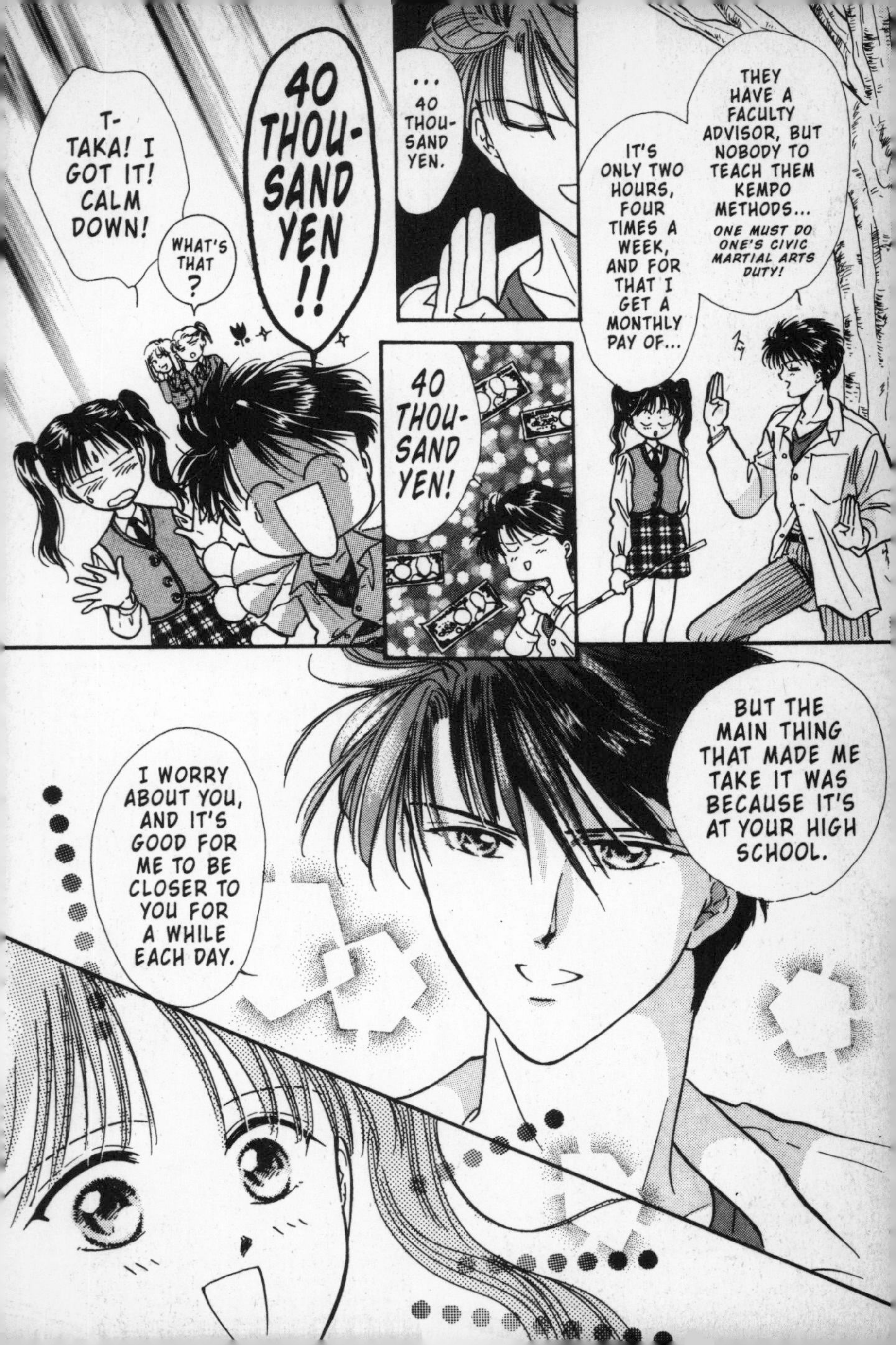
THEY HAVE A FACULTY ADVISOR, BUT NOBODY TO TEACH THEM KEMPO METHODS...
ONE MUST DO ONE'S CIVIC MARTIAL ARTS DUTY!
IT'S ONLY TWO HOURS, FOUR TIMES A WEEK, AND FOR THAT I GET A MONTHLY PAY OF...
... 40 THOUSAND YEN.
40 THOUSAND YEN!
40 THOUSAND YEN!!
T-TAKA! I GOT IT! CALM DOWN!
WHAT'S THAT?
BUT THE MAIN THING THAT MADE ME TAKE IT WAS BECAUSE IT'S AT YOUR HIGH SCHOOL.
I WORRY ABOUT YOU, AND IT'S GOOD FOR ME TO BE CLOSER TO YOU FOR A WHILE EACH DAY.

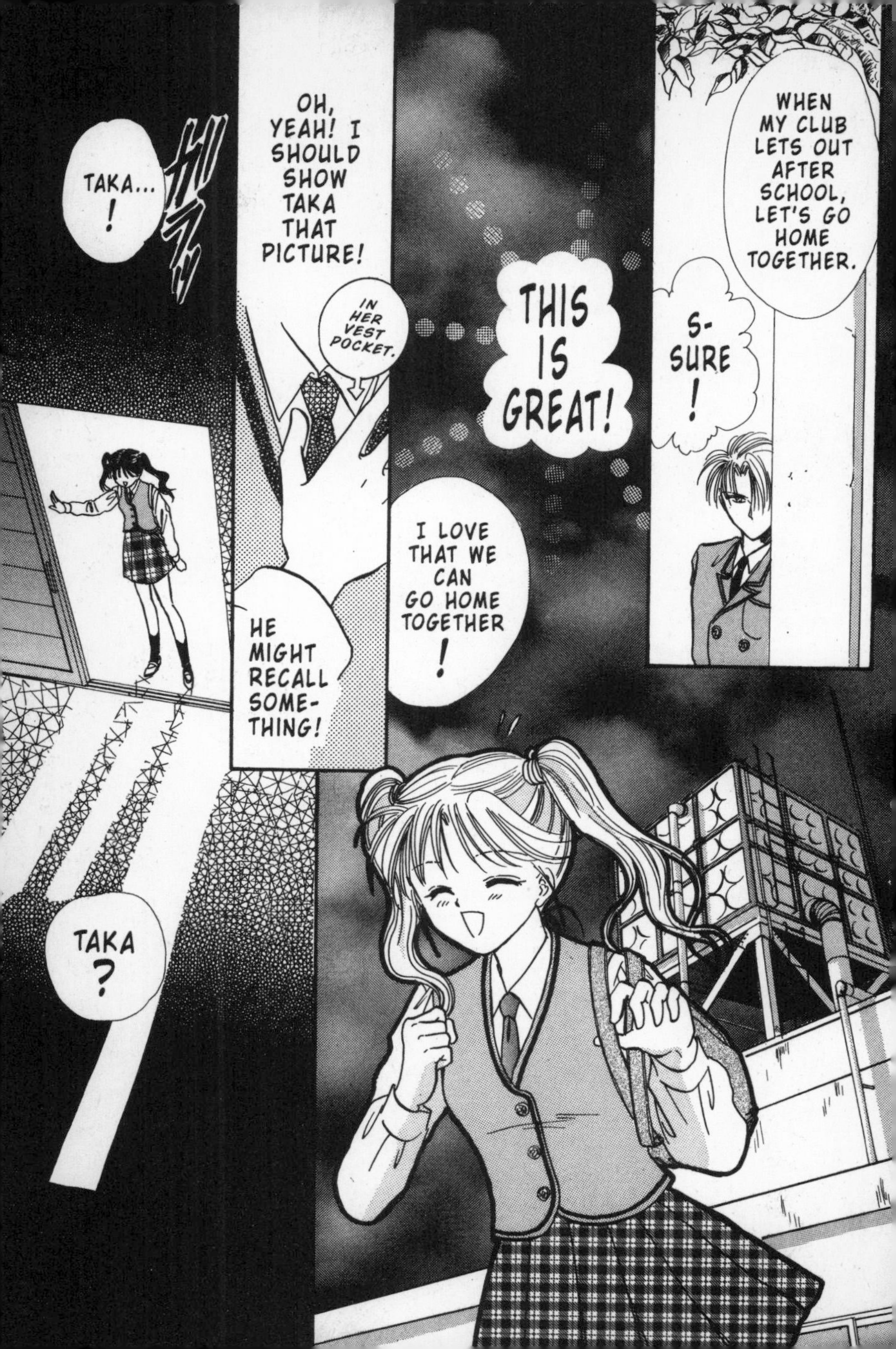
WHEN MY CLUB LETS OUT AFTER SCHOOL, LET'S GO HOME TOGETHER.
S-SURE!
THIS IS GREAT!
I LOVE THAT WE CAN GO HOME TOGETHER!
OH, YEAH! I SHOULD SHOW TAKA THAT PICTURE!
IN HER VEST POCKET.
HE MIGHT RECALL SOME-THING!
TAKA...!
TAKA?

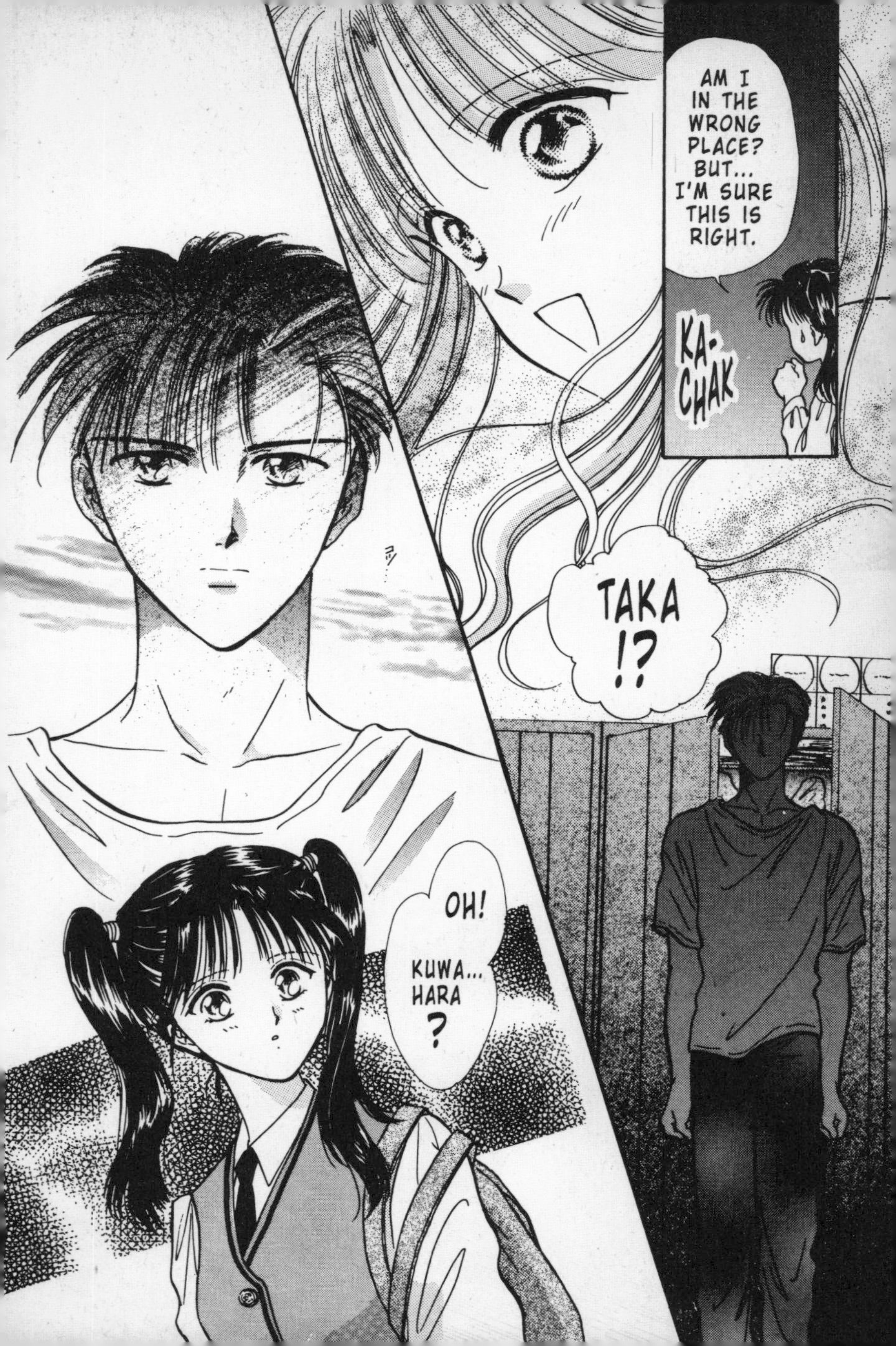
AM I IN THE WRONG PLACE? BUT... I'M SURE THIS IS RIGHT.
KA-CHAK
TAKA !?
OH!
KUWA... HARA ?

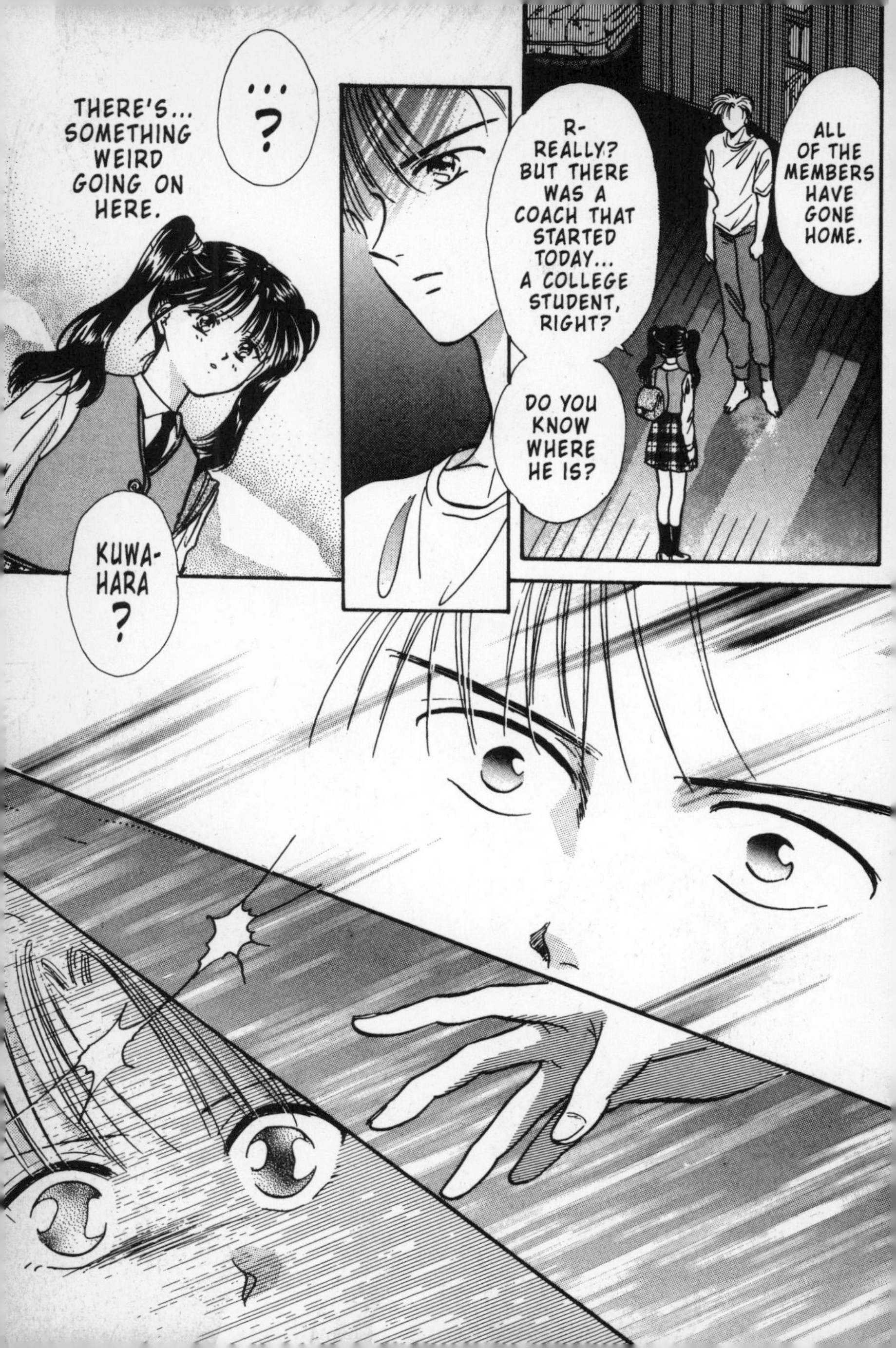
ALL OF THE MEMBERS HAVE GONE HOME.
R-REALLY? BUT THERE WAS A COACH THAT STARTED TODAY... A COLLEGE STUDENT, RIGHT?
DO YOU KNOW WHERE HE IS?
...?
THERE'S... SOMETHING WEIRD GOING ON HERE.
KUWAHARA?

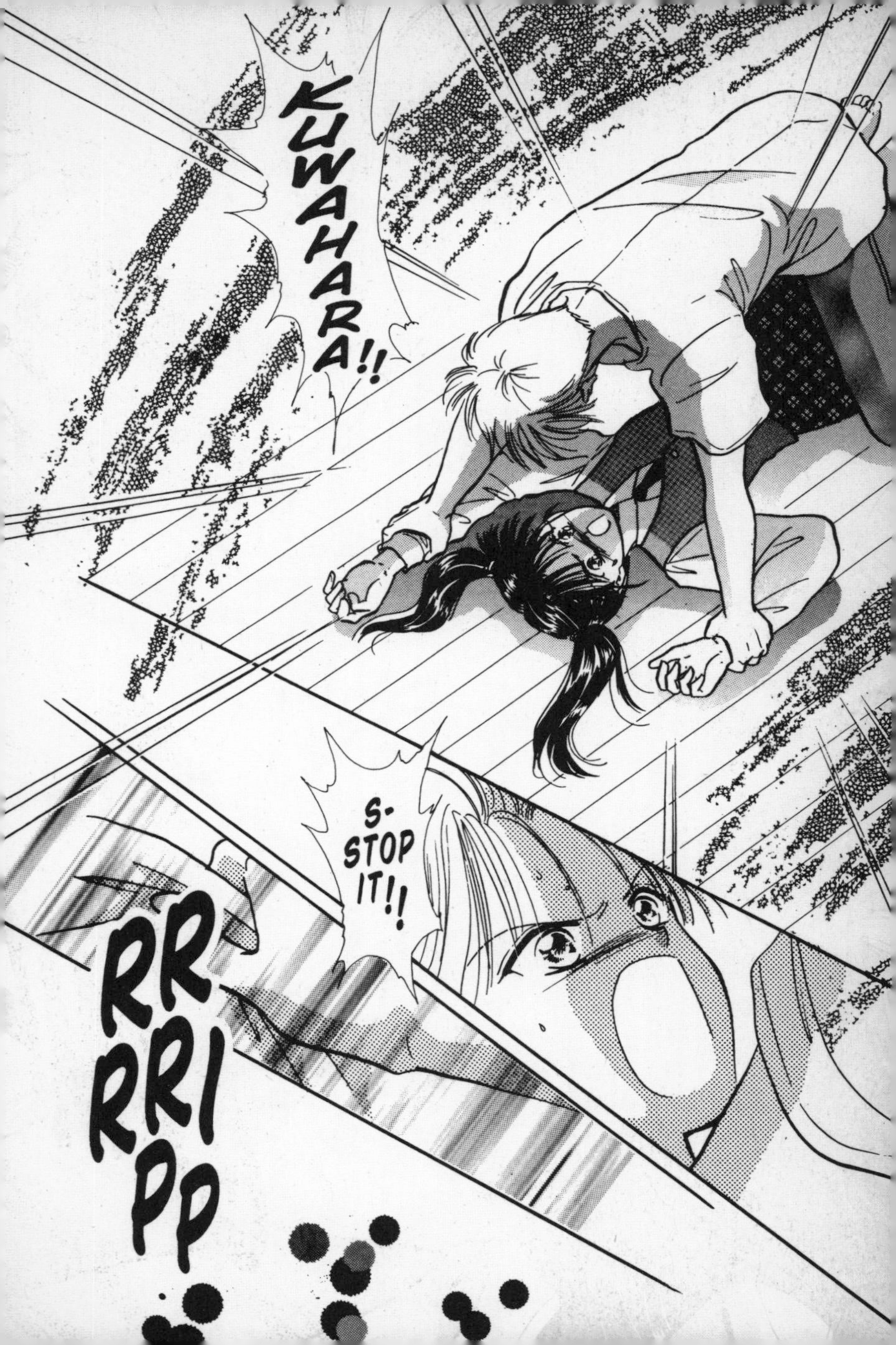
KUWAHARA!!
S-STOP IT!!
RRRRIPP

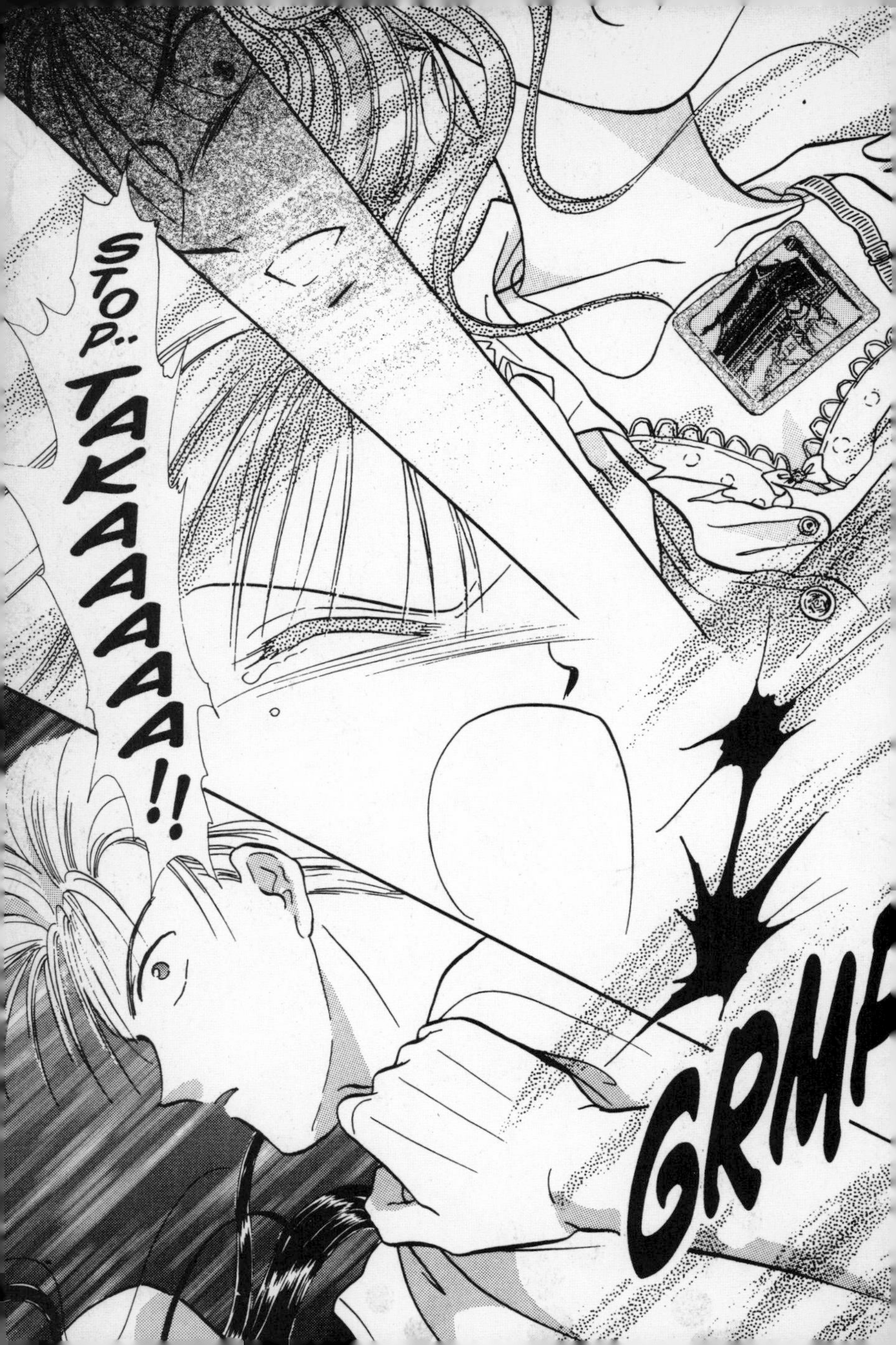
GRM
STOP.. TAKAAAAAA!!

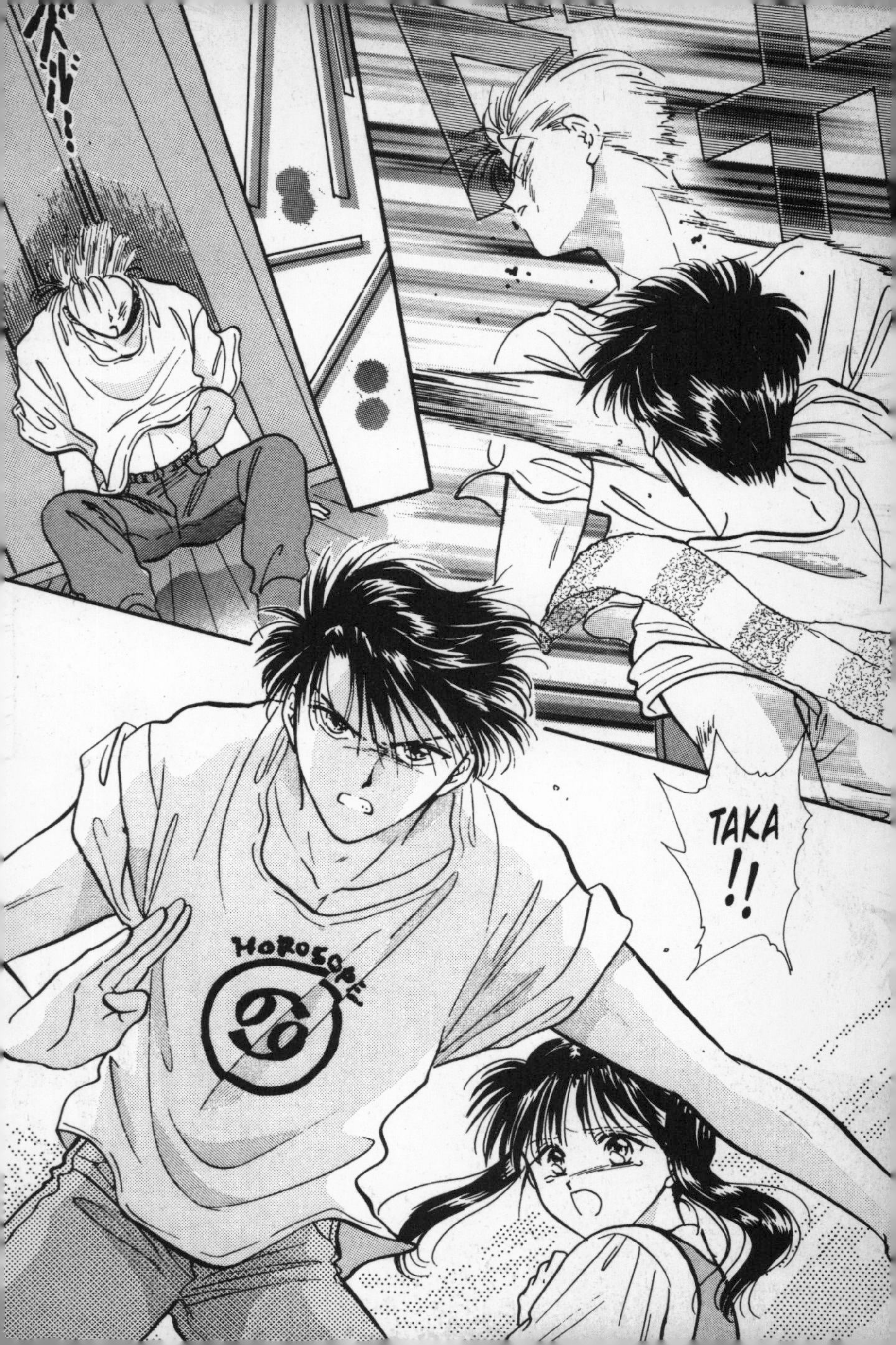
TAKA !!

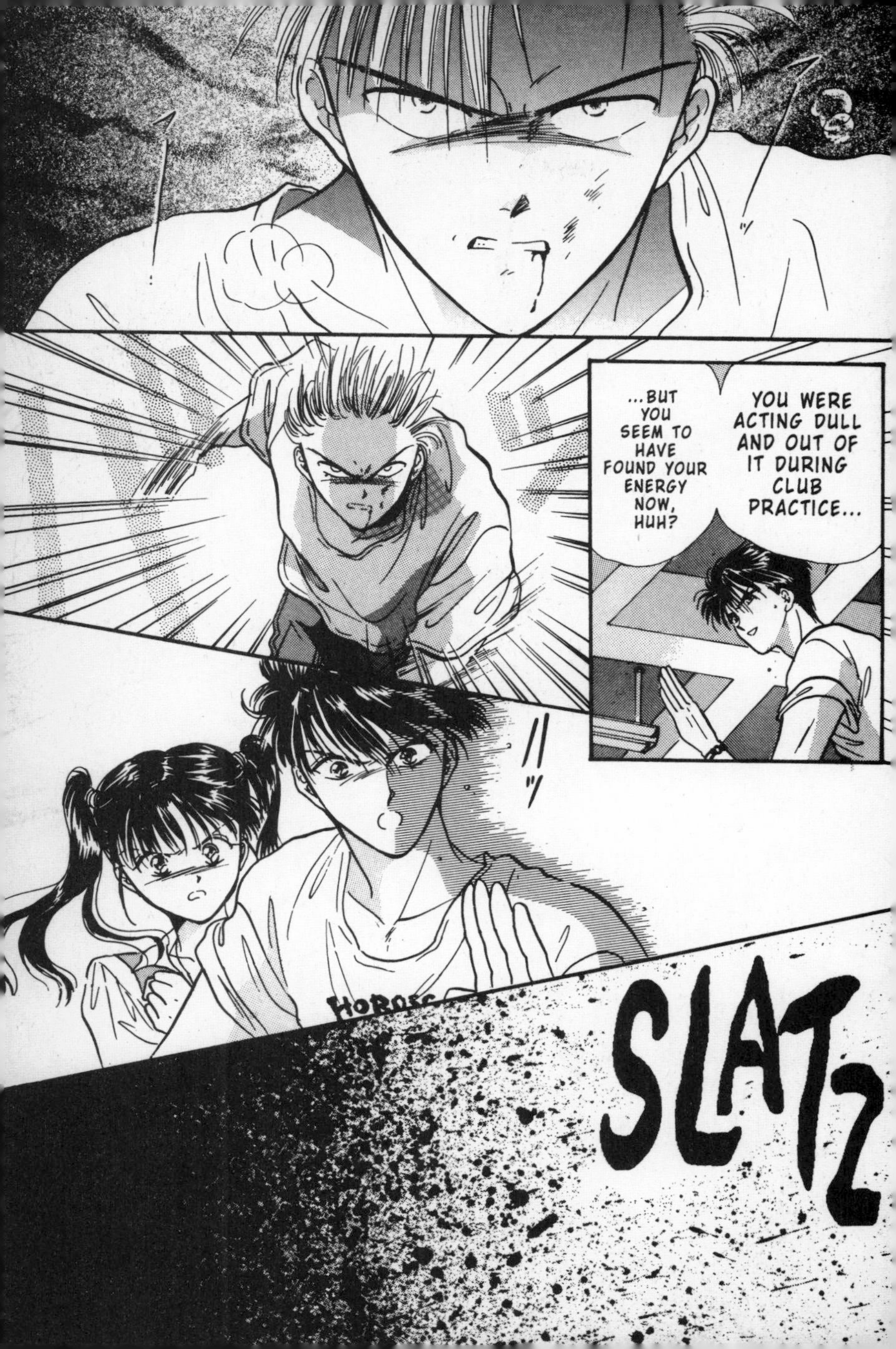
YOU WERE ACTING DULL AND OUT OF IT DURING CLUB PRACTICE...
...BUT YOU SEEM TO HAVE FOUND YOUR ENERGY NOW, HUH?
SLAT

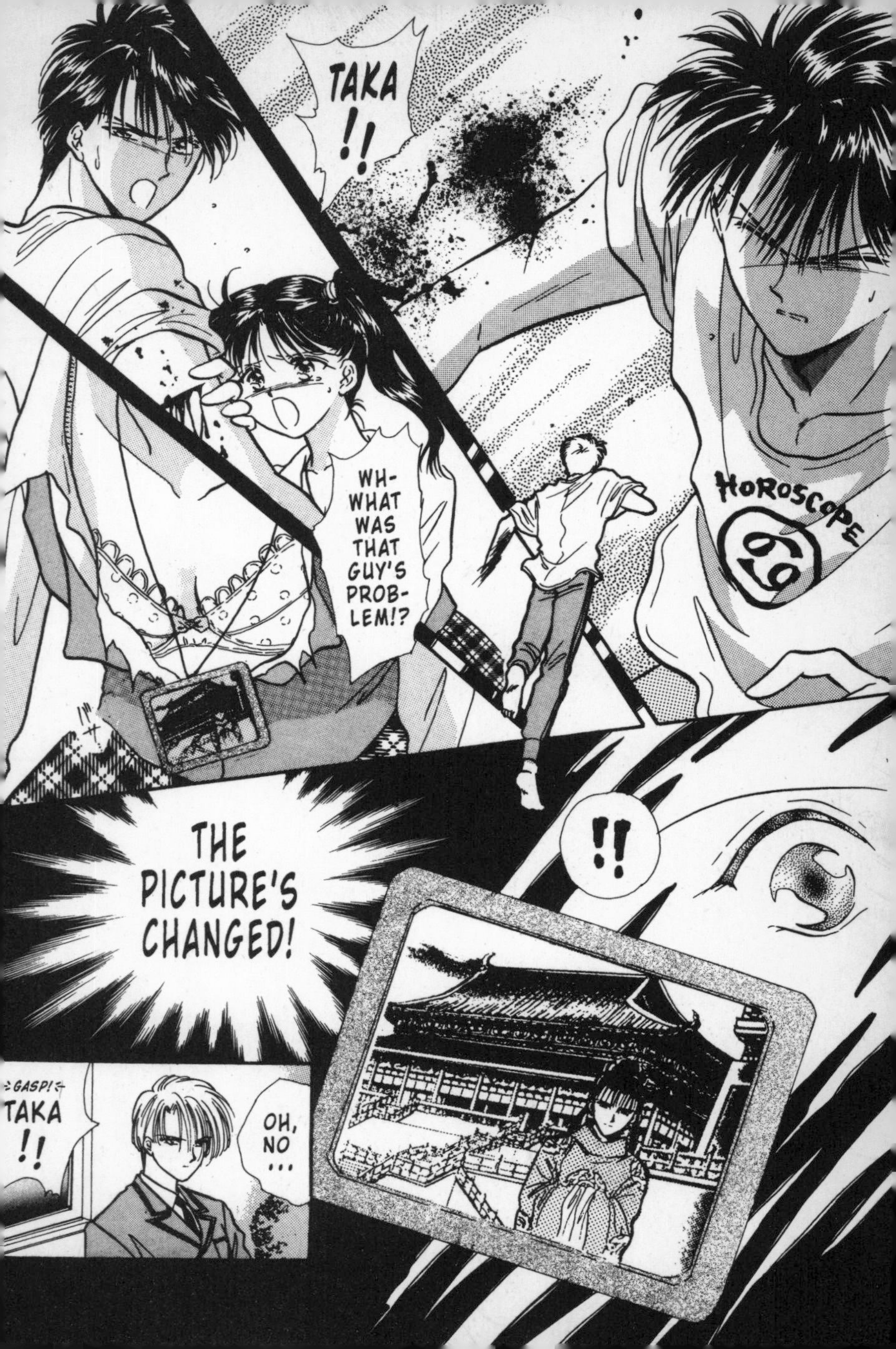
HOROSCOPE
TAKA !!
WH-WHAT WAS THAT GUY'S PROBLEM!?
!!
THE PICTURE'S CHANGED!
OH, NO...
GASP!
TAKA !!

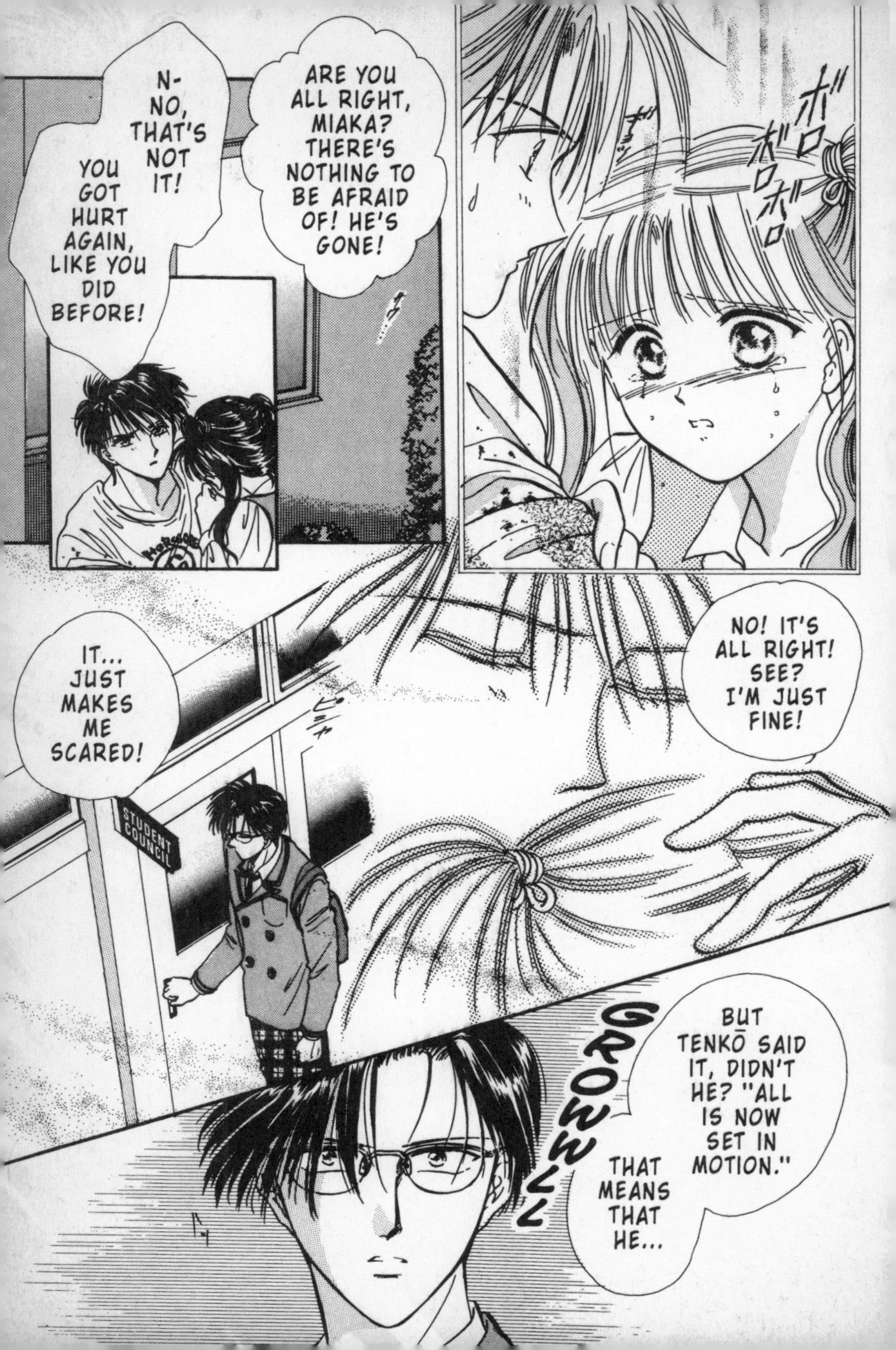
ARE YOU ALL RIGHT, MIAKA? THERE'S NOTHING TO BE AFRAID OF! HE'S GONE!
N-NO, THAT'S NOT IT!
YOU GOT HURT AGAIN, LIKE YOU DID BEFORE!
NO! IT'S ALL RIGHT! SEE? I'M JUST FINE!
IT... JUST MAKES ME SCARED!
STUDENT COUNCIL
BUT TENKŌ SAID IT, DIDN'T HE? "ALL IS NOW SET IN MOTION."
GROWWLLL
THAT MEANS THAT HE...

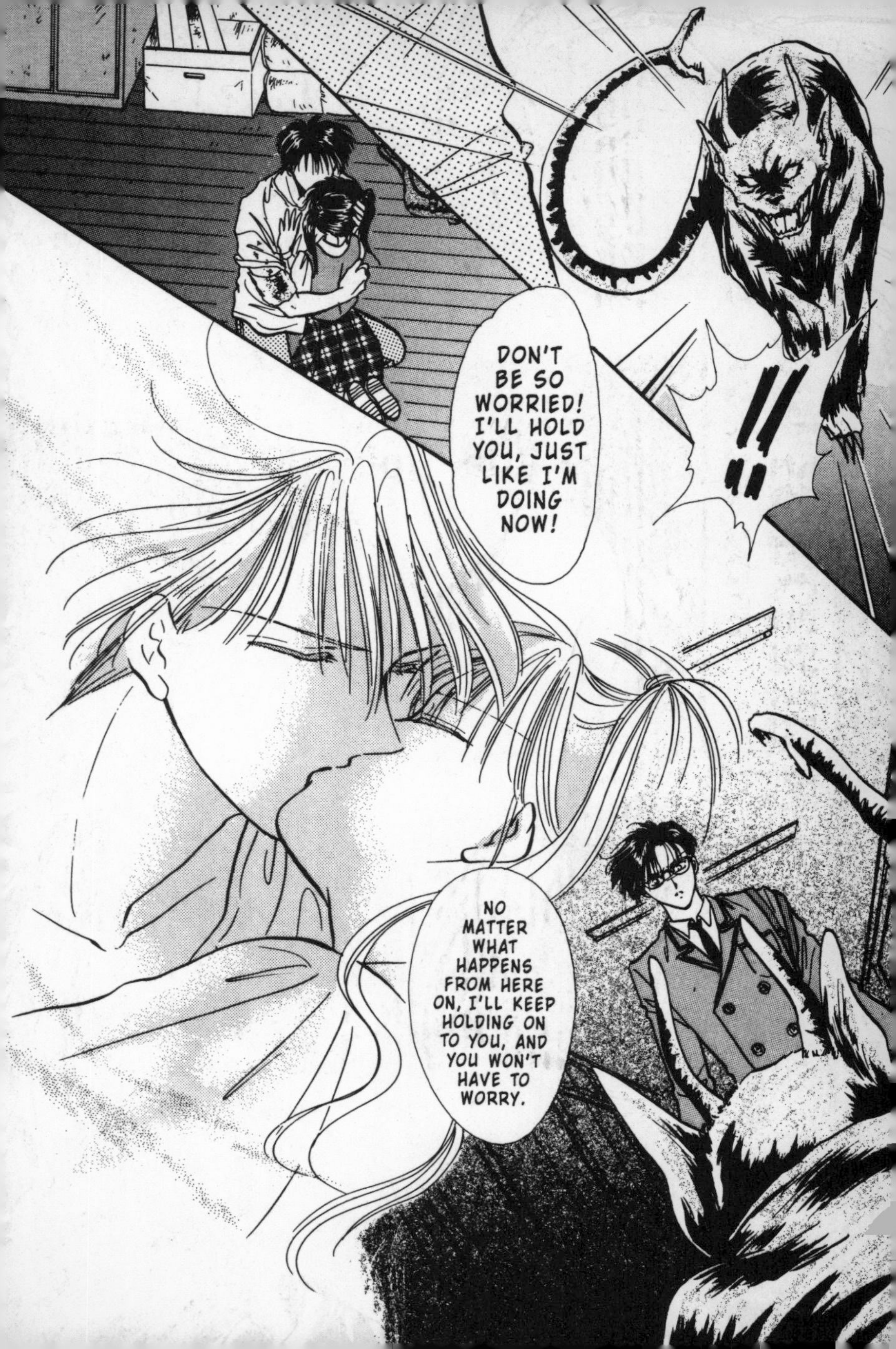
DON'T BE SO WORRIED! I'LL HOLD YOU, JUST LIKE I'M DOING NOW!
!!
NO MATTER WHAT HAPPENS FROM HERE ON, I'LL KEEP HOLDING ON TO YOU, AND YOU WON'T HAVE TO WORRY.

CHAPTER EIGHTY-FOUR
THE YOUNG SORCERER

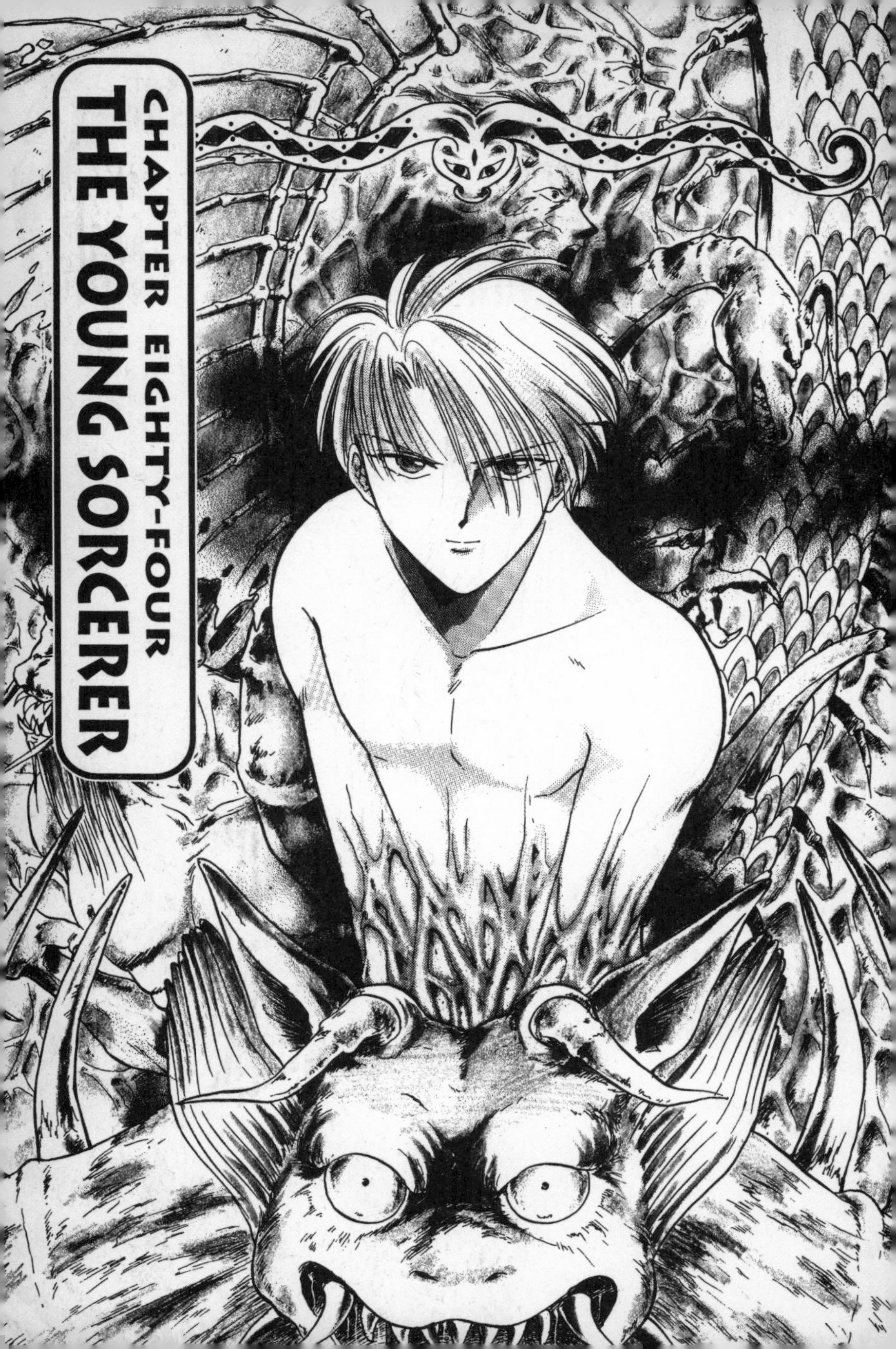

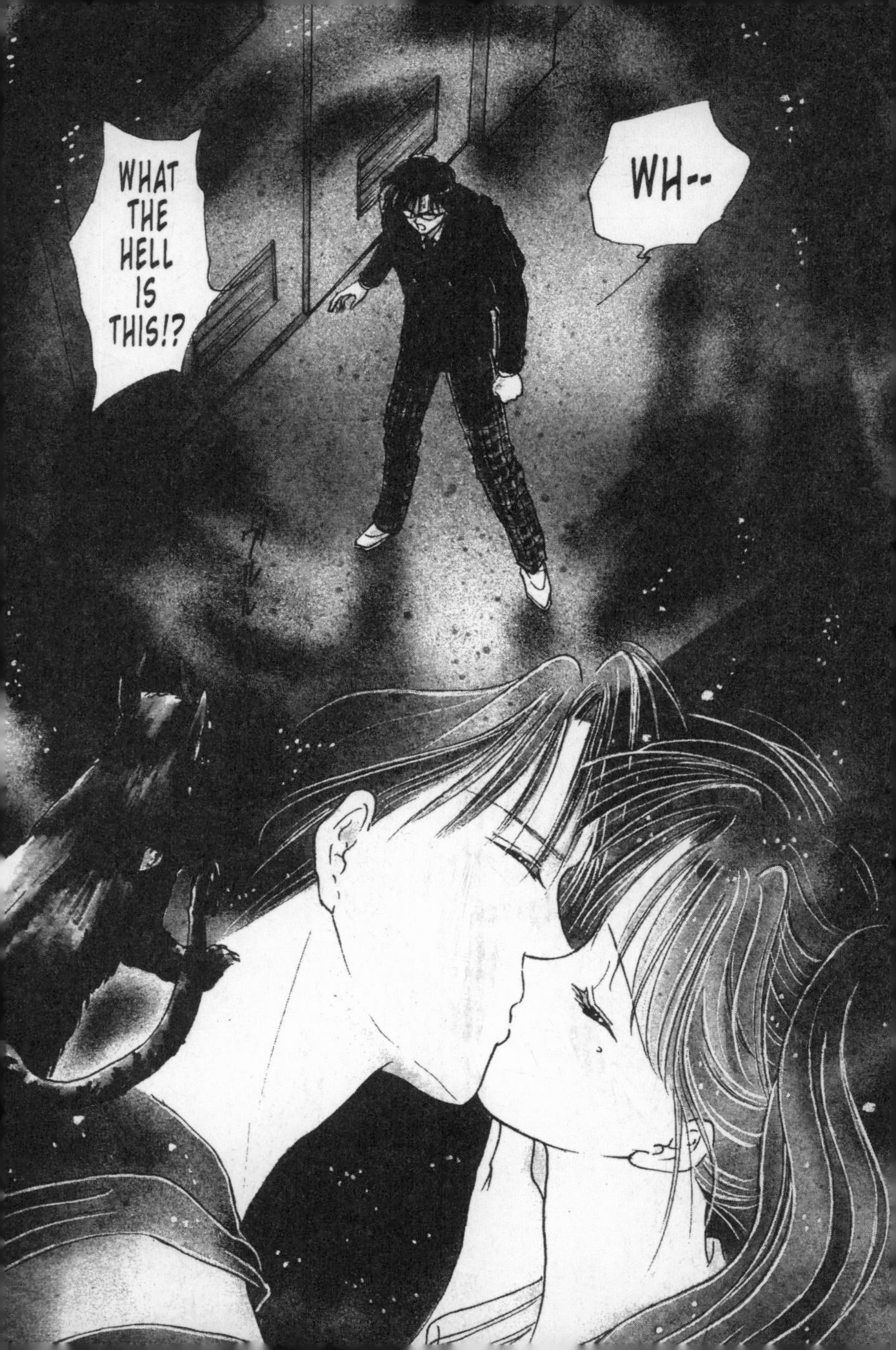
WH--
WHAT THE HELL IS THIS!?

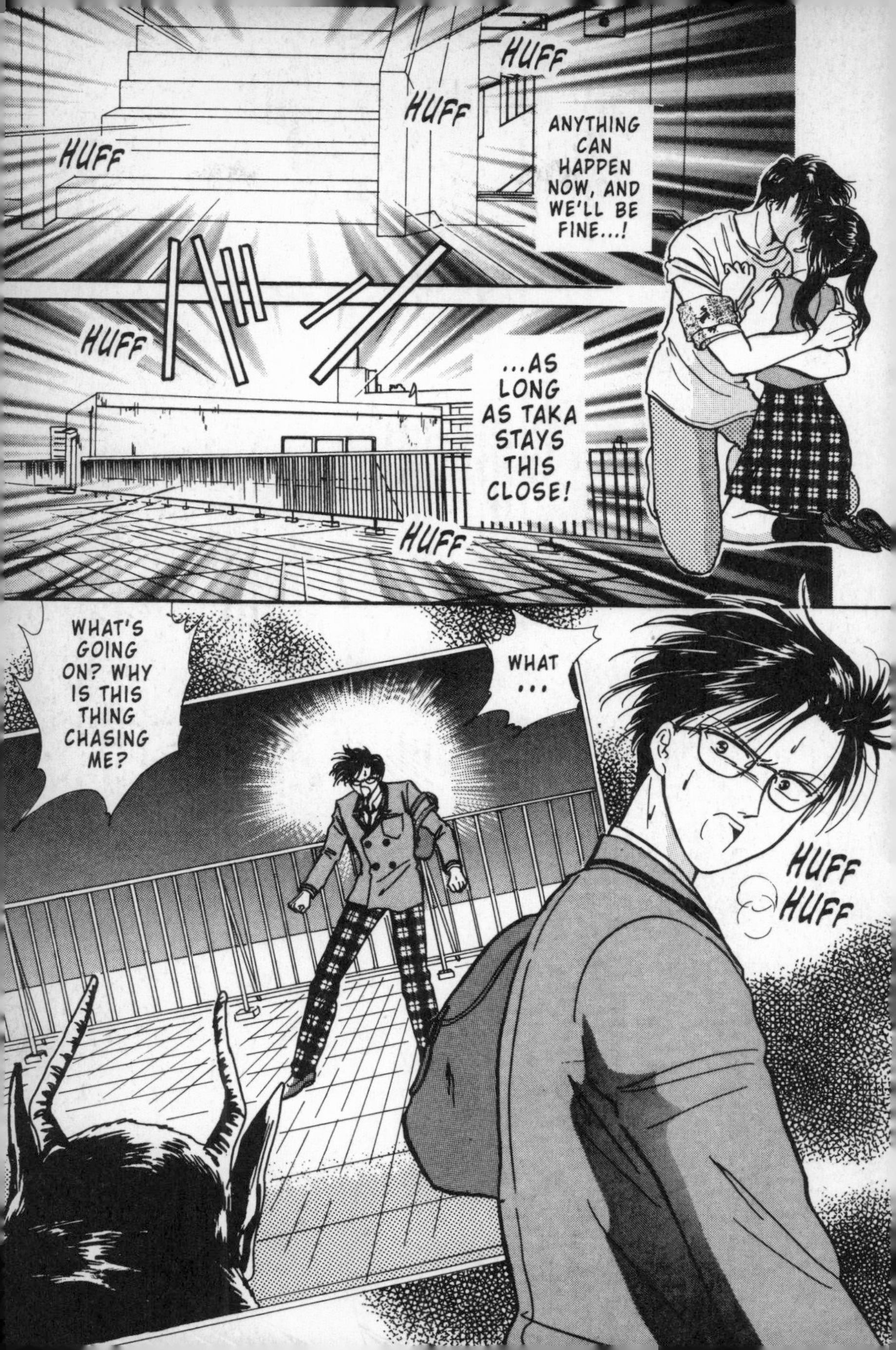
HUFF
HUFF
HUFF
ANYTHING CAN HAPPEN NOW, AND WE'LL BE FINE...!
...AS LONG AS TAKA STAYS THIS CLOSE!
HUFF
HUFF
HUFF HUFF
WHAT ...
WHAT'S GOING ON? WHY IS THIS THING CHASING ME?

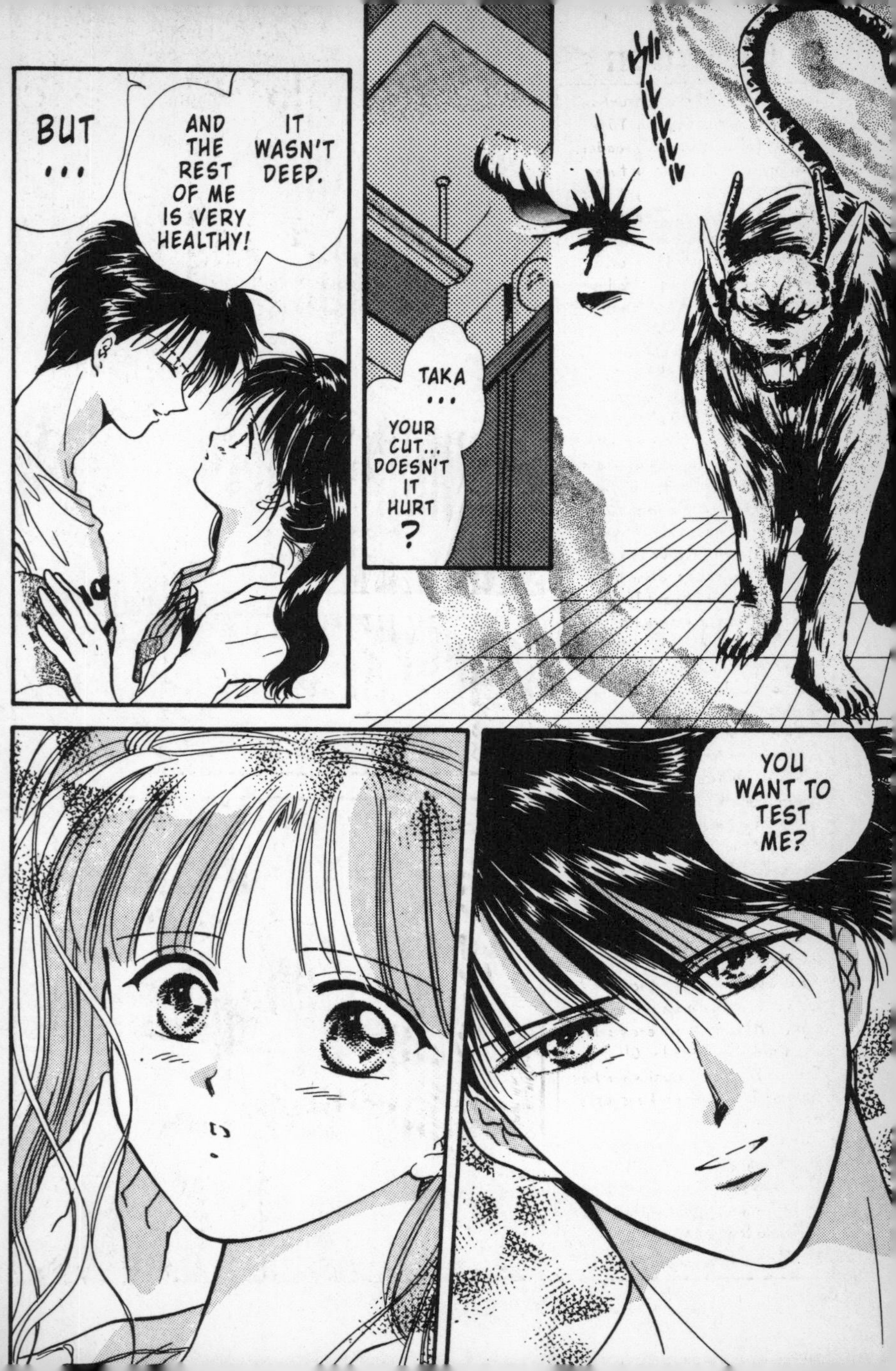
TAKA ... YOUR CUT... DOESN'T IT HURT?
IT WASN'T DEEP.
AND THE REST OF ME IS VERY HEALTHY!
BUT ...
YOU WANT TO TEST ME?

Guardian

To continue... At the Natsu-Komi, there was a lot of Fushigi Yūgi cosplay (all of it done by readers) that my assistant took pictures of. *But I haven't seen them yet!* And a friend of mine said, "There was this guy in a Hotohori costume that was so incredibly beautiful, one of my friends had to follow him." And when I heard that, it was like I was attacked! *(what's that mean?)* Listen, whoever did it, send me a picture...**NOW!** ☺ For anybody to play Hotohori, that takes self-confidence! My assistant also said there was a really cool Nuriko there. It was like if Nuriko actually lived, this is what he would be like. (In fact, Nuriko was played by a man!) I'll bet there are a lot of young women readers who are reacting by saying, "Really!? Kyaa! I wanna see!" ♥♥ Well, I wanted to see it too. But at that time, Watase wasn't even in Japan. I'll get into that later. At the signing, I was really surprised at the cosplay, but what really surprised me was between the hours of 1:00 and 2:00, the character designer for the anime, Mr. Motohashi, stopped by. I was so shocked! He was right there at the site of the signing! I'll bet none of you knew it! When he did a sketch, I went and asked him something stupid like, "Why is it that you can draw such pretty pictures!?" *Sniff, sniff!* After I went home, without realizing it, I started admiring my own work. He said they were working on episode 20. Episode 20!! Episode 20, with Tasuki when he's fighting Tamahome--he is just so cool, I could die!

And at the end of the month they'll be close to episode 30!

And they say they'll have even more Tasuki fighting action, so Tasuki fans, be sure to watch for it!

Entranced...

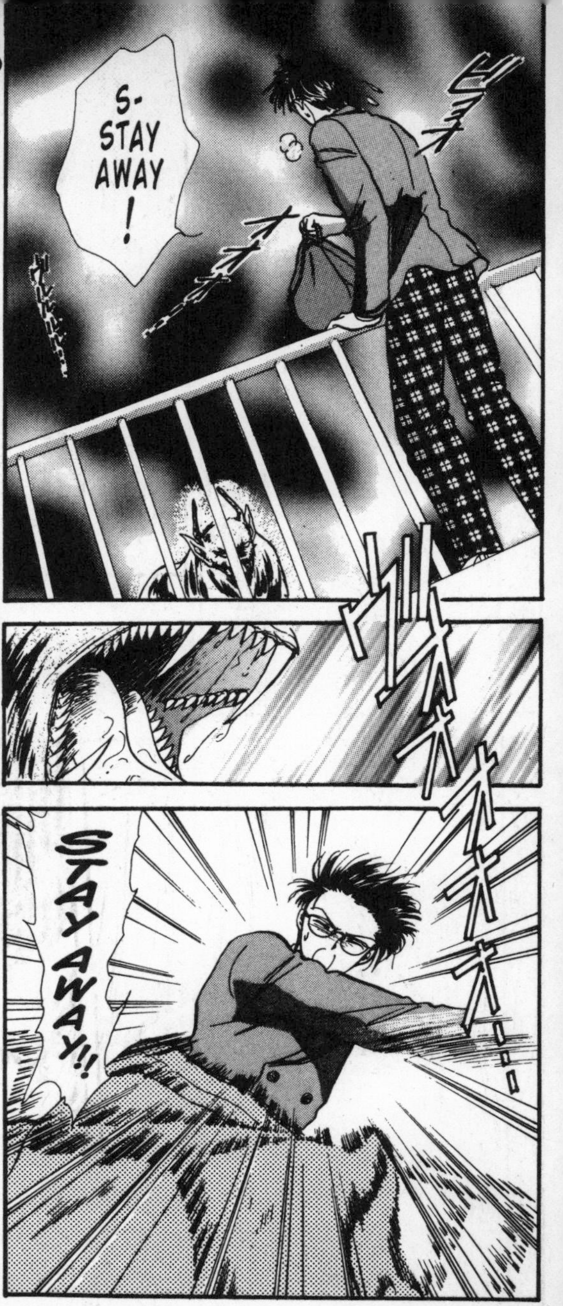
S-STAY AWAY!
STAY AWAY!!

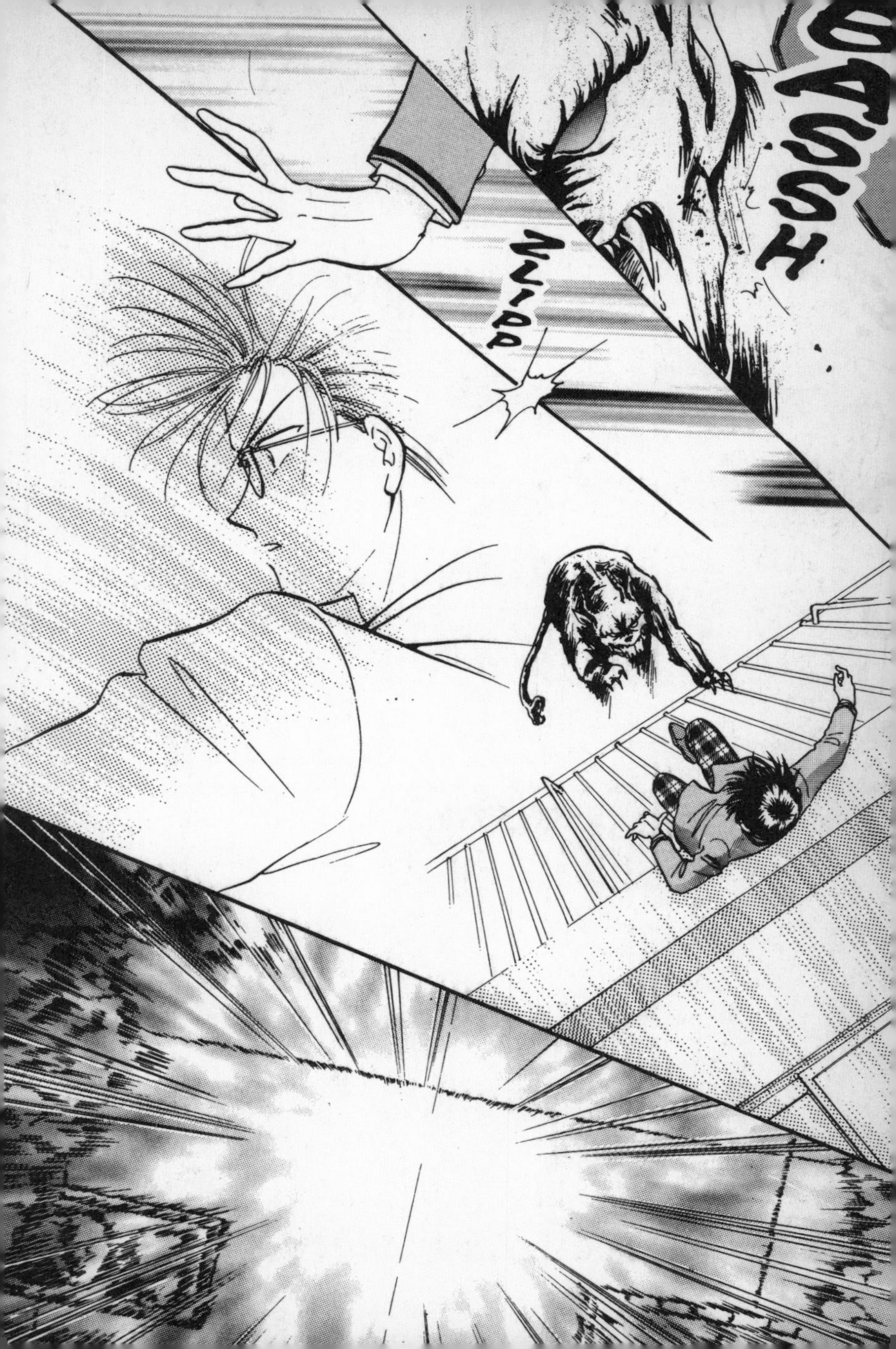
BASSH
ZZLIPP

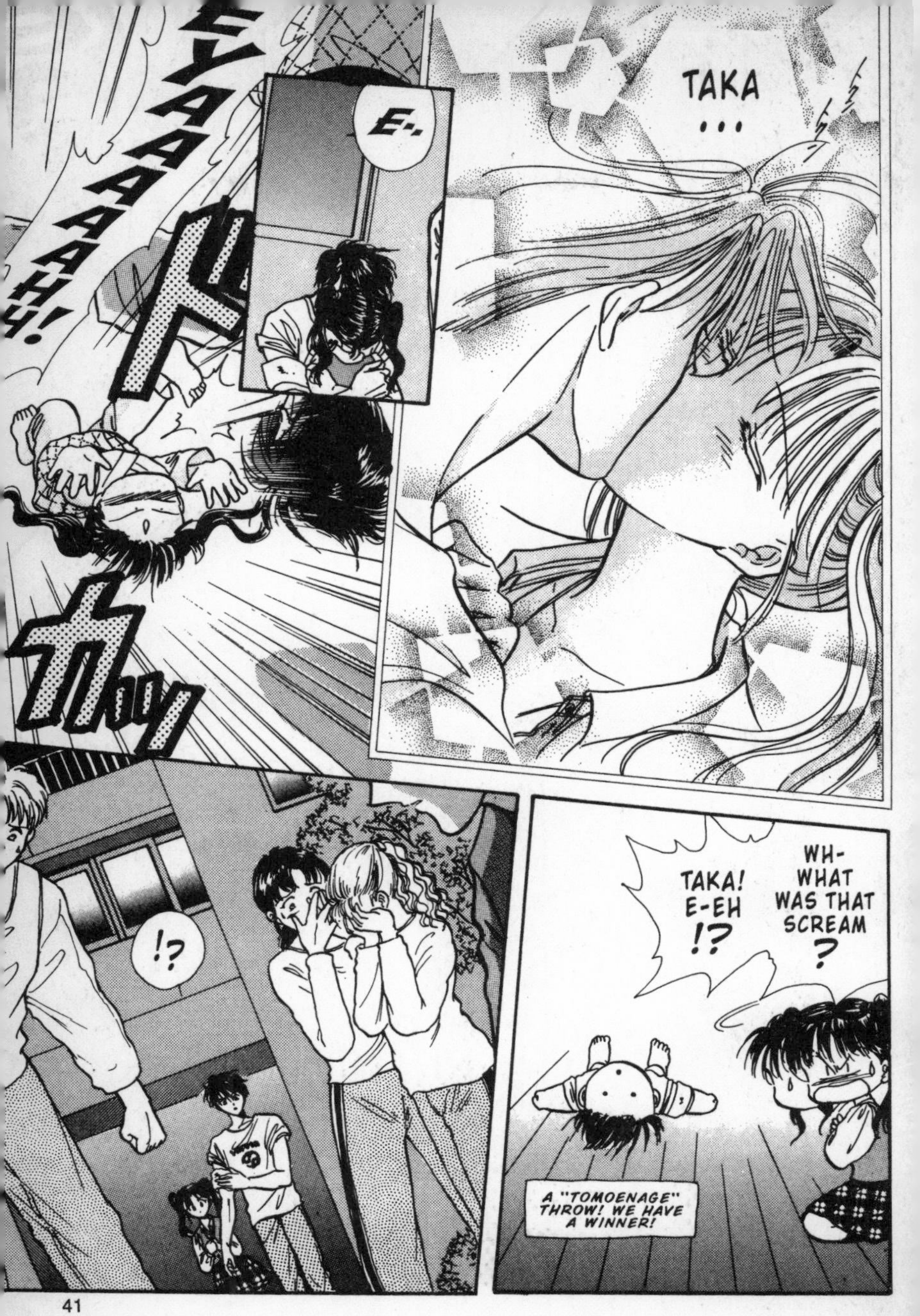

TAKA ...
E-.
EYAAAAAHH!
WH-WHAT WAS THAT SCREAM?
TAKA! E-EH!?
A "TOMOENAGE" THROW! WE HAVE A WINNER!
!?

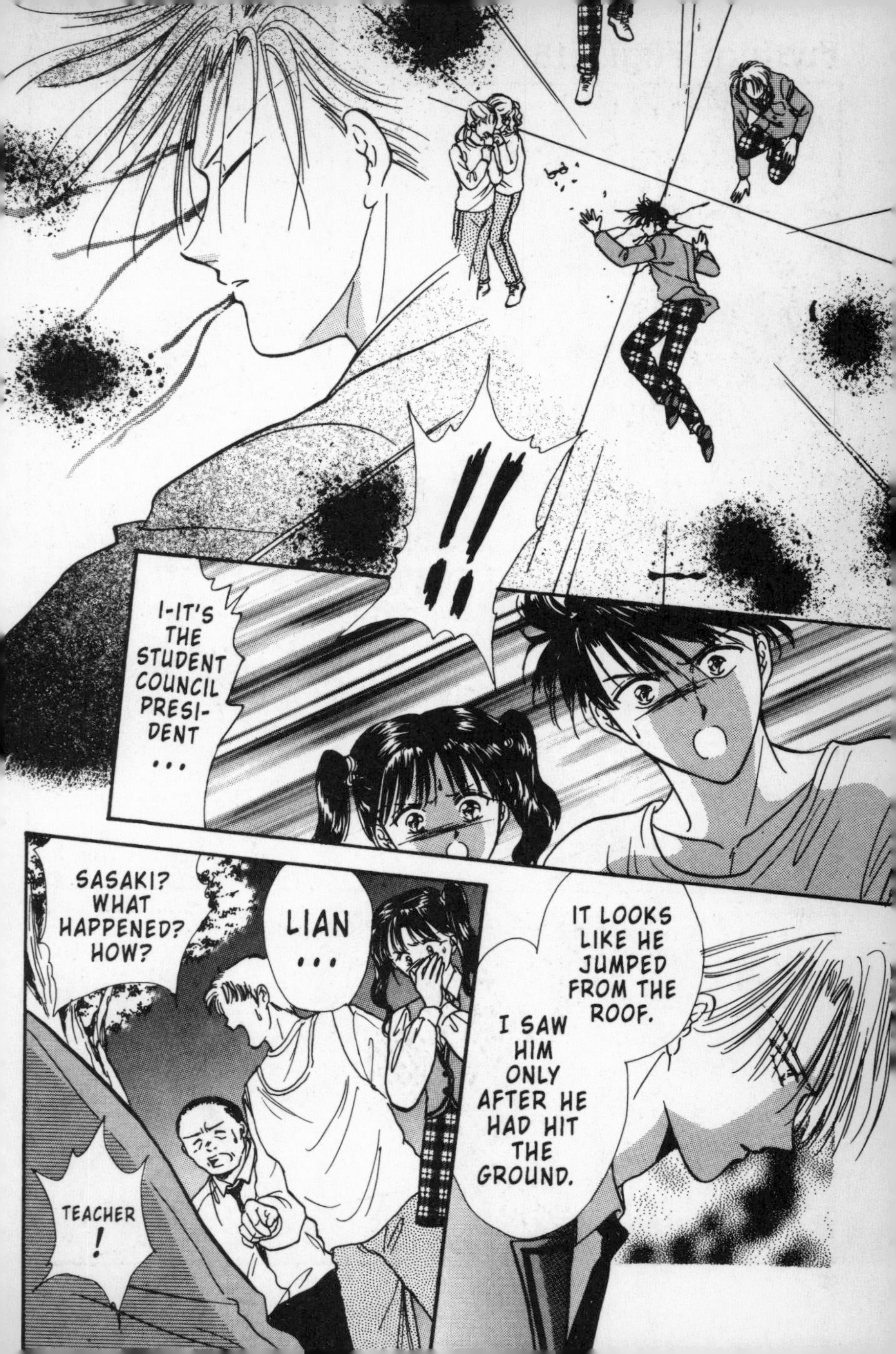
!!
I-IT'S THE STUDENT COUNCIL PRESIDENT...
IT LOOKS LIKE HE JUMPED FROM THE ROOF.
I SAW HIM ONLY AFTER HE HAD HIT THE GROUND.
LIAN...
SASAKI? WHAT HAPPENED? HOW?
TEACHER!

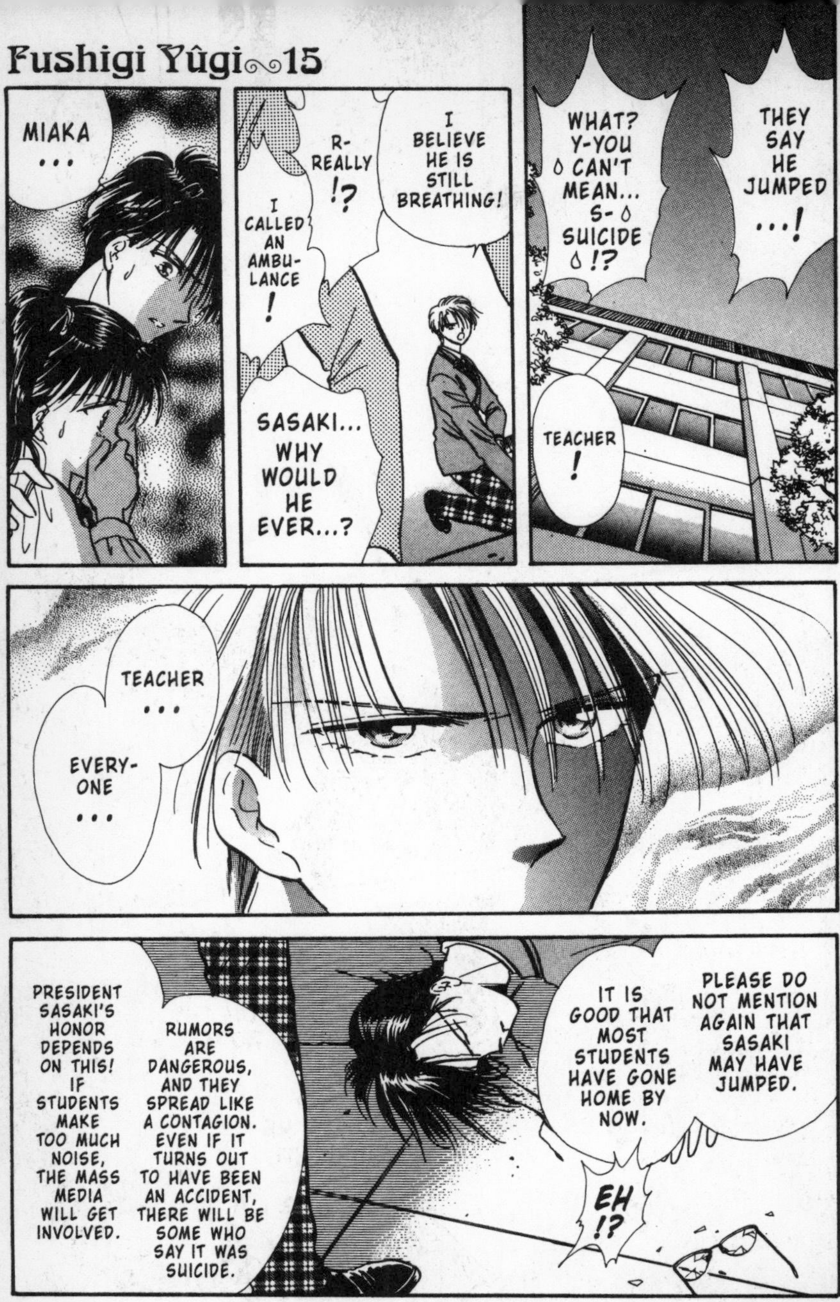
THEY SAY HE JUMPED ...!
WHAT? Y-YOU CAN'T MEAN... S-SUICIDE !?
TEACHER!
I BELIEVE HE IS STILL BREATHING!
R-REALLY !?
I CALLED AN AMBU-LANCE!
SASAKI... WHY WOULD HE EVER...?
MIAKA ...
TEACHER ...
EVERY-ONE ...
PLEASE DO NOT MENTION AGAIN THAT SASAKI MAY HAVE JUMPED.
IT IS GOOD THAT MOST STUDENTS HAVE GONE HOME BY NOW.
EH !?
RUMORS ARE DANGEROUS, AND THEY SPREAD LIKE A CONTAGION. EVEN IF IT TURNS OUT TO HAVE BEEN AN ACCIDENT, THERE WILL BE SOME WHO SAY IT WAS SUICIDE.
PRESIDENT SASAKI'S HONOR DEPENDS ON THIS! IF STUDENTS MAKE TOO MUCH NOISE, THE MASS MEDIA WILL GET INVOLVED.

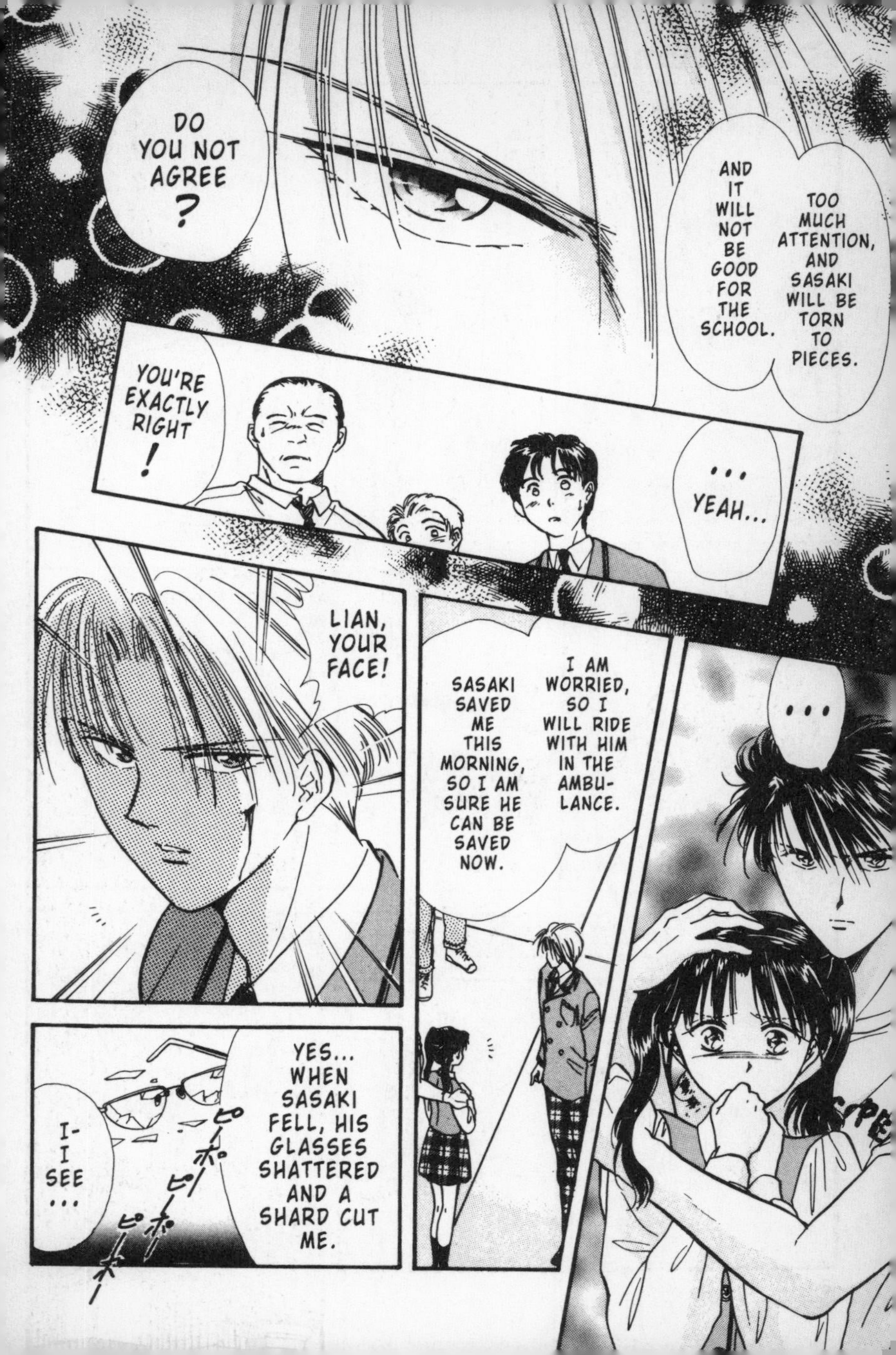
TOO MUCH ATTENTION, AND SASAKI WILL BE TORN TO PIECES.
AND IT WILL NOT BE GOOD FOR THE SCHOOL.
DO YOU NOT AGREE?
YOU'RE EXACTLY RIGHT!
... YEAH...
...
I AM WORRIED, SO I WILL RIDE WITH HIM IN THE AMBULANCE.
SASAKI SAVED ME THIS MORNING, SO I AM SURE HE CAN BE SAVED NOW.
LIAN, YOUR FACE!
YES... WHEN SASAKI FELL, HIS GLASSES SHATTERED AND A SHARD CUT ME.
ピーポーピーポーピーポー
I-I SEE...

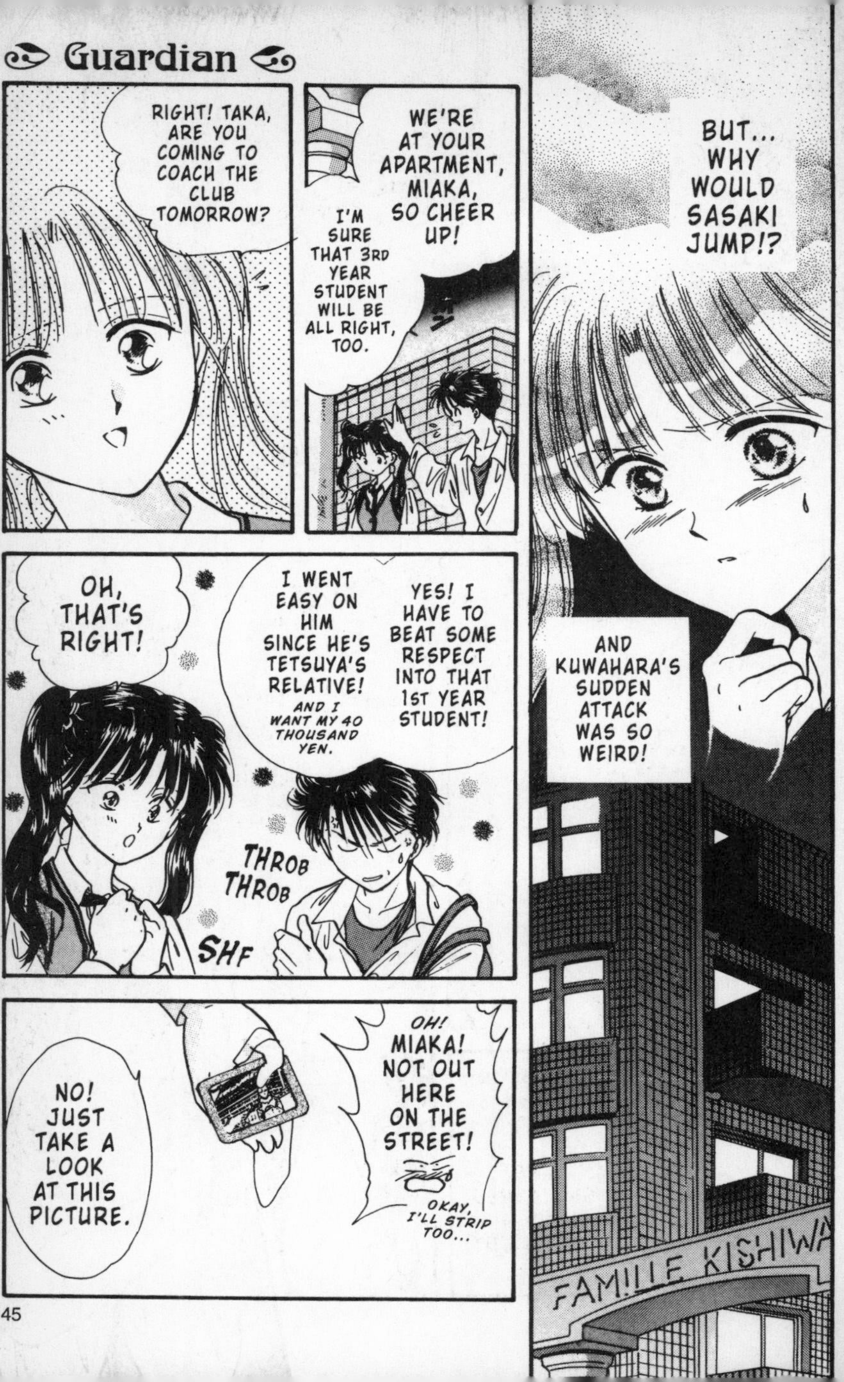
BUT... WHY WOULD SASAKI JUMP!?
AND KUWAHARA'S SUDDEN ATTACK WAS SO WEIRD!
FAMILLE KISHIWA
WE'RE AT YOUR APARTMENT, MIAKA, SO CHEER UP!
I'M SURE THAT 3RD YEAR STUDENT WILL BE ALL RIGHT, TOO.
RIGHT! TAKA, ARE YOU COMING TO COACH THE CLUB TOMORROW?
YES! I HAVE TO BEAT SOME RESPECT INTO THAT 1ST YEAR STUDENT!
I WENT EASY ON HIM SINCE HE'S TETSUYA'S RELATIVE!
AND I WANT MY 40 THOUSAND YEN.
OH, THAT'S RIGHT!
THROB THROB
SHF
OH! MIAKA! NOT OUT HERE ON THE STREET!
OKAY, I'LL STRIP TOO...
NO! JUST TAKE A LOOK AT THIS PICTURE.

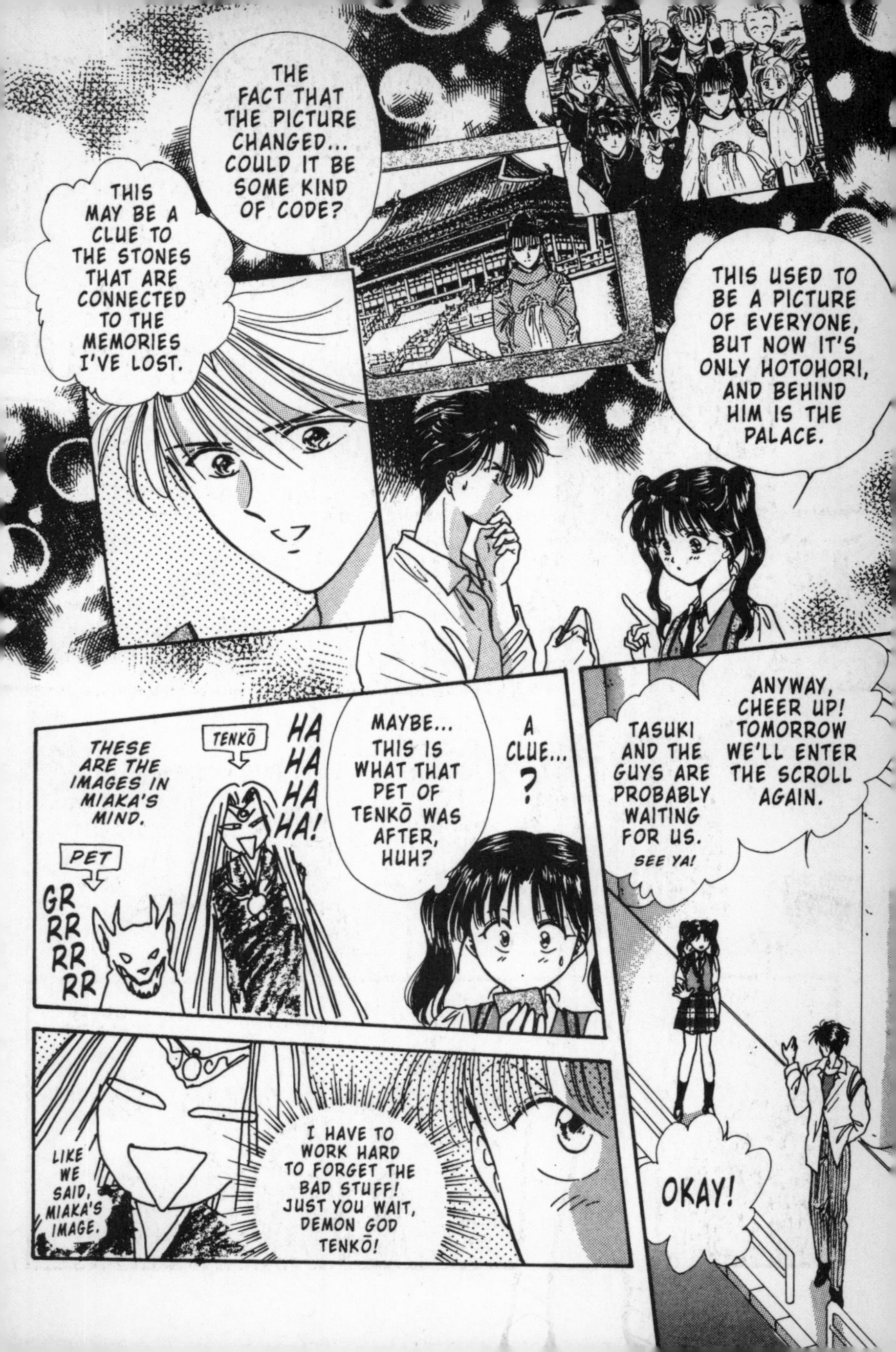
THIS USED TO BE A PICTURE OF EVERYONE, BUT NOW IT'S ONLY HOTOHORI, AND BEHIND HIM IS THE PALACE.
THE FACT THAT THE PICTURE CHANGED... COULD IT BE SOME KIND OF CODE?
THIS MAY BE A CLUE TO THE STONES THAT ARE CONNECTED TO THE MEMORIES I'VE LOST.
ANYWAY, CHEER UP! TOMORROW WE'LL ENTER THE SCROLL AGAIN.
TASUKI AND THE GUYS ARE PROBABLY WAITING FOR US.
SEE YA!
OKAY!
A CLUE...?
MAYBE... THIS IS WHAT THAT PET OF TENKŌ WAS AFTER, HUH?
HA HA HA HA!
TENKŌ
THESE ARE THE IMAGES IN MIAKA'S MIND.
PET
GR RR RR RR
I HAVE TO WORK HARD TO FORGET THE BAD STUFF! JUST YOU WAIT, DEMON GOD TENKŌ!
LIKE WE SAID, MIAKA'S IMAGE.

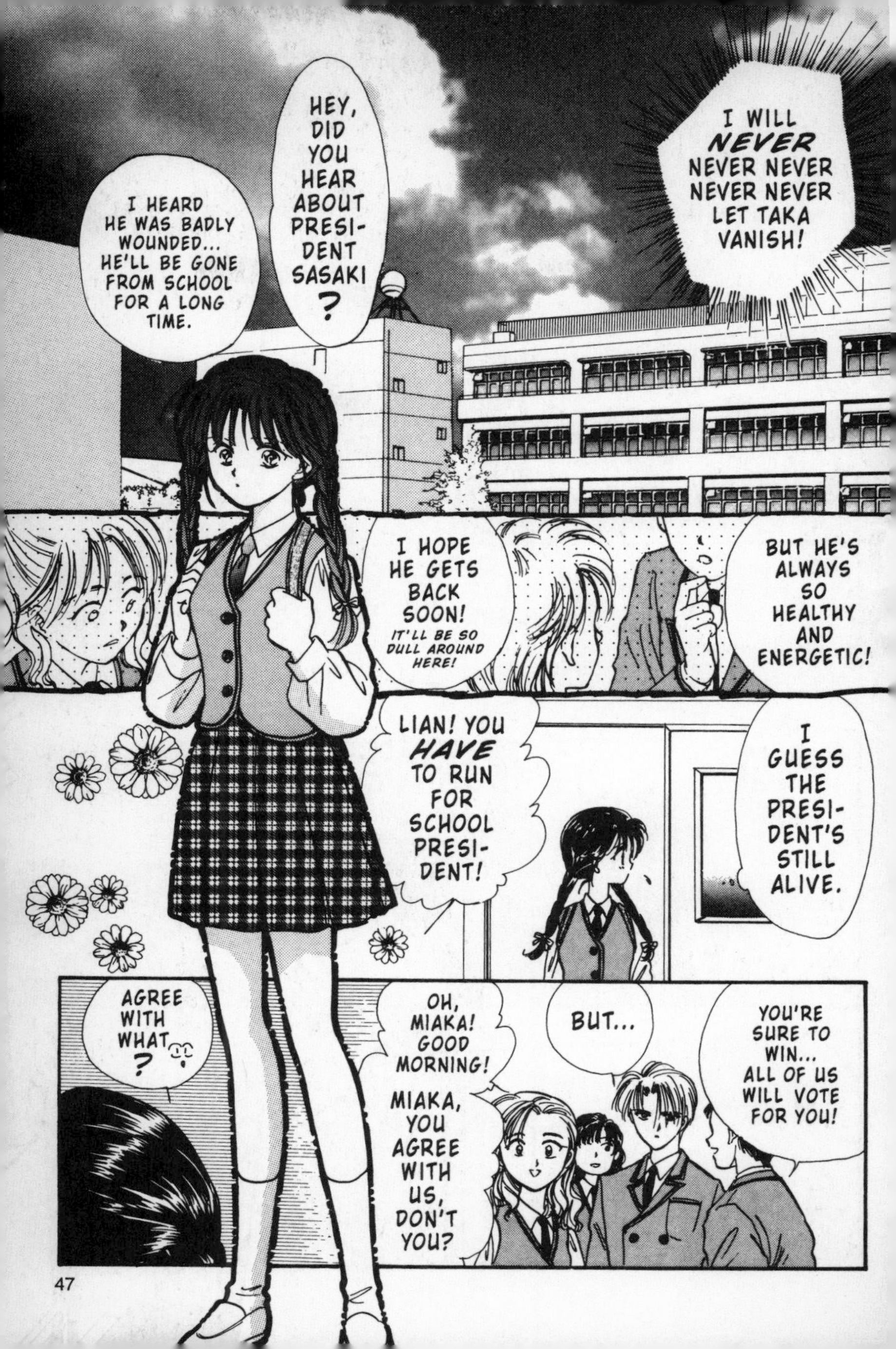

I WILL NEVER NEVER NEVER NEVER NEVER LET TAKA VANISH!
HEY, DID YOU HEAR ABOUT PRESIDENT SASAKI?
I HEARD HE WAS BADLY WOUNDED... HE'LL BE GONE FROM SCHOOL FOR A LONG TIME.
BUT HE'S ALWAYS SO HEALTHY AND ENERGETIC!
I HOPE HE GETS BACK SOON!
IT'LL BE SO DULL AROUND HERE!
I GUESS THE PRESIDENT'S STILL ALIVE.
LIAN! YOU HAVE TO RUN FOR SCHOOL PRESIDENT!
YOU'RE SURE TO WIN... ALL OF US WILL VOTE FOR YOU!
BUT...
OH, MIAKA! GOOD MORNING!
MIAKA, YOU AGREE WITH US, DON'T YOU?
AGREE WITH WHAT?

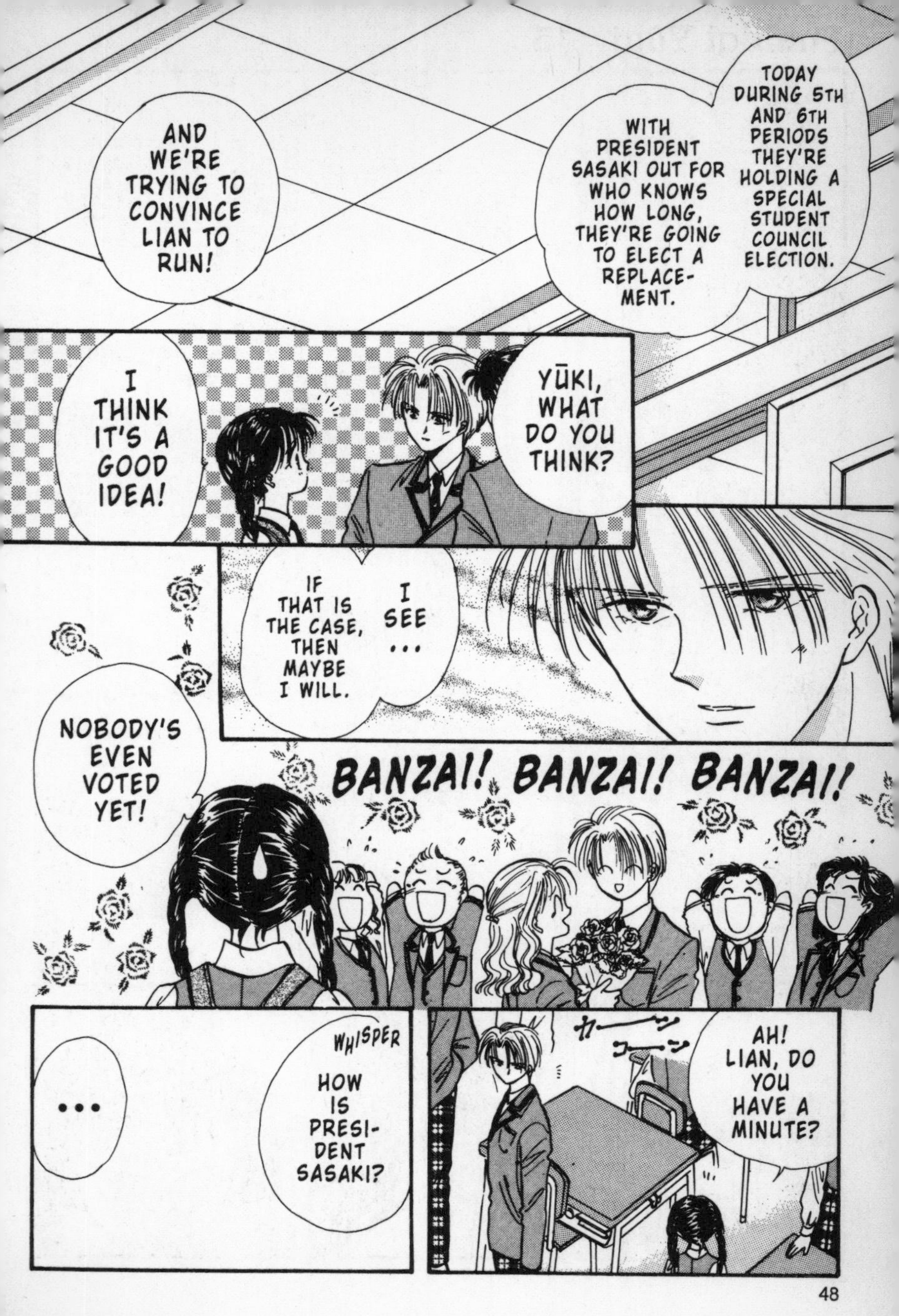
TODAY DURING 5TH AND 6TH PERIODS THEY'RE HOLDING A SPECIAL STUDENT COUNCIL ELECTION.
WITH PRESIDENT SASAKI OUT FOR WHO KNOWS HOW LONG, THEY'RE GOING TO ELECT A REPLACE-MENT.
AND WE'RE TRYING TO CONVINCE LIAN TO RUN!
YŪKI, WHAT DO YOU THINK?
I THINK IT'S A GOOD IDEA!
I SEE...
IF THAT IS THE CASE, THEN MAYBE I WILL.
BANZAI! BANZAI! BANZAI!
NOBODY'S EVEN VOTED YET!
カーン
コーン
AH! LIAN, DO YOU HAVE A MINUTE?
WHISPER
HOW IS PRESI-DENT SASAKI?
...

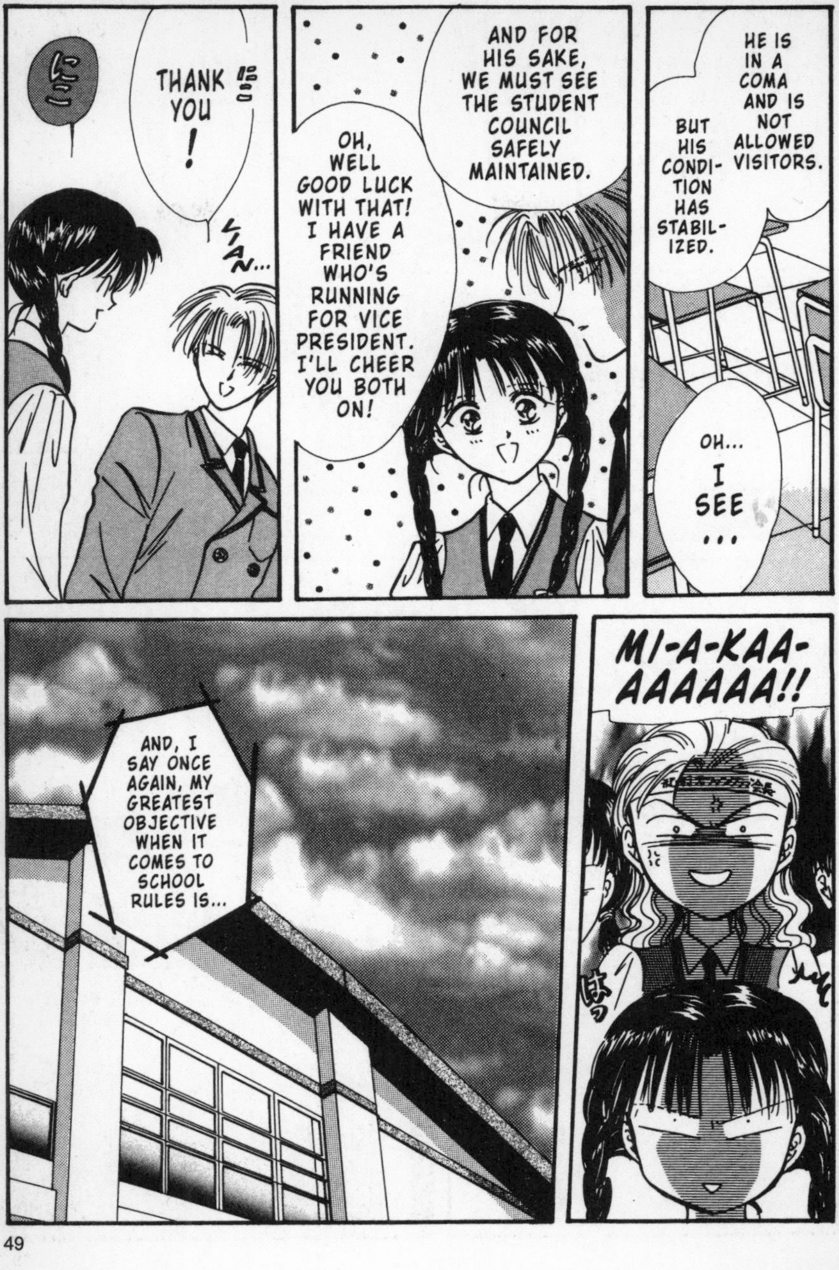
HE IS IN A COMA AND IS NOT ALLOWED VISITORS.
BUT HIS CONDITION HAS STABILIZED.
OH... I SEE...
AND FOR HIS SAKE, WE MUST SEE THE STUDENT COUNCIL SAFELY MAINTAINED.
OH, WELL GOOD LUCK WITH THAT! I HAVE A FRIEND WHO'S RUNNING FOR VICE PRESIDENT. I'LL CHEER YOU BOTH ON!
THANK YOU!
MI-A-KAA-AAAAAA!!
AND, I SAY ONCE AGAIN, MY GREATEST OBJECTIVE WHEN IT COMES TO SCHOOL RULES IS...

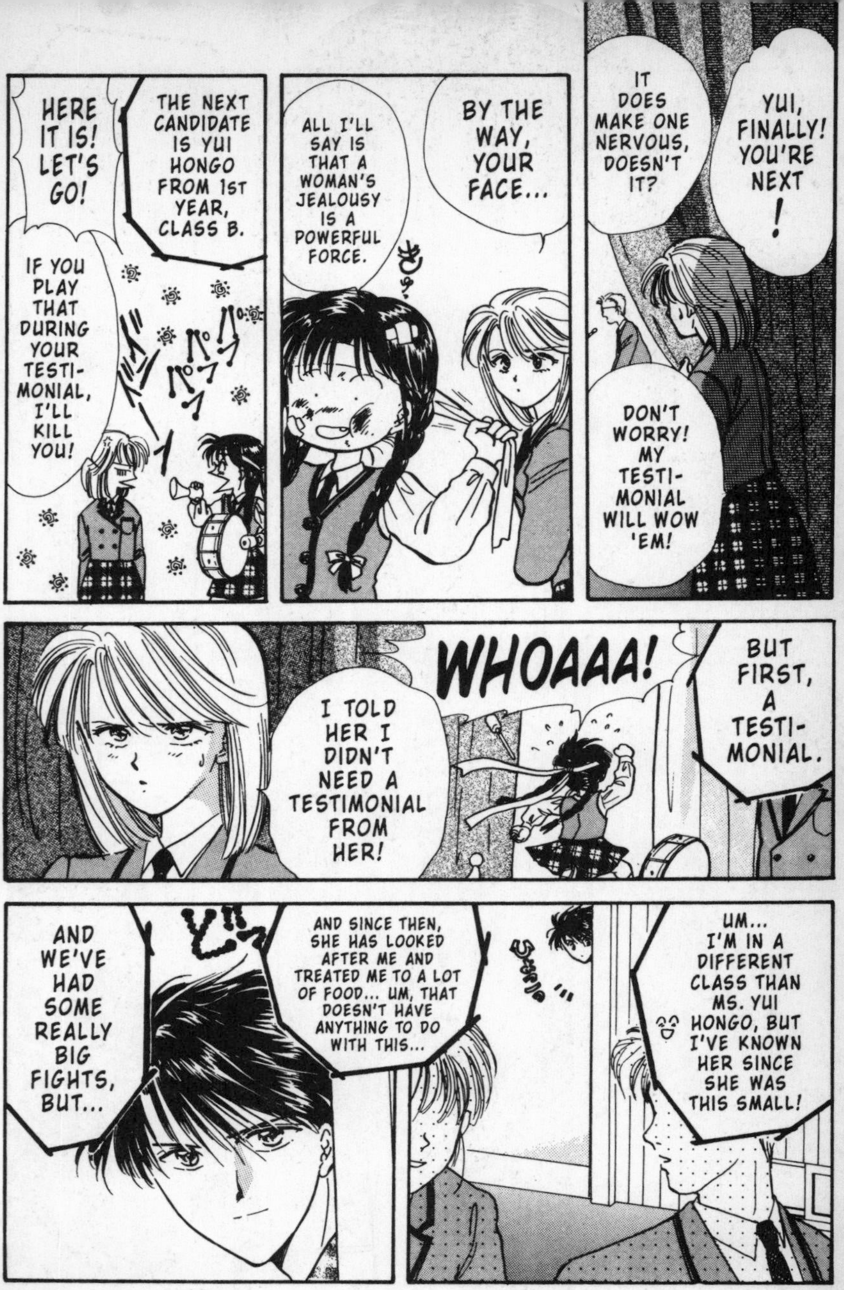
YUI, FINALLY! YOU'RE NEXT!
IT DOES MAKE ONE NERVOUS, DOESN'T IT?
DON'T WORRY! MY TESTIMONIAL WILL WOW 'EM!
BY THE WAY, YOUR FACE...
ALL I'LL SAY IS THAT A WOMAN'S JEALOUSY IS A POWERFUL FORCE.
THE NEXT CANDIDATE IS YUI HONGO FROM 1ST YEAR, CLASS B.
HERE IT IS! LET'S GO!
IF YOU PLAY THAT DURING YOUR TESTIMONIAL, I'LL KILL YOU!
BUT FIRST, A TESTIMONIAL.
WHOAAA!
I TOLD HER I DIDN'T NEED A TESTIMONIAL FROM HER!
UM... I'M IN A DIFFERENT CLASS THAN MS. YUI HONGO, BUT I'VE KNOWN HER SINCE SHE WAS THIS SMALL!
AND SINCE THEN, SHE HAS LOOKED AFTER ME AND TREATED ME TO A LOT OF FOOD... UM, THAT DOESN'T HAVE ANYTHING TO DO WITH THIS...
AND WE'VE HAD SOME REALLY BIG FIGHTS, BUT...

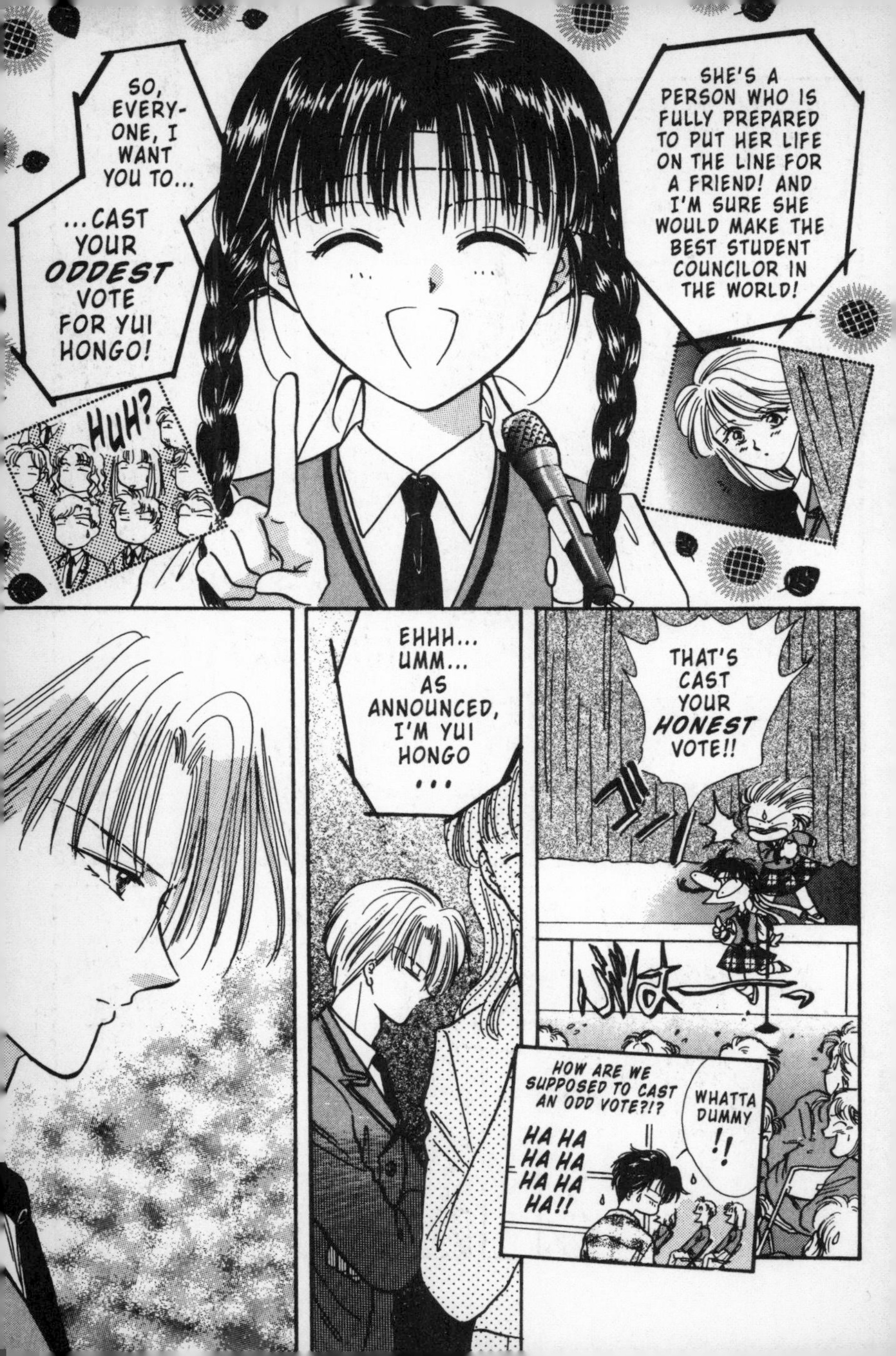
SHE'S A PERSON WHO IS FULLY PREPARED TO PUT HER LIFE ON THE LINE FOR A FRIEND! AND I'M SURE SHE WOULD MAKE THE BEST STUDENT COUNCILOR IN THE WORLD!
SO, EVERYONE, I WANT YOU TO...
...CAST YOUR ODDEST VOTE FOR YUI HONGO!
HUH?
THAT'S CAST YOUR HONEST VOTE!!
WHATTA DUMMY!!
HOW ARE WE SUPPOSED TO CAST AN ODD VOTE?!?
HA HA HA HA HA HA HA!!
EHHH... UMM... AS ANNOUNCED, I'M YUI HONGO...

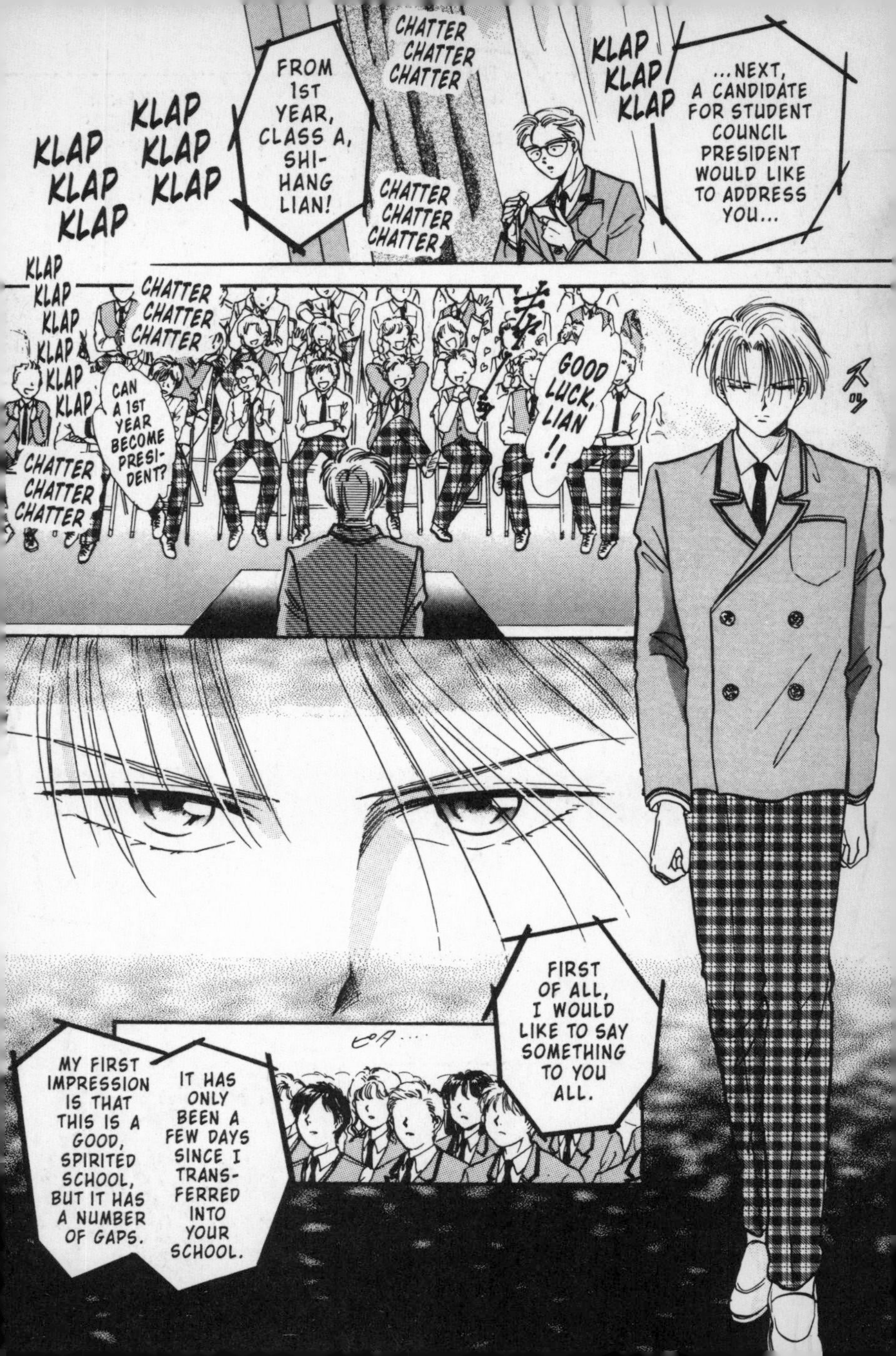
KLAP KLAP KLAP
...NEXT, A CANDIDATE FOR STUDENT COUNCIL PRESIDENT WOULD LIKE TO ADDRESS YOU...
CHATTER CHATTER CHATTER
FROM 1ST YEAR, CLASS A, SHI-HANG LIAN!
CHATTER CHATTER CHATTER
KLAP KLAP KLAP
KLAP KLAP KLAP
GOOD LUCK, LIAN!!
CHATTER CHATTER CHATTER
KLAP KLAP KLAP KLAP KLAP KLAP
CAN A 1ST YEAR BECOME PRESI-DENT?
CHATTER CHATTER CHATTER
FIRST OF ALL, I WOULD LIKE TO SAY SOMETHING TO YOU ALL.
IT HAS ONLY BEEN A FEW DAYS SINCE I TRANS-FERRED INTO YOUR SCHOOL.
MY FIRST IMPRESSION IS THAT THIS IS A GOOD, SPIRITED SCHOOL, BUT IT HAS A NUMBER OF GAPS.

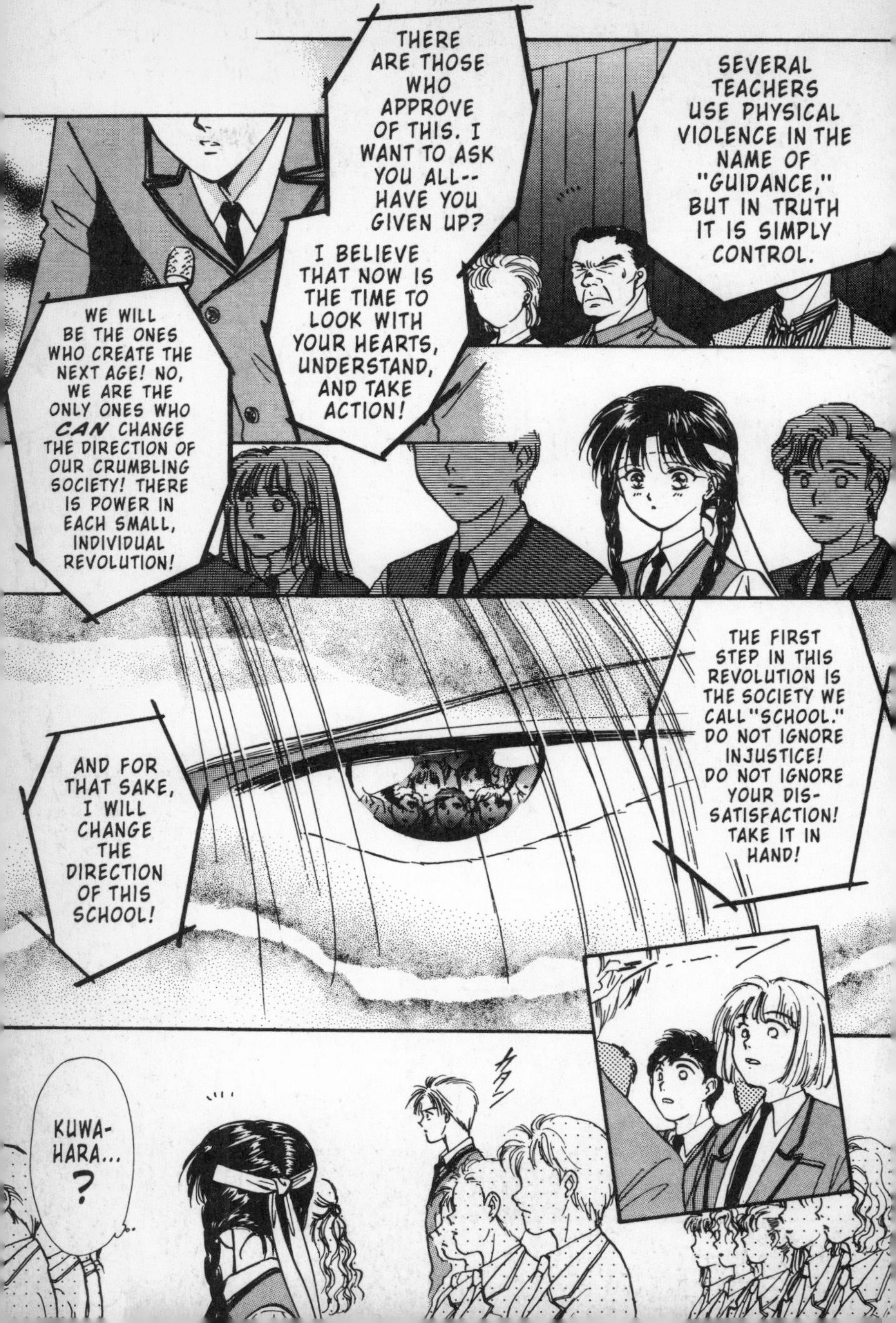

SEVERAL TEACHERS USE PHYSICAL VIOLENCE IN THE NAME OF "GUIDANCE," BUT IN TRUTH IT IS SIMPLY CONTROL.
THERE ARE THOSE WHO APPROVE OF THIS. I WANT TO ASK YOU ALL-- HAVE YOU GIVEN UP?
I BELIEVE THAT NOW IS THE TIME TO LOOK WITH YOUR HEARTS, UNDERSTAND, AND TAKE ACTION!
WE WILL BE THE ONES WHO CREATE THE NEXT AGE! NO, WE ARE THE ONLY ONES WHO CAN CHANGE THE DIRECTION OF OUR CRUMBLING SOCIETY! THERE IS POWER IN EACH SMALL, INDIVIDUAL REVOLUTION!
THE FIRST STEP IN THIS REVOLUTION IS THE SOCIETY WE CALL "SCHOOL." DO NOT IGNORE INJUSTICE! DO NOT IGNORE YOUR DIS-SATISFACTION! TAKE IT IN HAND!
AND FOR THAT SAKE, I WILL CHANGE THE DIRECTION OF THIS SCHOOL!
KUWA-HARA...?

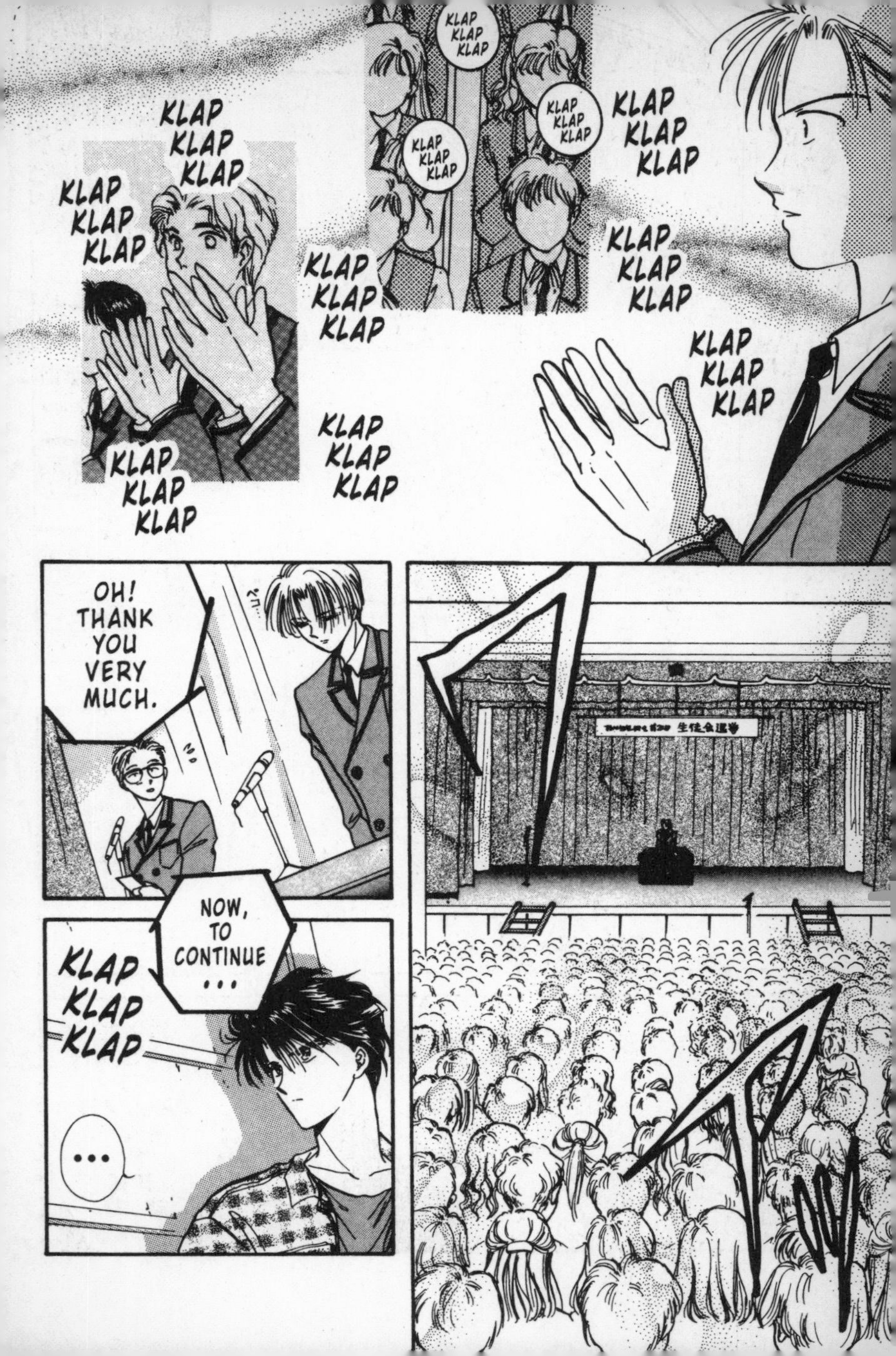
KLAP KLAP KLAP
KLAP KLAP KLAP
KLAP KLAP KLAP
KLAP KLAP KLAP
KLAP KLAP KLAP
KLAP KLAP KLAP
KLAP KLAP KLAP
KLAP KLAP KLAP
KLAP KLAP KLAP
KLAP KLAP KLAP
KLAP KLAP KLAP
OH! THANK YOU VERY MUCH.
NOW, TO CONTINUE ...
KLAP KLAP KLAP
...

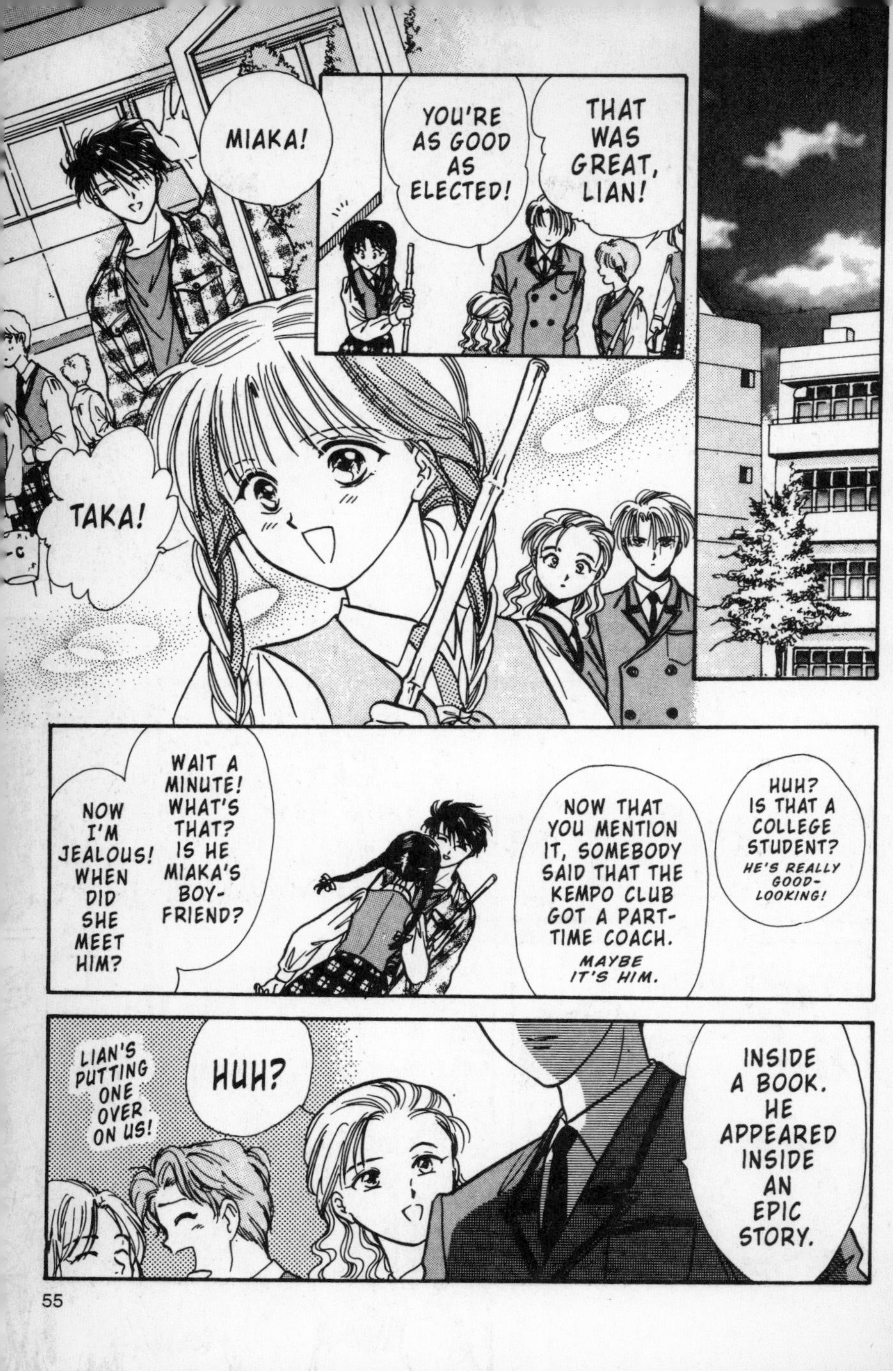
THAT WAS GREAT, LIAN!
YOU'RE AS GOOD AS ELECTED!
MIAKA!
TAKA!
HUH? IS THAT A COLLEGE STUDENT?
HE'S REALLY GOOD-LOOKING!
NOW THAT YOU MENTION IT, SOMEBODY SAID THAT THE KEMPO CLUB GOT A PART-TIME COACH.
MAYBE IT'S HIM.
WAIT A MINUTE! WHAT'S THAT? IS HE MIAKA'S BOY-FRIEND?
NOW I'M JEALOUS! WHEN DID SHE MEET HIM?
INSIDE A BOOK. HE APPEARED INSIDE AN EPIC STORY.
HUH?
LIAN'S PUTTING ONE OVER ON US!

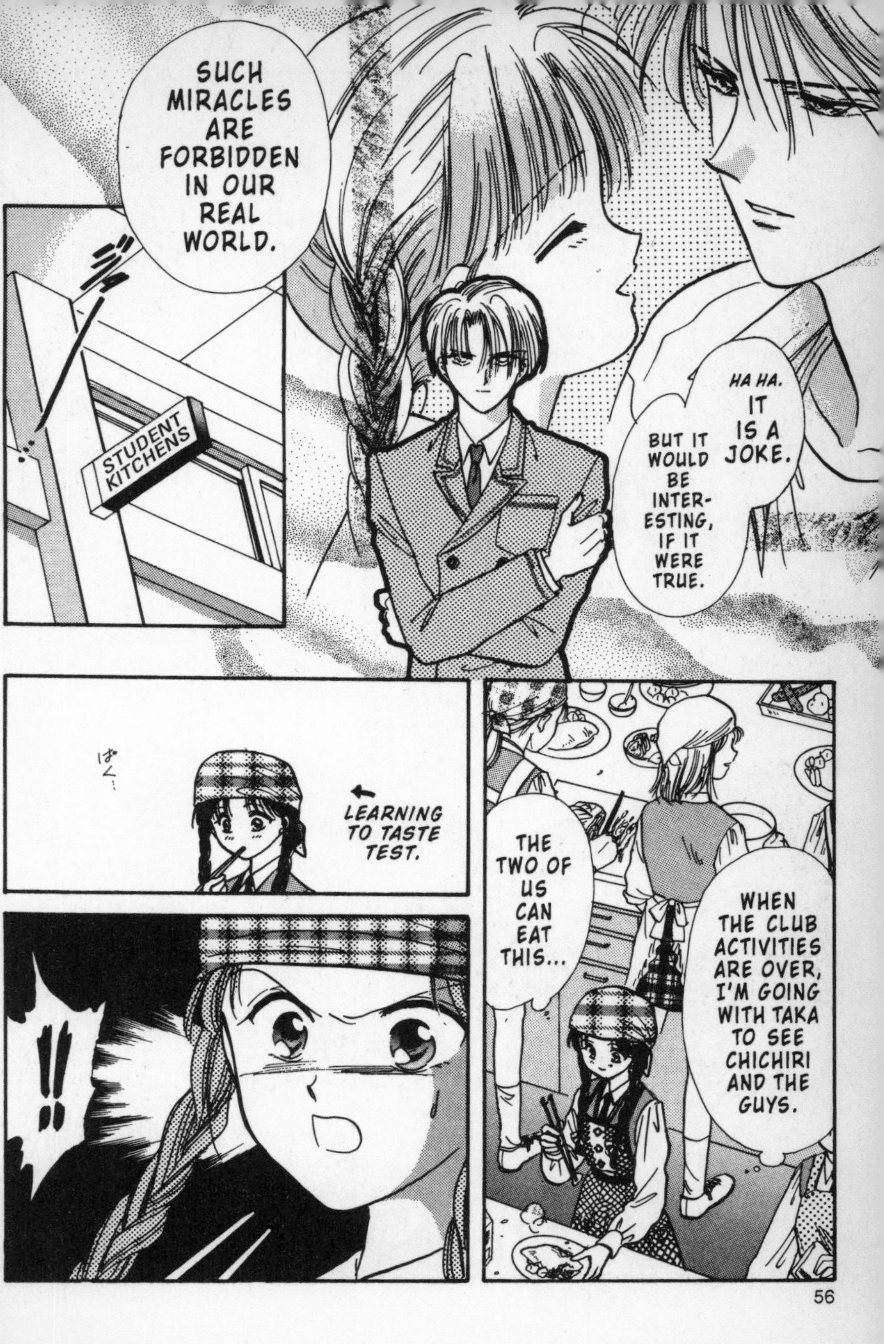
SUCH MIRACLES ARE FORBIDDEN IN OUR REAL WORLD.
HA HA. IT IS A JOKE.
BUT IT WOULD BE INTER-ESTING, IF IT WERE TRUE.
STUDENT KITCHENS
WHEN THE CLUB ACTIVITIES ARE OVER, I'M GOING WITH TAKA TO SEE CHICHIRI AND THE GUYS.
THE TWO OF US CAN EAT THIS...
ぱく…
LEARNING TO TASTE TEST.
!!

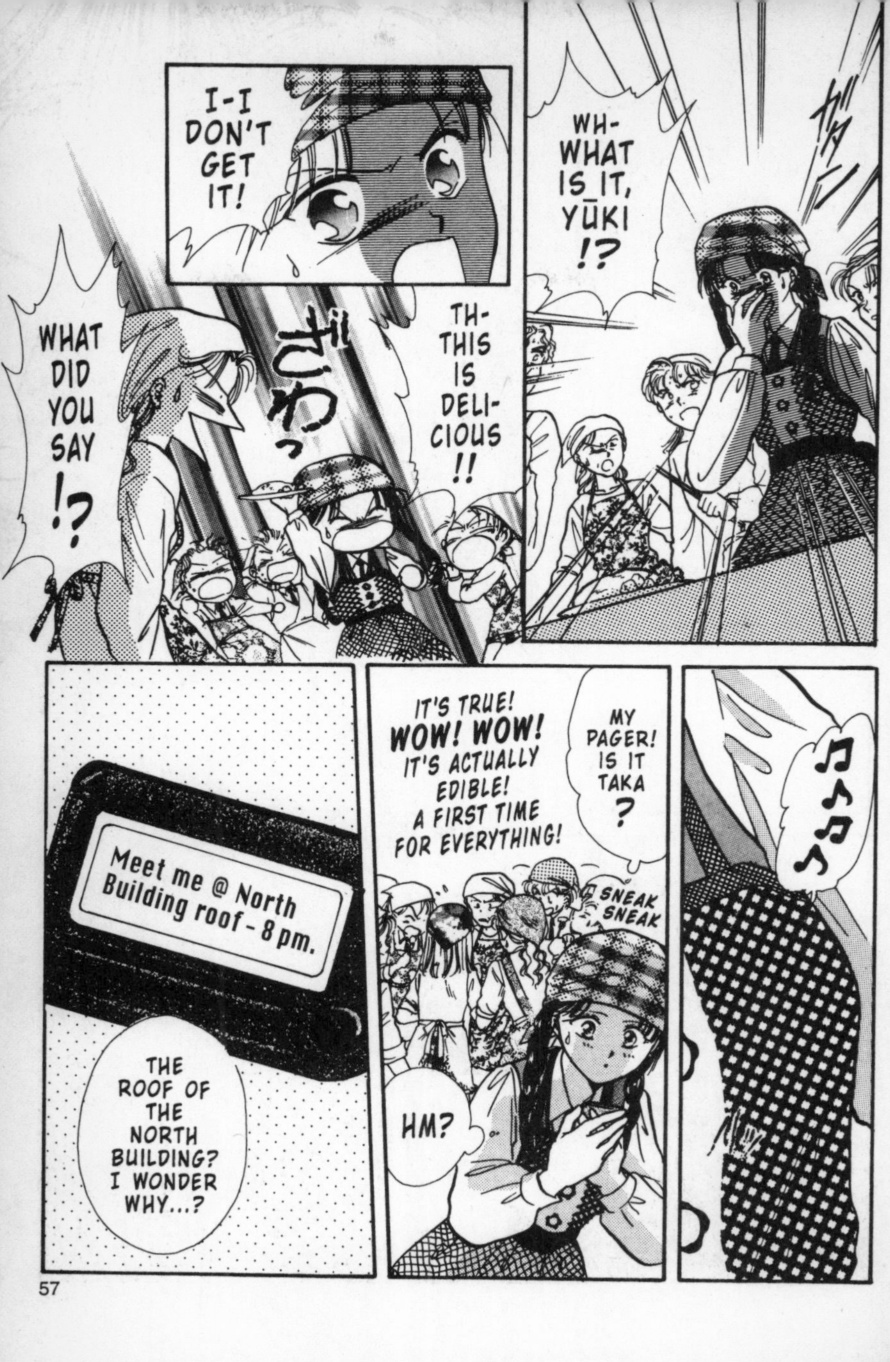

WH-WHAT IS IT, YŪKI!?
I-I DON'T GET IT!
TH-THIS IS DELICIOUS!!
ざわっ
WHAT DID YOU SAY!?
♫♪♫♪
MY PAGER! IS IT TAKA?
IT'S TRUE! WOW! WOW! IT'S ACTUALLY EDIBLE! A FIRST TIME FOR EVERYTHING!
SNEAK SNEAK
HM?
Meet me @ North Building roof - 8 pm.
THE ROOF OF THE NORTH BUILDING? I WONDER WHY...?

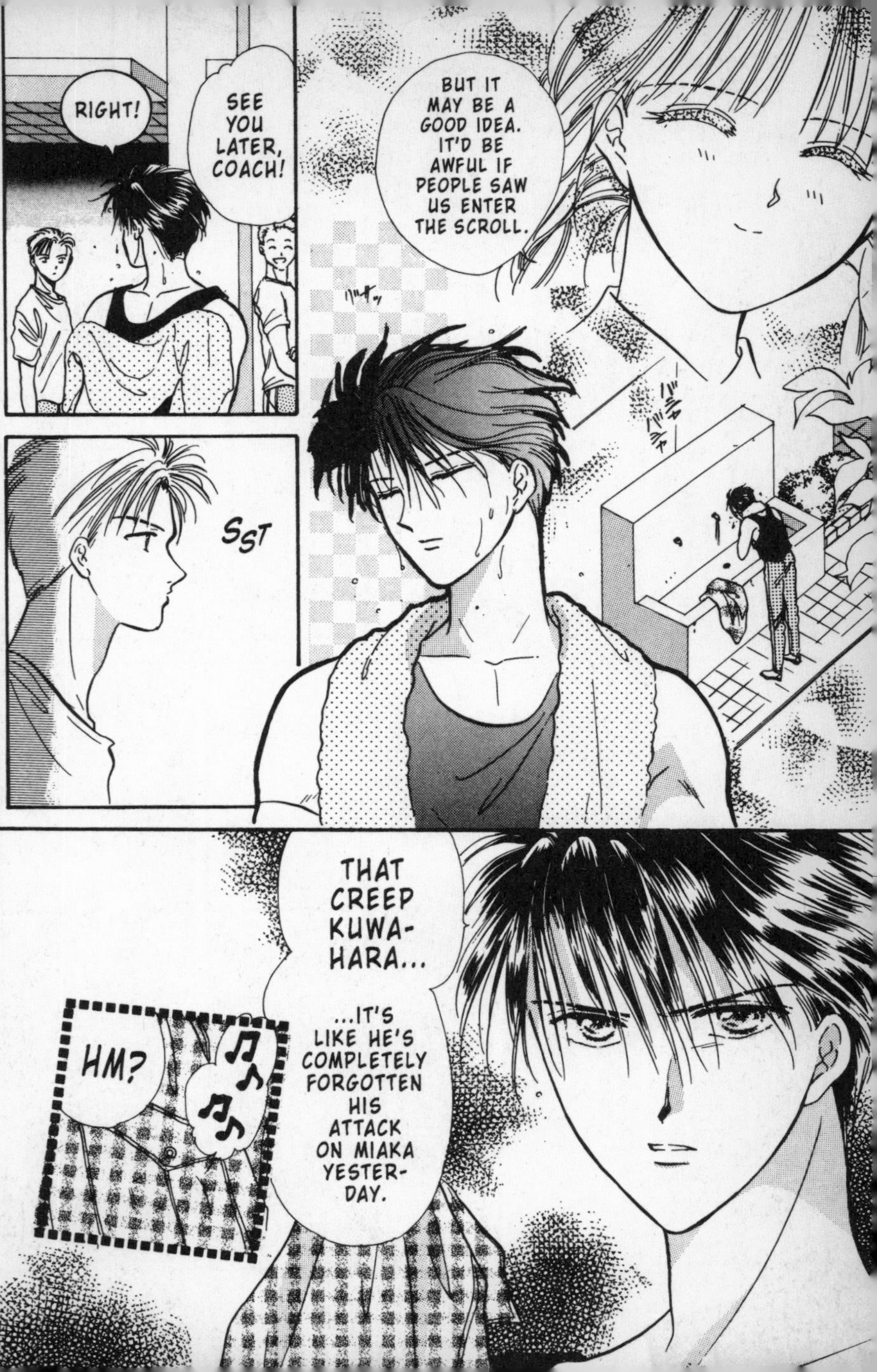
BUT IT MAY BE A GOOD IDEA. IT'D BE AWFUL IF PEOPLE SAW US ENTER THE SCROLL.
バシャ バシャ
SEE YOU LATER, COACH!
RIGHT!
SST
THAT CREEP KUWA-HARA...
...IT'S LIKE HE'S COMPLETELY FORGOTTEN HIS ATTACK ON MIAKA YESTER-DAY.
HM?

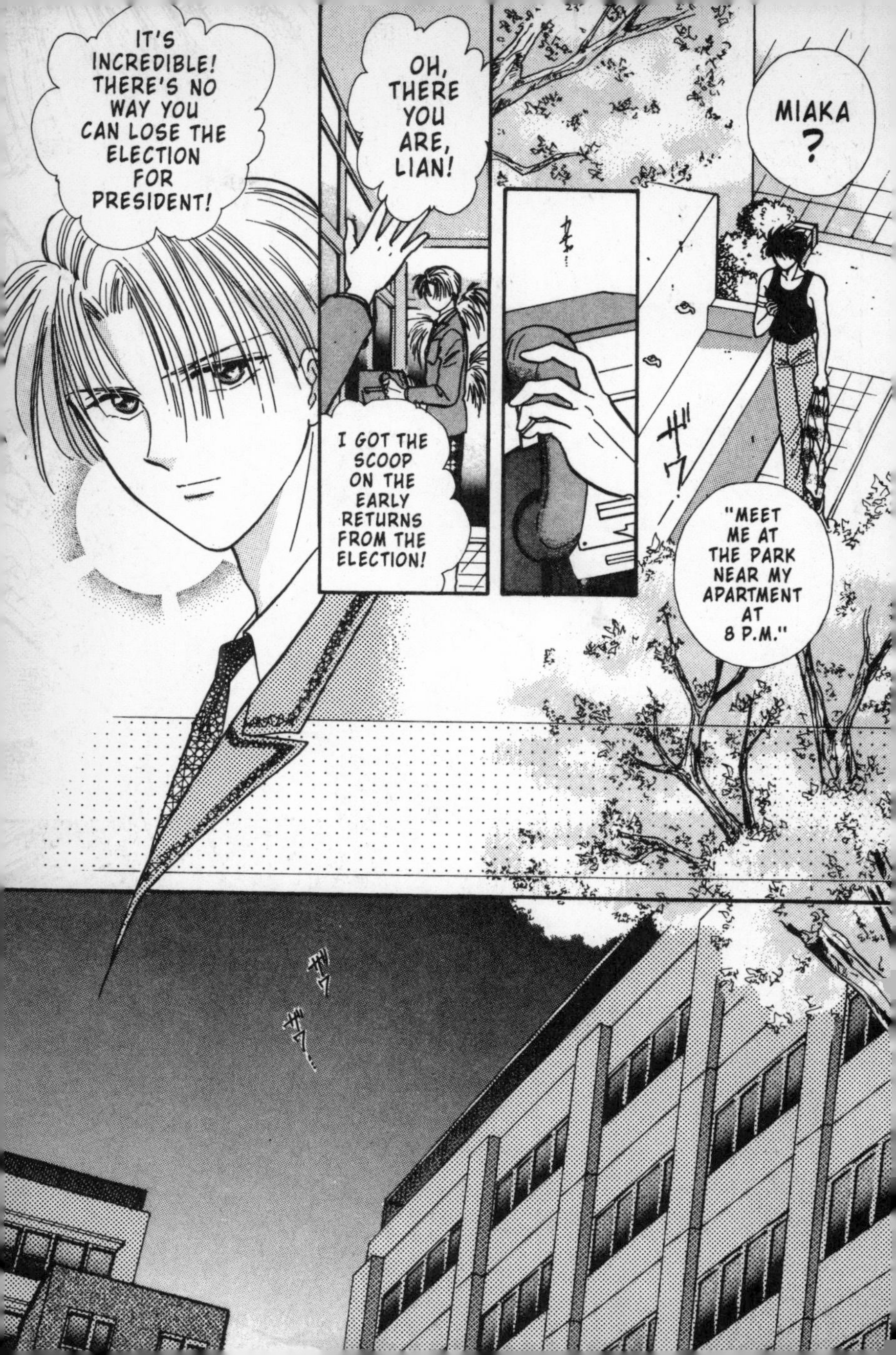
MIAKA ?
"MEET ME AT THE PARK NEAR MY APARTMENT AT 8 P.M."
OH, THERE YOU ARE, LIAN!
I GOT THE SCOOP ON THE EARLY RETURNS FROM THE ELECTION!
IT'S INCREDIBLE! THERE'S NO WAY YOU CAN LOSE THE ELECTION FOR PRESIDENT!

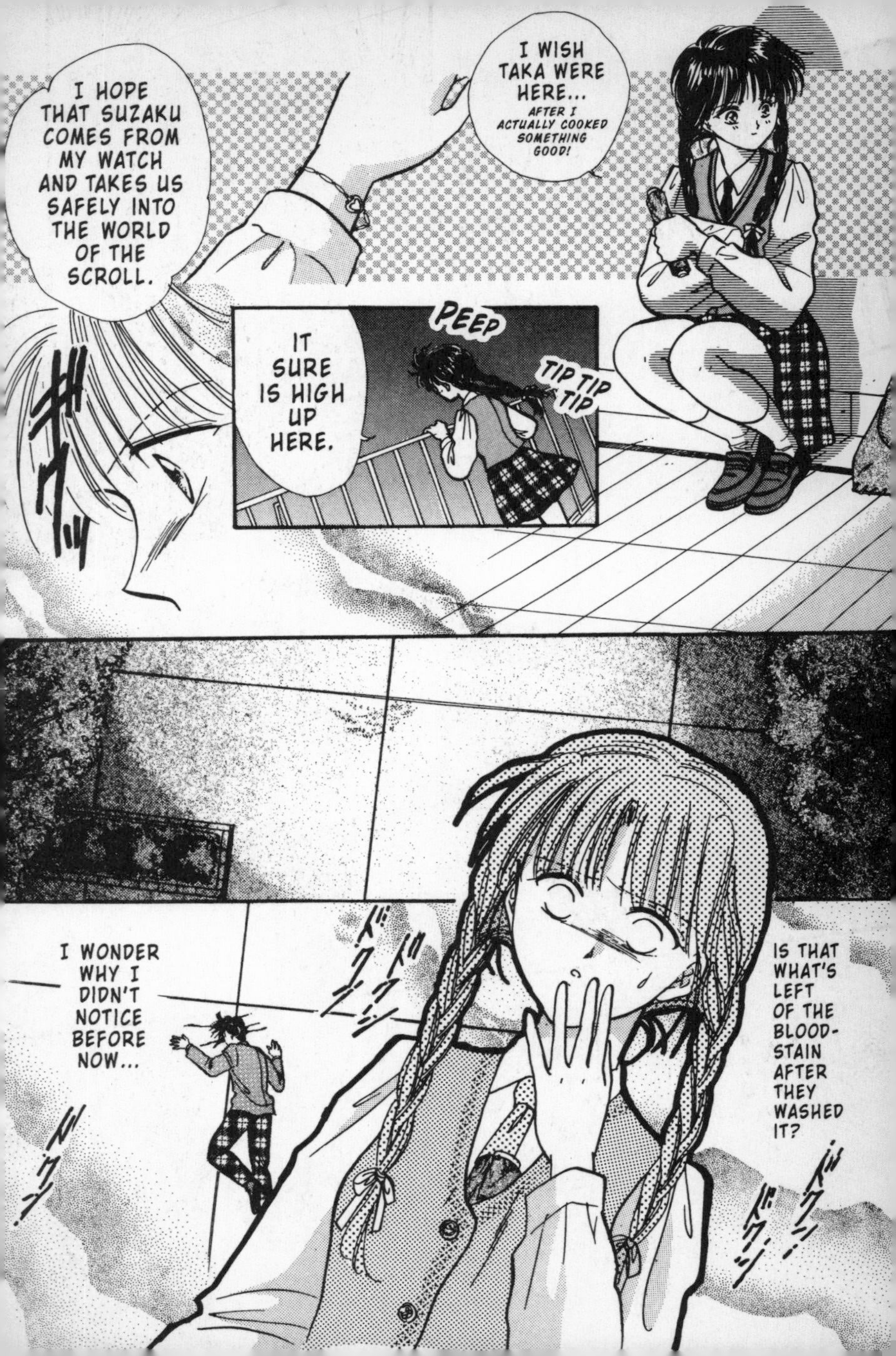

I WISH TAKA WERE HERE... AFTER I ACTUALLY COOKED SOMETHING GOOD!
PEEP
TIP TIP TIP
IT SURE IS HIGH UP HERE.
I HOPE THAT SUZAKU COMES FROM MY WATCH AND TAKES US SAFELY INTO THE WORLD OF THE SCROLL.
IS THAT WHAT'S LEFT OF THE BLOOD-STAIN AFTER THEY WASHED IT?
I WONDER WHY I DIDN'T NOTICE BEFORE NOW...

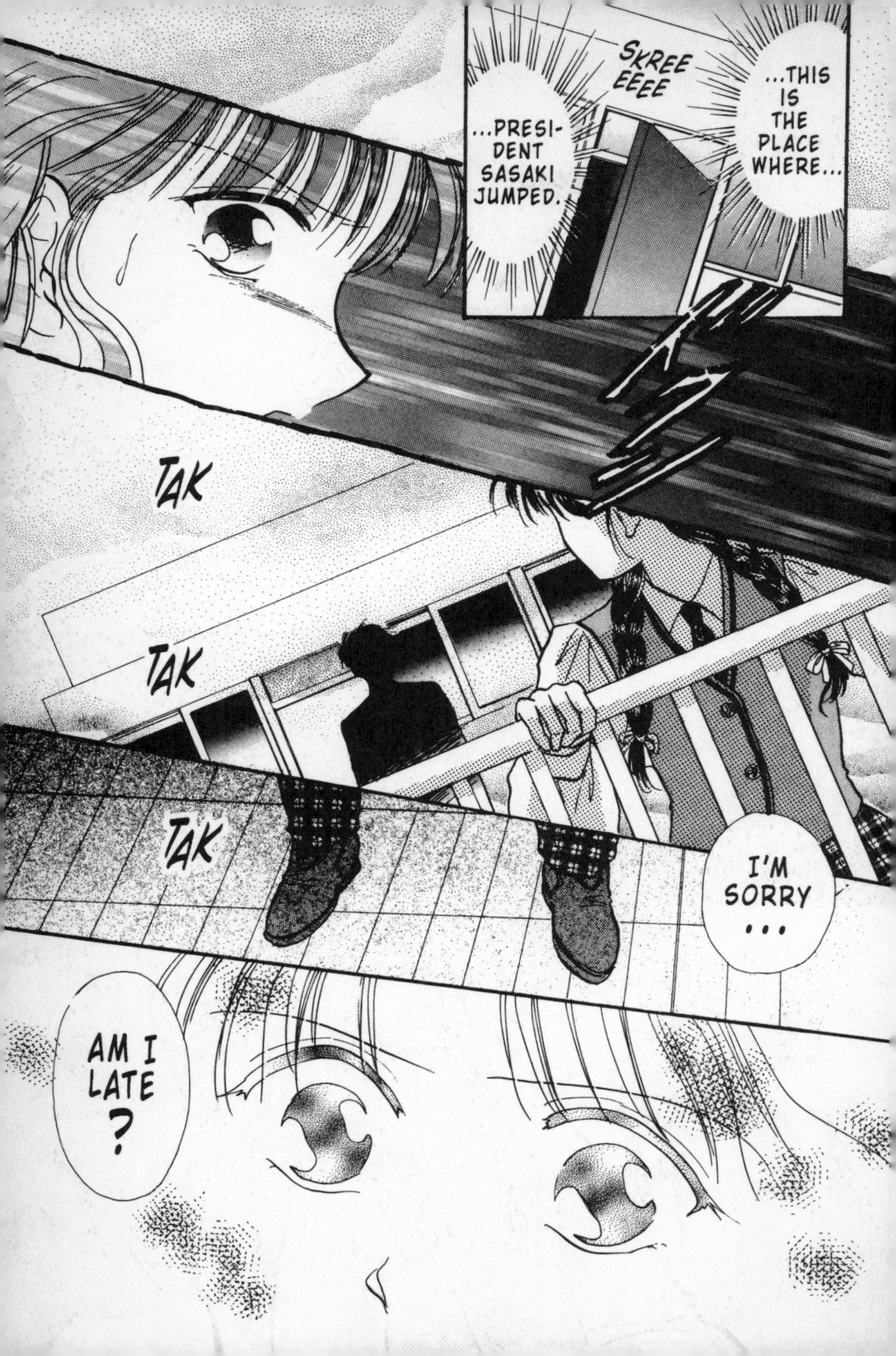
...THIS IS THE PLACE WHERE...
SKREE EEEE
...PRESIDENT SASAKI JUMPED.
TAK
TAK
TAK
I'M SORRY ...
AM I LATE ?

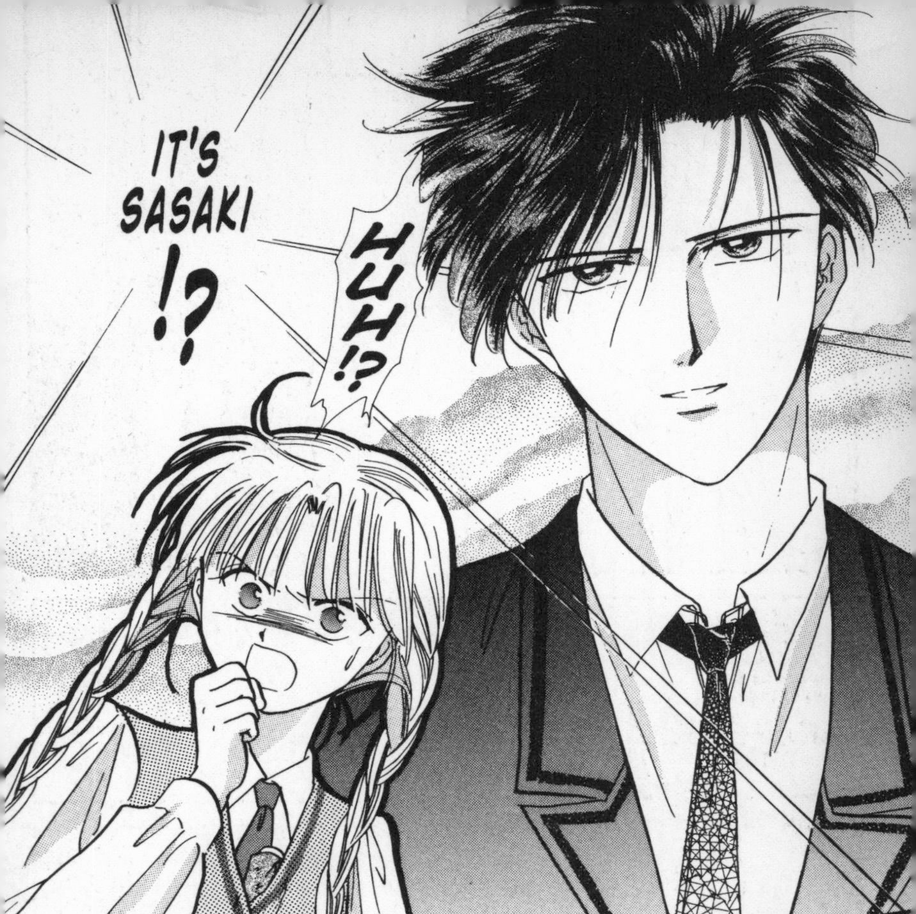
HUH!?
IT'S SASAKI !?
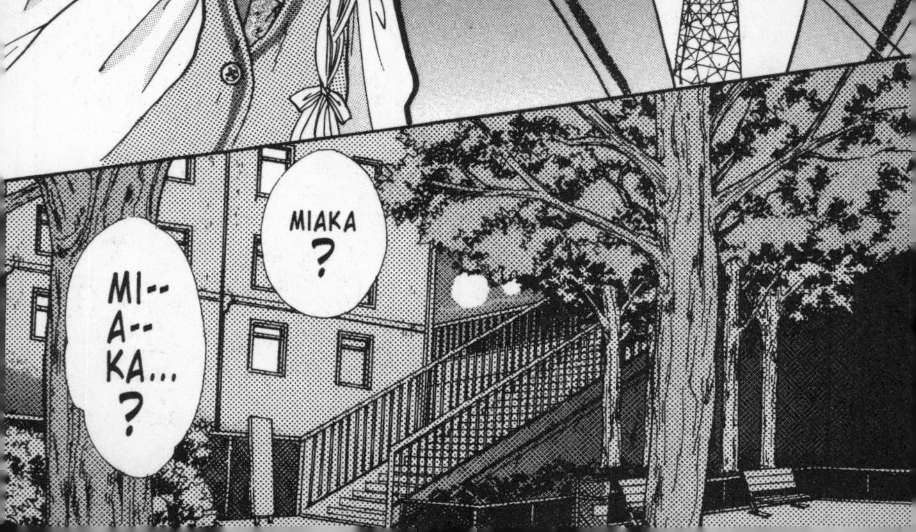
MIAKA ?
MI-- A-- KA... ?

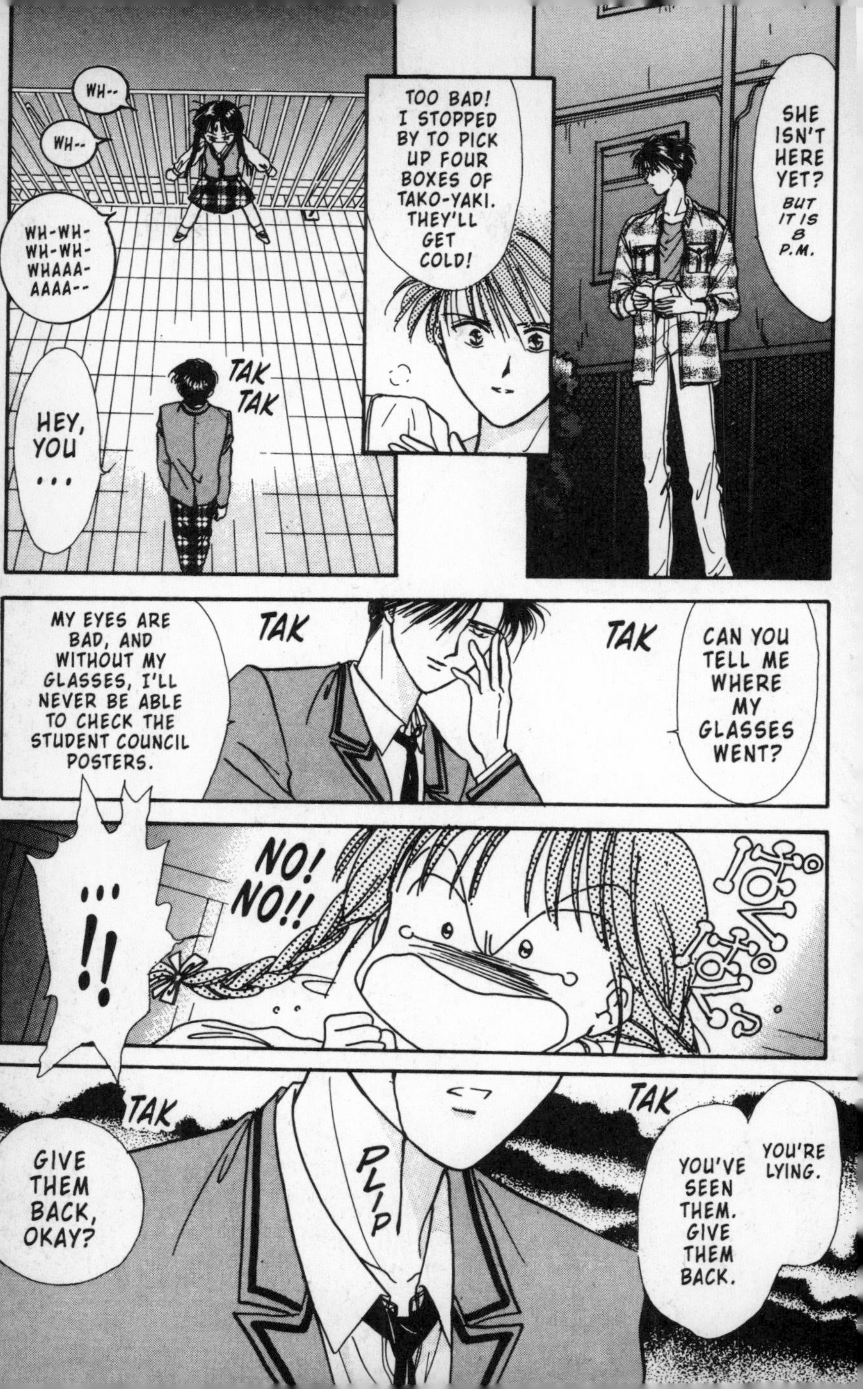
SHE ISN'T HERE YET?
BUT IT IS 8 P.M.
TOO BAD! I STOPPED BY TO PICK UP FOUR BOXES OF TAKO-YAKI. THEY'LL GET COLD!
WH--
WH--
WH-WH-WH-WH-WHAAA-AAAA--
TAK TAK
HEY, YOU . . .
CAN YOU TELL ME WHERE MY GLASSES WENT?
TAK
TAK
MY EYES ARE BAD, AND WITHOUT MY GLASSES, I'LL NEVER BE ABLE TO CHECK THE STUDENT COUNCIL POSTERS.
NO! NO!!
...!!
YOU'RE LYING.
YOU'VE SEEN THEM. GIVE THEM BACK.
TAK
PLIP
TAK
GIVE THEM BACK, OKAY?

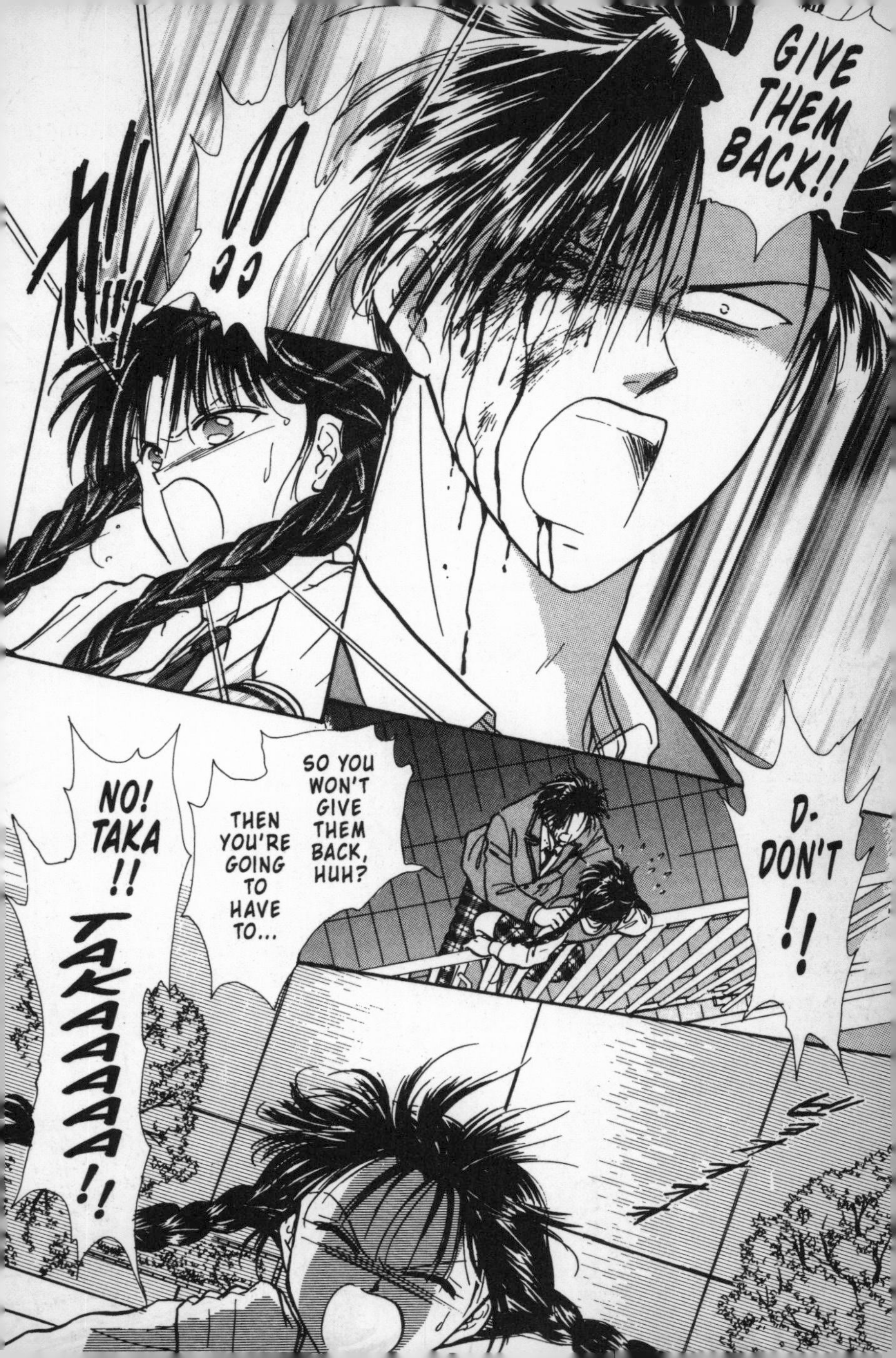
GIVE THEM BACK!!
D-DON'T!!
SO YOU WON'T GIVE THEM BACK, HUH?
THEN YOU'RE GOING TO HAVE TO...
NO! TAKA!!
TAKAAAAAA!!

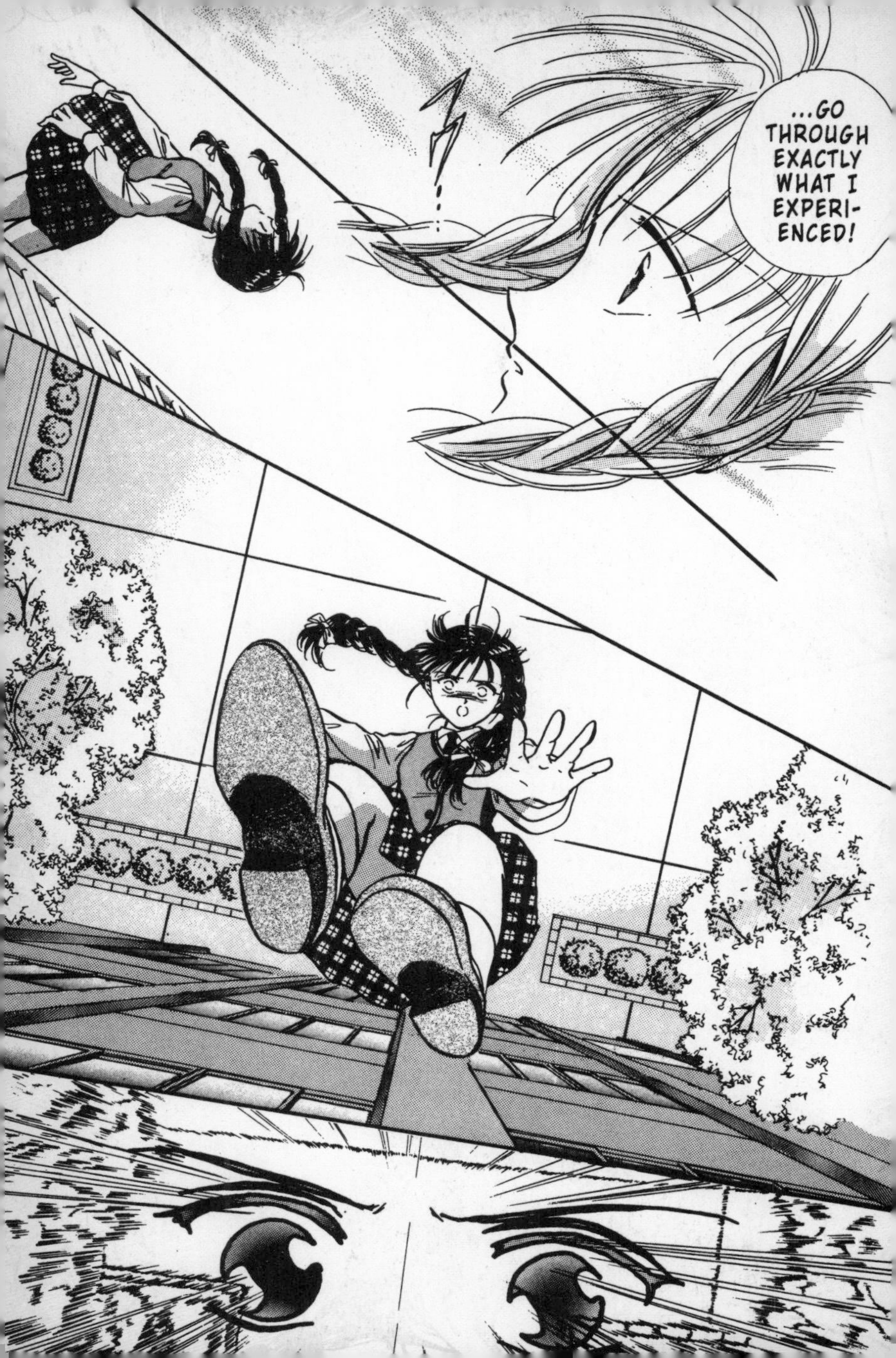
...GO THROUGH EXACTLY WHAT I EXPERIENCED!

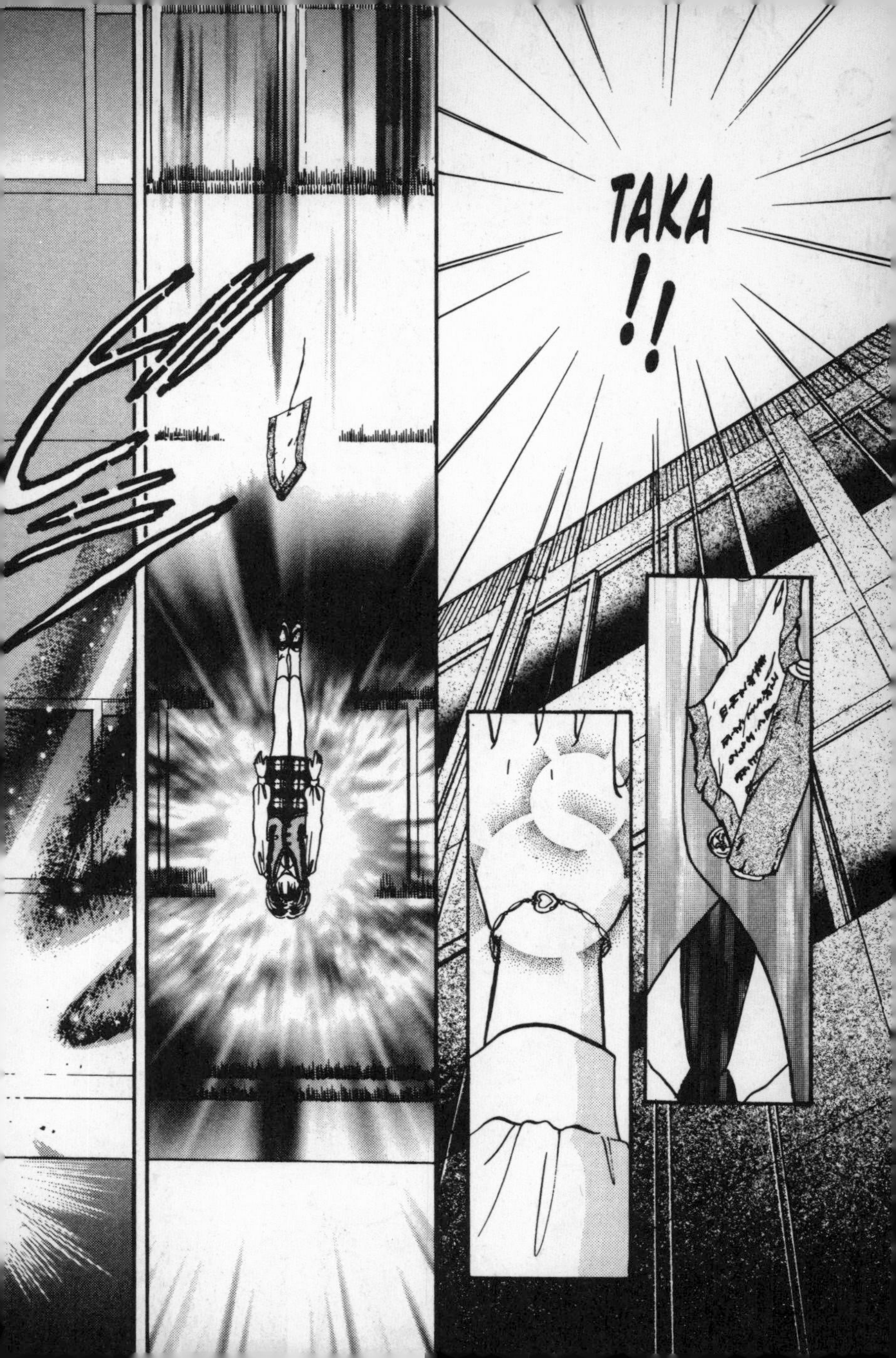
TAKA !!

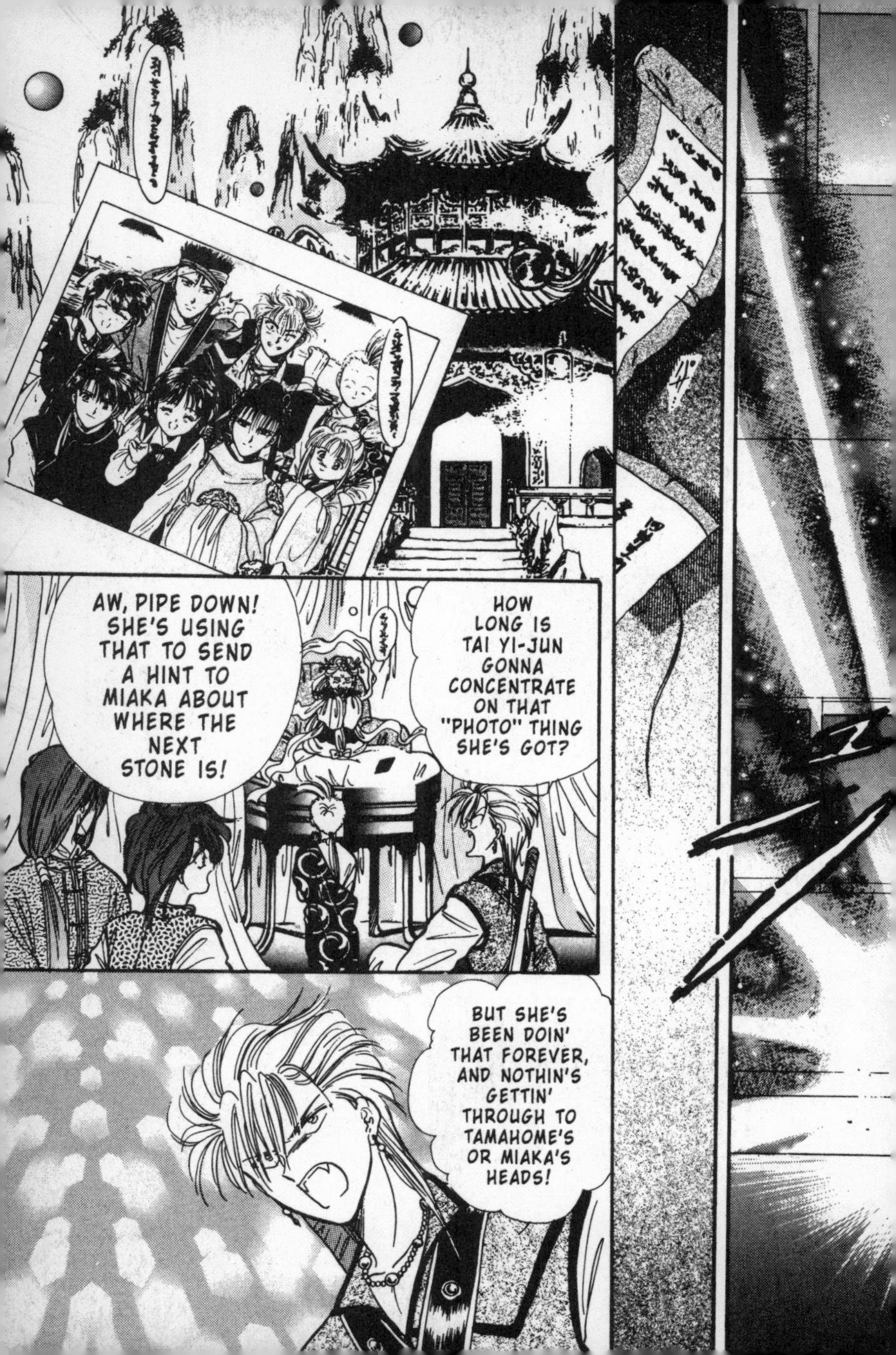
HOW LONG IS TAI YI-JUN GONNA CONCENTRATE ON THAT "PHOTO" THING SHE'S GOT?
AW, PIPE DOWN! SHE'S USING THAT TO SEND A HINT TO MIAKA ABOUT WHERE THE NEXT STONE IS!
BUT SHE'S BEEN DOIN' THAT FOREVER, AND NOTHIN'S GETTIN' THROUGH TO TAMAHOME'S OR MIAKA'S HEADS!

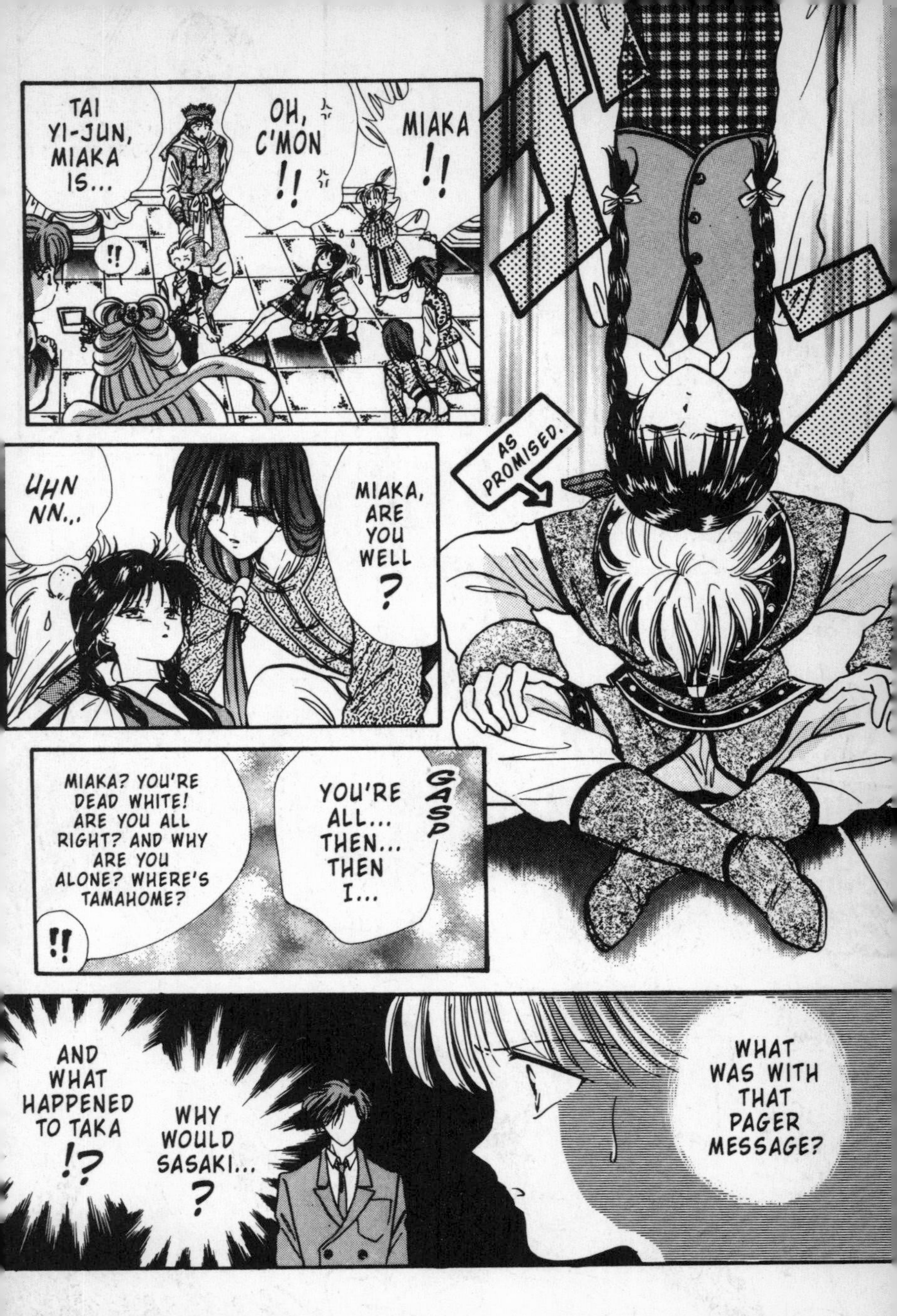
AS PROMISED.
MIAKA!!
OH, C'MON!!
TAI YI-JUN, MIAKA IS...
!!
MIAKA, ARE YOU WELL?
UHN NN...
GASP
YOU'RE ALL... THEN... THEN I...
MIAKA? YOU'RE DEAD WHITE! ARE YOU ALL RIGHT? AND WHY ARE YOU ALONE? WHERE'S TAMAHOME?
!!
WHAT WAS WITH THAT PAGER MESSAGE?
WHY WOULD SASAKI...?
AND WHAT HAPPENED TO TAKA!?

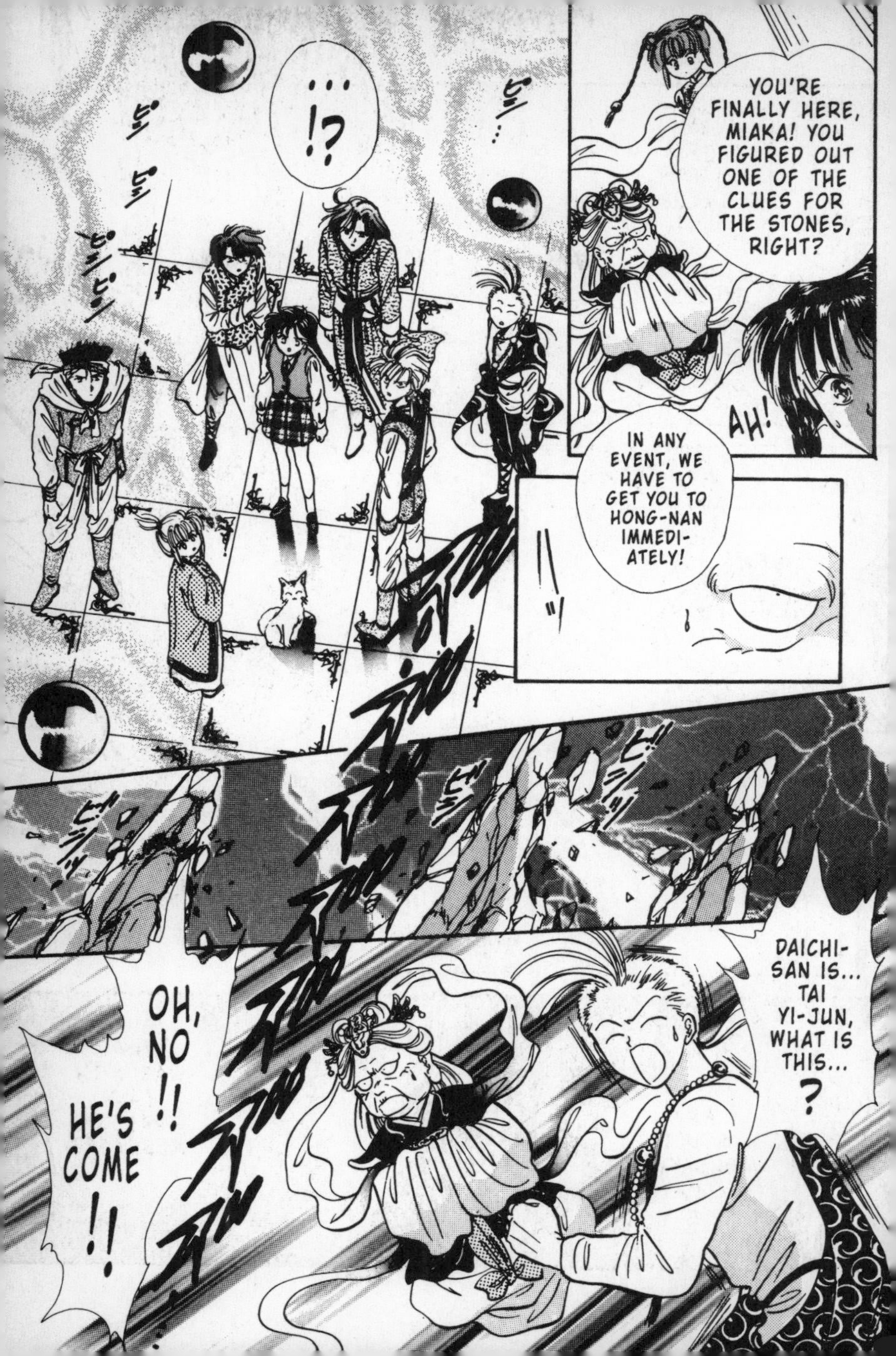

YOU'RE FINALLY HERE, MIAKA! YOU FIGURED OUT ONE OF THE CLUES FOR THE STONES, RIGHT?
AH!
IN ANY EVENT, WE HAVE TO GET YOU TO HONG-NAN IMMEDI-ATELY!
...!?
DAICHI-SAN IS... TAI YI-JUN, WHAT IS THIS...?
OH, NO!!
HE'S COME!!

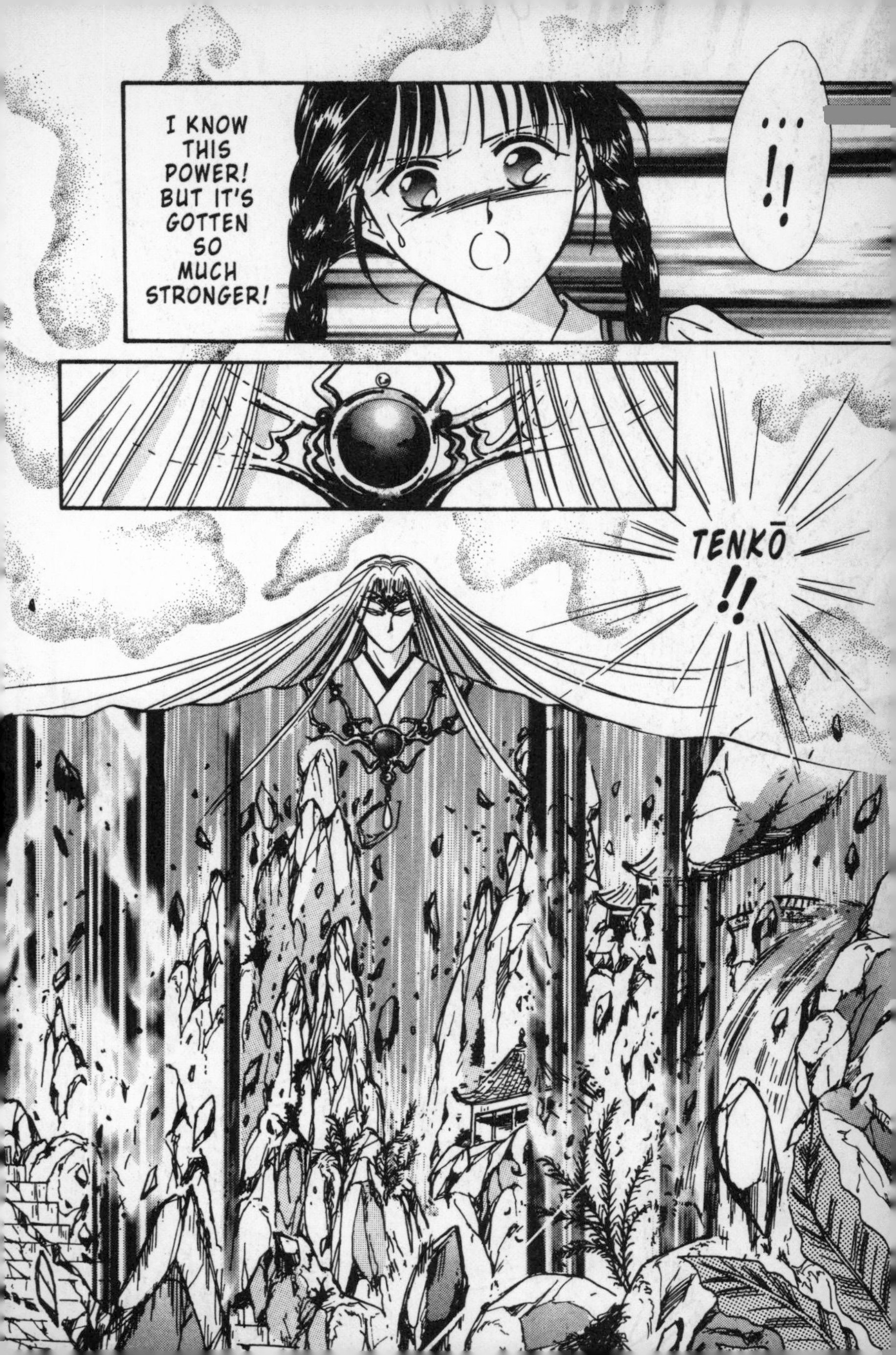

…!!
I KNOW THIS POWER! BUT IT'S GOTTEN SO MUCH STRONGER!
TENKŌ!!

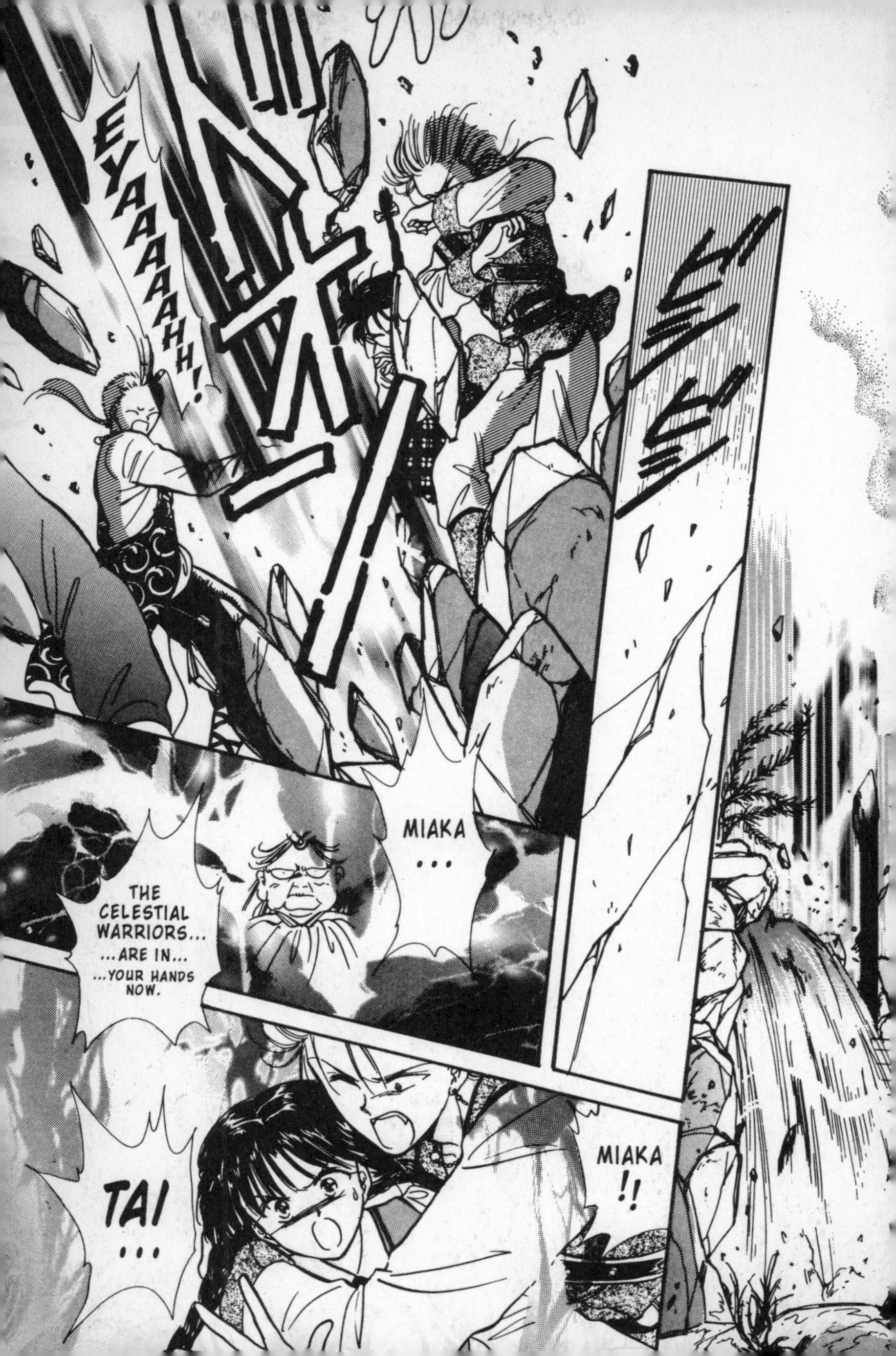
EYAAAAAAHH!
MIAKA ...
THE CELESTIAL WARRIORS... ...ARE IN... ...YOUR HANDS NOW.
MIAKA !!
TAI ...

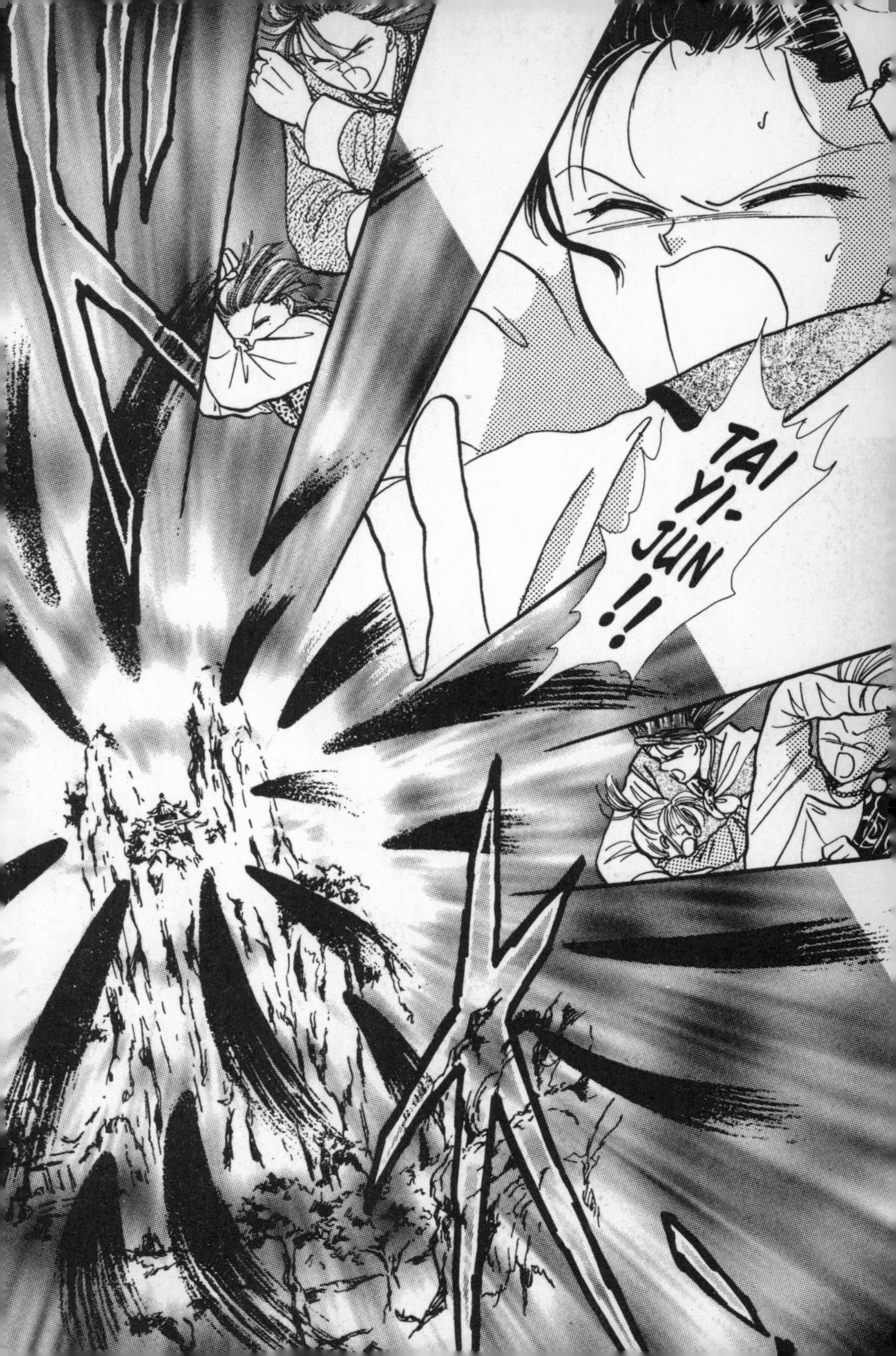
TAI YI-JUN!!!

CHAPTER EIGHTY-FIVE
THE SILENT CHILD

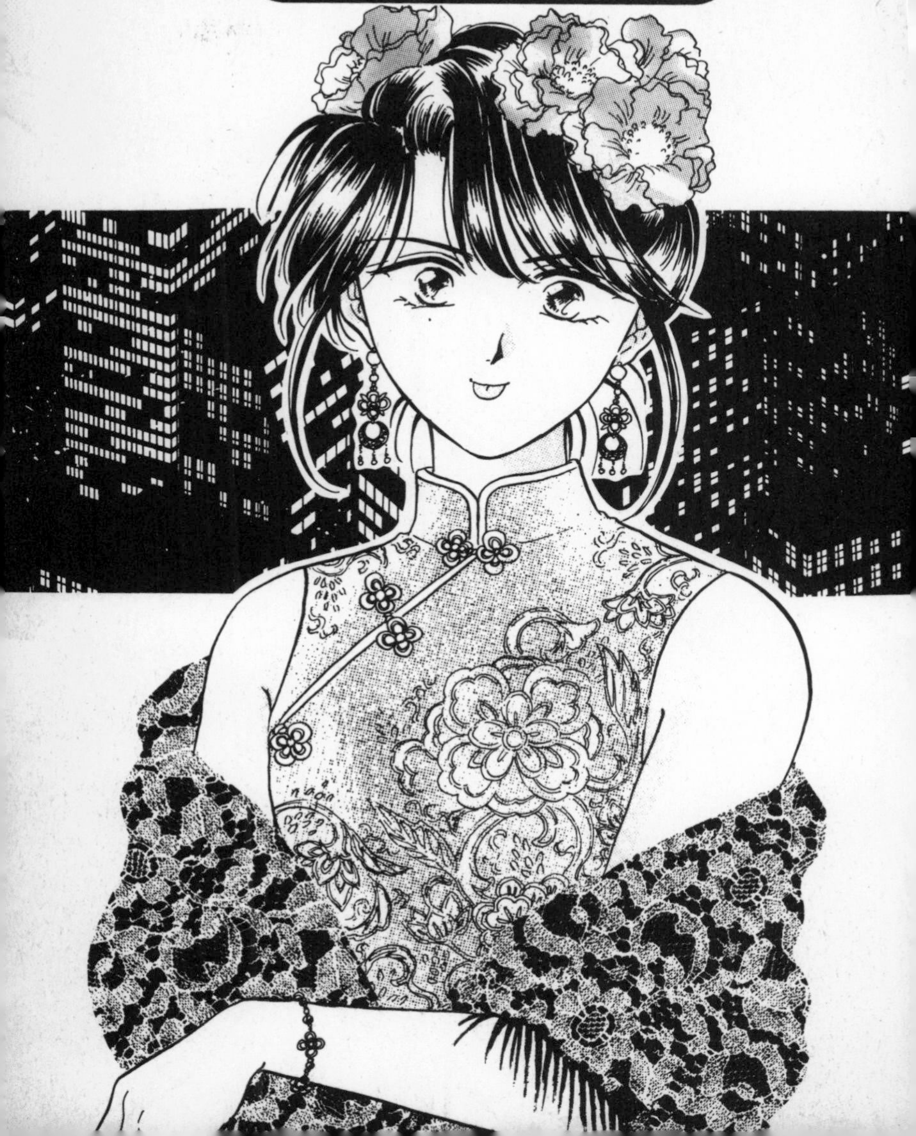

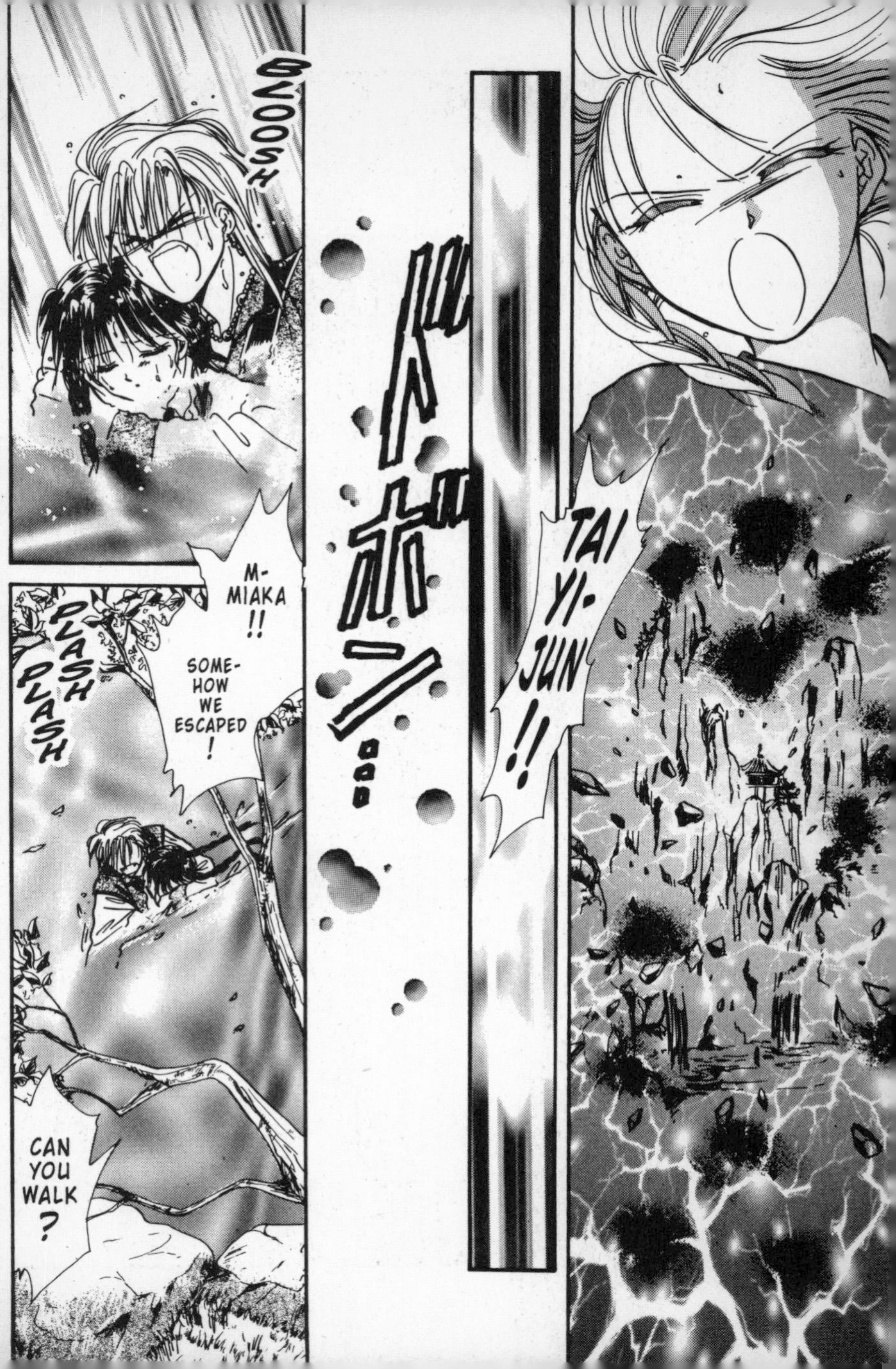
TAI YI-JUN!!
BVOOSH
M-MIAKA!!
SOMEHOW WE ESCAPED!
PLASH PLASH PLASH
CAN YOU WALK?

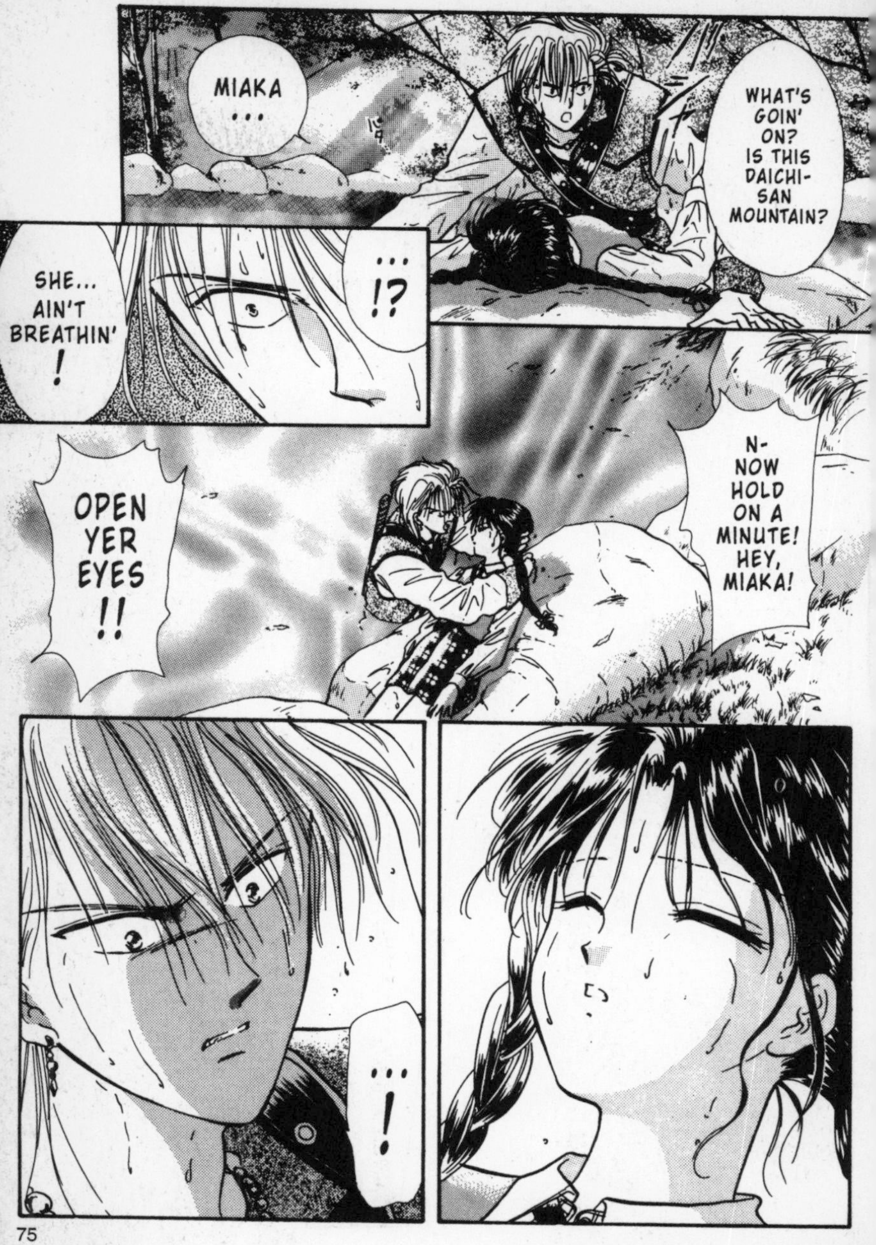

WHAT'S GOIN' ON? IS THIS DAICHI-SAN MOUNTAIN?
MIAKA...
...!?
SHE... AIN'T BREATHIN'!
N-NOW HOLD ON A MINUTE! HEY, MIAKA!
OPEN YER EYES!!
...!

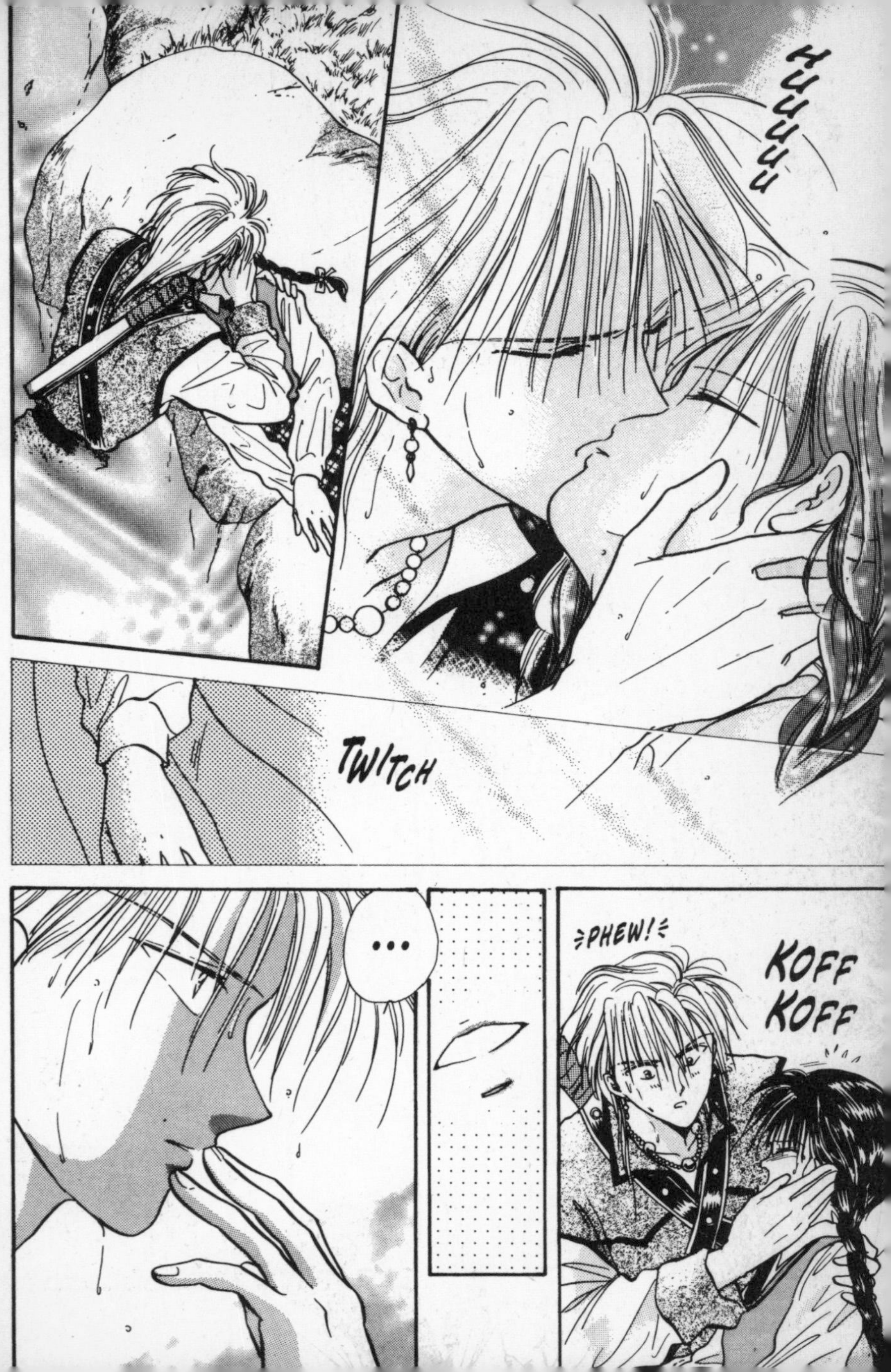
HUUUUU
TWITCH
PHEW!
KOFF KOFF
...

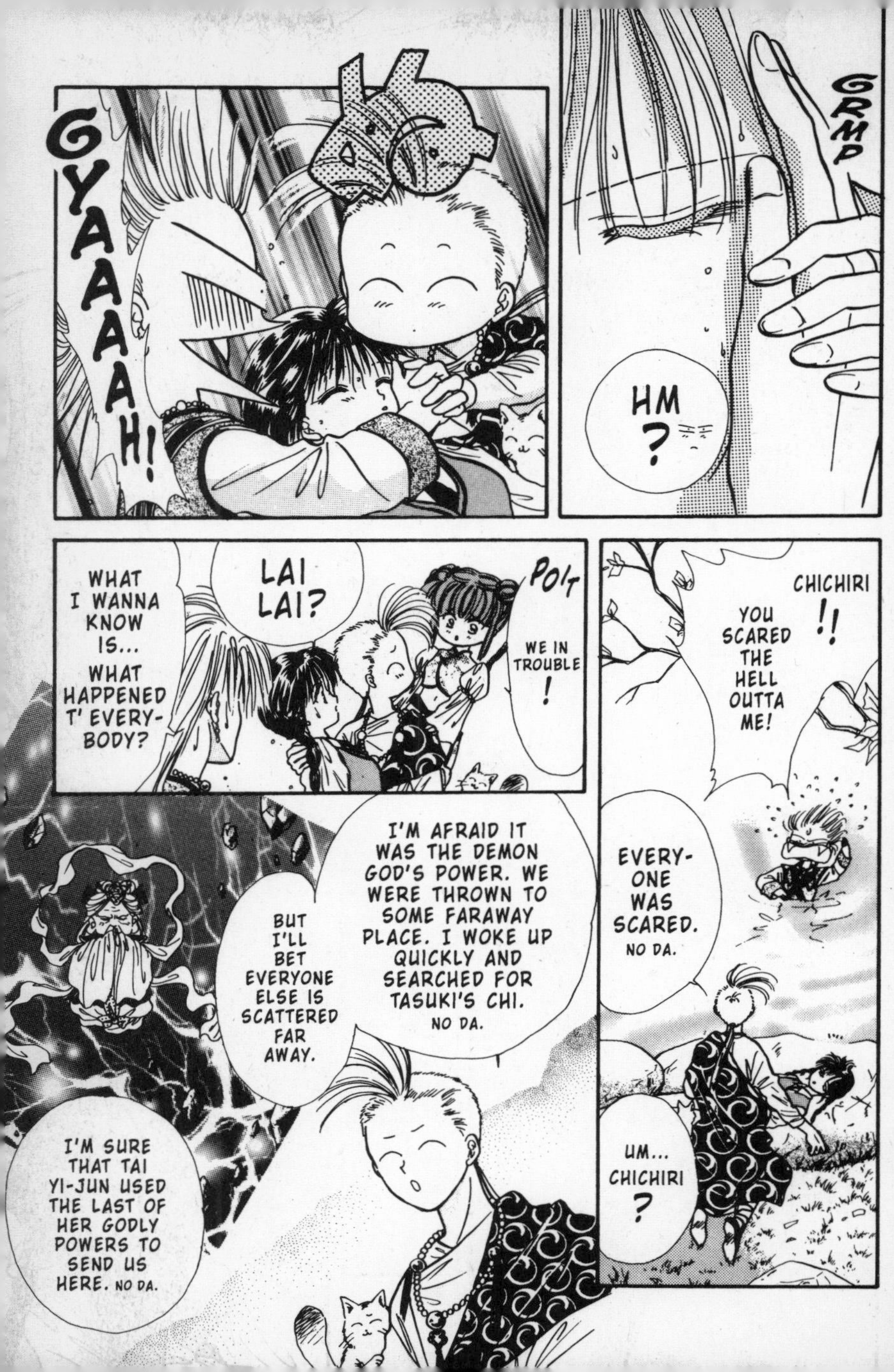
GRMP
HM?
GYAAAAH!
CHICHIRI!!
YOU SCARED THE HELL OUTTA ME!
EVERY-ONE WAS SCARED. NO DA.
UM... CHICHIRI?
POIT
LAI LAI?
WE IN TROUBLE!
WHAT I WANNA KNOW IS... WHAT HAPPENED T' EVERY-BODY?
I'M AFRAID IT WAS THE DEMON GOD'S POWER. WE WERE THROWN TO SOME FARAWAY PLACE. I WOKE UP QUICKLY AND SEARCHED FOR TASUKI'S CHI. NO DA.
BUT I'LL BET EVERYONE ELSE IS SCATTERED FAR AWAY.
I'M SURE THAT TAI YI-JUN USED THE LAST OF HER GODLY POWERS TO SEND US HERE. NO DA.

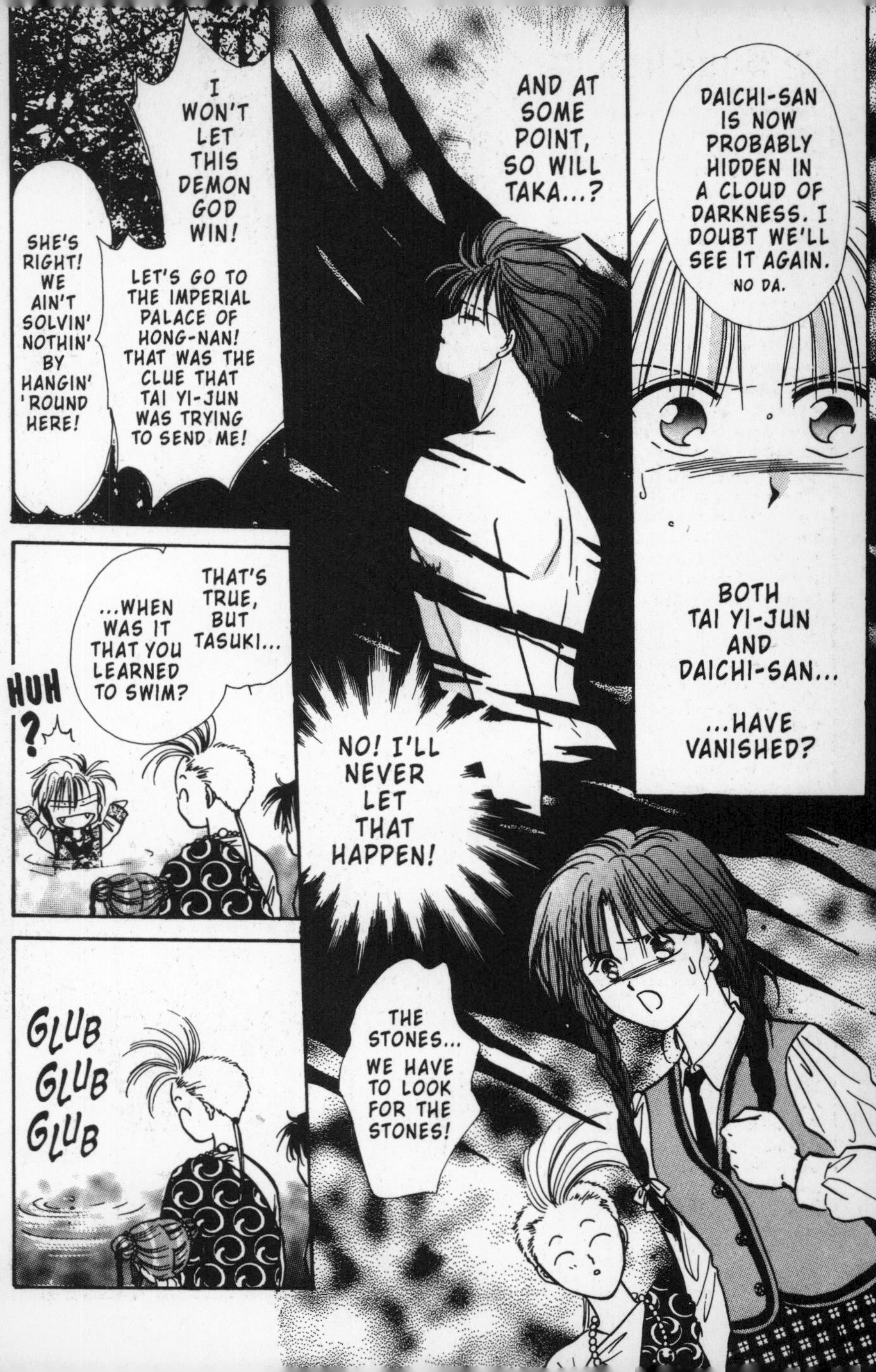
DAICHI-SAN IS NOW PROBABLY HIDDEN IN A CLOUD OF DARKNESS. I DOUBT WE'LL SEE IT AGAIN. NO DA.
BOTH TAI YI-JUN AND DAICHI-SAN...
...HAVE VANISHED?
AND AT SOME POINT, SO WILL TAKA...?
NO! I'LL NEVER LET THAT HAPPEN!
THE STONES... WE HAVE TO LOOK FOR THE STONES!
I WON'T LET THIS DEMON GOD WIN!
LET'S GO TO THE IMPERIAL PALACE OF HONG-NAN! THAT WAS THE CLUE THAT TAI YI-JUN WAS TRYING TO SEND ME!
SHE'S RIGHT! WE AIN'T SOLVIN' NOTHIN' BY HANGIN' 'ROUND HERE!
THAT'S TRUE, BUT TASUKI...
...WHEN WAS IT THAT YOU LEARNED TO SWIM?
HUH?
GLUB GLUB GLUB

Guardian

And on August 10th, I went to Hokkaido. It was so cool... I was surprised! It was only 18 degrees C (64 degrees F)! 06 And it was August! Maybe since it was raining... I think my strongest impression of the people of Hokkaido is that they have faces that look like they can accept both the good and the bad. At the signing, whenever anybody looked at me with a happy face, it made me very happy as well.
During one of the breaks, when I was eating lunch with my editors, there was a family eating next to us, and the older sister was talking to the younger sister. She said, "You've heard of *Fushigi Yûgi,* right? I'm collecting all the books!" I started to smile without realizing I was doing it. I'm sure she never knew that the manga artist was eating right next to her!
On a (sort of) related note, there was a time when I was in the arts & crafts section of Parco to buy some supplies, and on the paper where people can try out pens, one person had written "Tasuki! ♥"! Right next to it was, "I like Tamahome." And right next to that was another mark that said, "Hotohori for me." I just stood there alone, laughing. I was thinking of writing, "I love Nakago!" or "Lian, too!" ☺ but I didn't. It didn't seem like something a professional manga artist should do. Also, there were a bunch of girls standing over by the screen tone section. I doubt you're reading this, but if you saw a tall woman hanging out forever in the screen tone section with a tired look on her face, that was me. ☺
But Hokkaido was an easy place to hang out in. I wanted to stay longer. The crab was delicious, and I loved the Yuki-jirushi ("Snow-Brand") Parlors! I want to go there to vacation some time! It's one of the places I love within Japan!

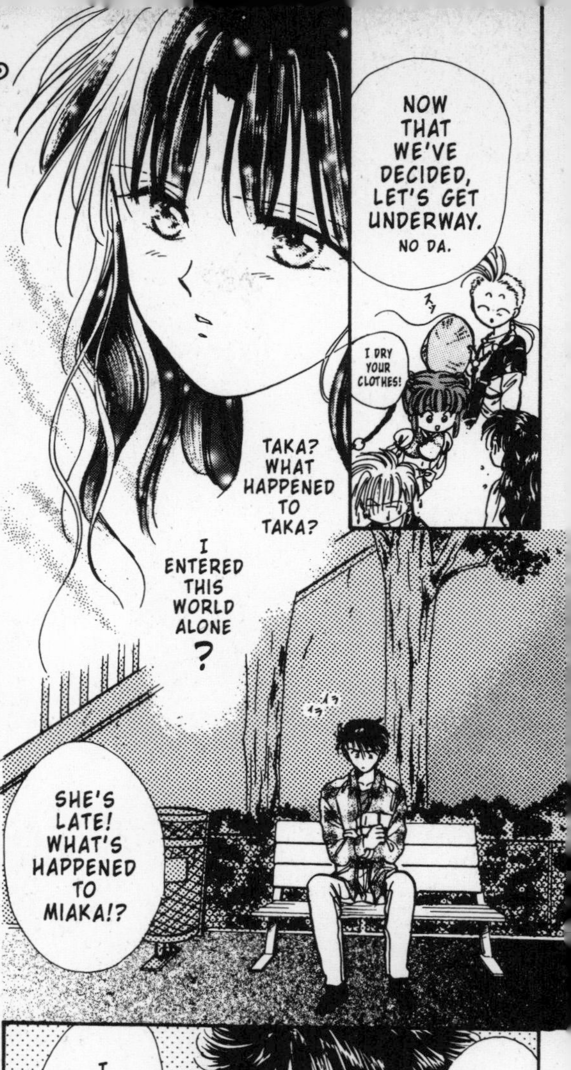
NOW THAT WE'VE DECIDED, LET'S GET UNDERWAY. NO DA.
I DRY YOUR CLOTHES!
TAKA? WHAT HAPPENED TO TAKA?
I ENTERED THIS WORLD ALONE?
SHE'S LATE! WHAT'S HAPPENED TO MIAKA!?
THIS IS WEIRD!
I SHOULD PROBABLY GO BACK TO HER SCHOOL...

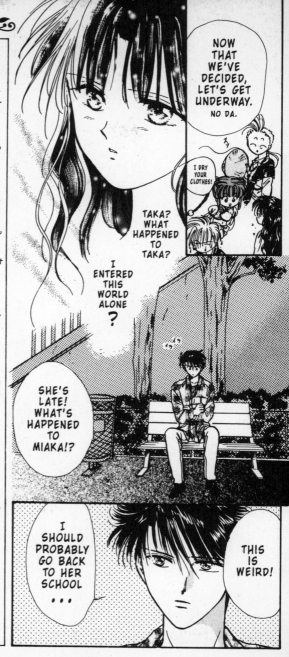

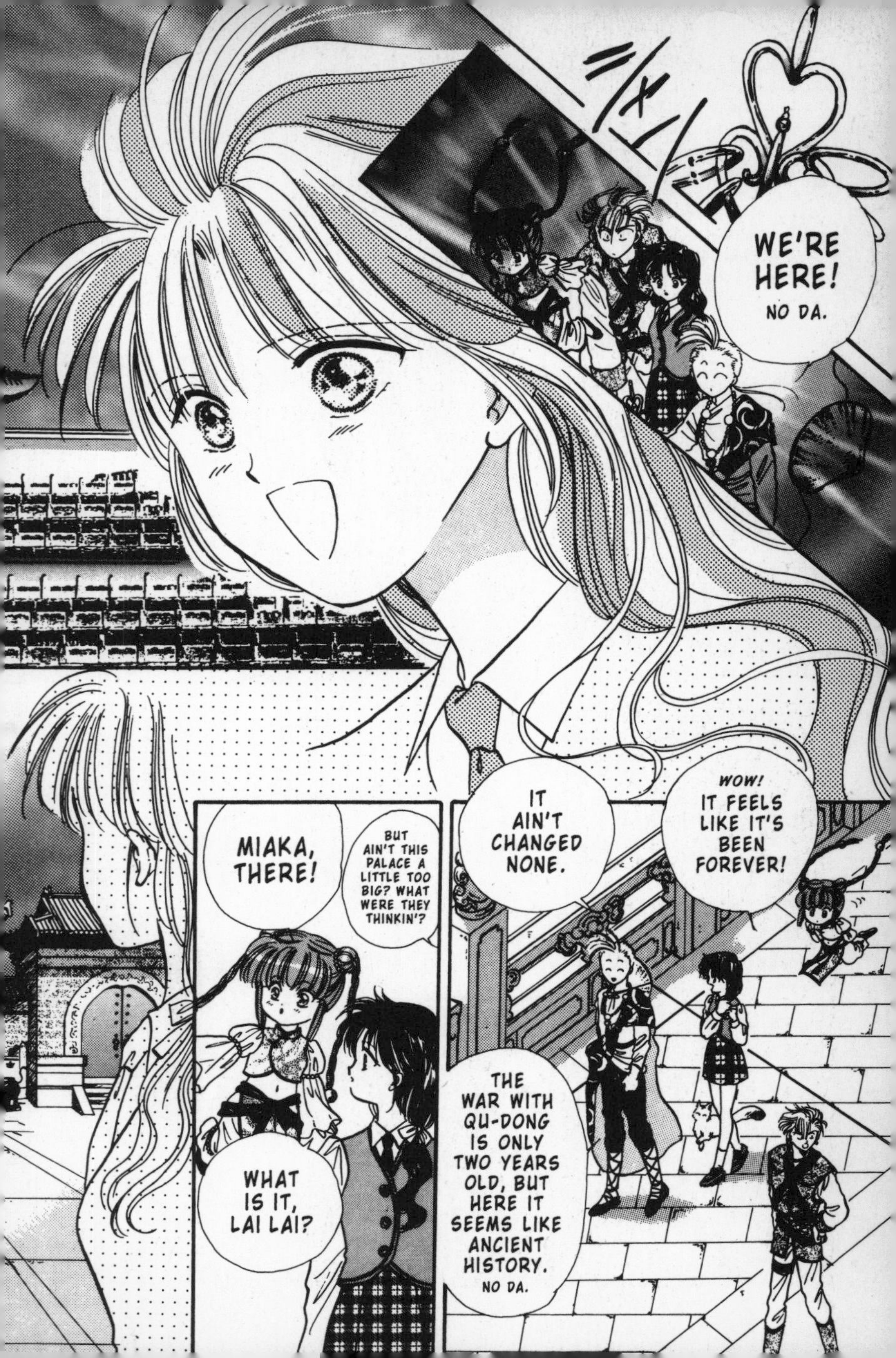
WE'RE HERE!
NO DA.
WOW! IT FEELS LIKE IT'S BEEN FOREVER!
IT AIN'T CHANGED NONE.
THE WAR WITH QU-DONG IS ONLY TWO YEARS OLD, BUT HERE IT SEEMS LIKE ANCIENT HISTORY.
NO DA.
BUT AIN'T THIS PALACE A LITTLE TOO BIG? WHAT WERE THEY THINKIN'?
MIAKA, THERE!
WHAT IS IT, LAI LAI?

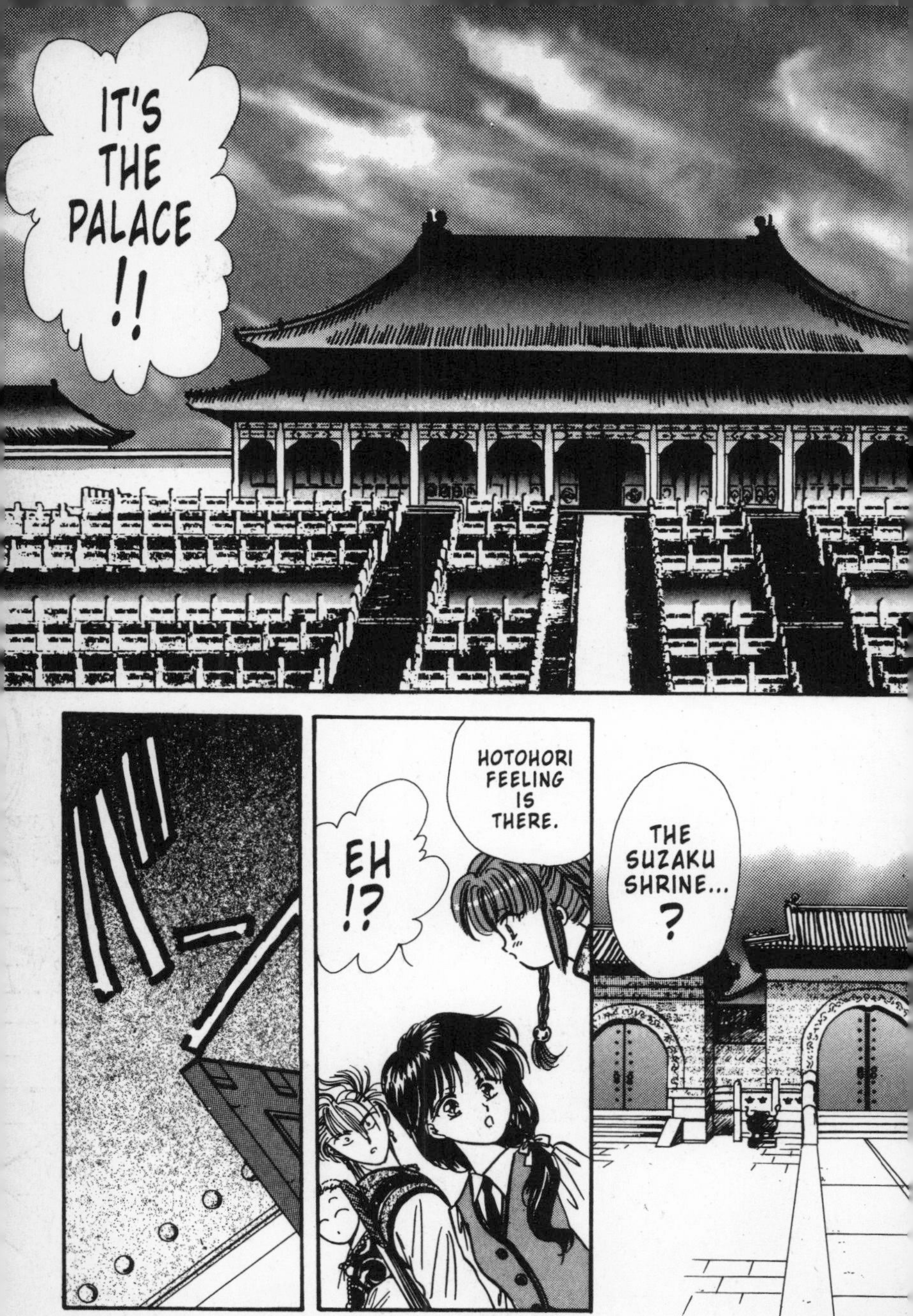
IT'S THE PALACE !!
THE SUZAKU SHRINE... ?
HOTOHORI FEELING IS THERE.
EH !?

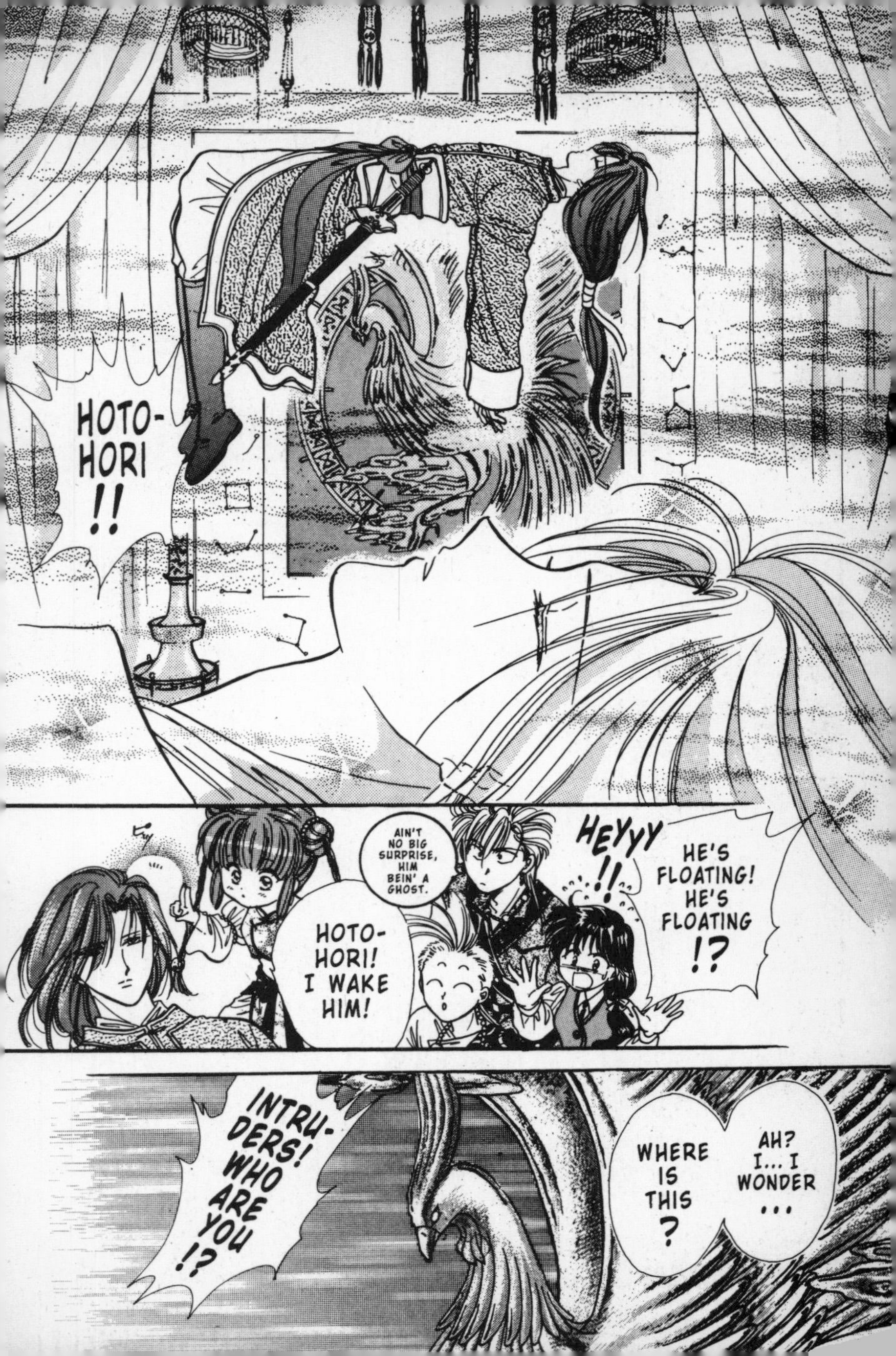
HOTO-HORI!!
HE'S FLOATING! HE'S FLOATING!?
HEYYY!!
AIN'T NO BIG SURPRISE, HIM BEIN' A GHOST.
HOTO-HORI! I WAKE HIM!
AH? I... I WONDER...
WHERE IS THIS?
INTRU-DERS! WHO ARE YOU!?

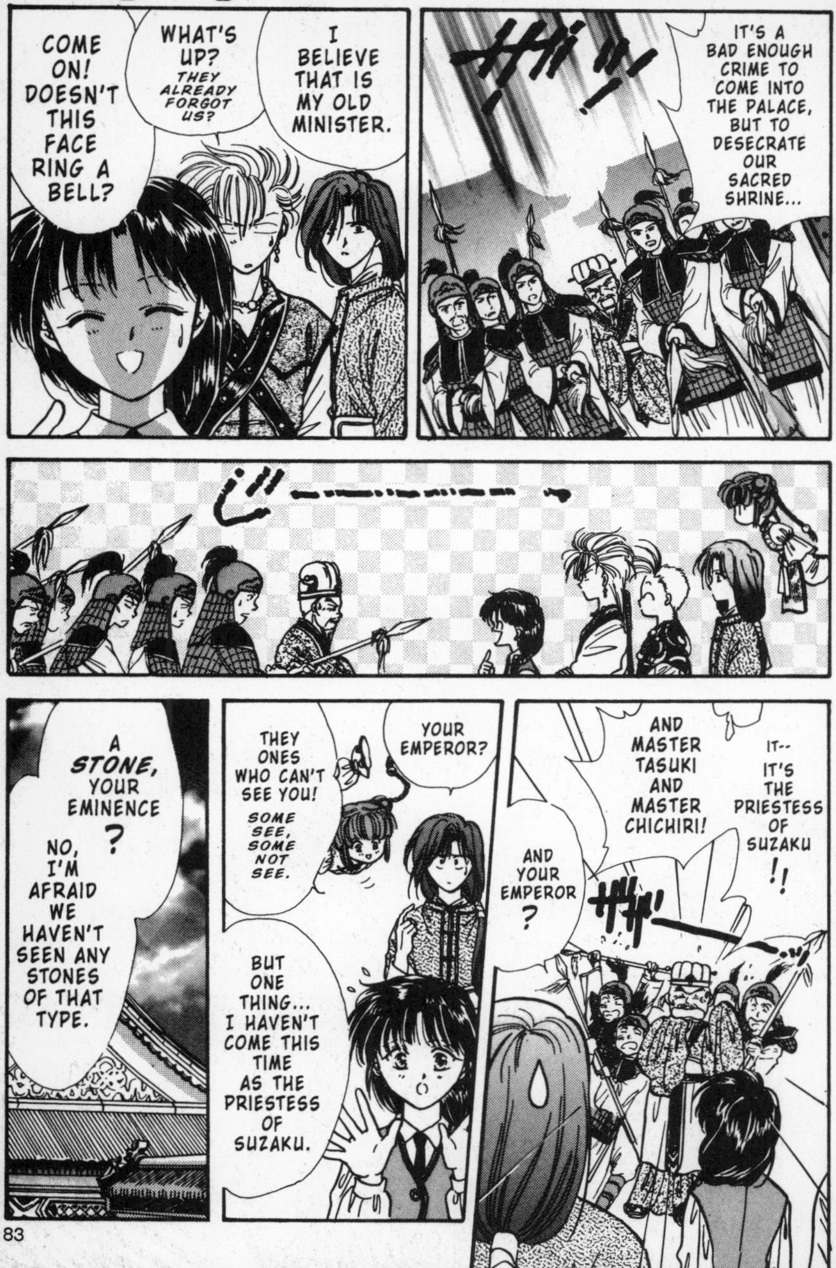
IT'S A BAD ENOUGH CRIME TO COME INTO THE PALACE, BUT TO DESECRATE OUR SACRED SHRINE...
I BELIEVE THAT IS MY OLD MINISTER.
WHAT'S UP? THEY ALREADY FORGOT US?
COME ON! DOESN'T THIS FACE RING A BELL?
IT-- IT'S THE PRIESTESS OF SUZAKU !!
AND MASTER TASUKI AND MASTER CHICHIRI!
AND YOUR EMPEROR ?
YOUR EMPEROR?
THEY ONES WHO CAN'T SEE YOU!
SOME SEE, SOME NOT SEE.
BUT ONE THING... I HAVEN'T COME THIS TIME AS THE PRIESTESS OF SUZAKU.
A STONE, YOUR EMINENCE ?
NO, I'M AFRAID WE HAVEN'T SEEN ANY STONES OF THAT TYPE.

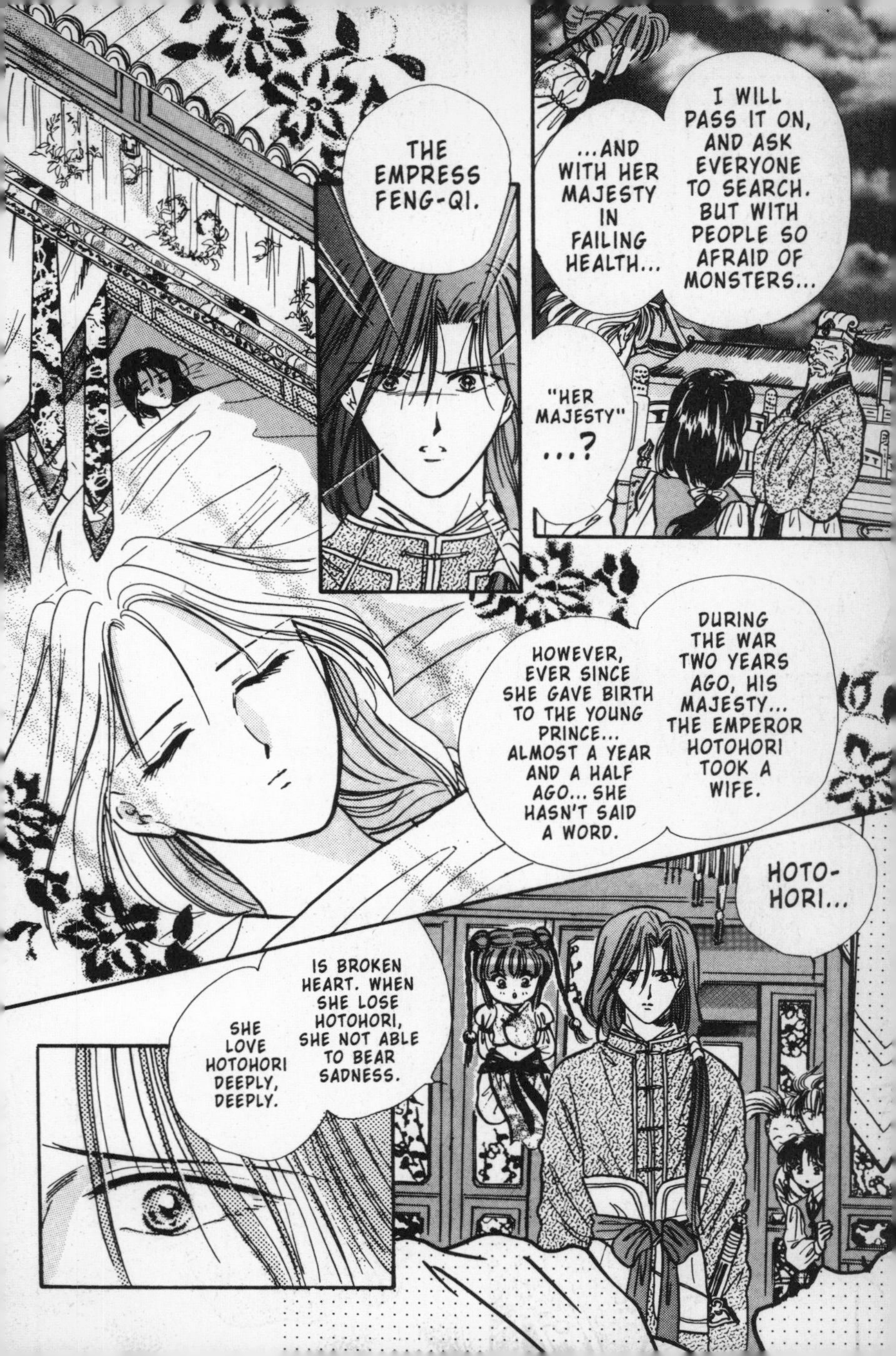

I WILL PASS IT ON, AND ASK EVERYONE TO SEARCH. BUT WITH PEOPLE SO AFRAID OF MONSTERS...
...AND WITH HER MAJESTY IN FAILING HEALTH...
"HER MAJESTY" ...?
THE EMPRESS FENG-QI.
DURING THE WAR TWO YEARS AGO, HIS MAJESTY... THE EMPEROR HOTOHORI TOOK A WIFE.
HOWEVER, EVER SINCE SHE GAVE BIRTH TO THE YOUNG PRINCE... ALMOST A YEAR AND A HALF AGO... SHE HASN'T SAID A WORD.
HOTO-HORI...
SHE LOVE HOTOHORI DEEPLY, DEEPLY.
IS BROKEN HEART. WHEN SHE LOSE HOTOHORI, SHE NOT ABLE TO BEAR SADNESS.

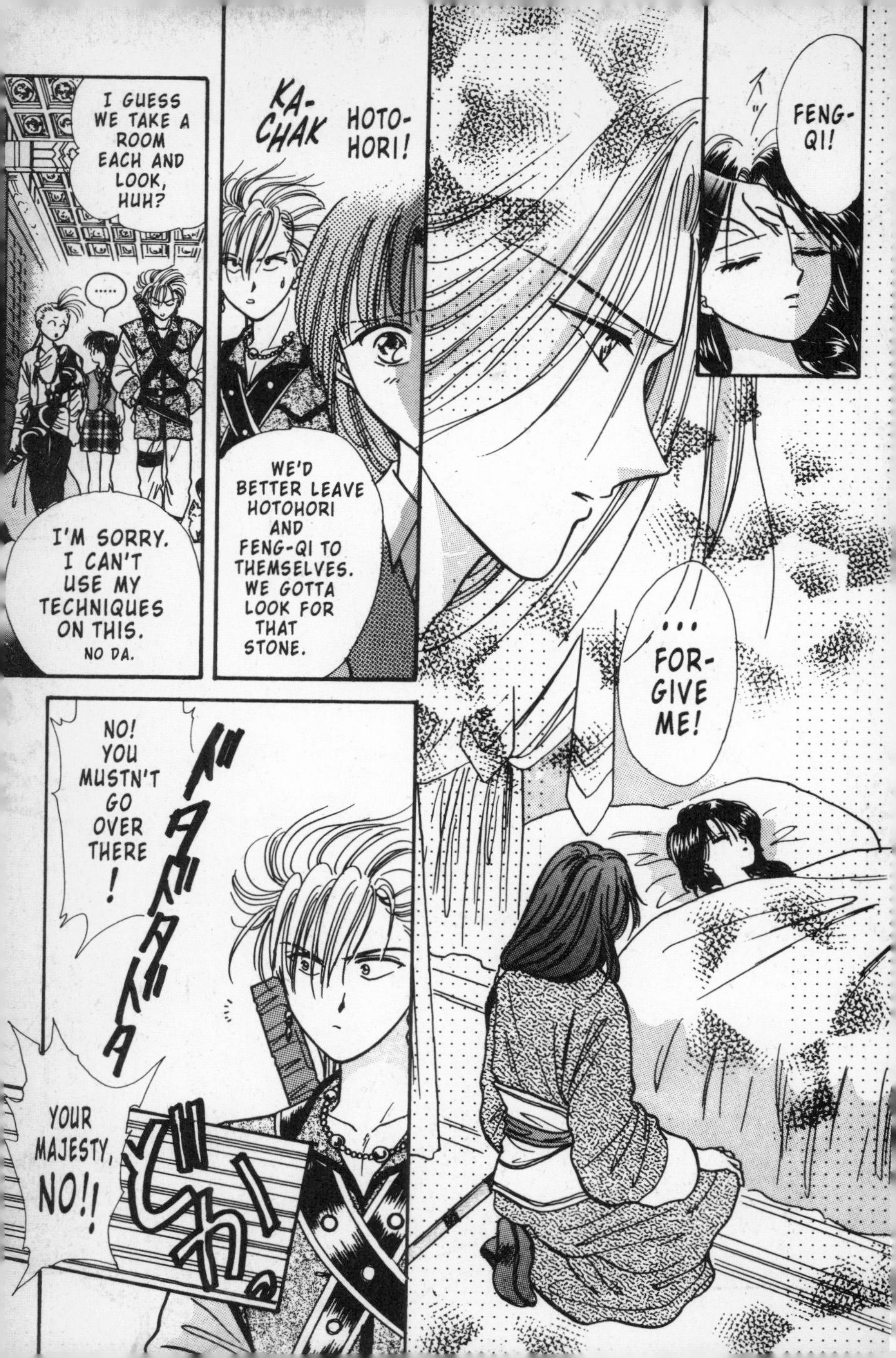
スッ
FENG-QI!
...FOR-GIVE ME!
KA-CHAK
HOTO-HORI!
WE'D BETTER LEAVE HOTOHORI AND FENG-QI TO THEMSELVES. WE GOTTA LOOK FOR THAT STONE.
I GUESS WE TAKE A ROOM EACH AND LOOK, HUH?
......
I'M SORRY. I CAN'T USE MY TECHNIQUES ON THIS. NO DA.
NO! YOU MUSTN'T GO OVER THERE!
YOUR MAJESTY, NO!!

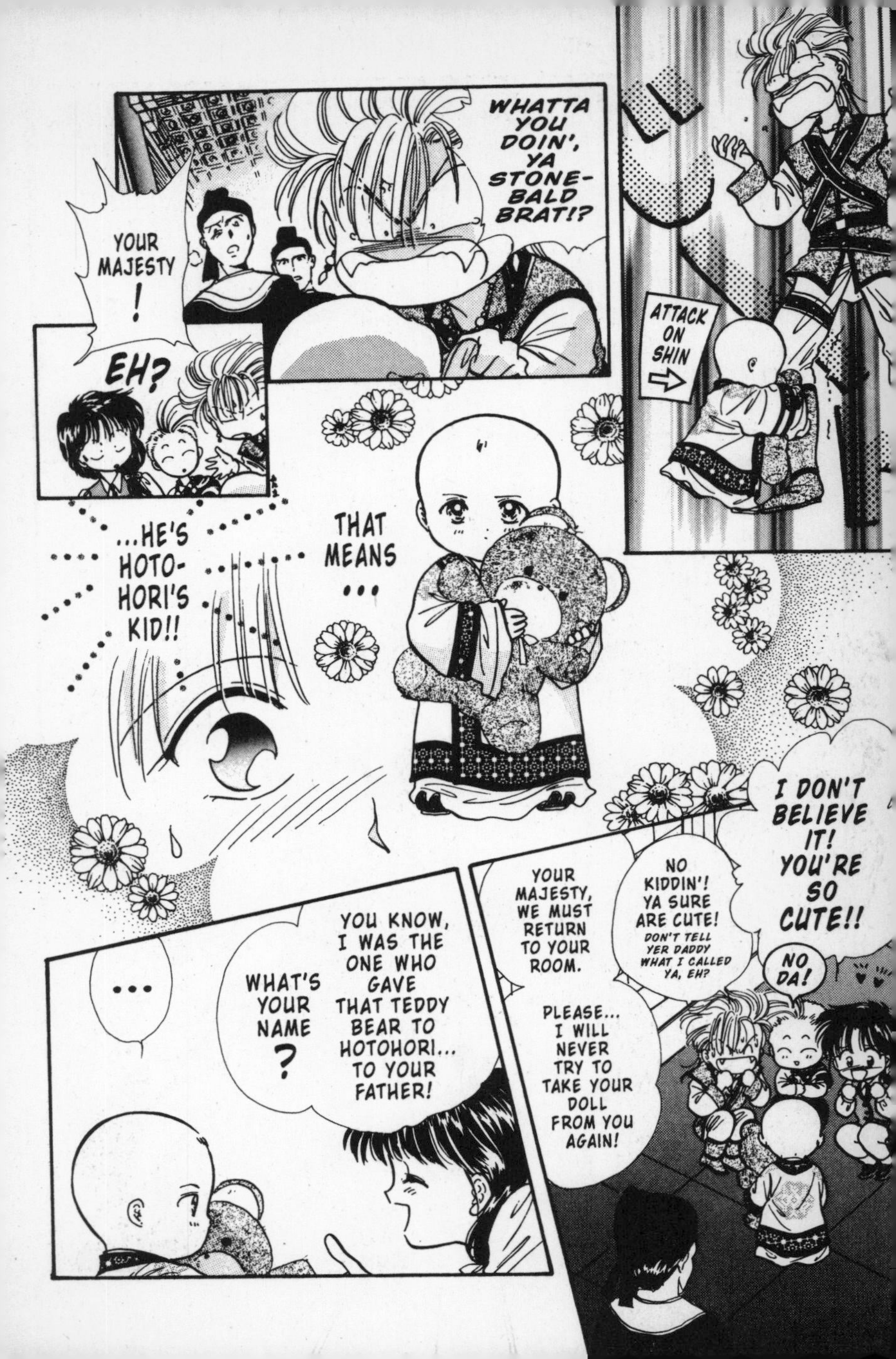
ATTACK ON SHIN
WHATTA YOU DOIN', YA STONE-BALD BRAT!?
YOUR MAJESTY!
EH?
THAT MEANS...
...HE'S HOTOHORI'S KID!!
I DON'T BELIEVE IT! YOU'RE SO CUTE!!
NO KIDDIN'! YA SURE ARE CUTE! DON'T TELL YER DADDY WHAT I CALLED YA, EH?
YOUR MAJESTY, WE MUST RETURN TO YOUR ROOM.
NO DA!
PLEASE... I WILL NEVER TRY TO TAKE YOUR DOLL FROM YOU AGAIN!
YOU KNOW, I WAS THE ONE WHO GAVE THAT TEDDY BEAR TO HOTOHORI... TO YOUR FATHER!
WHAT'S YOUR NAME?
...

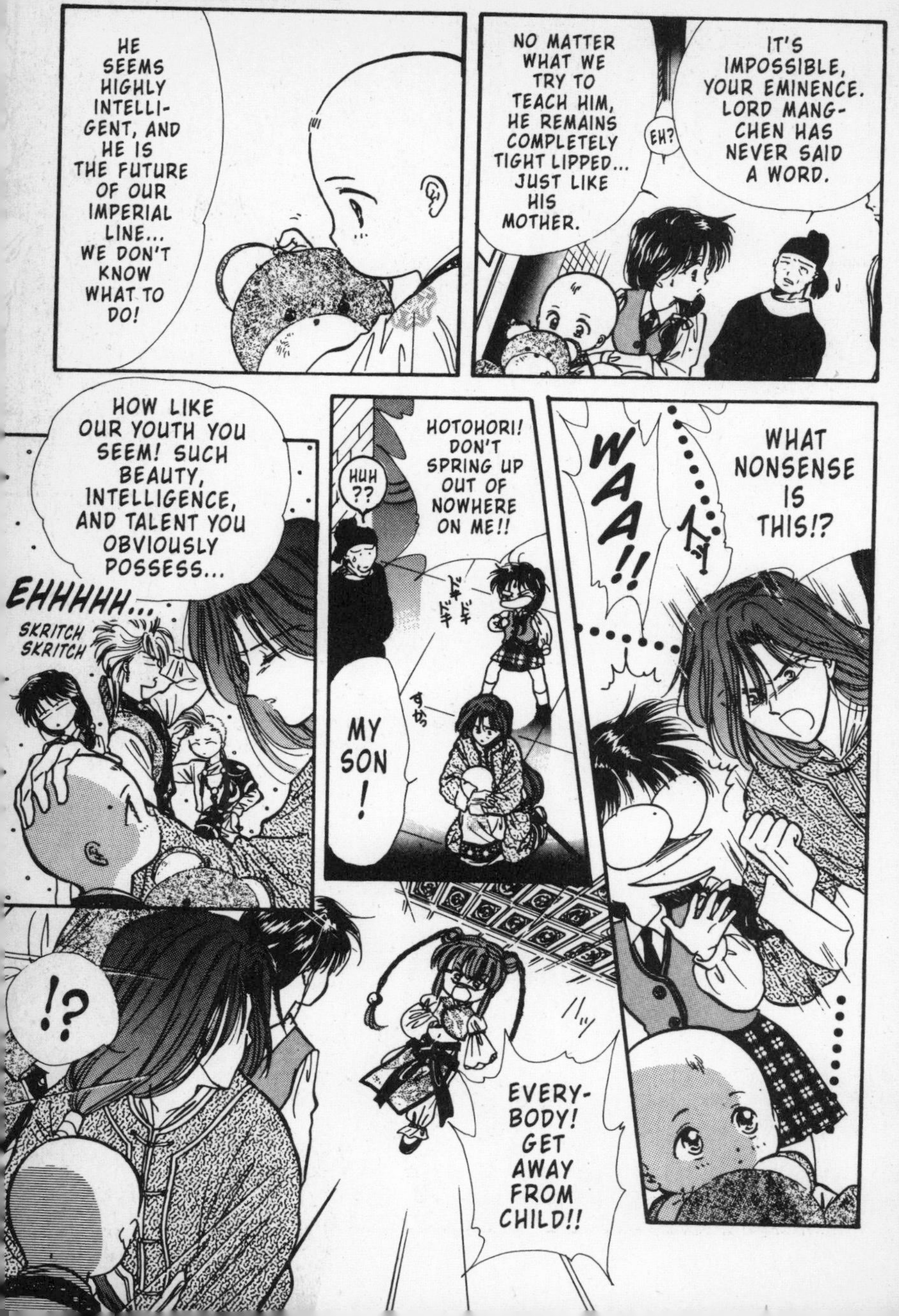
IT'S IMPOSSIBLE, YOUR EMINENCE. LORD MANG-CHEN HAS NEVER SAID A WORD.
EH?
NO MATTER WHAT WE TRY TO TEACH HIM, HE REMAINS COMPLETELY TIGHT LIPPED... JUST LIKE HIS MOTHER.
HE SEEMS HIGHLY INTELLI-GENT, AND HE IS THE FUTURE OF OUR IMPERIAL LINE... WE DON'T KNOW WHAT TO DO!
WHAT NONSENSE IS THIS!?
WAA!!
HOTOHORI! DON'T SPRING UP OUT OF NOWHERE ON ME!!
HUH ??
MY SON !
HOW LIKE OUR YOUTH YOU SEEM! SUCH BEAUTY, INTELLIGENCE, AND TALENT YOU OBVIOUSLY POSSESS...
EHHHHH...
SKRITCH SKRITCH
EVERY-BODY! GET AWAY FROM CHILD!!
!?

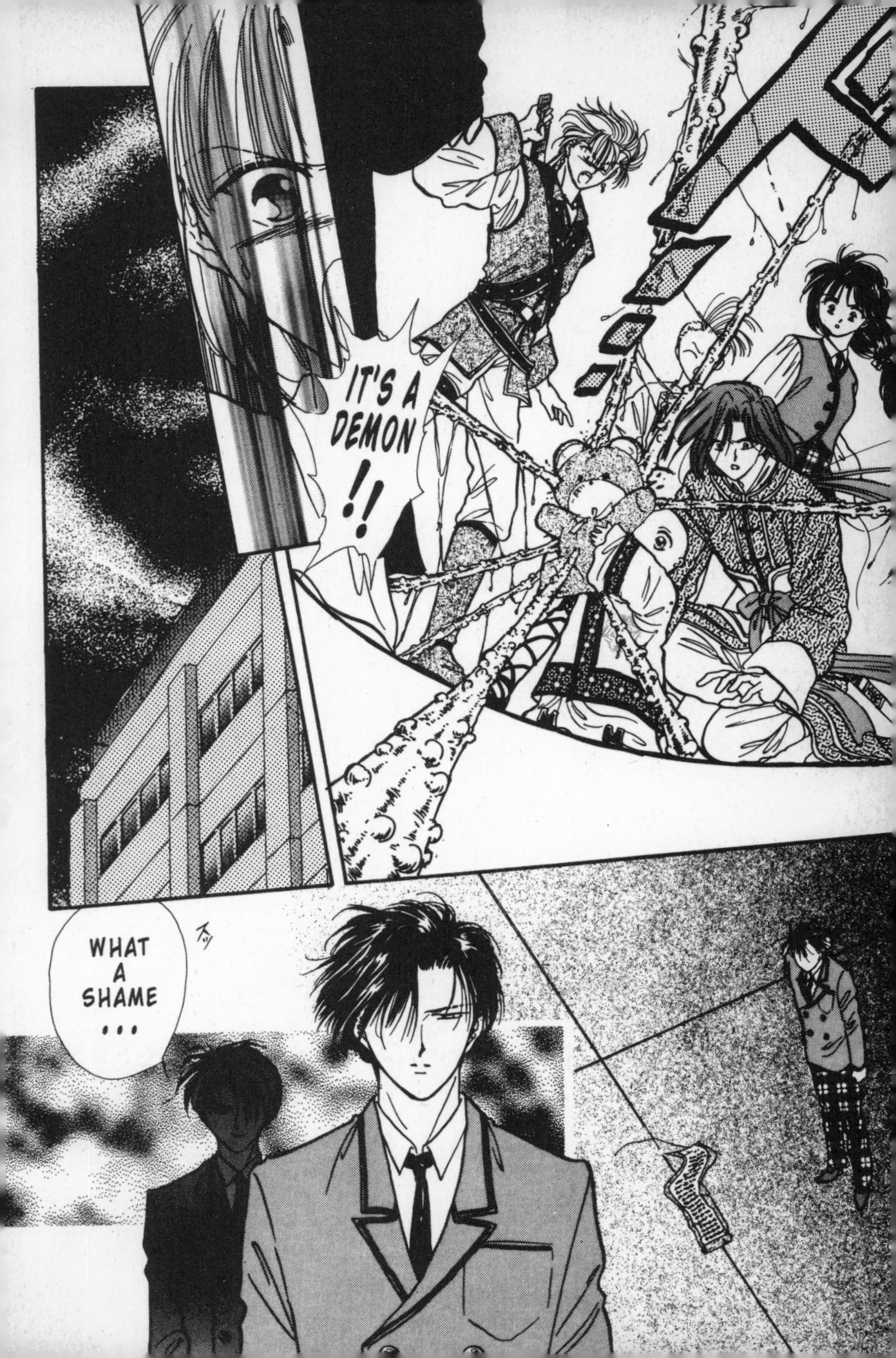
IT'S A DEMON !!
WHAT A SHAME ...

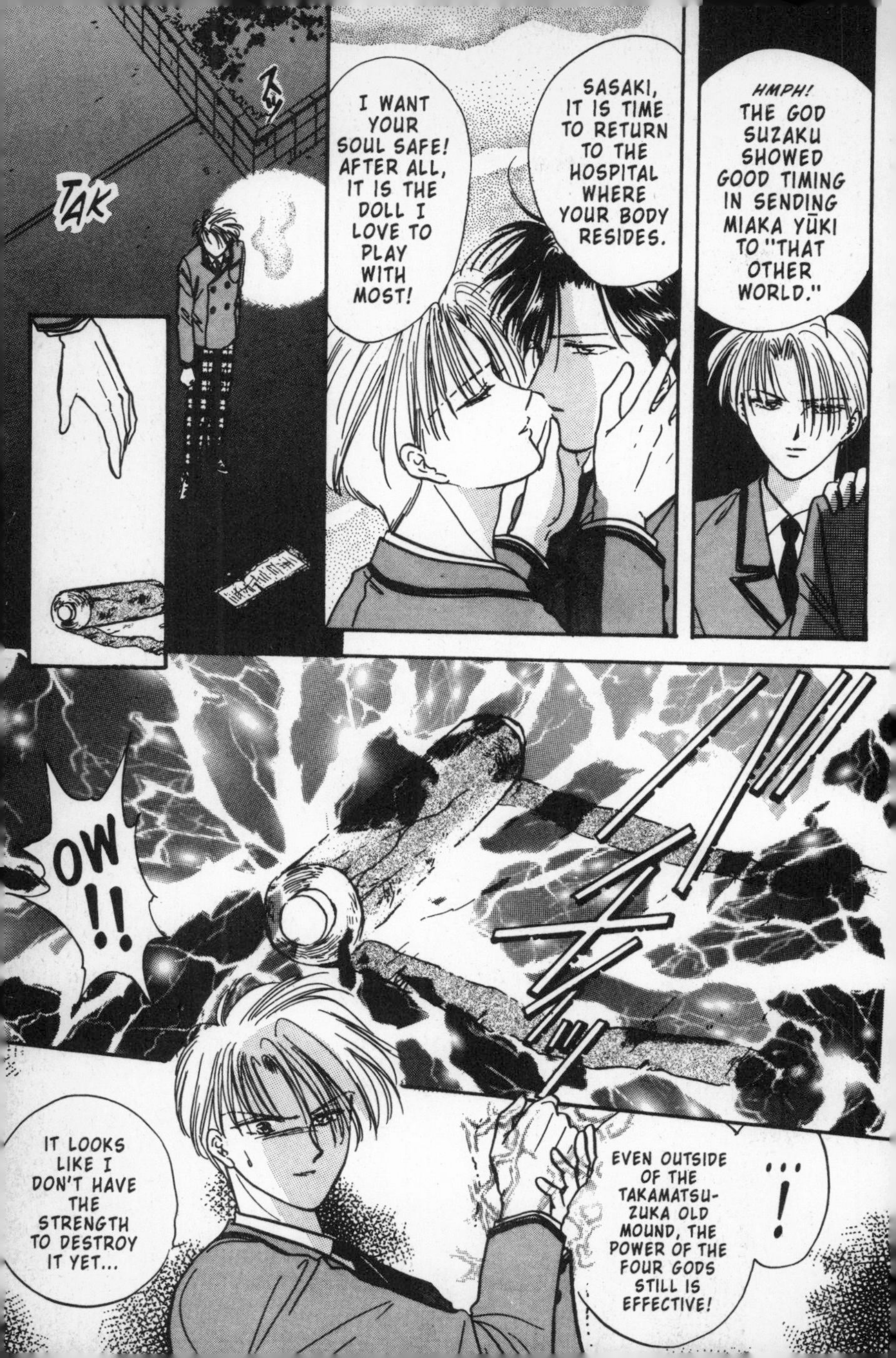
HMPH! THE GOD SUZAKU SHOWED GOOD TIMING IN SENDING MIAKA YŪKI TO "THAT OTHER WORLD."
SASAKI, IT IS TIME TO RETURN TO THE HOSPITAL WHERE YOUR BODY RESIDES.
I WANT YOUR SOUL SAFE! AFTER ALL, IT IS THE DOLL I LOVE TO PLAY WITH MOST!
TAK
OW!!
...!
EVEN OUTSIDE OF THE TAKAMATSU-ZUKA OLD MOUND, THE POWER OF THE FOUR GODS STILL IS EFFECTIVE!
IT LOOKS LIKE I DON'T HAVE THE STRENGTH TO DESTROY IT YET...

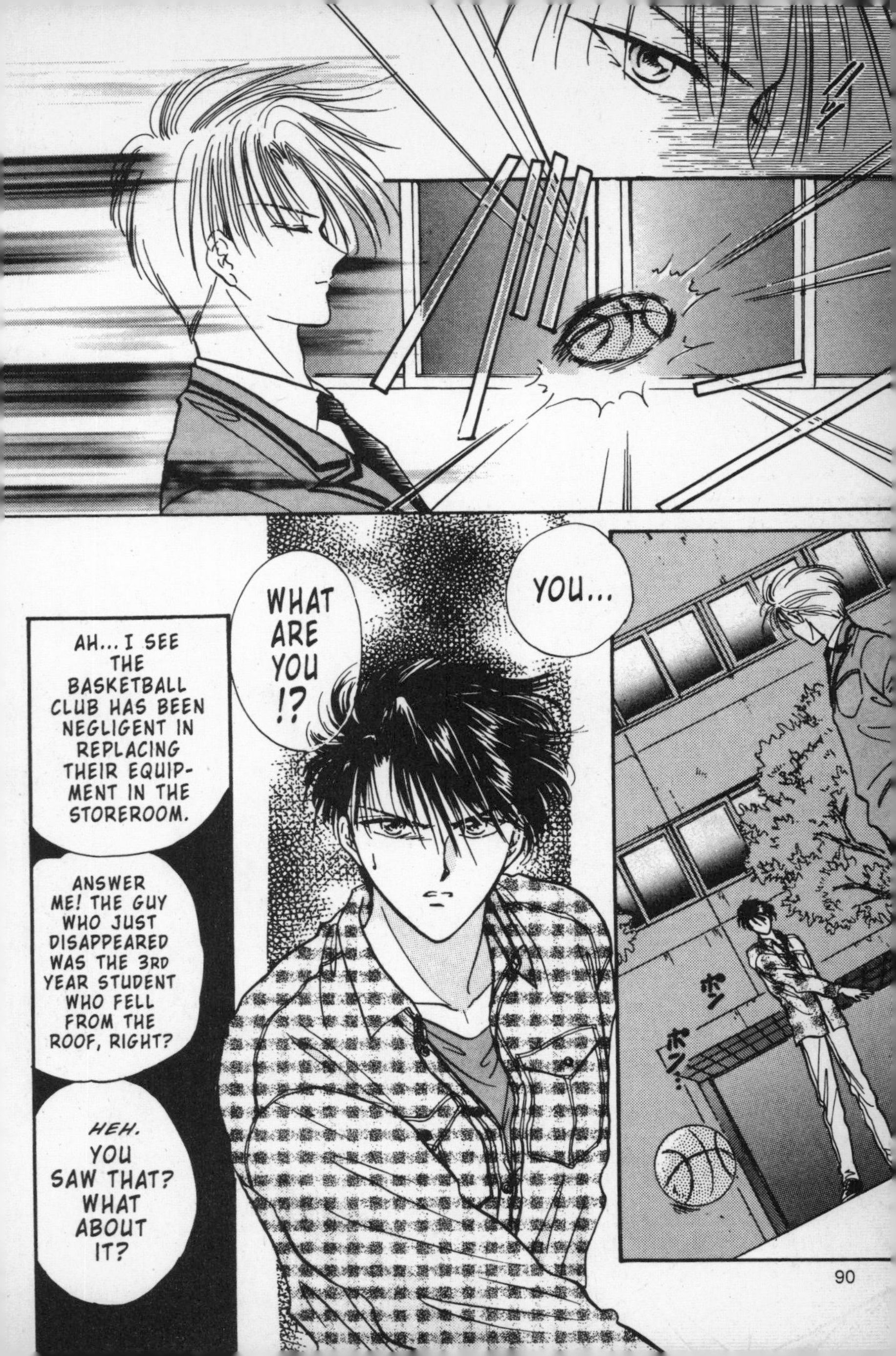
ポン
ポン…
YOU...
WHAT ARE YOU !?
AH... I SEE THE BASKETBALL CLUB HAS BEEN NEGLIGENT IN REPLACING THEIR EQUIPMENT IN THE STOREROOM.
ANSWER ME! THE GUY WHO JUST DISAPPEARED WAS THE 3RD YEAR STUDENT WHO FELL FROM THE ROOF, RIGHT?
HEH. YOU SAW THAT? WHAT ABOUT IT?

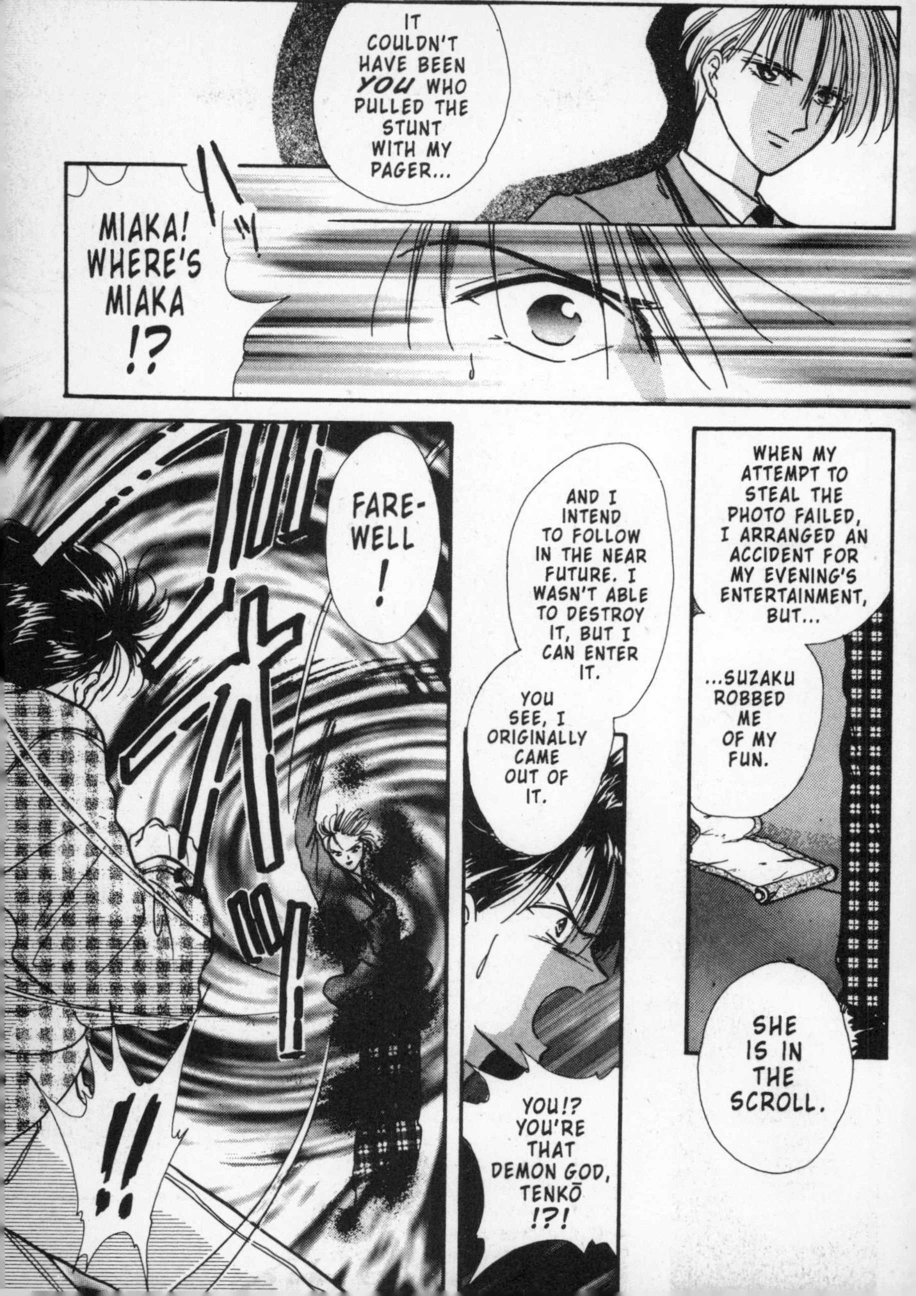
IT COULDN'T HAVE BEEN *YOU* WHO PULLED THE STUNT WITH MY PAGER...
MIAKA! WHERE'S MIAKA !?
WHEN MY ATTEMPT TO STEAL THE PHOTO FAILED, I ARRANGED AN ACCIDENT FOR MY EVENING'S ENTERTAINMENT, BUT...
...SUZAKU ROBBED ME OF MY FUN.
SHE IS IN THE SCROLL.
AND I INTEND TO FOLLOW IN THE NEAR FUTURE. I WASN'T ABLE TO DESTROY IT, BUT I CAN ENTER IT.
YOU SEE, I ORIGINALLY CAME OUT OF IT.
YOU!? YOU'RE THAT DEMON GOD, TENKŌ !?!
FARE-WELL !
!!

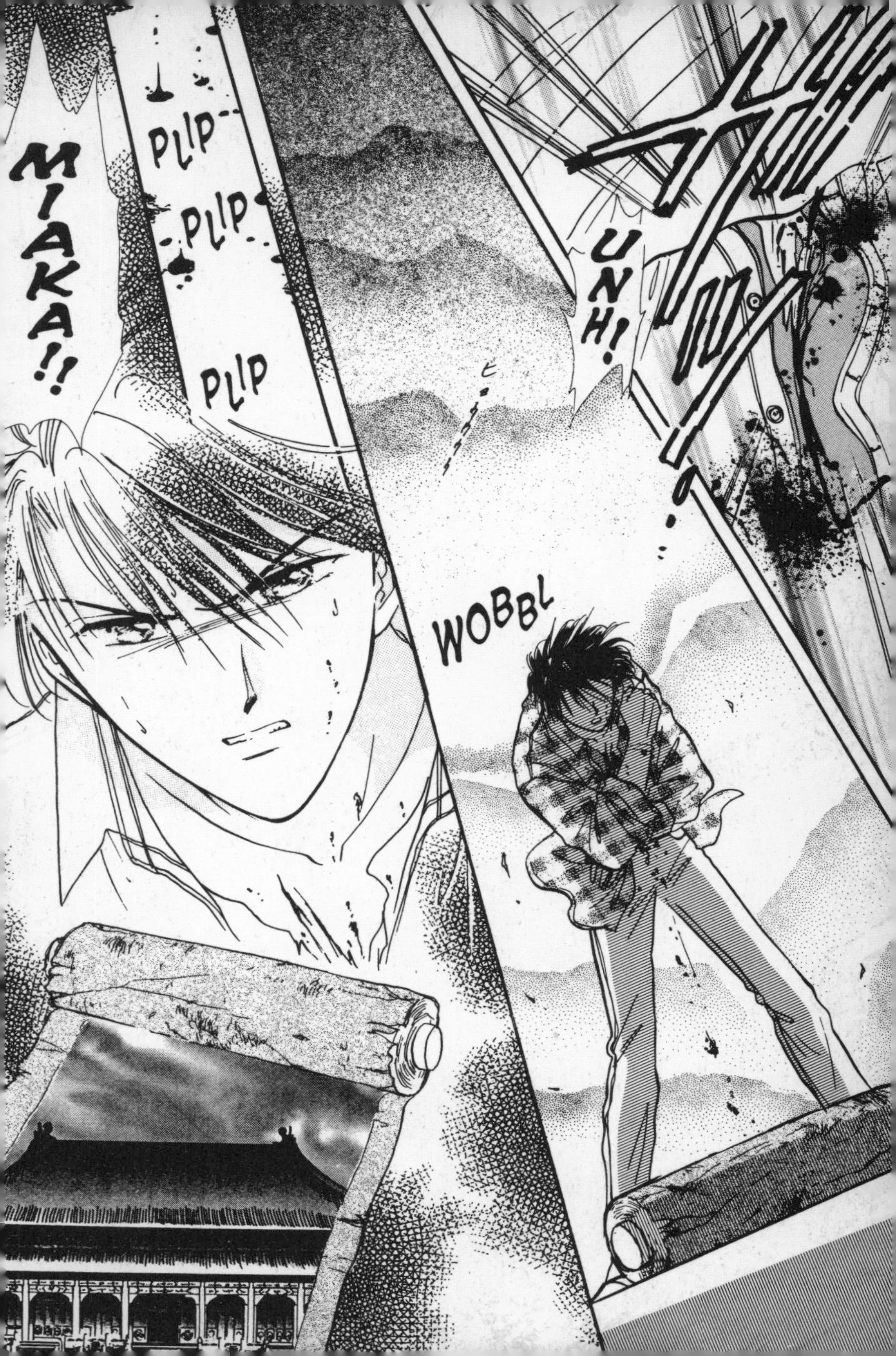
UNH!
WOBBL
PLIP
PLIP
PLIP
MIAKA!!

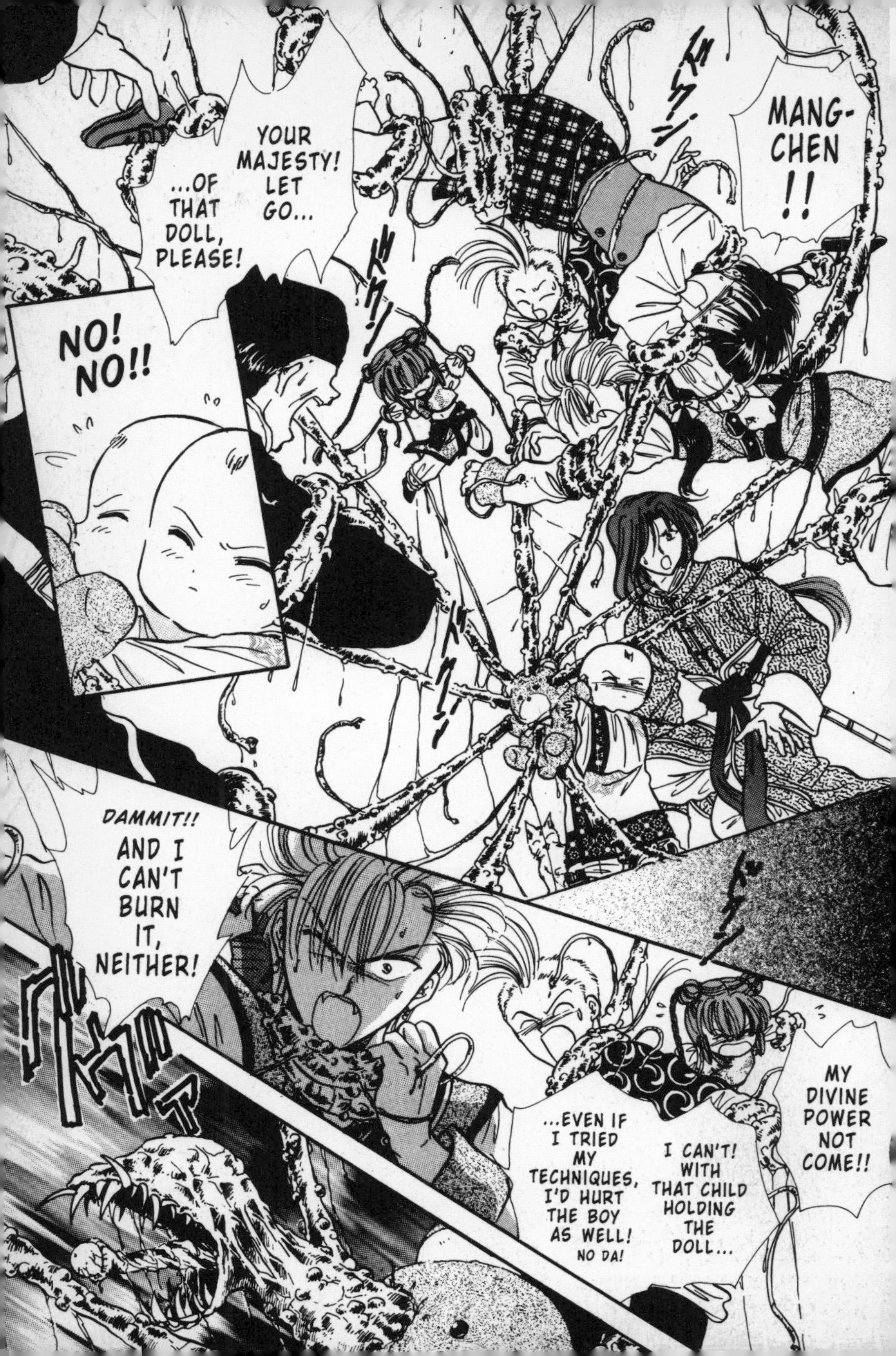
MANG-CHEN!!
YOUR MAJESTY! LET GO...
...OF THAT DOLL, PLEASE!
NO! NO!!
MY DIVINE POWER NOT COME!!
I CAN'T! WITH THAT CHILD HOLDING THE DOLL...
...EVEN IF I TRIED MY TECHNIQUES, I'D HURT THE BOY AS WELL! NO DA!
DAMMIT!! AND I CAN'T BURN IT, NEITHER!

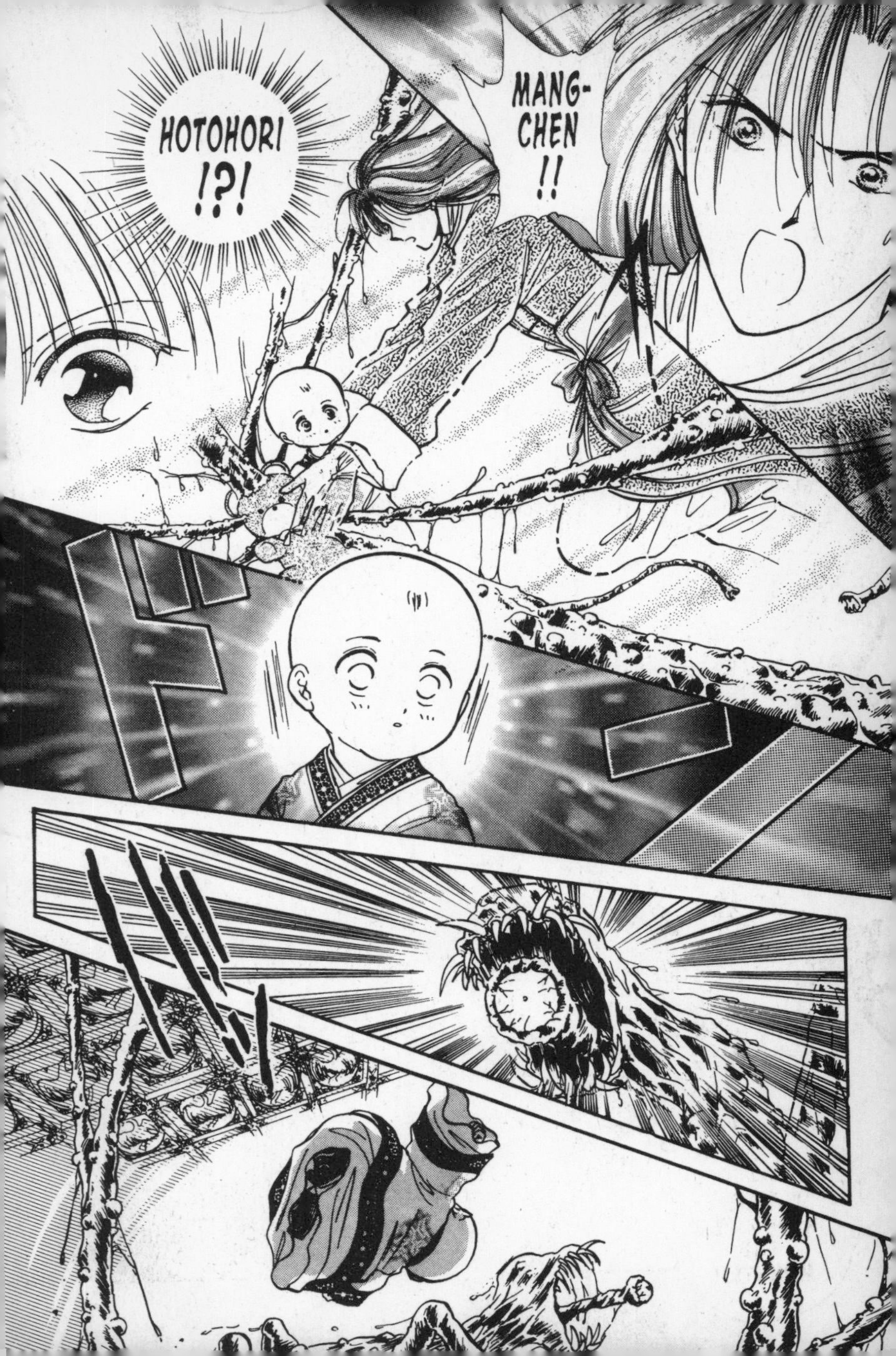
MANG-CHEN !!
HOTOHORI !?!

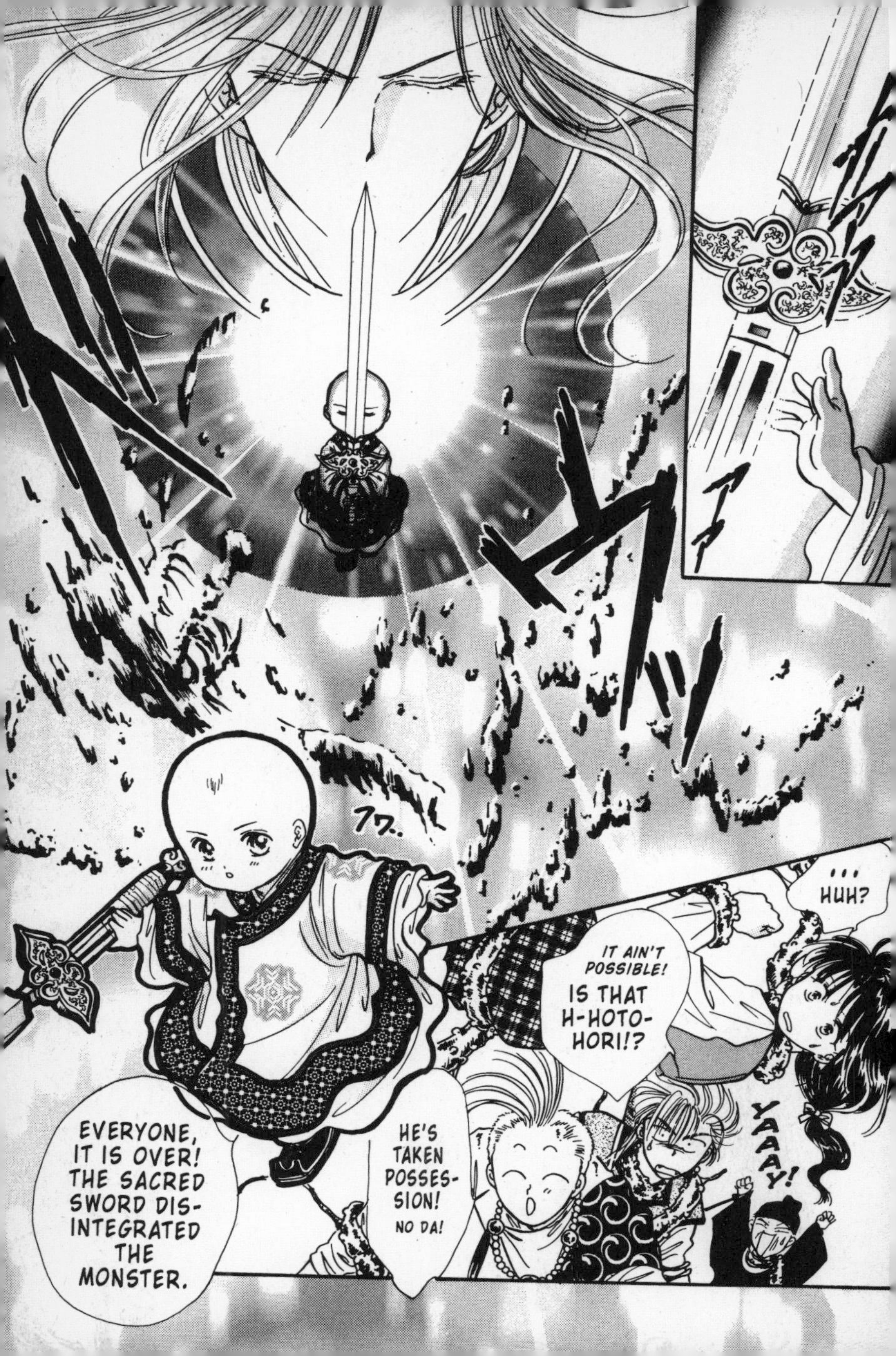
フワ..
... HUH?
IT AIN'T POSSIBLE! IS THAT H-HOTO-HORI!?
YAAAY!
HE'S TAKEN POSSES-SION! NO DA!
EVERYONE, IT IS OVER! THE SACRED SWORD DIS-INTEGRATED THE MONSTER.

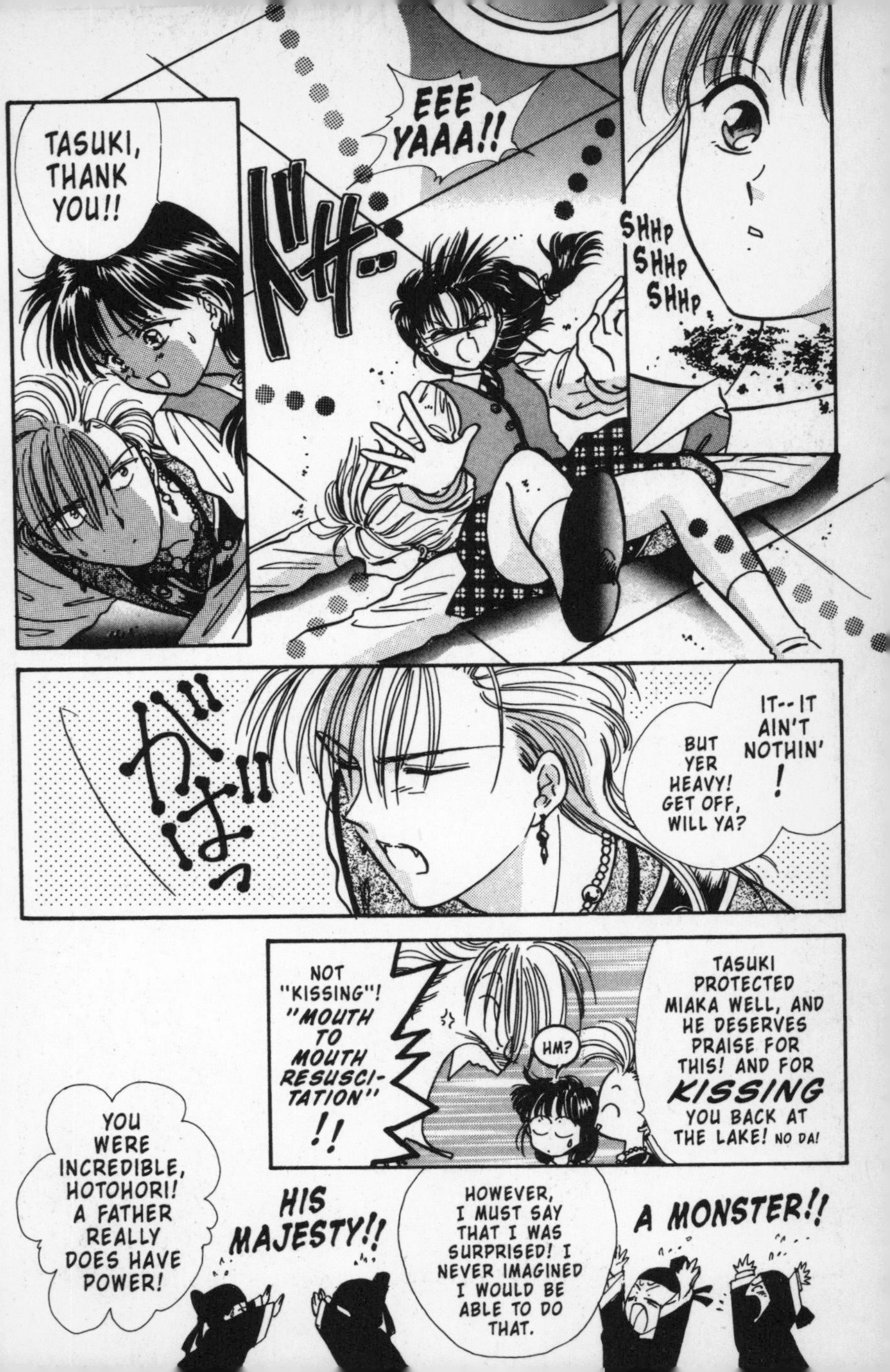
SHHp
SHHp
SHHp
EEE YAAA!!
ドザー
TASUKI, THANK YOU!!
IT-- IT AIN'T NOTHIN' !
BUT YER HEAVY! GET OFF, WILL YA?
がばっ
TASUKI PROTECTED MIAKA WELL, AND HE DESERVES PRAISE FOR THIS! AND FOR KISSING YOU BACK AT THE LAKE! NO DA!
HM?
NOT "KISSING"! "MOUTH TO MOUTH RESUSCI- TATION" !!
A MONSTER!!
HOWEVER, I MUST SAY THAT I WAS SURPRISED! I NEVER IMAGINED I WOULD BE ABLE TO DO THAT.
HIS MAJESTY!!
YOU WERE INCREDIBLE, HOTOHORI! A FATHER REALLY DOES HAVE POWER!

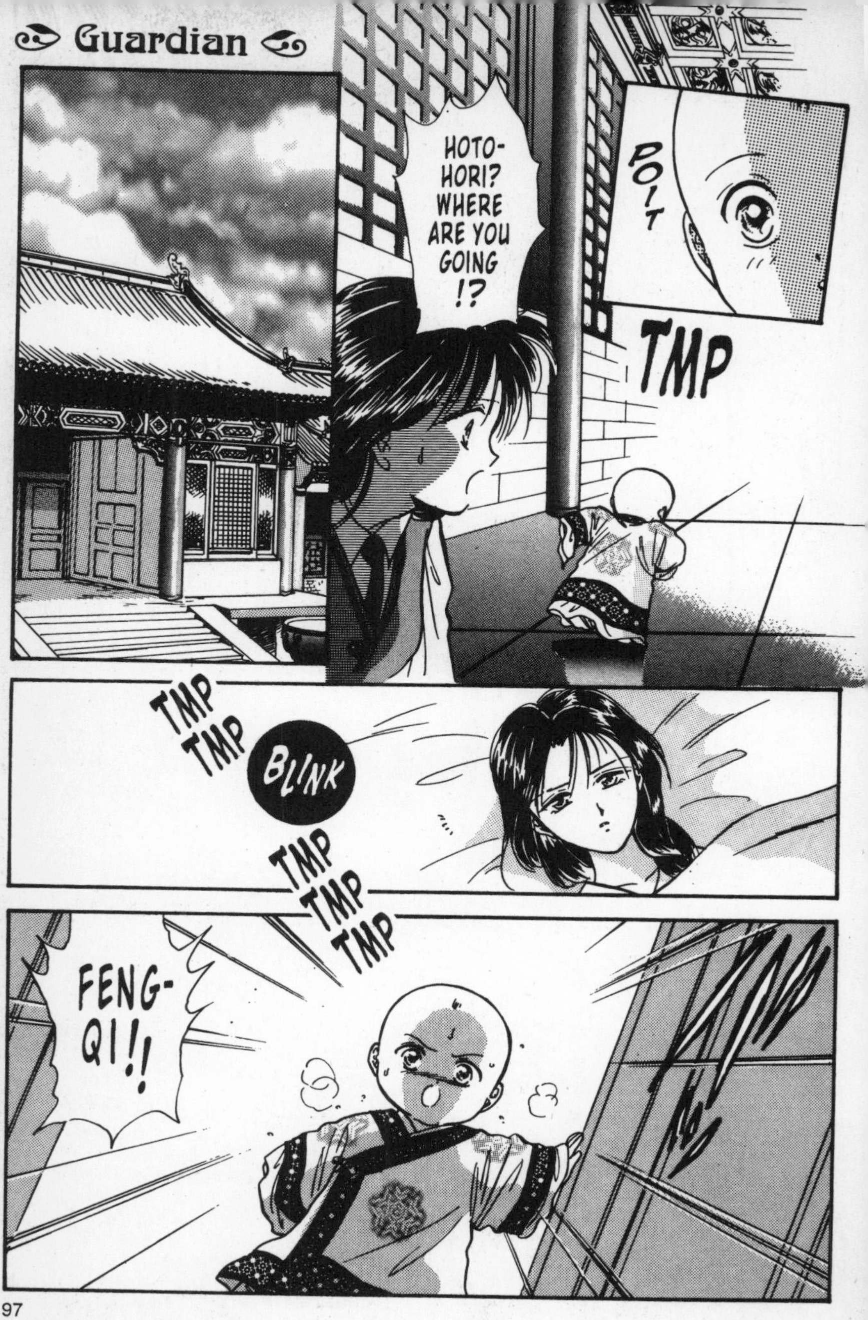
POIT
HOTO-HORI? WHERE ARE YOU GOING!?
TMP
TMP TMP
BLINK
TMP TMP TMP
FENG-QI!!

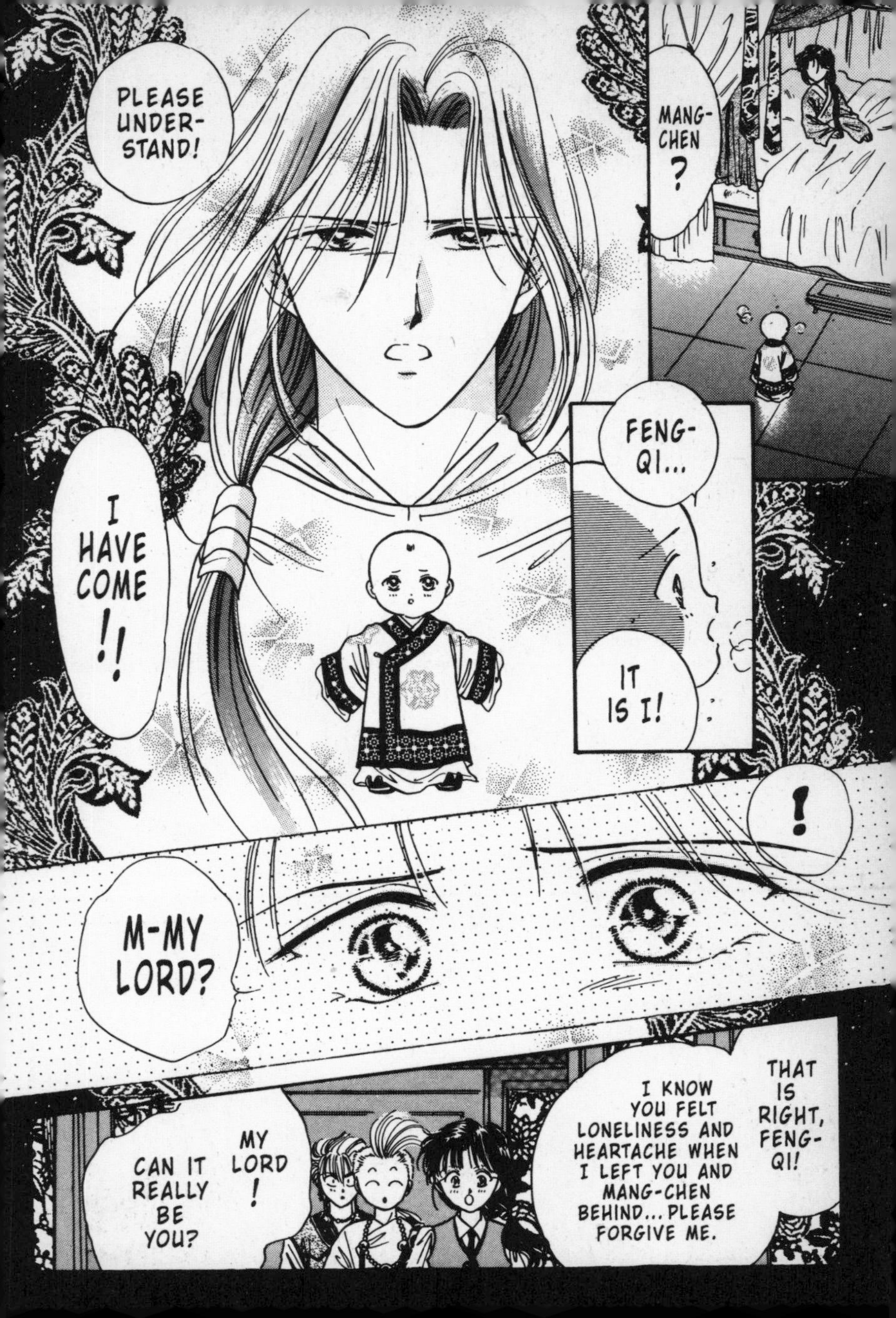
MANG-CHEN?
FENG-QI...
IT IS I!
PLEASE UNDER-STAND!
I HAVE COME!!
!
M-MY LORD?
THAT IS RIGHT, FENG-QI!
I KNOW YOU FELT LONELINESS AND HEARTACHE WHEN I LEFT YOU AND MANG-CHEN BEHIND... PLEASE FORGIVE ME.
MY LORD!
CAN IT REALLY BE YOU?

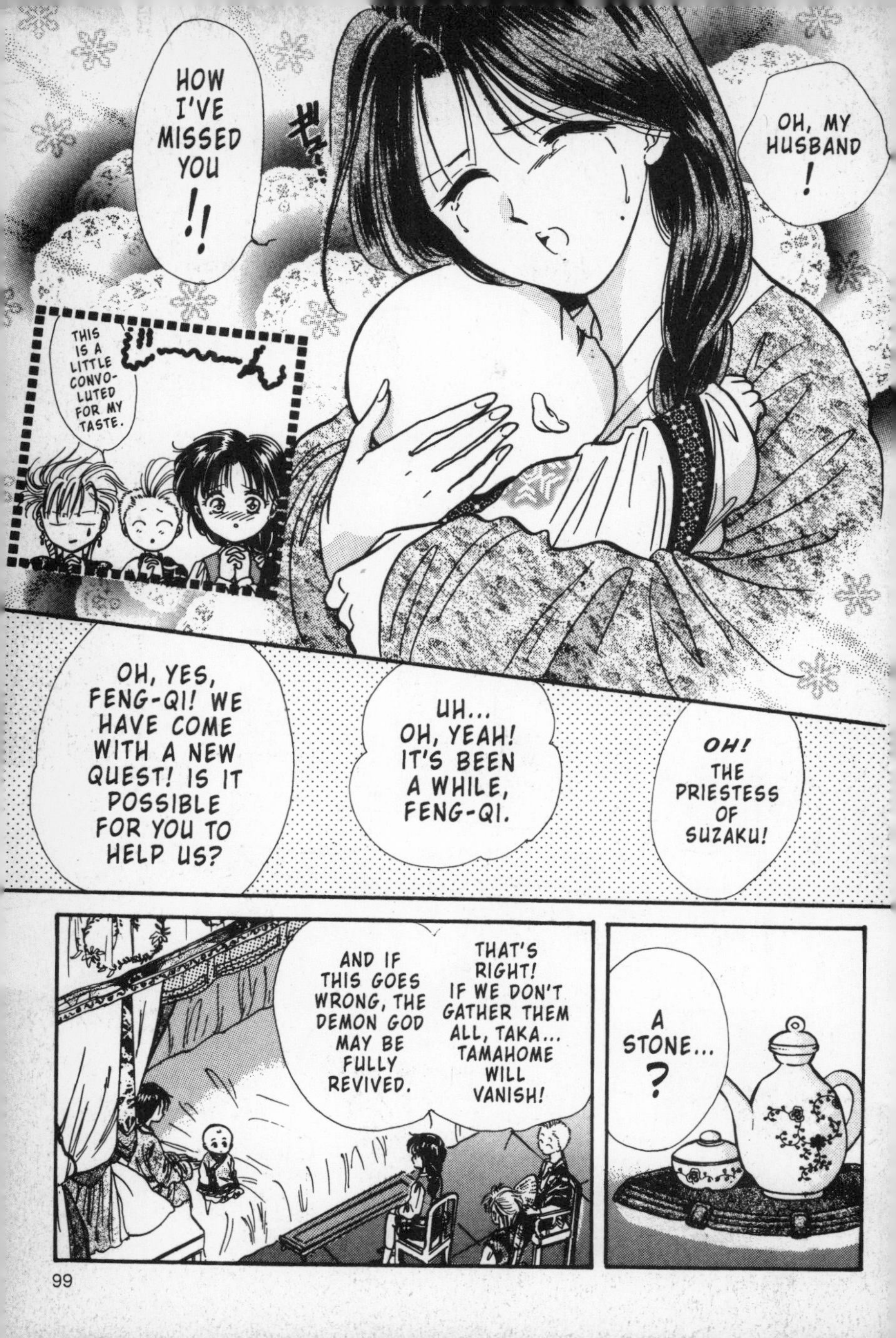
OH, MY HUSBAND!
HOW I'VE MISSED YOU!!
THIS IS A LITTLE CONVOLUTED FOR MY TASTE.
OH! THE PRIESTESS OF SUZAKU!
UH... OH, YEAH! IT'S BEEN A WHILE, FENG-QI.
OH, YES, FENG-QI! WE HAVE COME WITH A NEW QUEST! IS IT POSSIBLE FOR YOU TO HELP US?
A STONE...?
THAT'S RIGHT! IF WE DON'T GATHER THEM ALL, TAKA... TAMAHOME WILL VANISH!
AND IF THIS GOES WRONG, THE DEMON GOD MAY BE FULLY REVIVED.

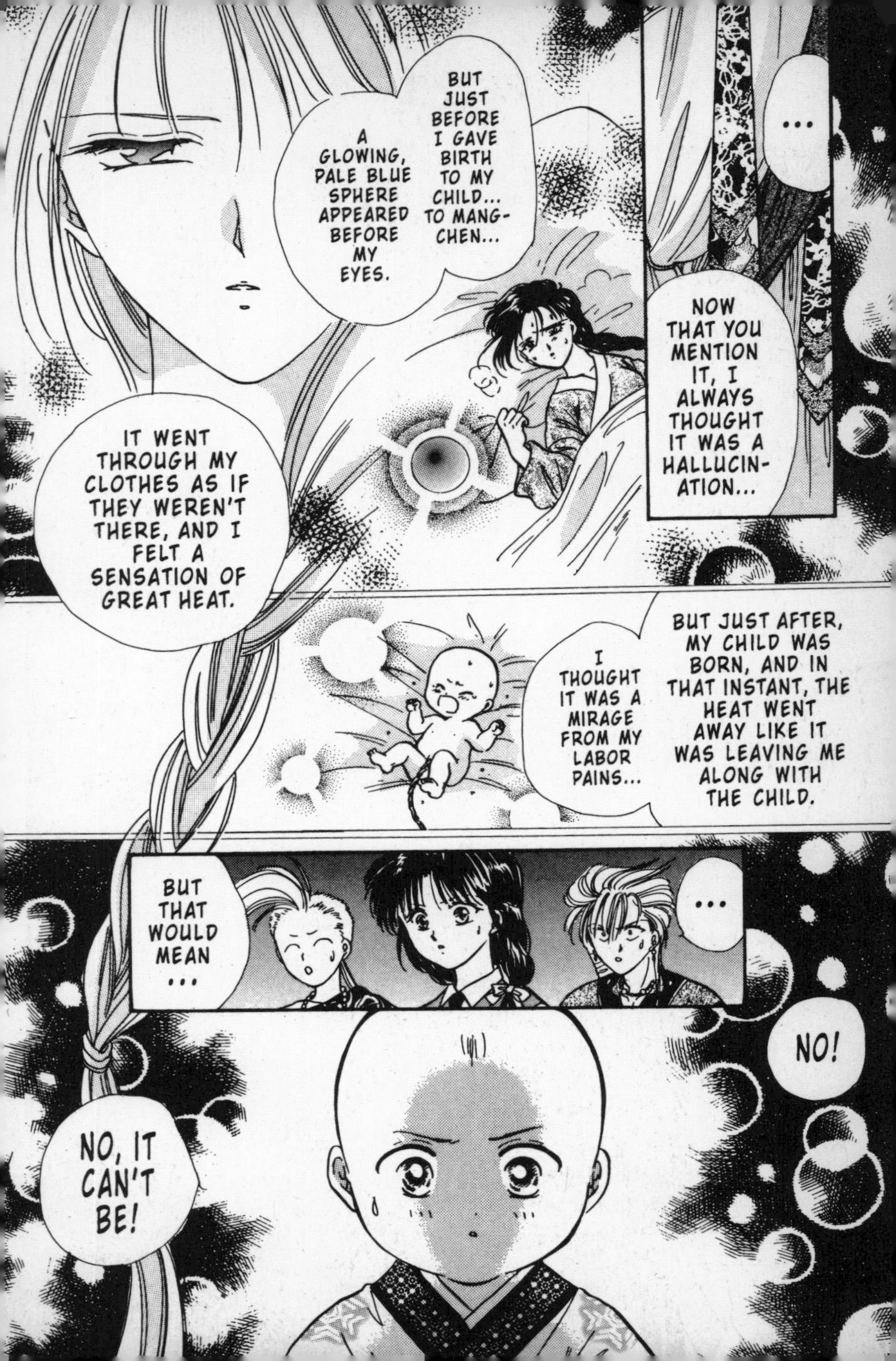
...
NOW THAT YOU MENTION IT, I ALWAYS THOUGHT IT WAS A HALLUCIN-ATION...
BUT JUST BEFORE I GAVE BIRTH TO MY CHILD... TO MANG-CHEN...
A GLOWING, PALE BLUE SPHERE APPEARED BEFORE MY EYES.
IT WENT THROUGH MY CLOTHES AS IF THEY WEREN'T THERE, AND I FELT A SENSATION OF GREAT HEAT.
I THOUGHT IT WAS A MIRAGE FROM MY LABOR PAINS...
BUT JUST AFTER, MY CHILD WAS BORN, AND IN THAT INSTANT, THE HEAT WENT AWAY LIKE IT WAS LEAVING ME ALONG WITH THE CHILD.
...
BUT THAT WOULD MEAN ...
NO!
NO, IT CAN'T BE!

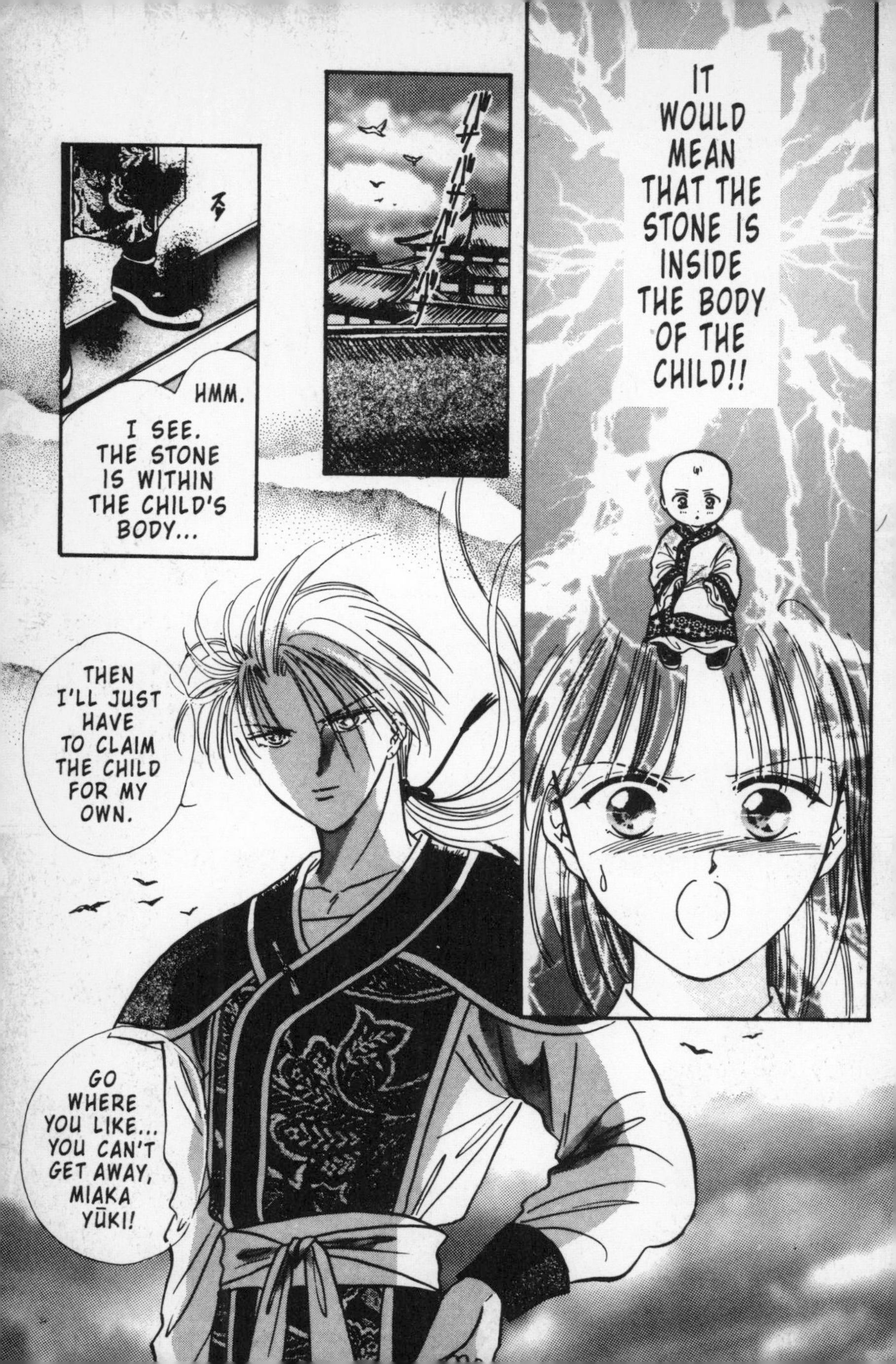
IT WOULD MEAN THAT THE STONE IS INSIDE THE BODY OF THE CHILD!!
HMM.
I SEE. THE STONE IS WITHIN THE CHILD'S BODY...
THEN I'LL JUST HAVE TO CLAIM THE CHILD FOR MY OWN.
GO WHERE YOU LIKE... YOU CAN'T GET AWAY, MIAKA YŪKI!

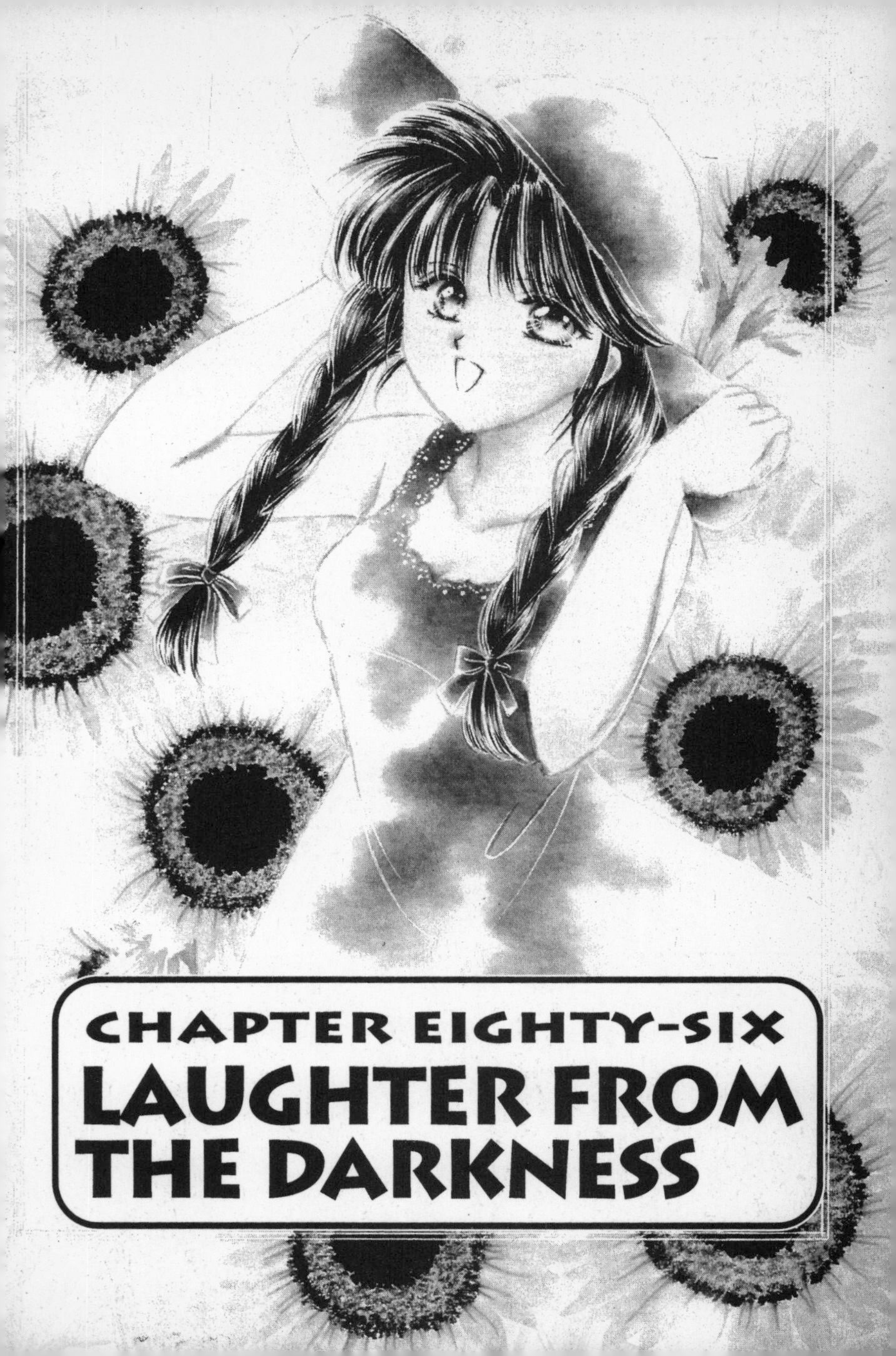

CHAPTER EIGHTY-SIX

LAUGHTER FROM THE DARKNESS

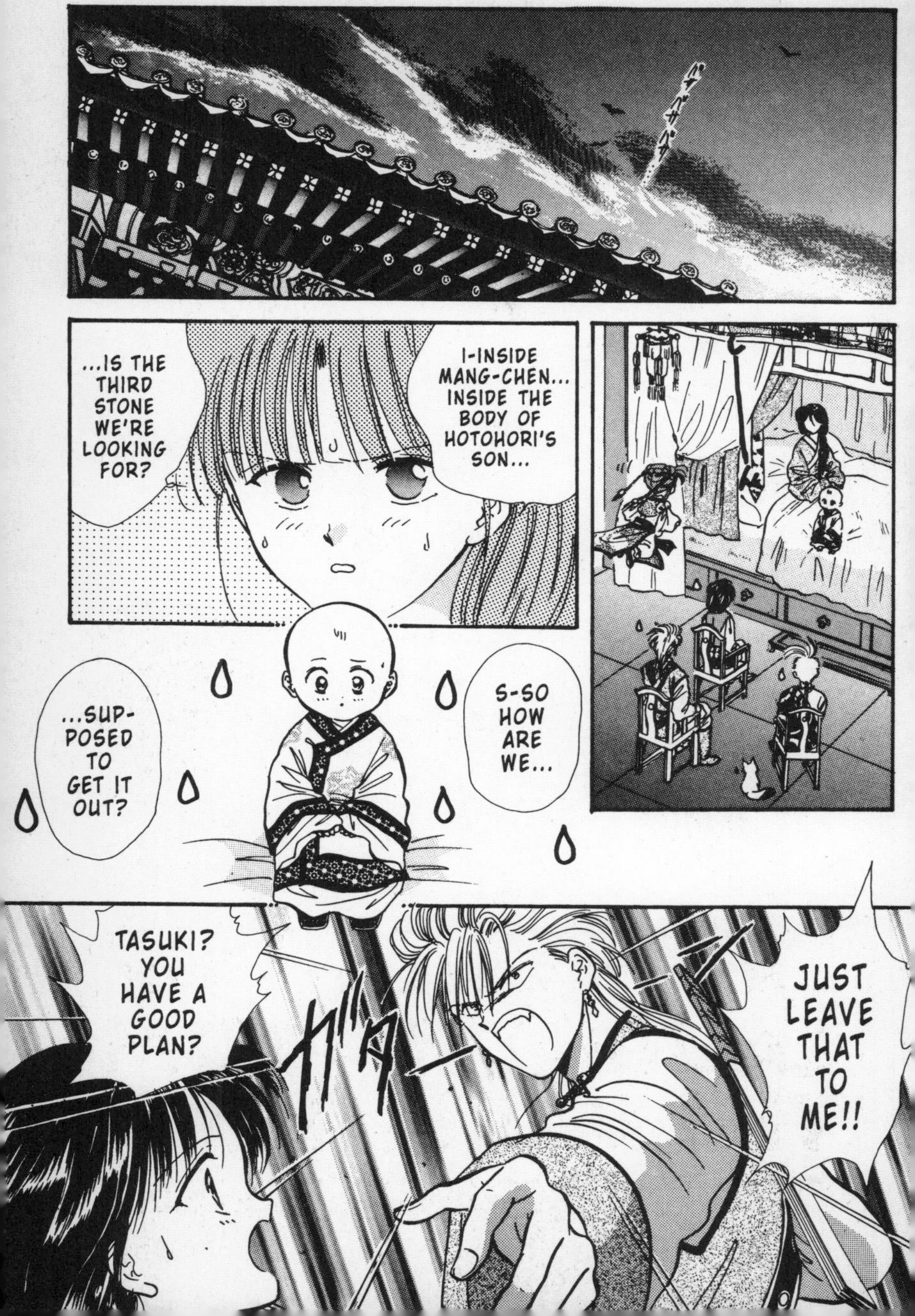
I-INSIDE MANG-CHEN... INSIDE THE BODY OF HOTOHORI'S SON...
...IS THE THIRD STONE WE'RE LOOKING FOR?
S-SO HOW ARE WE...
...SUP-POSED TO GET IT OUT?
JUST LEAVE THAT TO ME!!
TASUKI? YOU HAVE A GOOD PLAN?

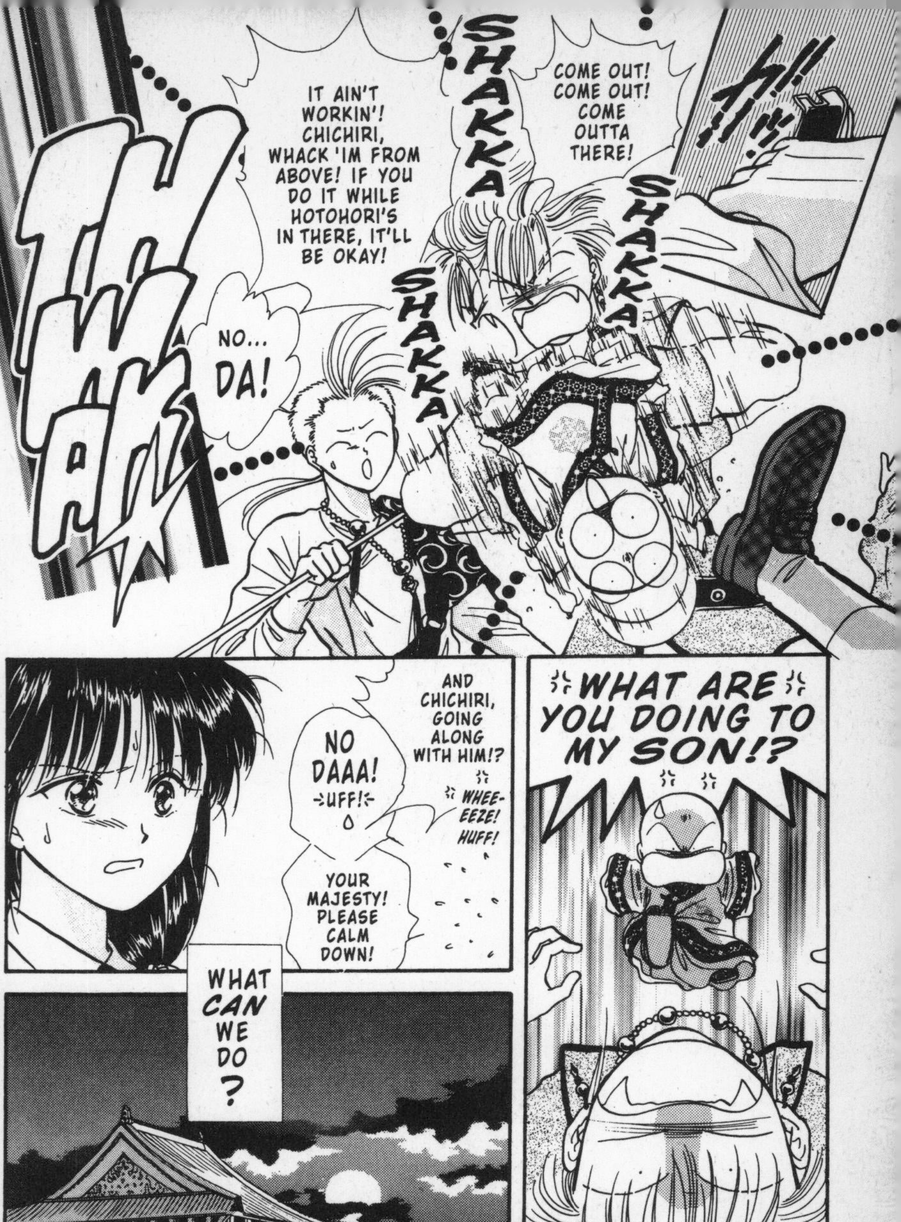
COME OUT! COME OUT! COME OUTTA THERE!
SHAKKA
IT AIN'T WORKIN'! CHICHIRI, WHACK 'IM FROM ABOVE! IF YOU DO IT WHILE HOTOHORI'S IN THERE, IT'LL BE OKAY!
SHAKKA
SHAKKA
NO... DA!
WHAT ARE YOU DOING TO MY SON!?
AND CHICHIRI, GOING ALONG WITH HIM!?
WHEE-EEZE! HUFF!
NO DAAA! -UFF!-
YOUR MAJESTY! PLEASE CALM DOWN!
WHAT CAN WE DO?

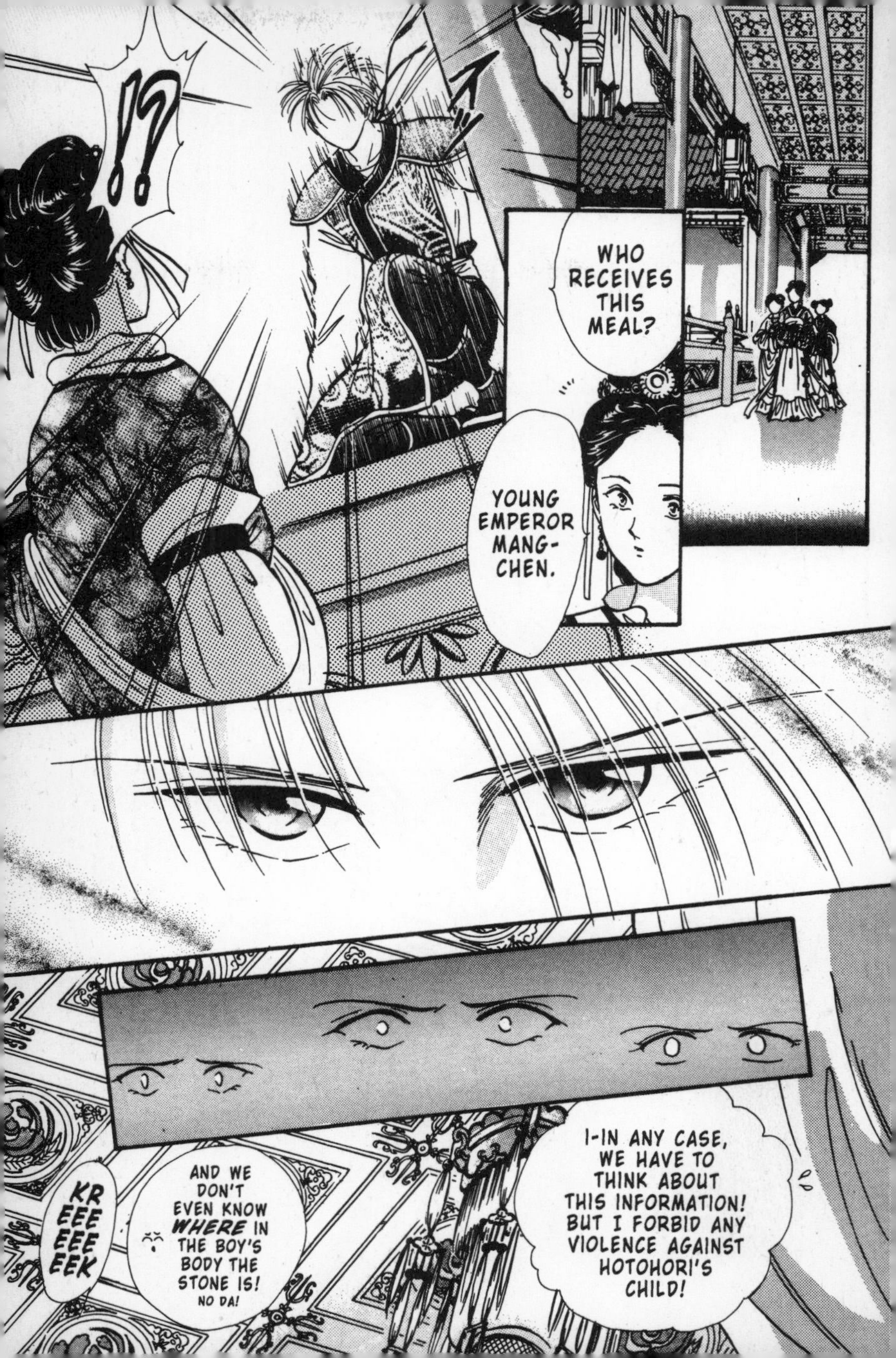
WHO RECEIVES THIS MEAL?
YOUNG EMPEROR MANG-CHEN.
!?
I-IN ANY CASE, WE HAVE TO THINK ABOUT THIS INFORMATION! BUT I FORBID ANY VIOLENCE AGAINST HOTOHORI'S CHILD!
AND WE DON'T EVEN KNOW *WHERE* IN THE BOY'S BODY THE STONE IS! NO DA!
KREEEEEEEEEEEK

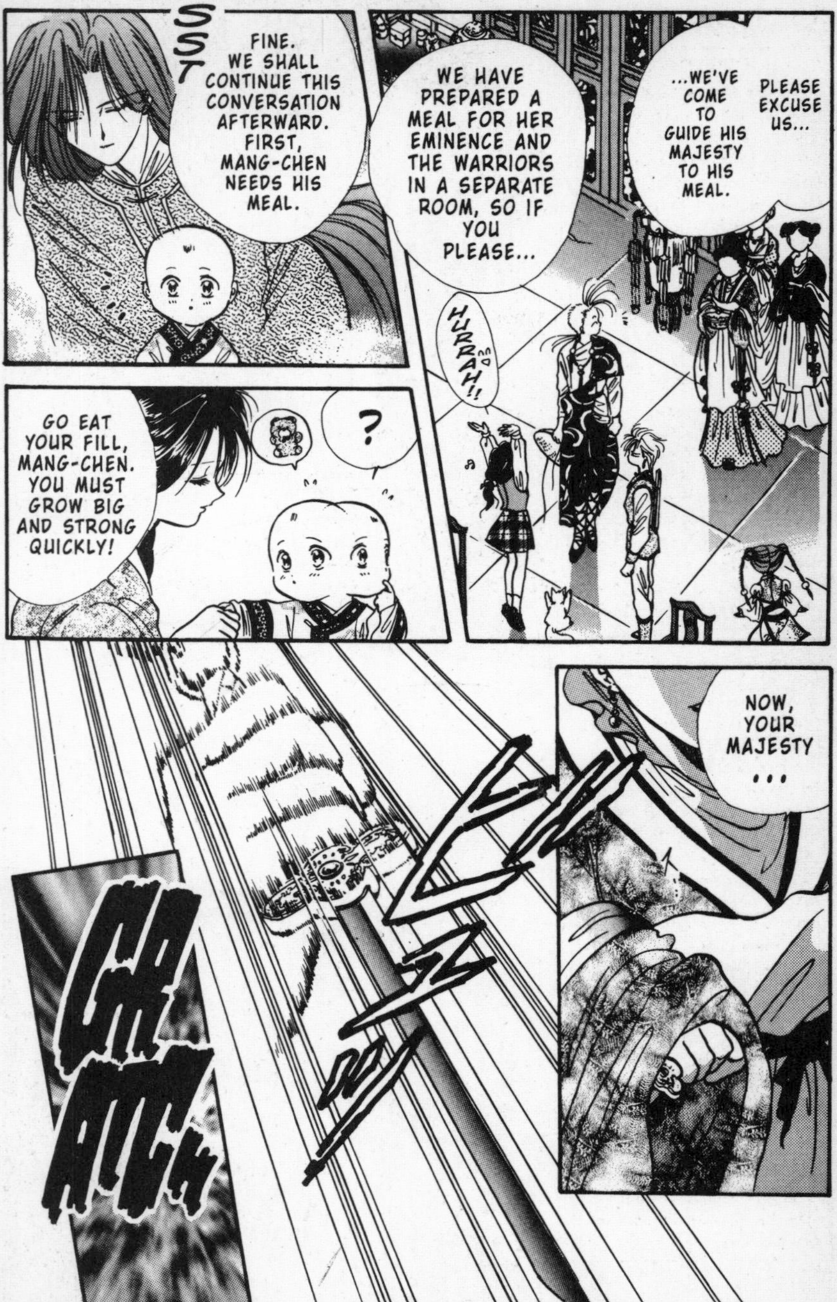
PLEASE EXCUSE US...
...WE'VE COME TO GUIDE HIS MAJESTY TO HIS MEAL.
WE HAVE PREPARED A MEAL FOR HER EMINENCE AND THE WARRIORS IN A SEPARATE ROOM, SO IF YOU PLEASE...
HURRAH!!
SST
FINE. WE SHALL CONTINUE THIS CONVERSATION AFTERWARD. FIRST, MANG-CHEN NEEDS HIS MEAL.
?
GO EAT YOUR FILL, MANG-CHEN. YOU MUST GROW BIG AND STRONG QUICKLY!
NOW, YOUR MAJESTY ...

Guardian

Now, on 8/18 (1995), I took part in a Bandai event. But I'm so timid☺ that I had to think that with the voice actors there, there was no need for me to be. I didn't have much to say, and I'm not much to look at.☺ And I'm really bad in front of crowds. Ah! There was some great Chichiri cosplay! (I had gone to the rest room at the time, so I didn't know.) During the "talk" period, it was really fun hearing the speech by Mr. Koyasu, who plays Hotohori. And I said some stuff that didn't make much sense.☺ Oh, yeah! It was then I got some really surprising news. One of the people from Bandai mentioned to me earlier that when Ms. Takeuchi, the manga artist who created Sailor Moon, was there, she said that she would like to meet me. "Dammit! I missed her!" I thought.☺ And in the end, we never did meet. I sent her a book of illustrations--I hope she got it all right. Was it really me she wanted to meet? *I get the feeling I'm just flattering myself.*

But even after all that, the biggest event of the summer (for me) was a signing in Taiwan! On 8/19, I was on my way there! (Actually, I had just finished my manga pages on 8/17, so I felt that I was near death with exhaustion! I could write forever about the view, it was so wonderful! But to summarize, it really reminded me of Osaka!☺ And the people who live there are nothing if not energetic! Really! Just like Japan! I mean... somehow their image when viewed from Japan seems "fake," and "dull," and "gray." That's how some people think of them, so when I got there, I was so surprised! And all the people from the Taiwanese publisher treated me so well!

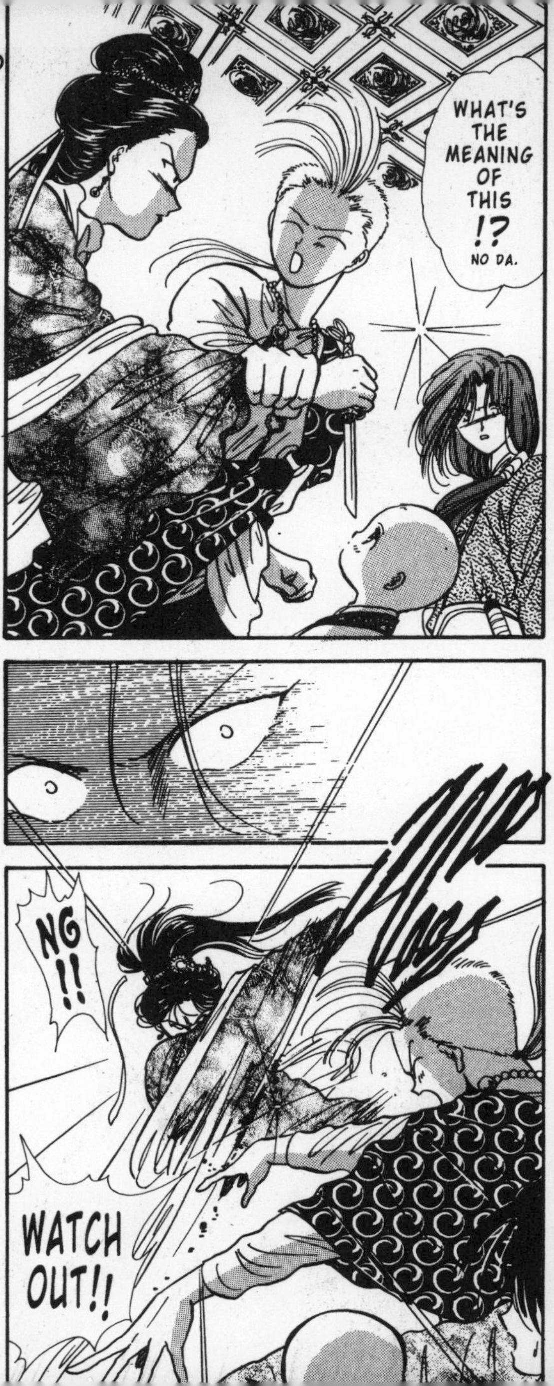

WHAT'S THE MEANING OF THIS !? NO DA.
NG !!
WATCH OUT!!

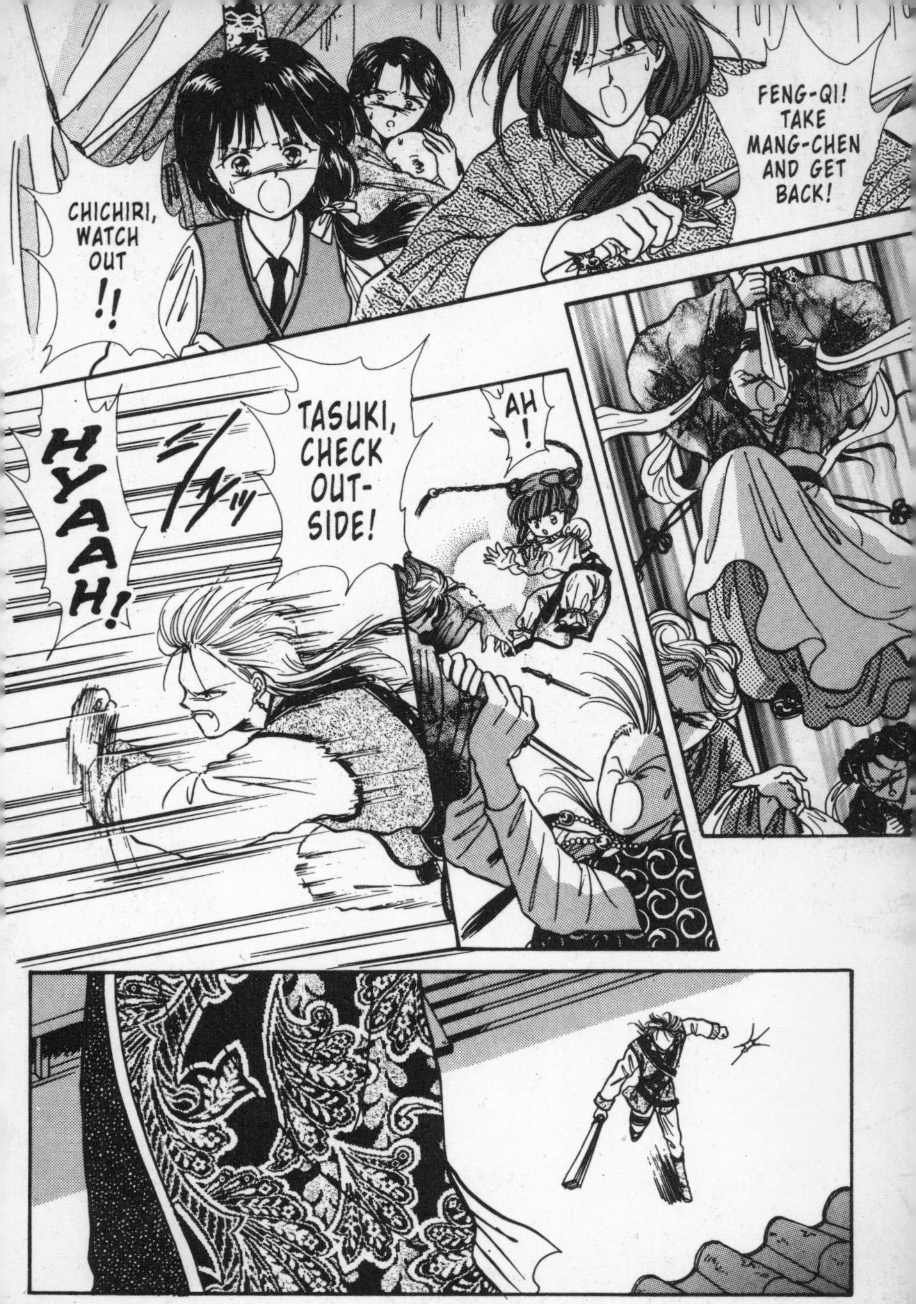
FENG-QI! TAKE MANG-CHEN AND GET BACK!
CHICHIRI, WATCH OUT !!
AH!
TASUKI, CHECK OUT-SIDE!
HYAAH!

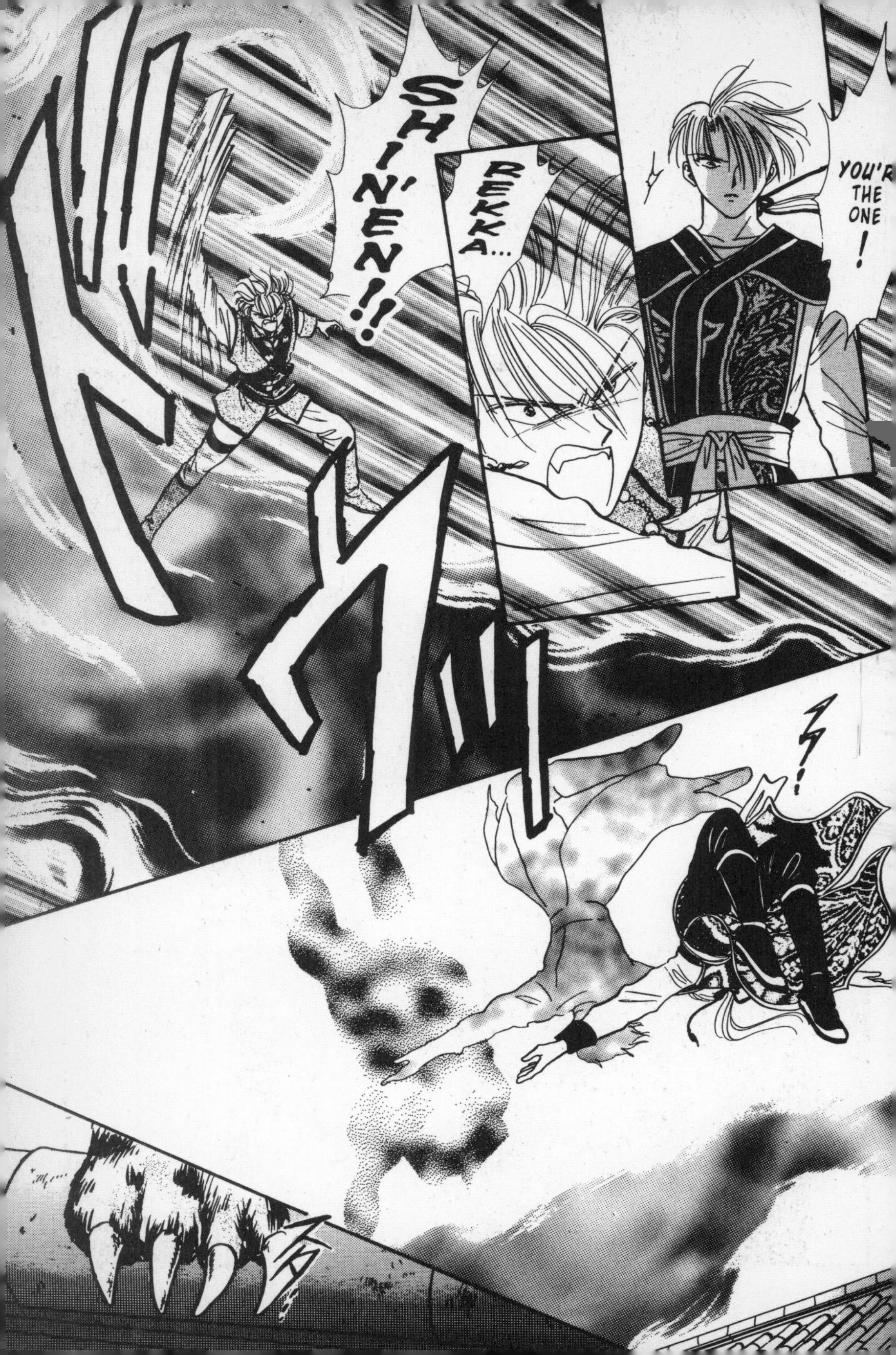
YOU'R THE ONE!
REKKA...
SHIN'NEN!!

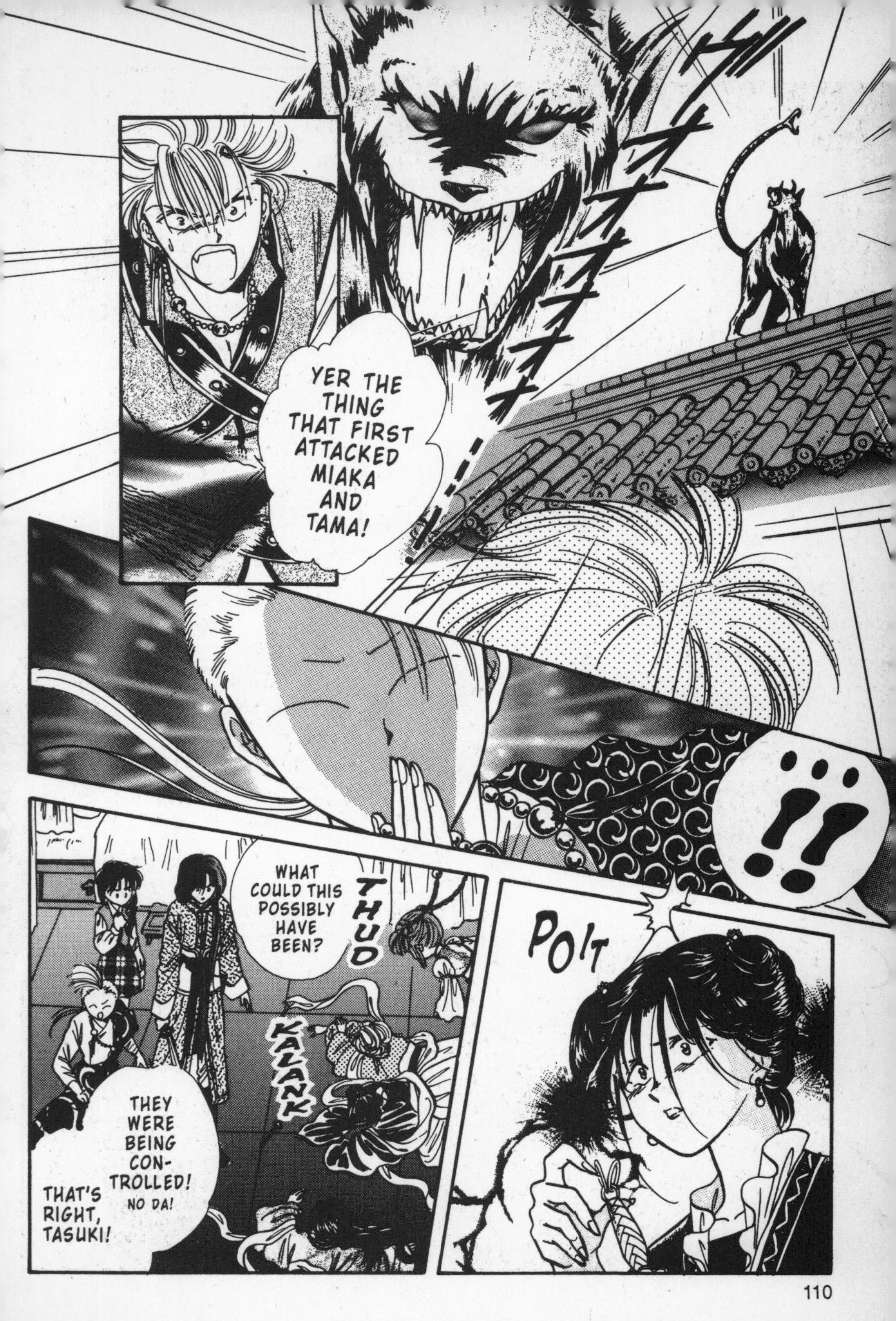
YER THE THING THAT FIRST ATTACKED MIAKA AND TAMA!
!!
POIT
THUD
WHAT COULD THIS POSSIBLY HAVE BEEN?
KALANK
THEY WERE BEING CON-TROLLED! NO DA!
THAT'S RIGHT, TASUKI!

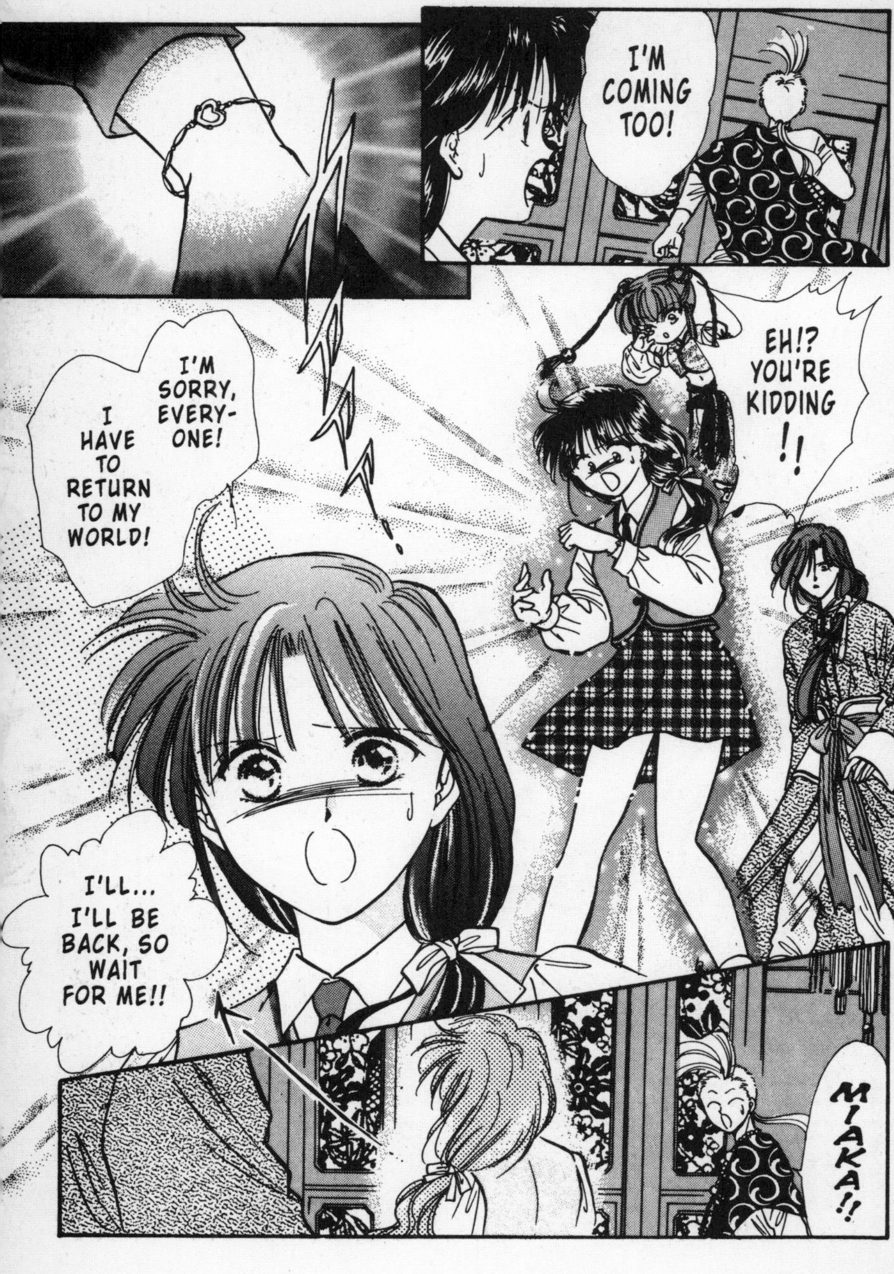
I'M COMING TOO!
EH!? YOU'RE KIDDING!!
I'M SORRY, EVERYONE! I HAVE TO RETURN TO MY WORLD!
I'LL... I'LL BE BACK, SO WAIT FOR ME!!
MIAKA!!

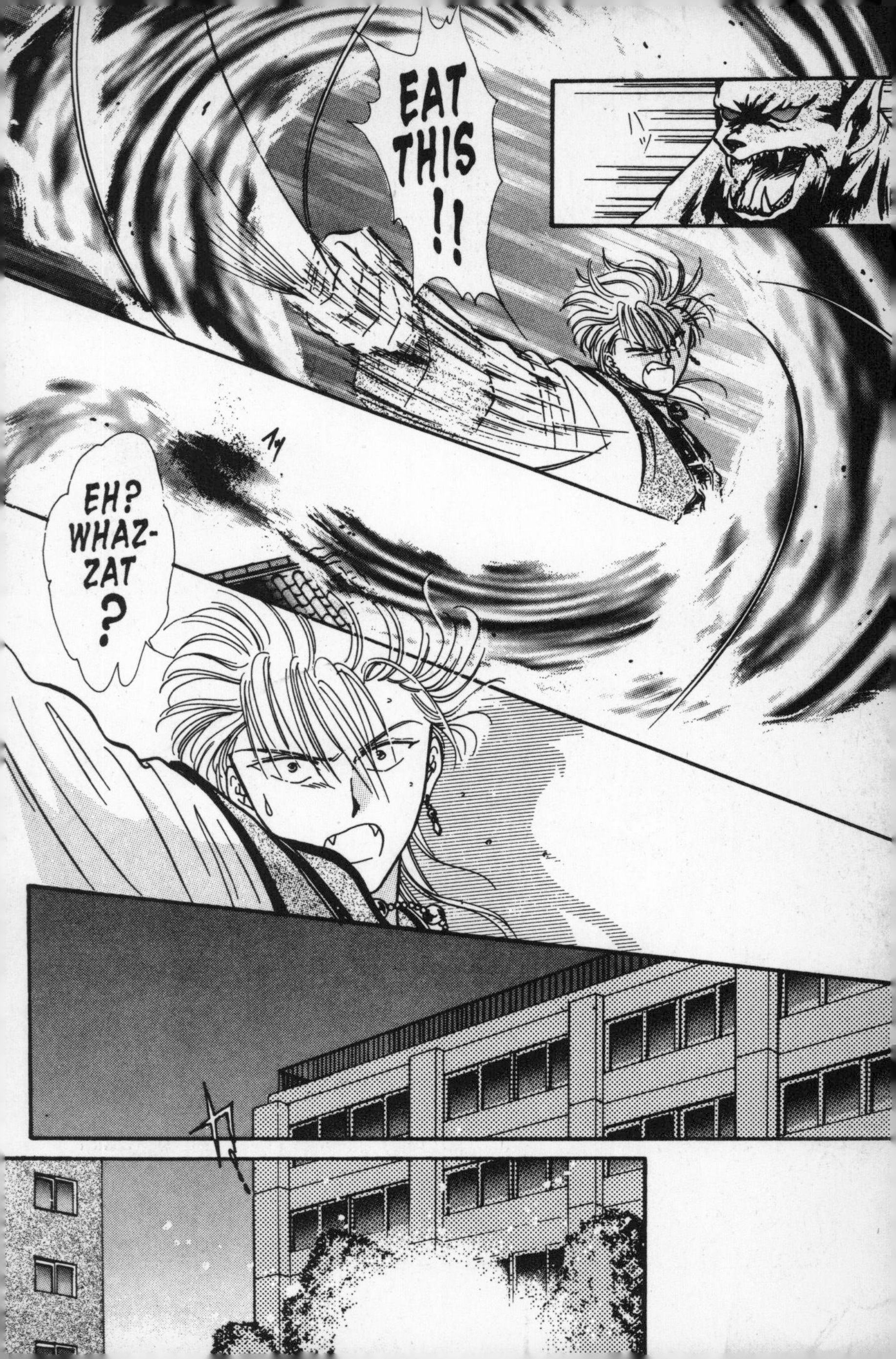
EAT THIS !!
EH? WHAZ-ZAT ?

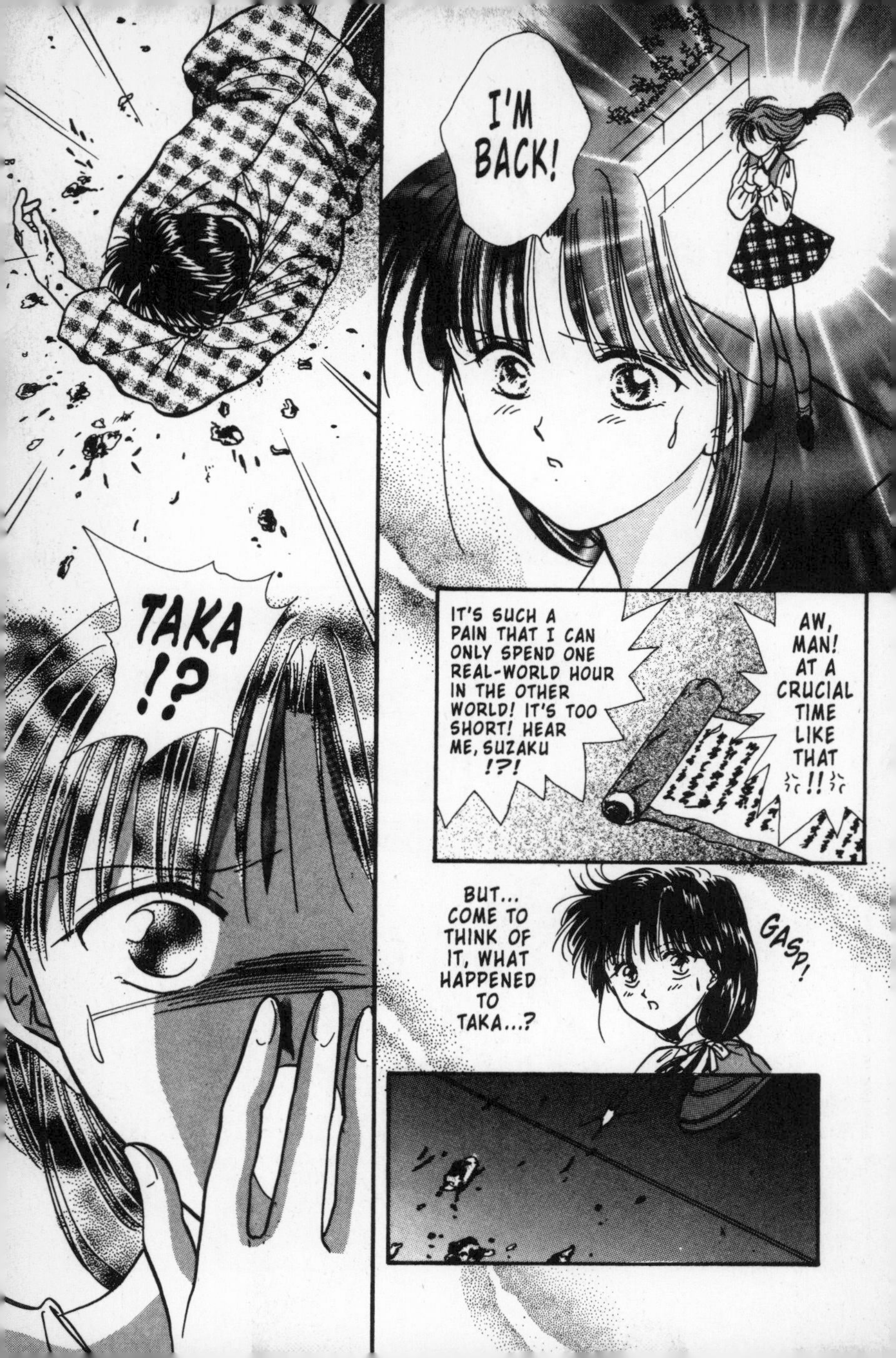
I'M BACK!
AW, MAN! AT A CRUCIAL TIME LIKE THAT!!
IT'S SUCH A PAIN THAT I CAN ONLY SPEND ONE REAL-WORLD HOUR IN THE OTHER WORLD! IT'S TOO SHORT! HEAR ME, SUZAKU!?!
GASP!
BUT... COME TO THINK OF IT, WHAT HAPPENED TO TAKA...?
TAKA!?

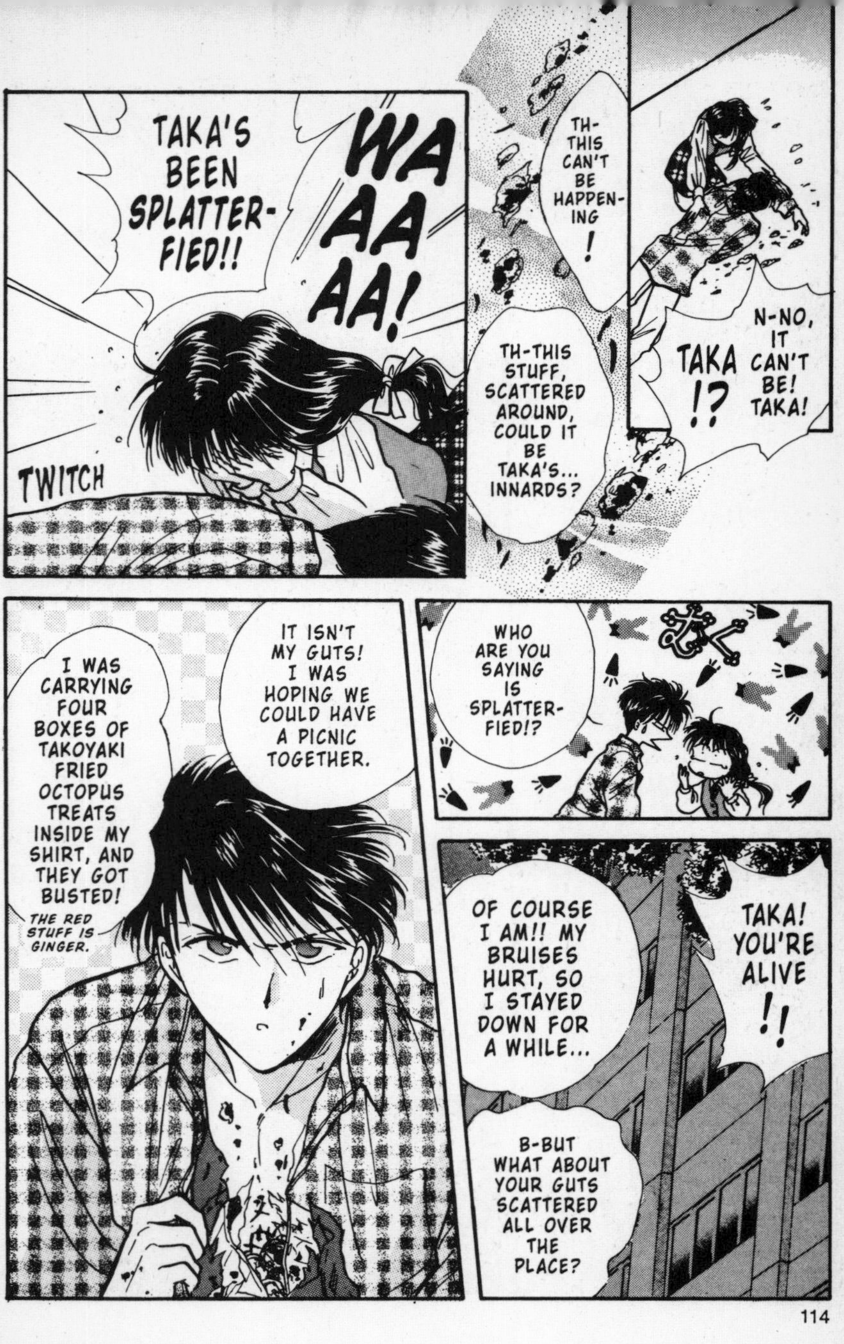

N-NO, IT CAN'T BE! TAKA!
TAKA!?
TH-THIS CAN'T BE HAPPEN-ING!
TH-THIS STUFF, SCATTERED AROUND, COULD IT BE TAKA'S... INNARDS?
WAAAAAA!
TAKA'S BEEN SPLATTER-FIED!!
TWITCH
WHO ARE YOU SAYING IS SPLATTER-FIED!?
TAKA! YOU'RE ALIVE!!
OF COURSE I AM!! MY BRUISES HURT, SO I STAYED DOWN FOR A WHILE...
B-BUT WHAT ABOUT YOUR GUTS SCATTERED ALL OVER THE PLACE?
IT ISN'T MY GUTS! I WAS HOPING WE COULD HAVE A PICNIC TOGETHER.
I WAS CARRYING FOUR BOXES OF TAKOYAKI FRIED OCTOPUS TREATS INSIDE MY SHIRT, AND THEY GOT BUSTED!
THE RED STUFF IS GINGER.

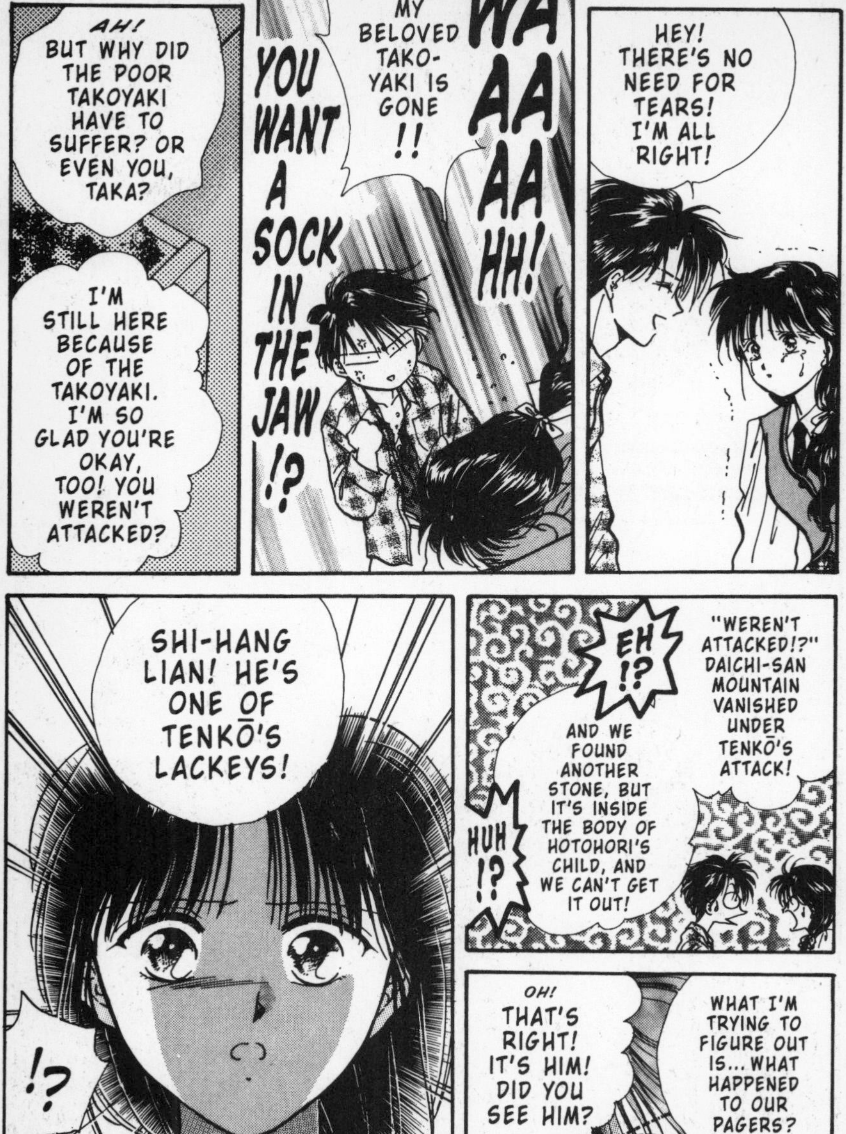

HEY! THERE'S NO NEED FOR TEARS! I'M ALL RIGHT!
...
WAAAAAAHH!
MY BELOVED TAKO-YAKI IS GONE!!
YOU WANT A SOCK IN THE JAW!?
AH! BUT WHY DID THE POOR TAKOYAKI HAVE TO SUFFER? OR EVEN YOU, TAKA?
I'M STILL HERE BECAUSE OF THE TAKOYAKI. I'M SO GLAD YOU'RE OKAY, TOO! YOU WEREN'T ATTACKED?
"WEREN'T ATTACKED!?" DAICHI-SAN MOUNTAIN VANISHED UNDER TENKŌ'S ATTACK!
EH!?
AND WE FOUND ANOTHER STONE, BUT IT'S INSIDE THE BODY OF HOTOHORI'S CHILD, AND WE CAN'T GET IT OUT!
HUH!?
WHAT I'M TRYING TO FIGURE OUT IS... WHAT HAPPENED TO OUR PAGERS?
OH! THAT'S RIGHT! IT'S HIM! DID YOU SEE HIM?
SHI-HANG LIAN! HE'S ONE OF TENKŌ'S LACKEYS!
!?

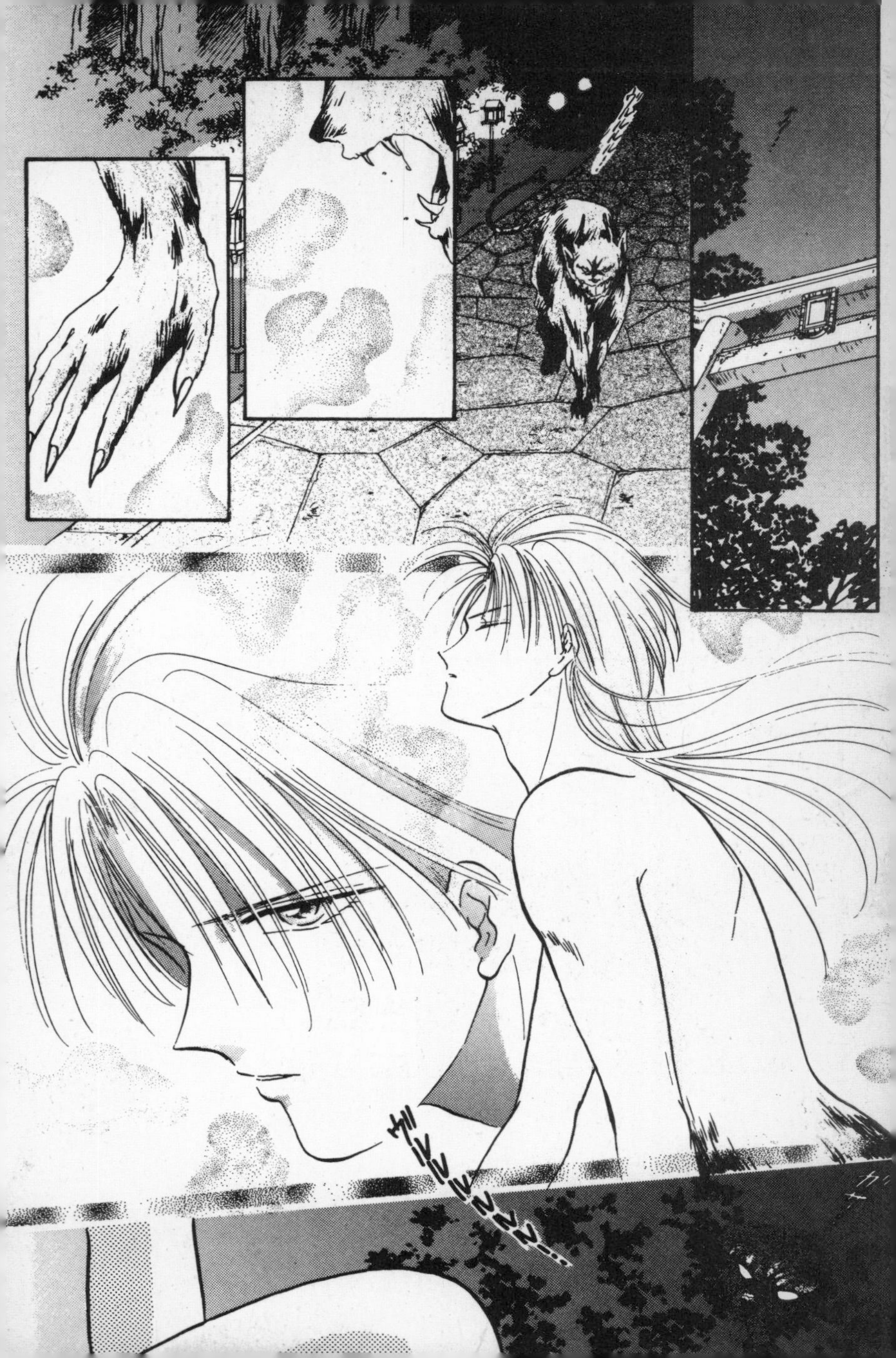

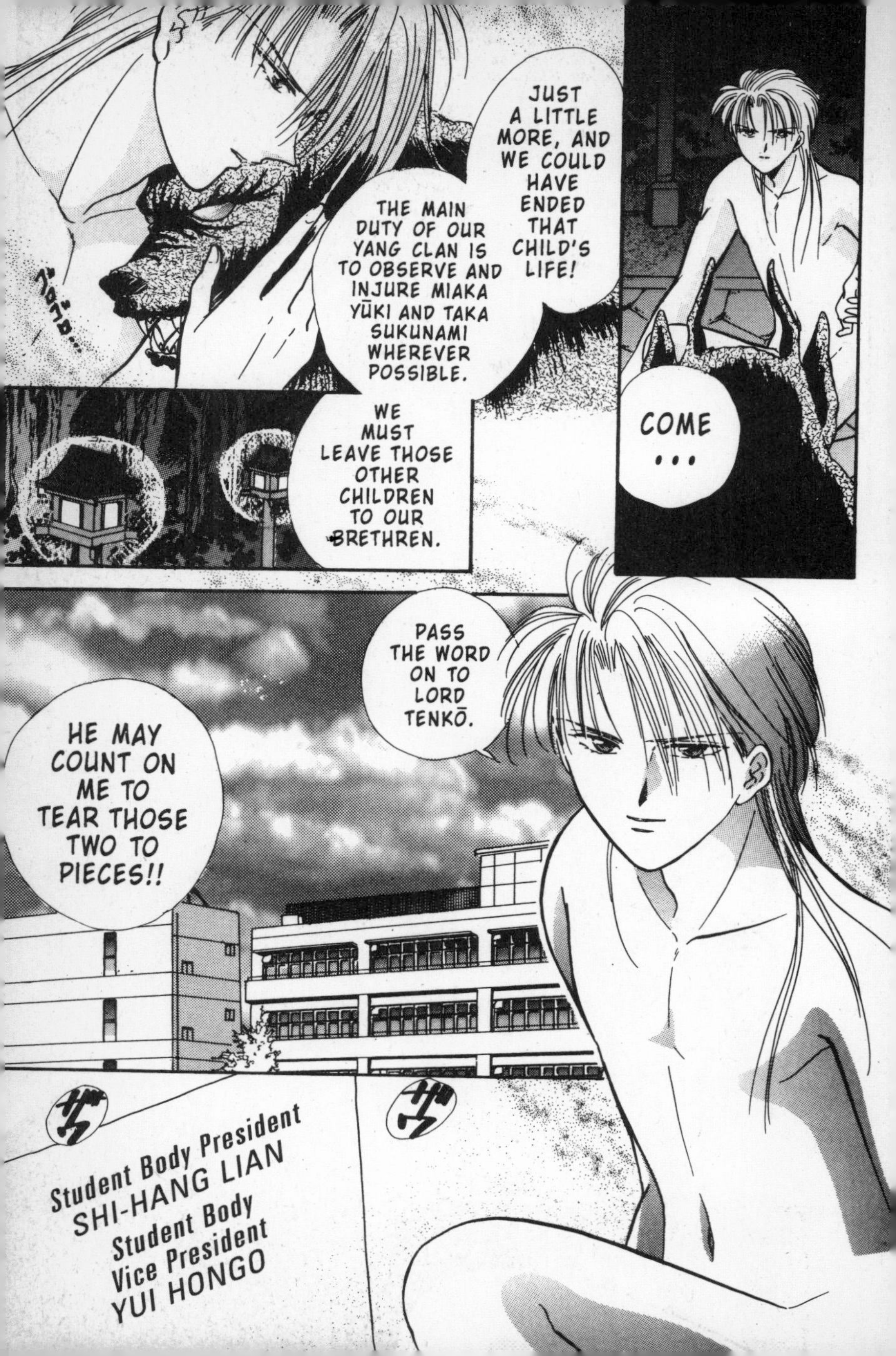
COME ...
JUST A LITTLE MORE, AND WE COULD HAVE ENDED THAT CHILD'S LIFE!
THE MAIN DUTY OF OUR YANG CLAN IS TO OBSERVE AND INJURE MIAKA YŪKI AND TAKA SUKUNAMI WHEREVER POSSIBLE.
WE MUST LEAVE THOSE OTHER CHILDREN TO OUR BRETHREN.
PASS THE WORD ON TO LORD TENKŌ.
HE MAY COUNT ON ME TO TEAR THOSE TWO TO PIECES!!
Student Body President
SHI-HANG LIAN
Student Body Vice President
YUI HONGO

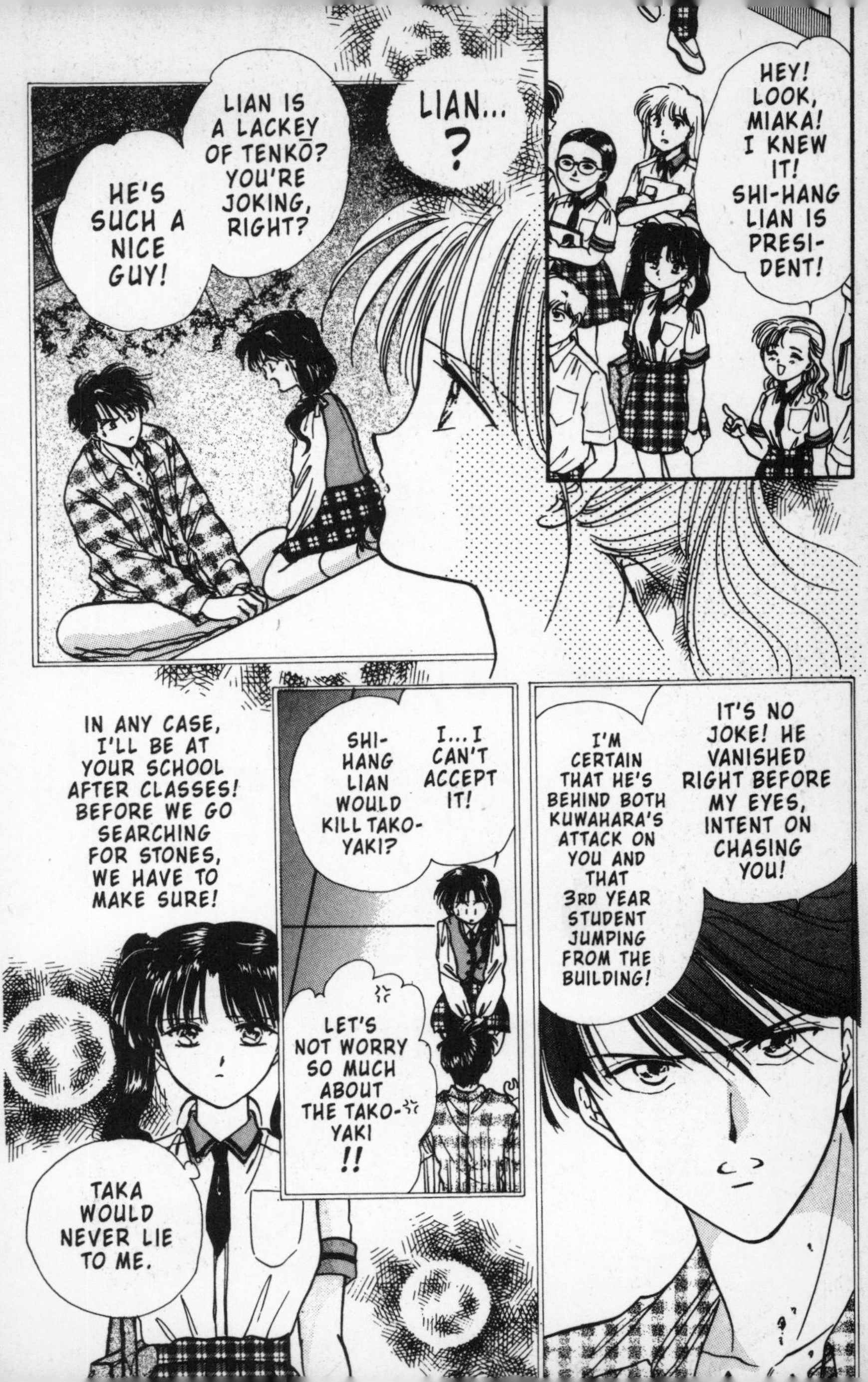
HEY! LOOK, MIAKA! I KNEW IT! SHI-HANG LIAN IS PRESIDENT!
LIAN...?
LIAN IS A LACKEY OF TENKŌ? YOU'RE JOKING, RIGHT?
HE'S SUCH A NICE GUY!
IT'S NO JOKE! HE VANISHED RIGHT BEFORE MY EYES, INTENT ON CHASING YOU!
I'M CERTAIN THAT HE'S BEHIND BOTH KUWAHARA'S ATTACK ON YOU AND THAT 3RD YEAR STUDENT JUMPING FROM THE BUILDING!
I... I CAN'T ACCEPT IT!
SHI-HANG LIAN WOULD KILL TAKO-YAKI?
LET'S NOT WORRY SO MUCH ABOUT THE TAKO-YAKI!!
IN ANY CASE, I'LL BE AT YOUR SCHOOL AFTER CLASSES! BEFORE WE GO SEARCHING FOR STONES, WE HAVE TO MAKE SURE!
TAKA WOULD NEVER LIE TO ME.

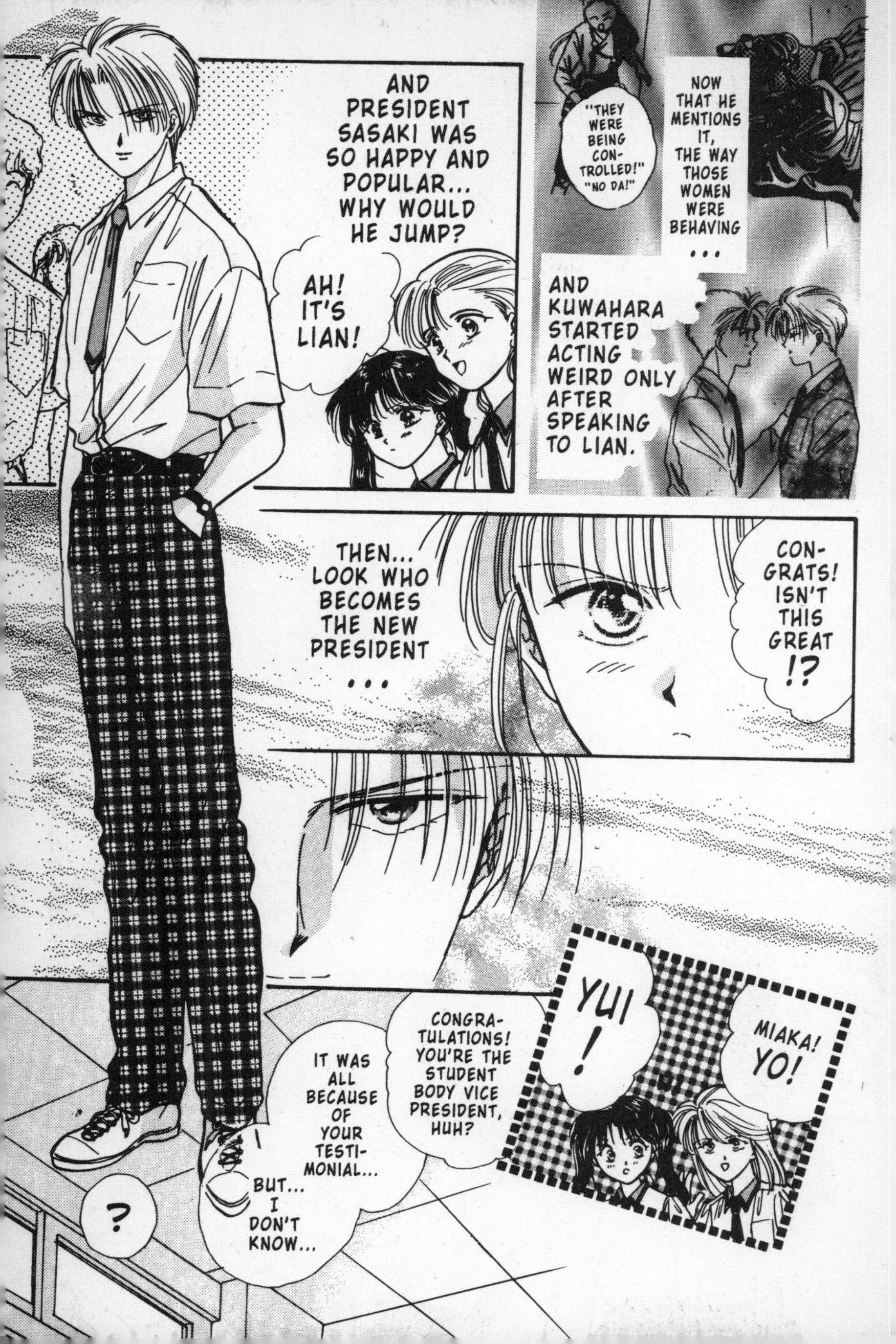
NOW THAT HE MENTIONS IT, THE WAY THOSE WOMEN WERE BEHAVING...
"THEY WERE BEING CON-TROLLED!" "NO DA!"
AND KUWAHARA STARTED ACTING WEIRD ONLY AFTER SPEAKING TO LIAN.
AND PRESIDENT SASAKI WAS SO HAPPY AND POPULAR... WHY WOULD HE JUMP?
AH! IT'S LIAN!
CON-GRATS! ISN'T THIS GREAT!?
THEN... LOOK WHO BECOMES THE NEW PRESIDENT...
MIAKA! YO!
YUI!
CONGRA-TULATIONS! YOU'RE THE STUDENT BODY VICE PRESIDENT, HUH?
IT WAS ALL BECAUSE OF YOUR TESTI-MONIAL...
BUT... I DON'T KNOW...
?

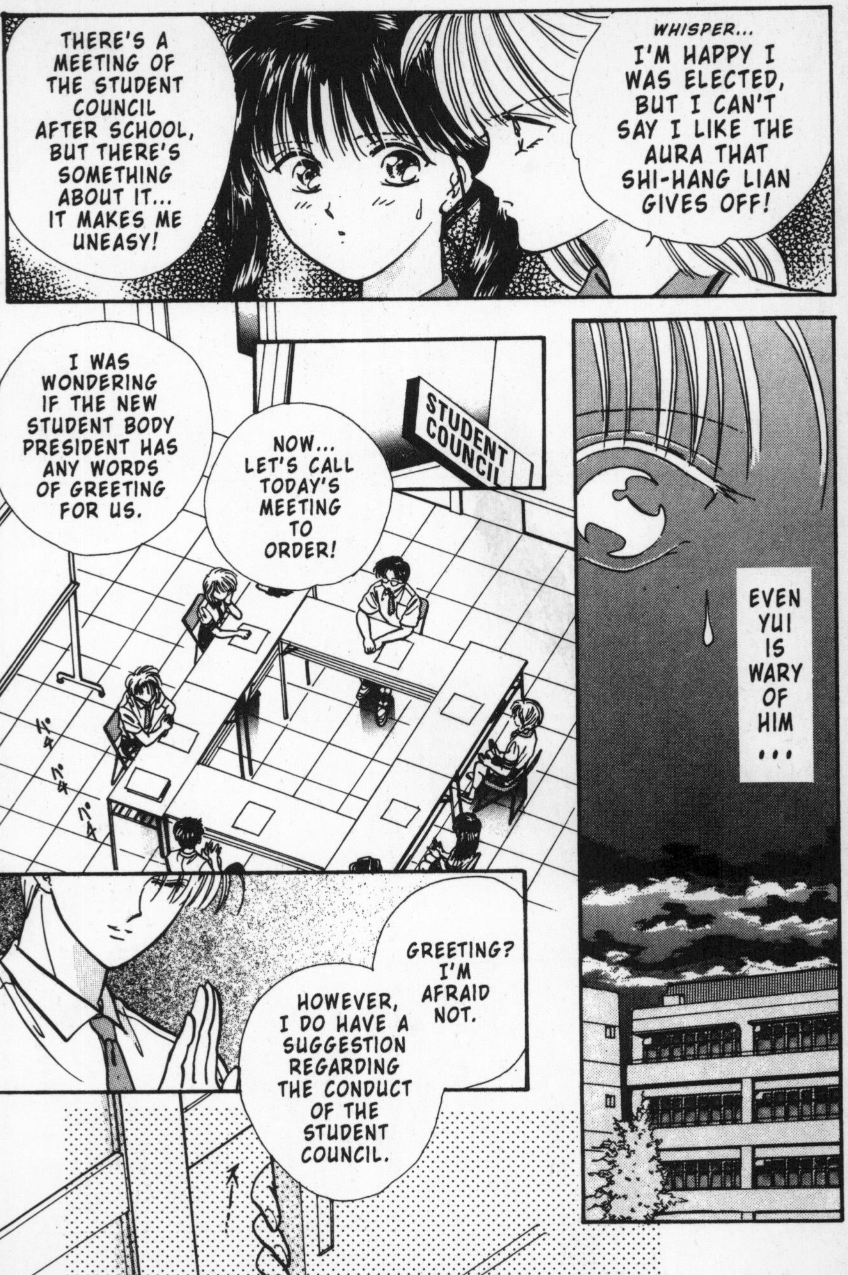
WHISPER... I'M HAPPY I WAS ELECTED, BUT I CAN'T SAY I LIKE THE AURA THAT SHI-HANG LIAN GIVES OFF!
THERE'S A MEETING OF THE STUDENT COUNCIL AFTER SCHOOL, BUT THERE'S SOMETHING ABOUT IT... IT MAKES ME UNEASY!
EVEN YUI IS WARY OF HIM...
STUDENT COUNCIL
NOW... LET'S CALL TODAY'S MEETING TO ORDER!
I WAS WONDERING IF THE NEW STUDENT BODY PRESIDENT HAS ANY WORDS OF GREETING FOR US.
GREETING? I'M AFRAID NOT.
HOWEVER, I DO HAVE A SUGGESTION REGARDING THE CONDUCT OF THE STUDENT COUNCIL.

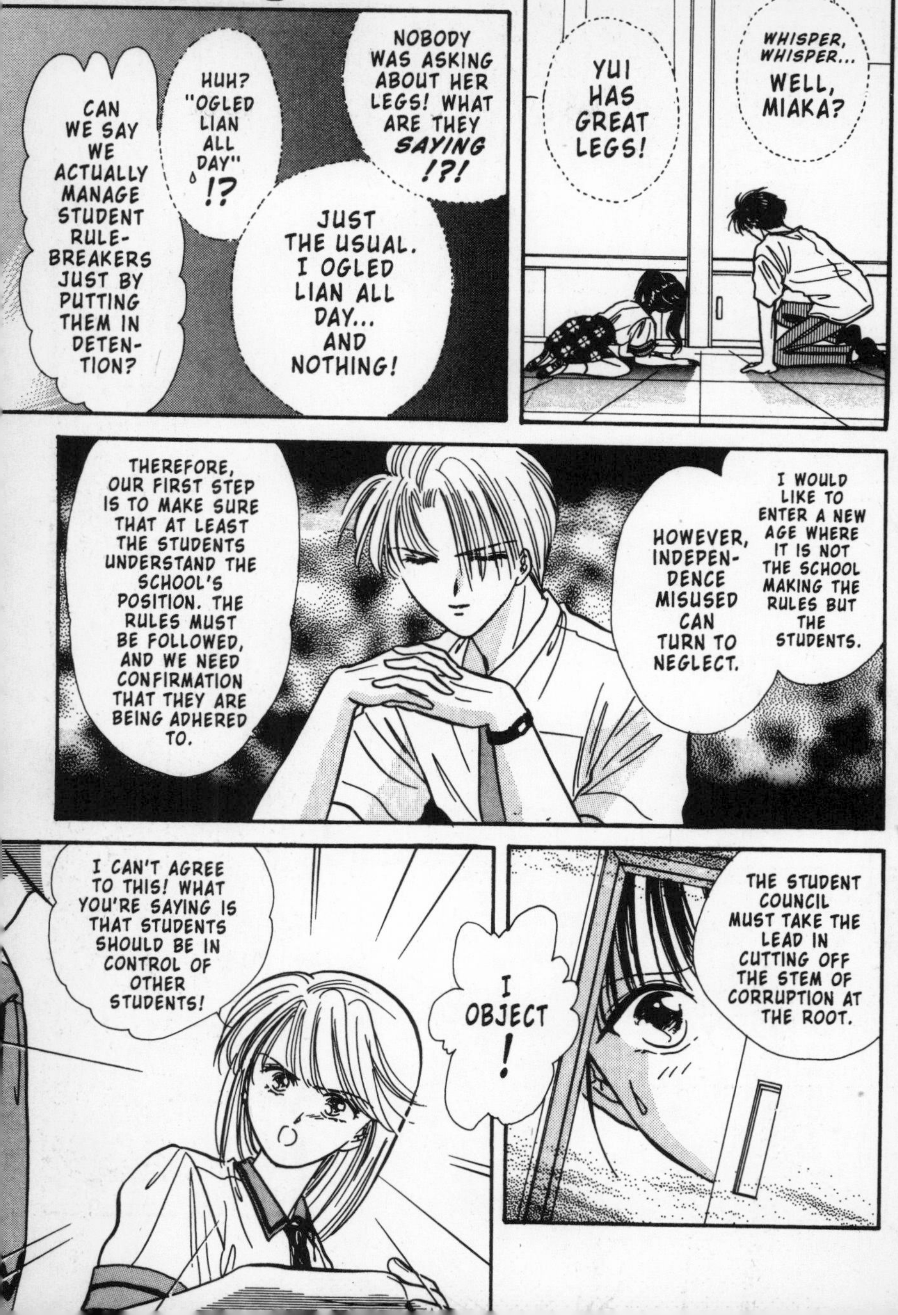
WHISPER, WHISPER... WELL, MIAKA?
YUI HAS GREAT LEGS!
NOBODY WAS ASKING ABOUT HER LEGS! WHAT ARE THEY SAYING !?!
JUST THE USUAL. I OGLED LIAN ALL DAY... AND NOTHING!
HUH? "OGLED LIAN ALL DAY" !?
CAN WE SAY WE ACTUALLY MANAGE STUDENT RULE-BREAKERS JUST BY PUTTING THEM IN DETEN-TION?
I WOULD LIKE TO ENTER A NEW AGE WHERE IT IS NOT THE SCHOOL MAKING THE RULES BUT THE STUDENTS.
HOWEVER, INDEPEN-DENCE MISUSED CAN TURN TO NEGLECT.
THEREFORE, OUR FIRST STEP IS TO MAKE SURE THAT AT LEAST THE STUDENTS UNDERSTAND THE SCHOOL'S POSITION. THE RULES MUST BE FOLLOWED, AND WE NEED CONFIRMATION THAT THEY ARE BEING ADHERED TO.
THE STUDENT COUNCIL MUST TAKE THE LEAD IN CUTTING OFF THE STEM OF CORRUPTION AT THE ROOT.
I OBJECT !
I CAN'T AGREE TO THIS! WHAT YOU'RE SAYING IS THAT STUDENTS SHOULD BE IN CONTROL OF OTHER STUDENTS!

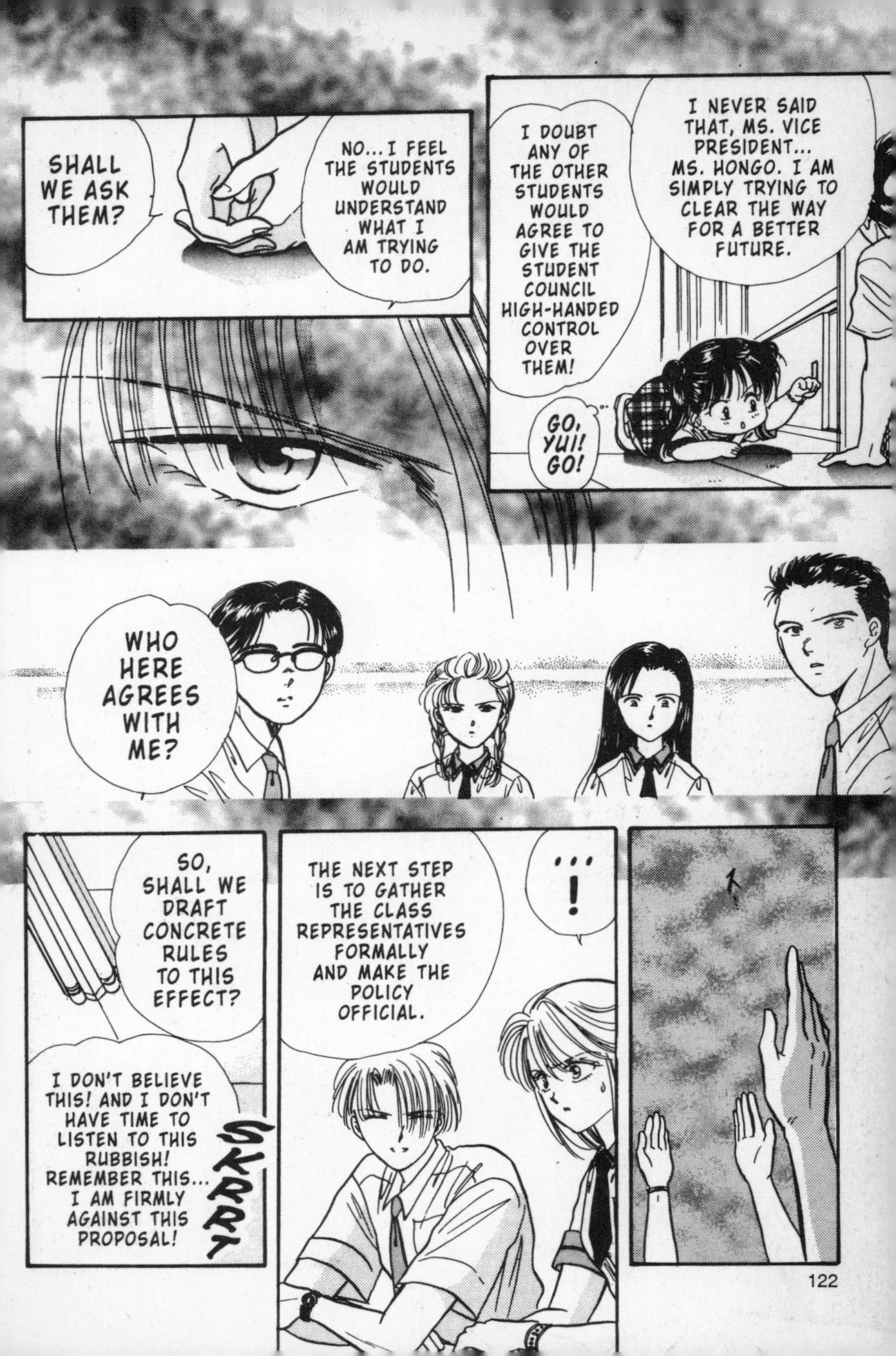
I NEVER SAID THAT, MS. VICE PRESIDENT... MS. HONGO. I AM SIMPLY TRYING TO CLEAR THE WAY FOR A BETTER FUTURE.
I DOUBT ANY OF THE OTHER STUDENTS WOULD AGREE TO GIVE THE STUDENT COUNCIL HIGH-HANDED CONTROL OVER THEM!
GO, YUI! GO!
NO... I FEEL THE STUDENTS WOULD UNDERSTAND WHAT I AM TRYING TO DO.
SHALL WE ASK THEM?
WHO HERE AGREES WITH ME?
...!
THE NEXT STEP IS TO GATHER THE CLASS REPRESENTATIVES FORMALLY AND MAKE THE POLICY OFFICIAL.
SO, SHALL WE DRAFT CONCRETE RULES TO THIS EFFECT?
I DON'T BELIEVE THIS! AND I DON'T HAVE TIME TO LISTEN TO THIS RUBBISH! REMEMBER THIS... I AM FIRMLY AGAINST THIS PROPOSAL!
SKRRT

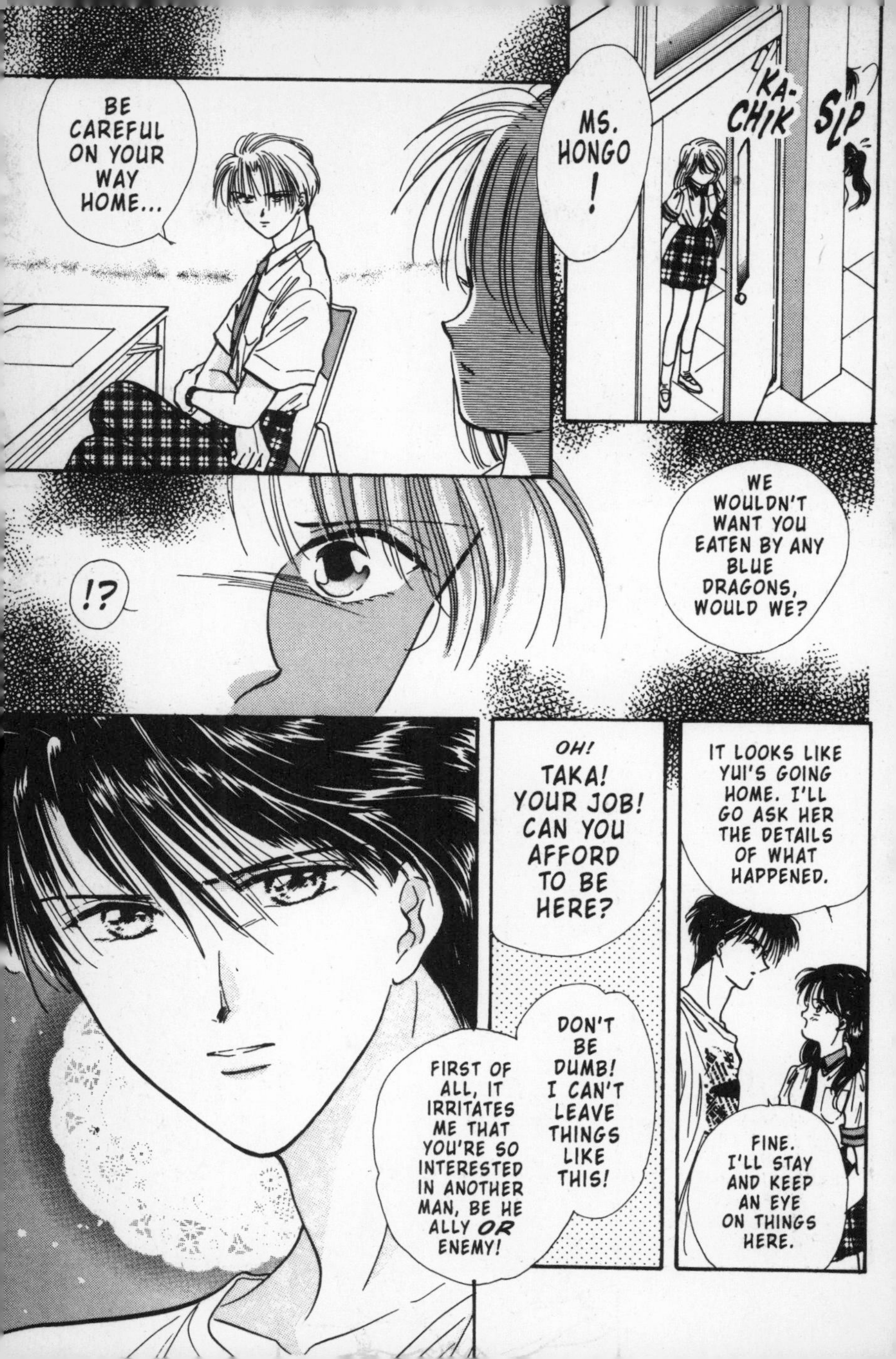
SLIP
KA-CHIK
MS. HONGO!
BE CAREFUL ON YOUR WAY HOME...
WE WOULDN'T WANT YOU EATEN BY ANY BLUE DRAGONS, WOULD WE?
!?
IT LOOKS LIKE YUI'S GOING HOME. I'LL GO ASK HER THE DETAILS OF WHAT HAPPENED.
FINE. I'LL STAY AND KEEP AN EYE ON THINGS HERE.
OH! TAKA! YOUR JOB! CAN YOU AFFORD TO BE HERE?
DON'T BE DUMB! I CAN'T LEAVE THINGS LIKE THIS!
FIRST OF ALL, IT IRRITATES ME THAT YOU'RE SO INTERESTED IN ANOTHER MAN, BE HE ALLY OR ENEMY!

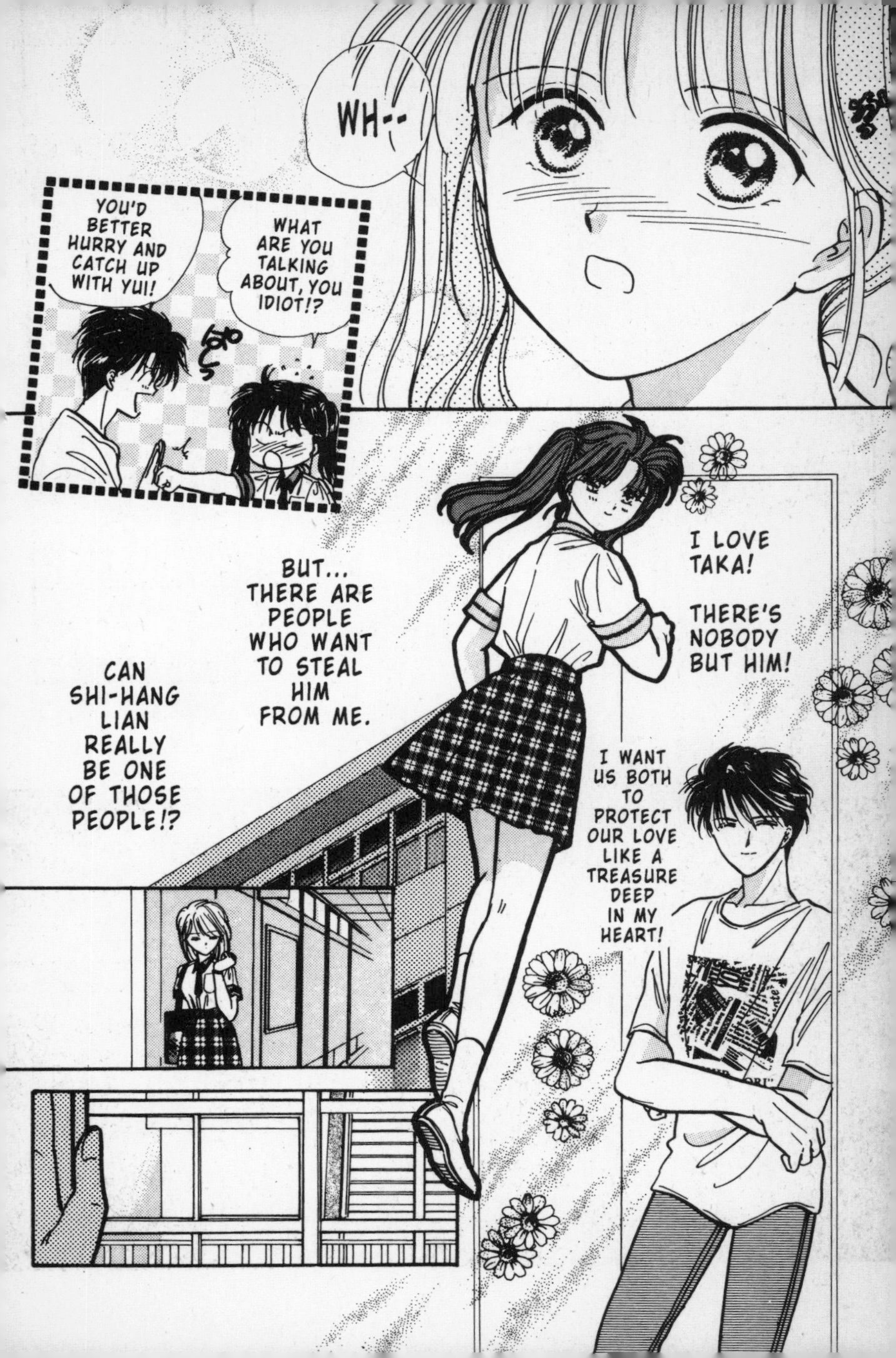

WH--
YOU'D BETTER HURRY AND CATCH UP WITH YUI!
WHAT ARE YOU TALKING ABOUT, YOU IDIOT!?
I LOVE TAKA!
THERE'S NOBODY BUT HIM!
I WANT US BOTH TO PROTECT OUR LOVE LIKE A TREASURE DEEP IN MY HEART!
BUT... THERE ARE PEOPLE WHO WANT TO STEAL HIM FROM ME.
CAN SHI-HANG LIAN REALLY BE ONE OF THOSE PEOPLE!?

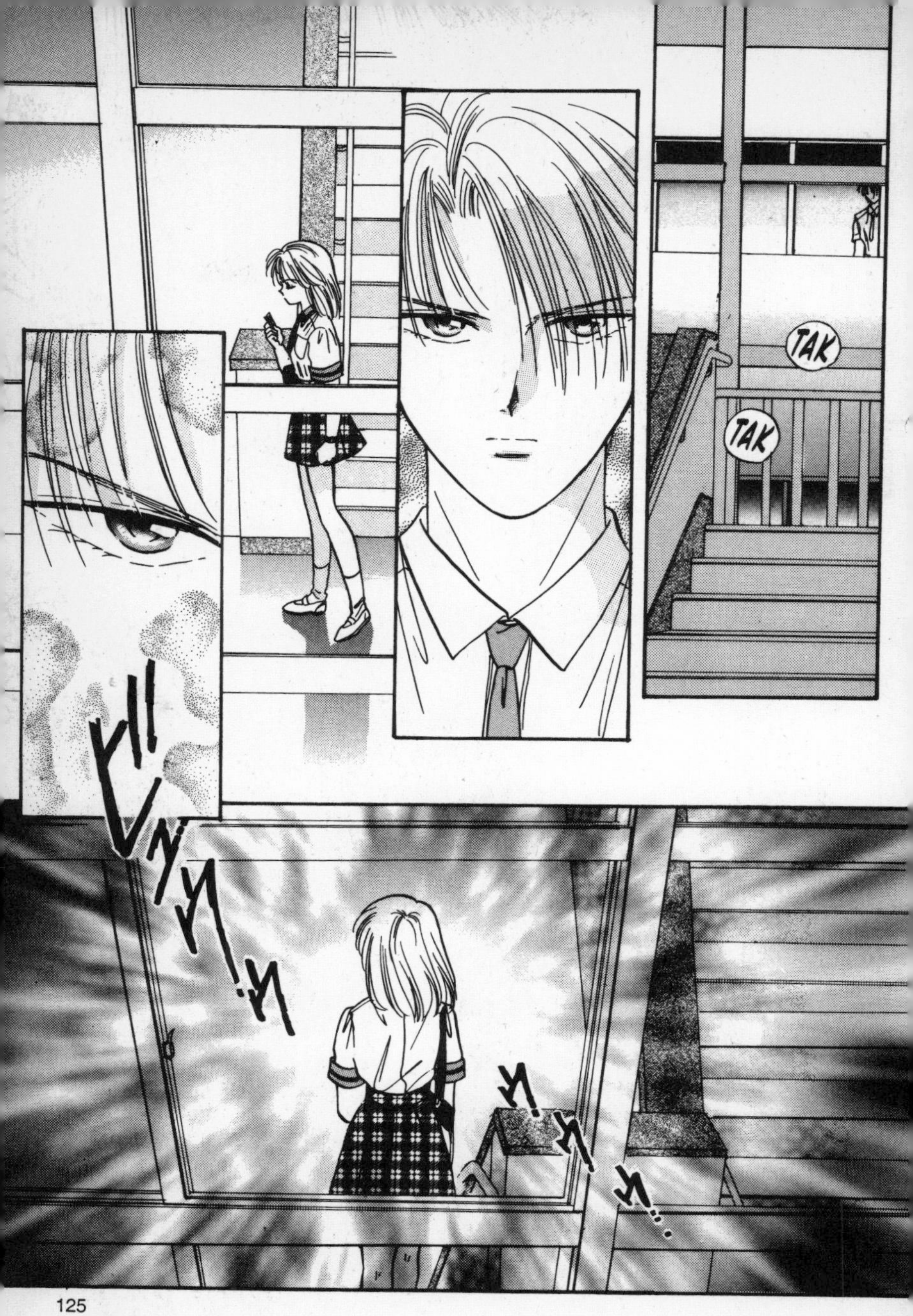
TAK
TAK

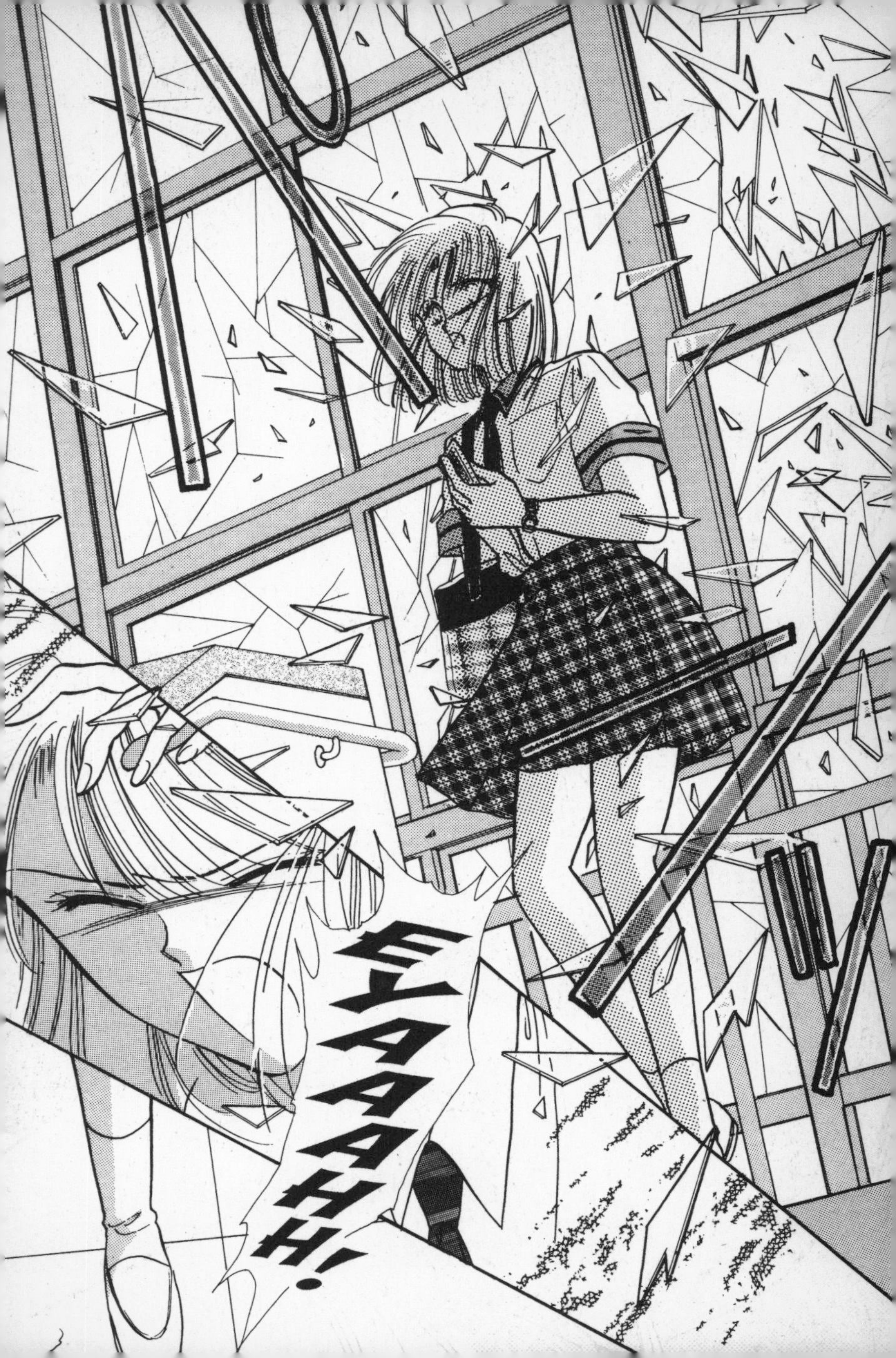
EYAAAHH!

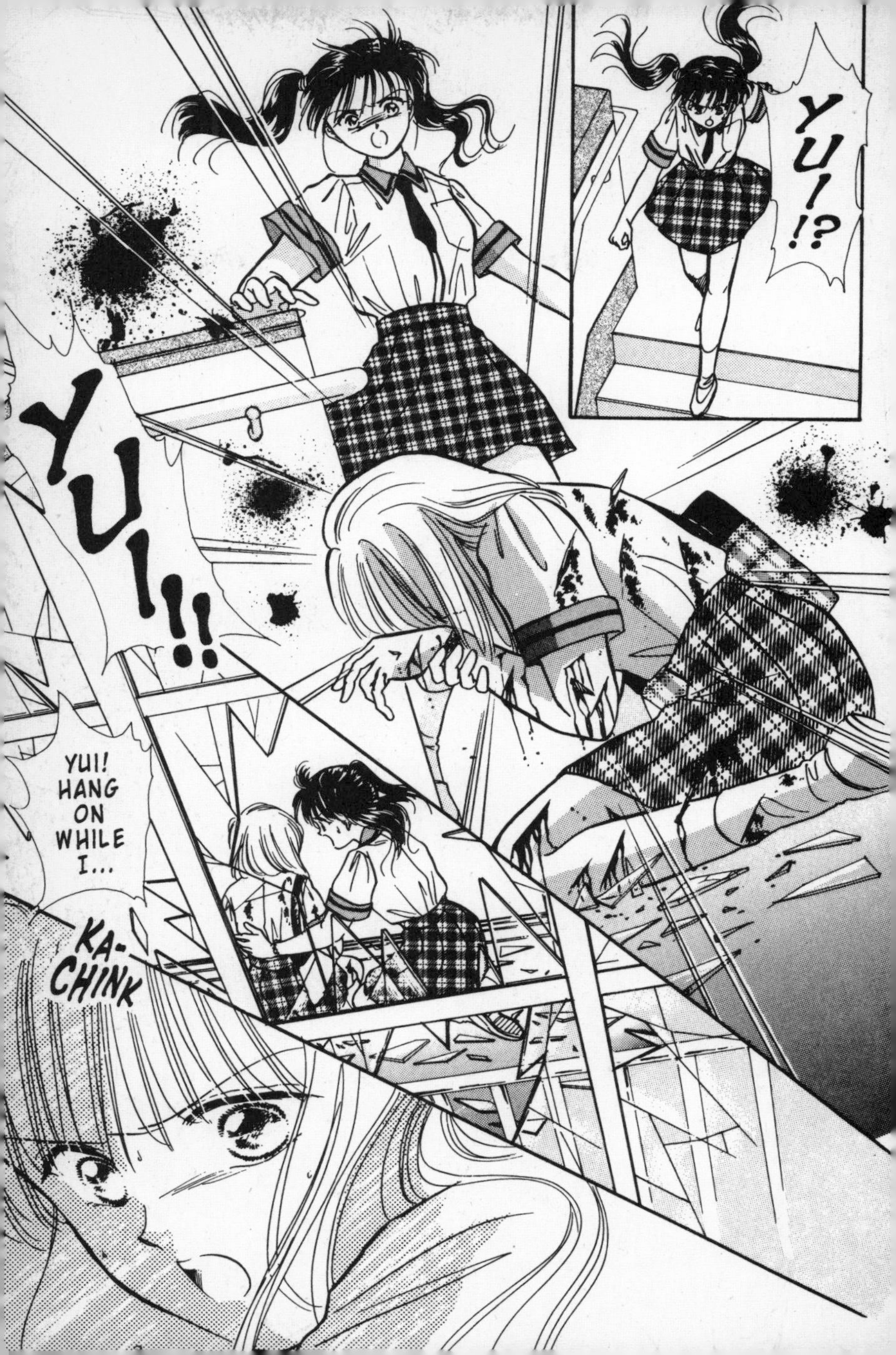
YUI!?
YUI!!
YUI! HANG ON WHILE I...
KA-CHINK

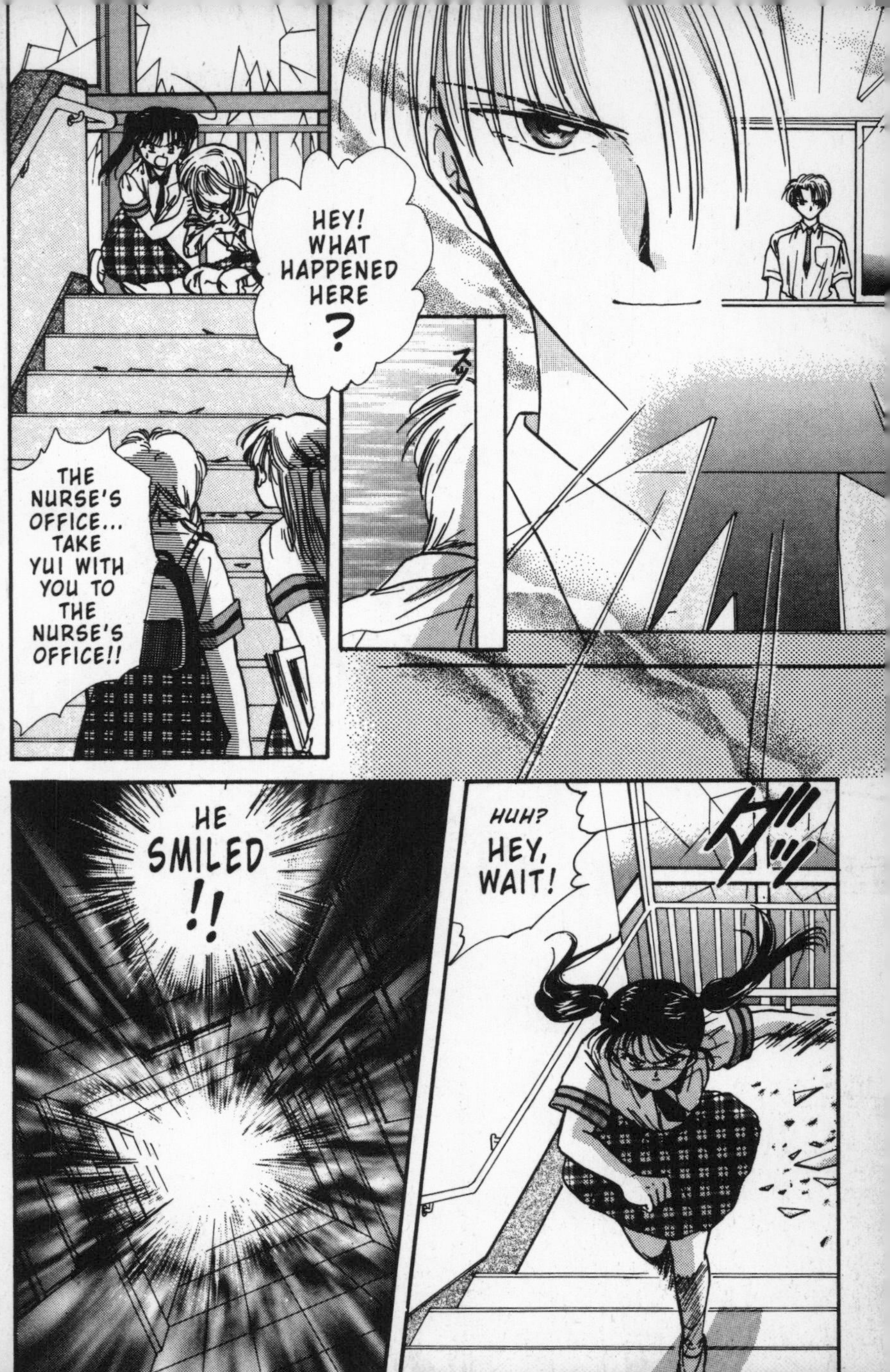
HEY! WHAT HAPPENED HERE?
THE NURSE'S OFFICE... TAKE YUI WITH YOU TO THE NURSE'S OFFICE!!
HUH? HEY, WAIT!
HE SMILED!!

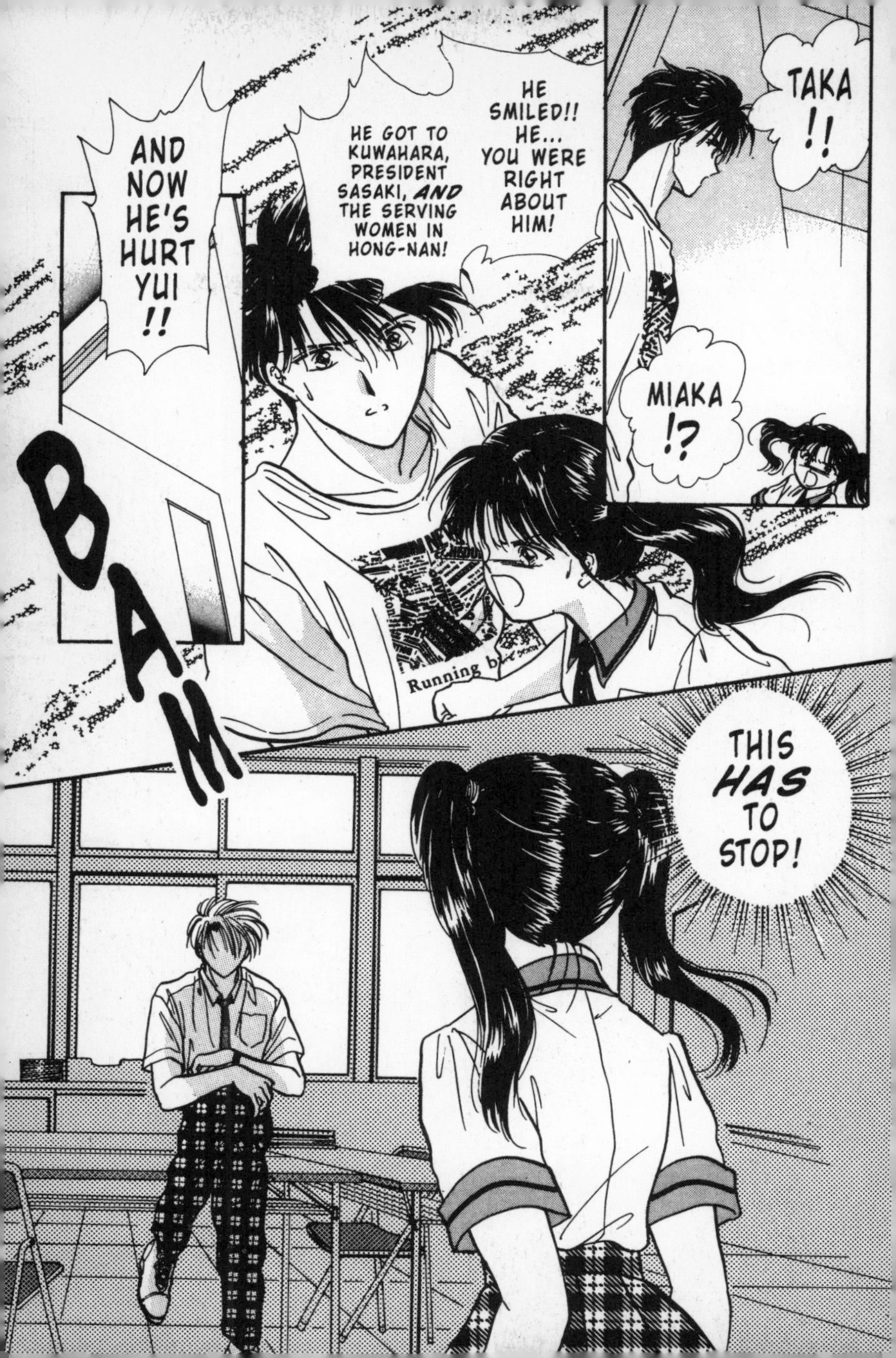
TAKA!!
MIAKA!?
HE SMILED!! HE... YOU WERE RIGHT ABOUT HIM!
HE GOT TO KUWAHARA, PRESIDENT SASAKI, AND THE SERVING WOMEN IN HONG-NAN!
AND NOW HE'S HURT YUI!!
BAM
Running b
THIS HAS TO STOP!

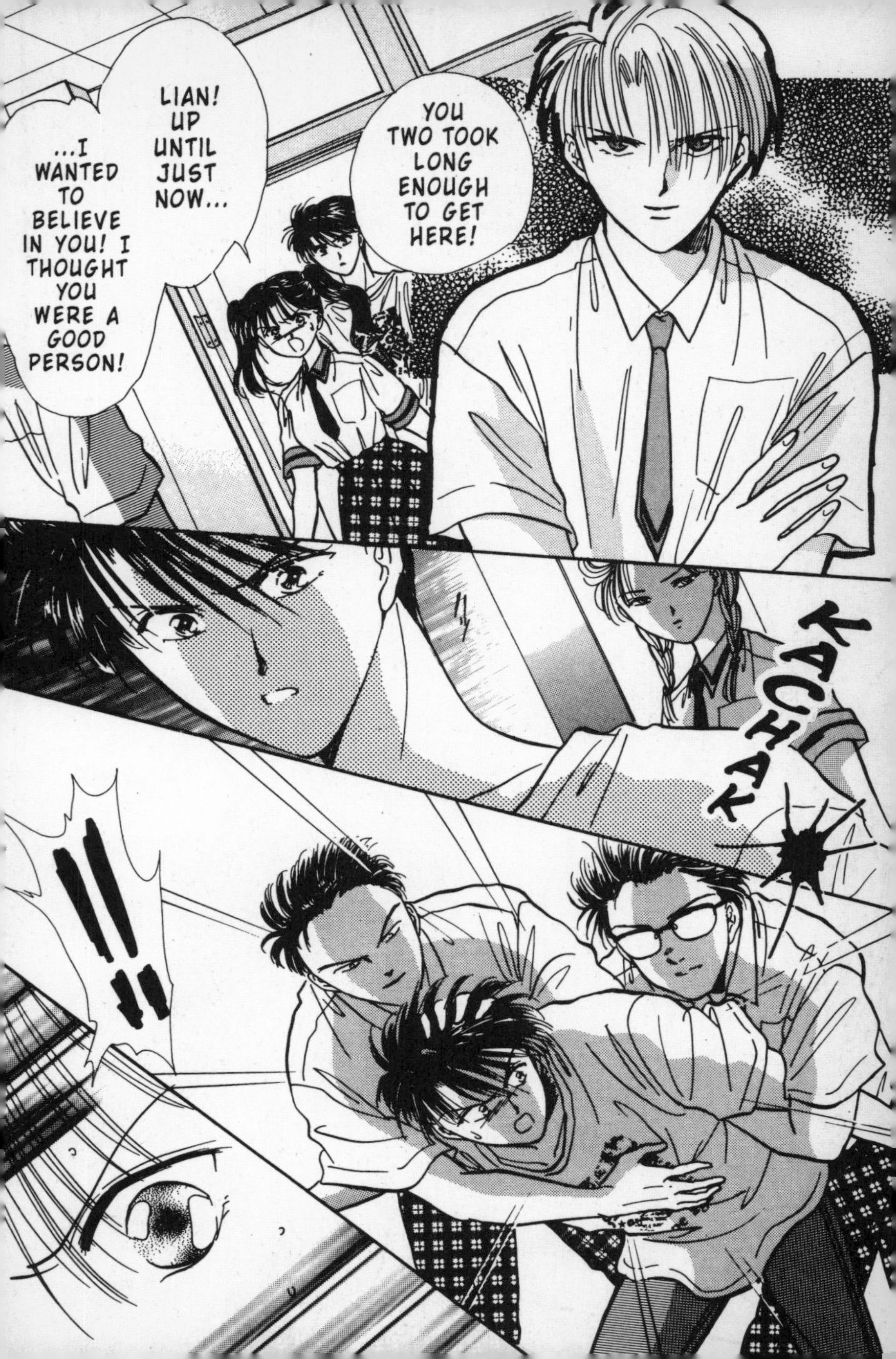
YOU TWO TOOK LONG ENOUGH TO GET HERE!
LIAN! UP UNTIL JUST NOW...
...I WANTED TO BELIEVE IN YOU! I THOUGHT YOU WERE A GOOD PERSON!
KACHAK
!!

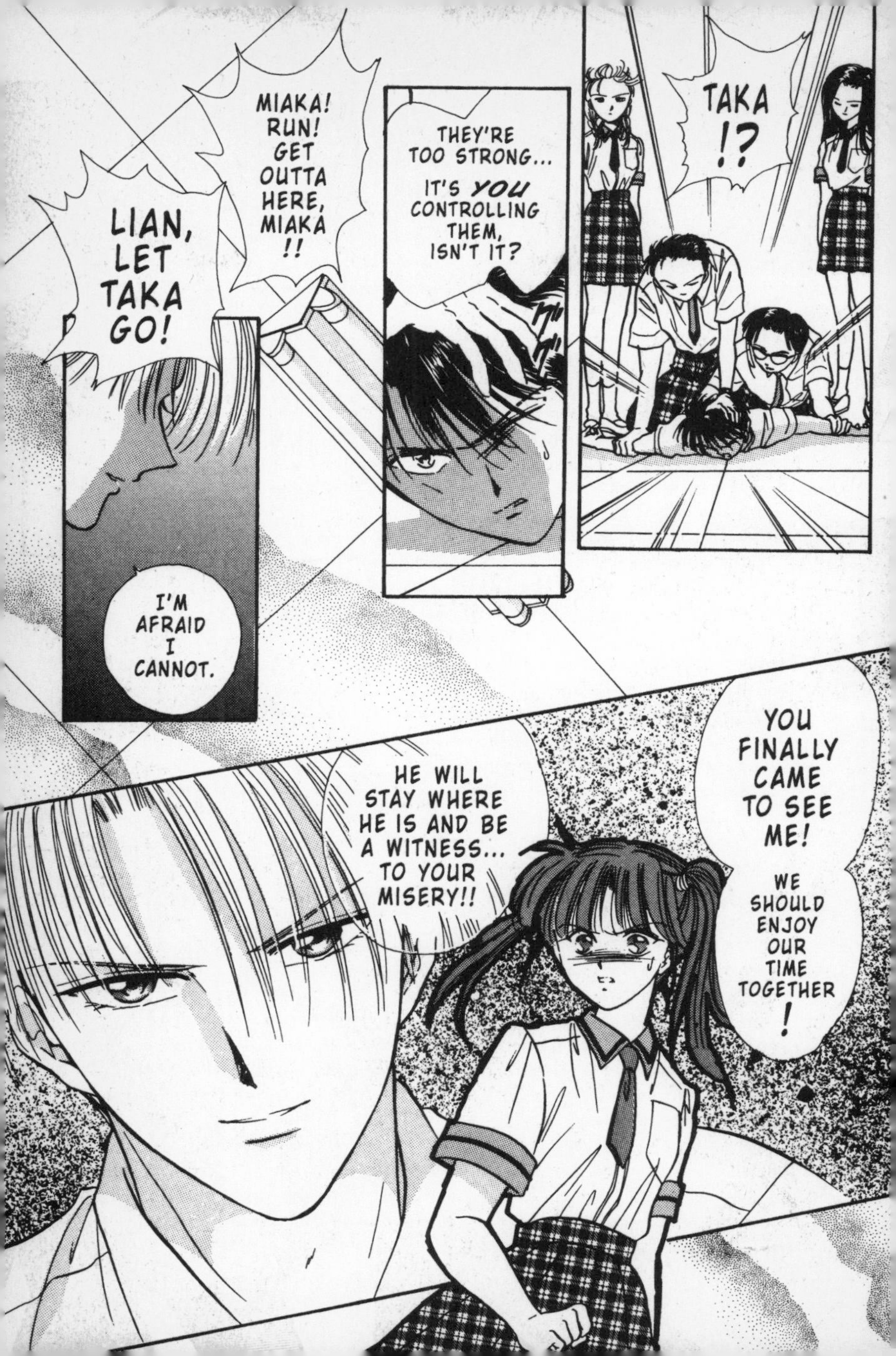
TAKA !?
THEY'RE TOO STRONG...
IT'S *YOU* CONTROLLING THEM, ISN'T IT?
MIAKA! RUN! GET OUTTA HERE, MIAKA!!
LIAN, LET TAKA GO!
I'M AFRAID I CANNOT.
YOU FINALLY CAME TO SEE ME!
WE SHOULD ENJOY OUR TIME TOGETHER!
HE WILL STAY WHERE HE IS AND BE A WITNESS... TO YOUR MISERY!!

\ \/ / \ \/ / /
SUDDENLY...

Q: Tell us about the character goods that are available now ('95) for Fushigi Yūgi!

A: Well, if you insist, I'll tell you! *Although there may be some that I don't know about.*

● First, there's the "Universe of the Four Gods" set (I don't remember the actual name! ◊) from Bandai! It has a huge Suzaku on the cover, and inside is this transparent binder or file holder. What's really incredible is that inside there is a game where the seven warriors have ways of testing a prospective priestess! It was really fun! I only skimmed it, but with this, I think I could really experience what it's like to be the Priestess of Suzaku! *I didn't know they could do that with stationery products!! They even have fighting techniques!!* The pictures are beautiful, and it's so cool that I just think "Sold!"

> Oh, there're also cards in there and lots of character data written in!

Let's see, there are these huge stickers (sold separately)! And key chains with Miaka (2 versions), Tamahome, Hotohori, Nuriko, and Tasuki! I heard they put out a Tasuki "harisen" fan ☺ and a compact with the anime version of Miaka on it! Oh, and a diary! ⌐ **IS THIS TRUE?**

> Hey! This stuff is NOT available in the anime shops!! I want my local [toy store] to carry it!! To those who say, "I want to see them in the Animate Shop that's near me!!" Go to the toy store instead! It's all there!

● Next is all the stuff by Seika Notebooks and Movic. There's so much fun stuff!! Notebooks, pencil boards, erasers, pencils, mechanical pencils, bookmarks, clear file holders, wall hangings, video boxes, rubber key chains, stationery sets, posters, sticky notes, foldable letter notebooks (or something like that...), forks, lunch boxes, and there's a lot more! There are coloring books! That could help me! ☺

> These are available in a stationery shop or anime shop near you! They should stock them in stationery shops all over Japan!

● Next: Fushigi where you don't expect it! Starting in September at all the Gei-Sen amusement parks in the country, there will be Miaka and the Warriors stuffed dolls called "Toru-toru Catchers," and also figurines! ↰ (I want the Seiryu version!) *I'm told that four warriors have figurines.*

● Aside from those, there's a bath mat (really huge!). It's a picture of Miaka and the warriors, and it's really pretty, so... maybe it'll substitute for a poster? ◊◊ → *Setting aside Miaka, the thought of having the warriors in the place where I wash makes my heart race a bit.* And towels, handkerchiefs, etc. ...

> I think that for these, you'll have to go to your local department store or bed & bath store. Or maybe where you buy your lingerie.

So everybody, do your best to get them! ☺ If you manage to get all of them, write me! *I'll praise you!*

I also heard they've started a fan club! It looks like everyone around me has gotten themselves into something big! ☺

By the way, all of the goods above are listed from memory, and I may have remembered some stuff wrong. There may also be things I'm forgetting. But just go out there and show your fannish guts!! (What!? ◊◊◊)

★ This is information from Japan circa September 1995.

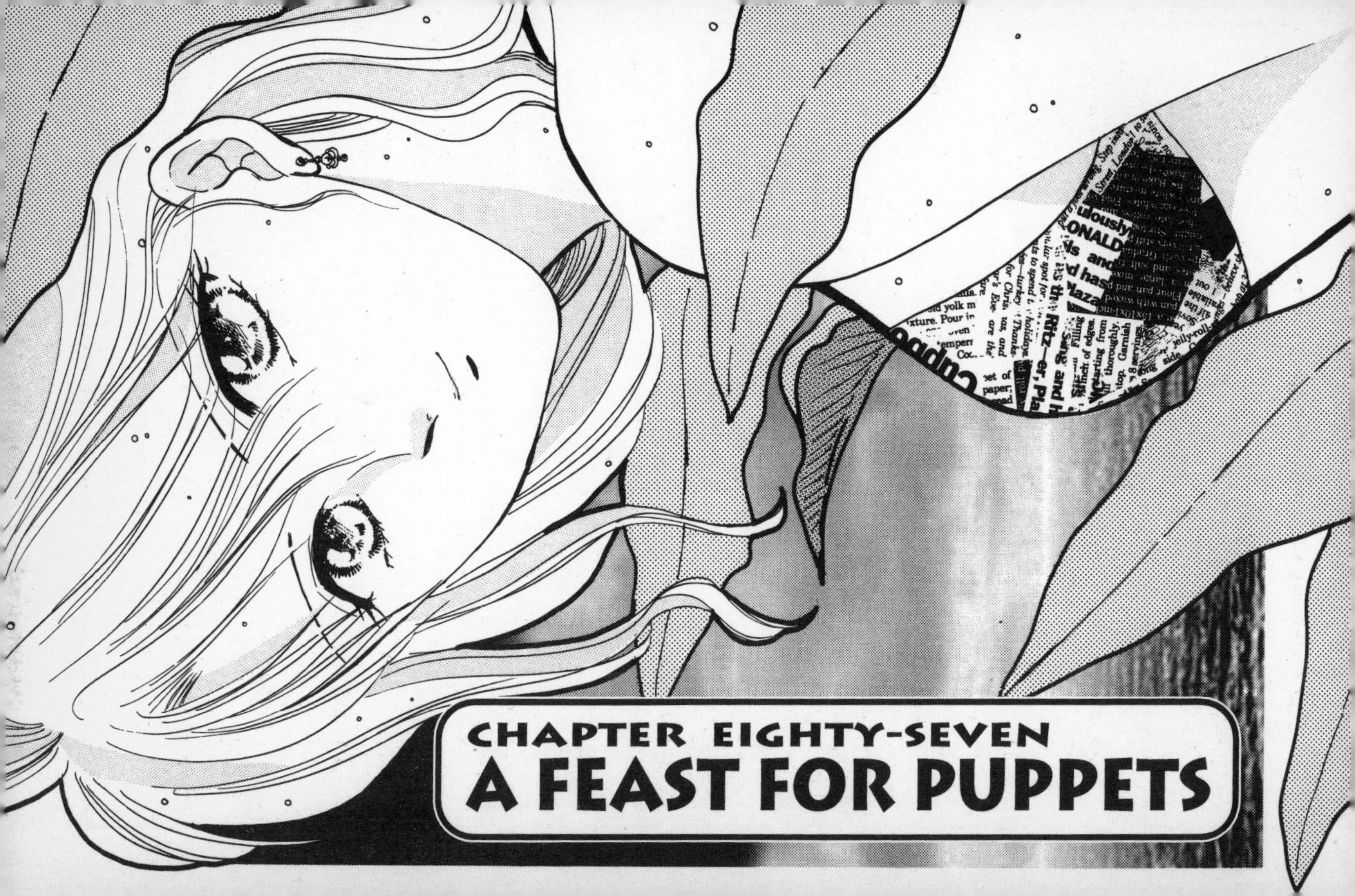
CHAPTER EIGHTY-SEVEN
A FEAST FOR PUPPETS

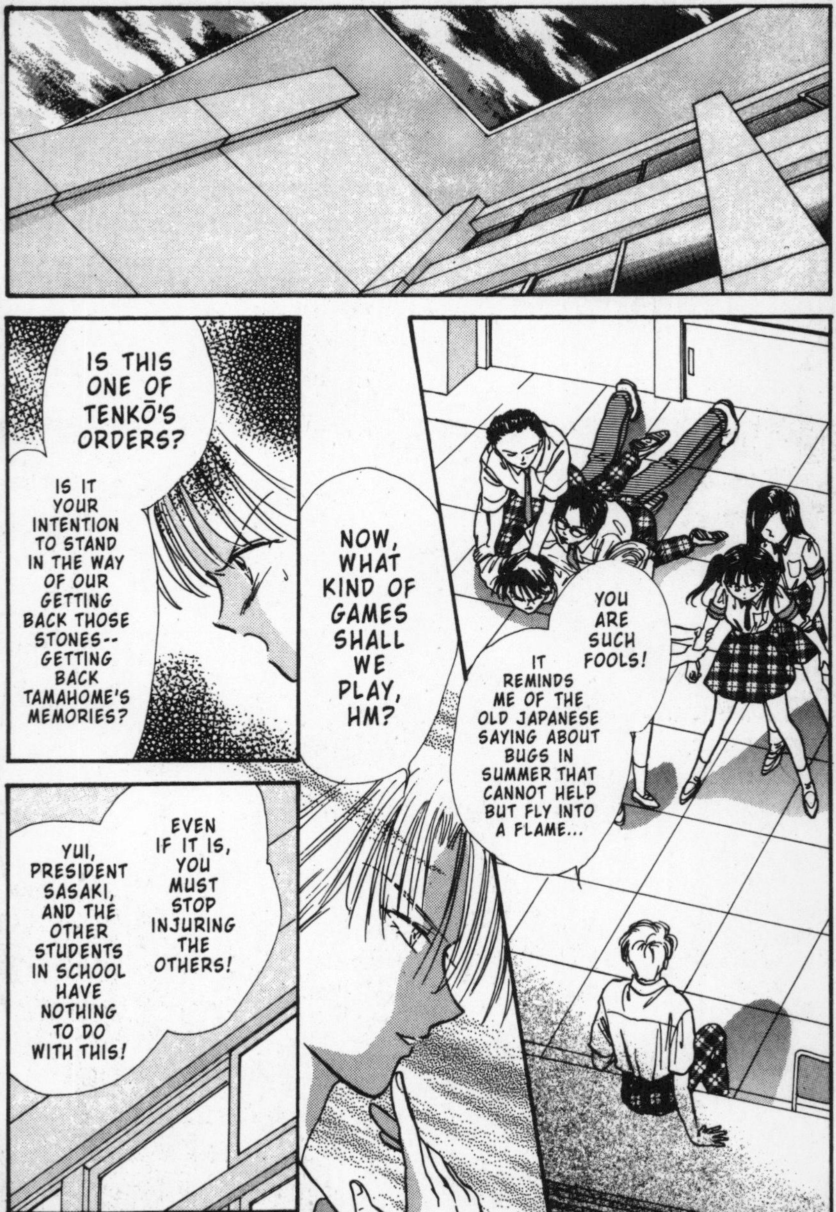
YOU ARE SUCH FOOLS!
IT REMINDS ME OF THE OLD JAPANESE SAYING ABOUT BUGS IN SUMMER THAT CANNOT HELP BUT FLY INTO A FLAME...
NOW, WHAT KIND OF GAMES SHALL WE PLAY, HM?
IS THIS ONE OF TENKŌ'S ORDERS?
IS IT YOUR INTENTION TO STAND IN THE WAY OF OUR GETTING BACK THOSE STONES-- GETTING BACK TAMAHOME'S MEMORIES?
EVEN IF IT IS, YOU MUST STOP INJURING THE OTHERS!
YUI, PRESIDENT SASAKI, AND THE OTHER STUDENTS IN SCHOOL HAVE NOTHING TO DO WITH THIS!

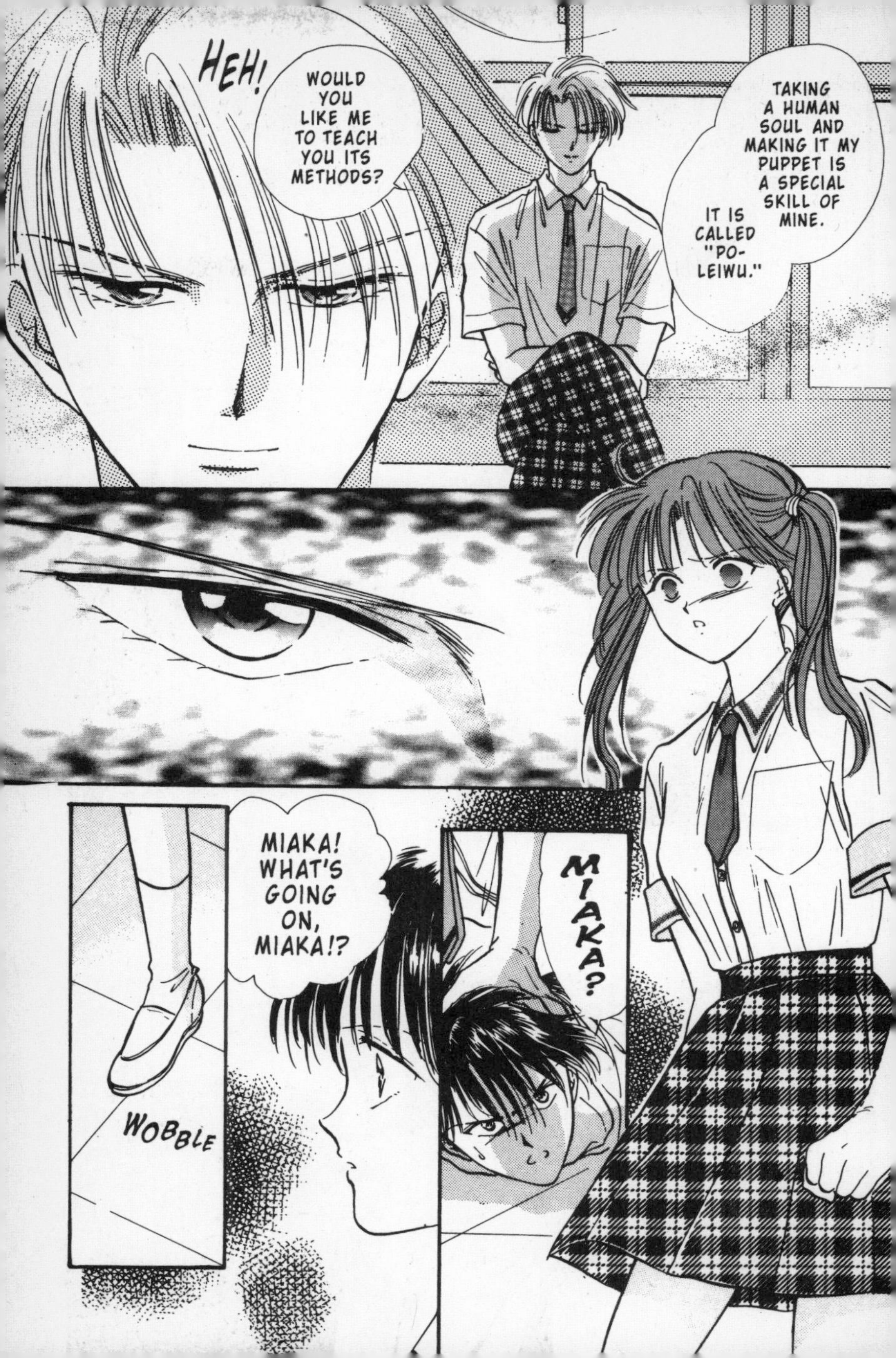
TAKING A HUMAN SOUL AND MAKING IT MY PUPPET IS A SPECIAL SKILL OF MINE.
IT IS CALLED "PO-LEIWU."
HEH!
WOULD YOU LIKE ME TO TEACH YOU ITS METHODS?
MIAKA?
MIAKA! WHAT'S GOING ON, MIAKA!?
WOBBLE

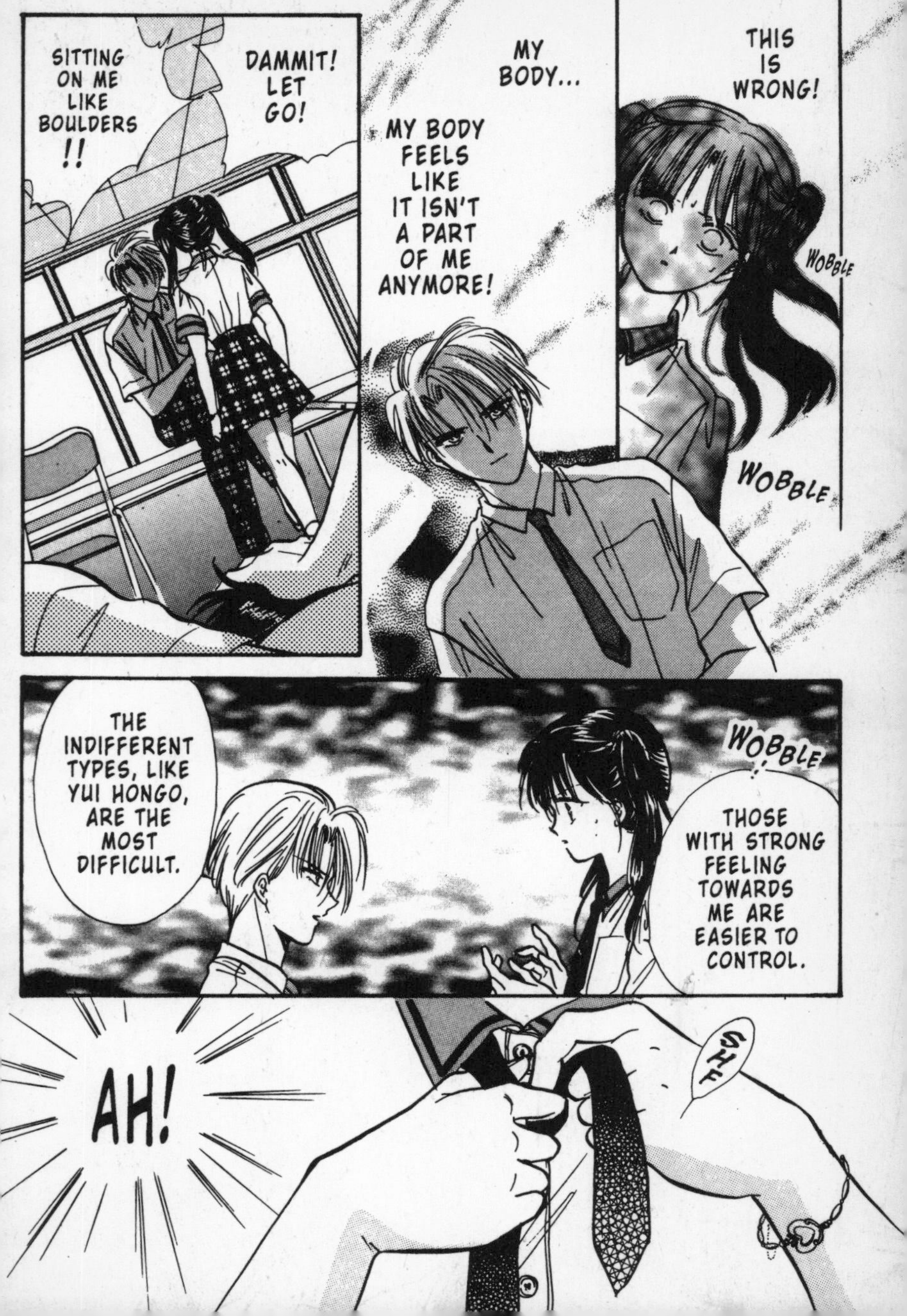

THIS IS WRONG!
WOBBLE
WOBBLE
MY BODY...
MY BODY FEELS LIKE IT ISN'T A PART OF ME ANYMORE!
DAMMIT! LET GO!
SITTING ON ME LIKE BOULDERS !!
WOBBLE!
THOSE WITH STRONG FEELING TOWARDS ME ARE EASIER TO CONTROL.
THE INDIFFERENT TYPES, LIKE YUI HONGO, ARE THE MOST DIFFICULT.
SHF
AH!

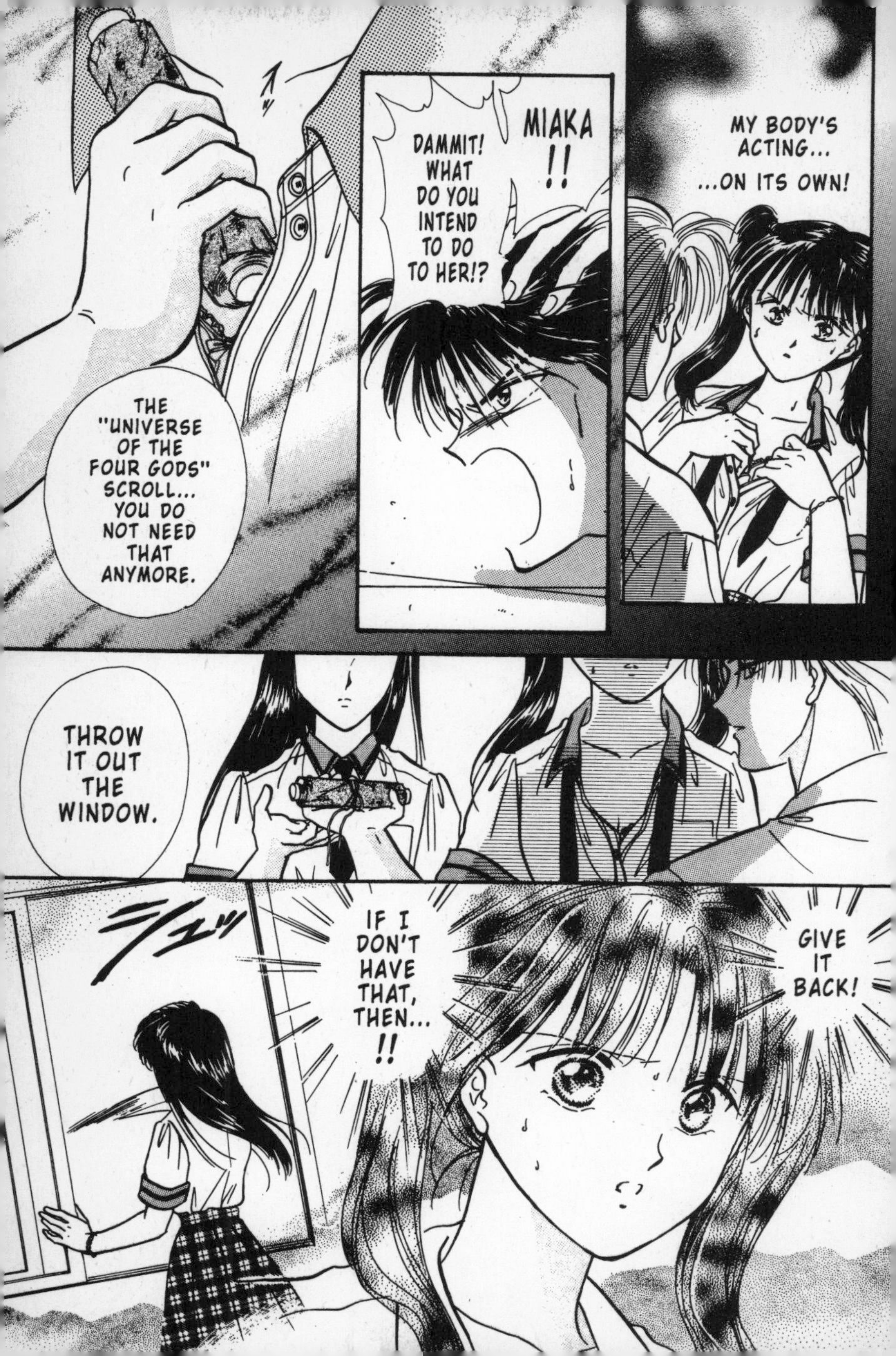
MY BODY'S ACTING...
...ON ITS OWN!
MIAKA !!
DAMMIT! WHAT DO YOU INTEND TO DO TO HER!?
THE "UNIVERSE OF THE FOUR GODS" SCROLL... YOU DO NOT NEED THAT ANYMORE.
THROW IT OUT THE WINDOW.
GIVE IT BACK!
IF I DON'T HAVE THAT, THEN... !!

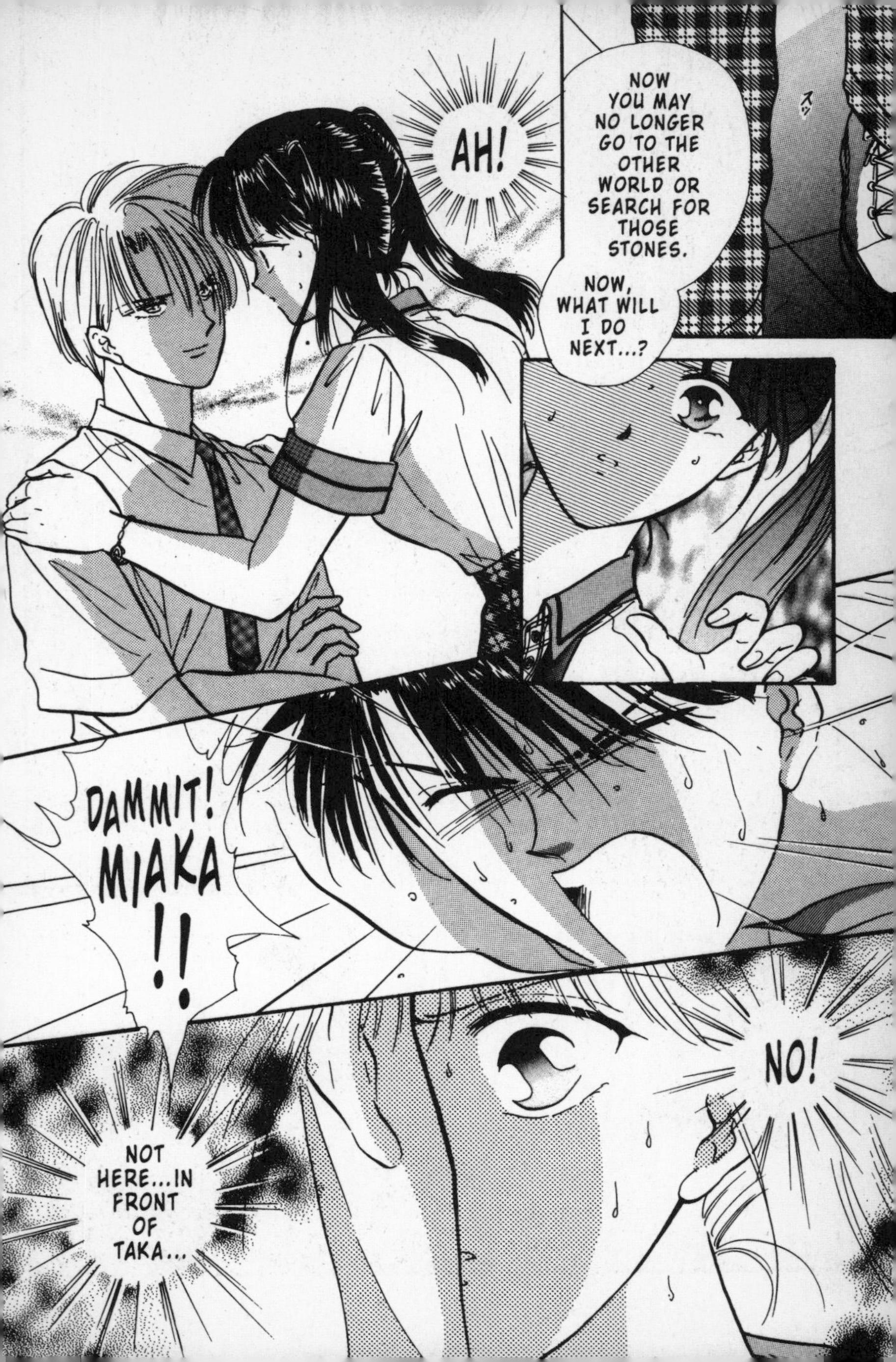
NOW YOU MAY NO LONGER GO TO THE OTHER WORLD OR SEARCH FOR THOSE STONES.
NOW, WHAT WILL I DO NEXT...?
AH!
DAMMIT! MIAKA!!
NO!
NOT HERE...IN FRONT OF TAKA...

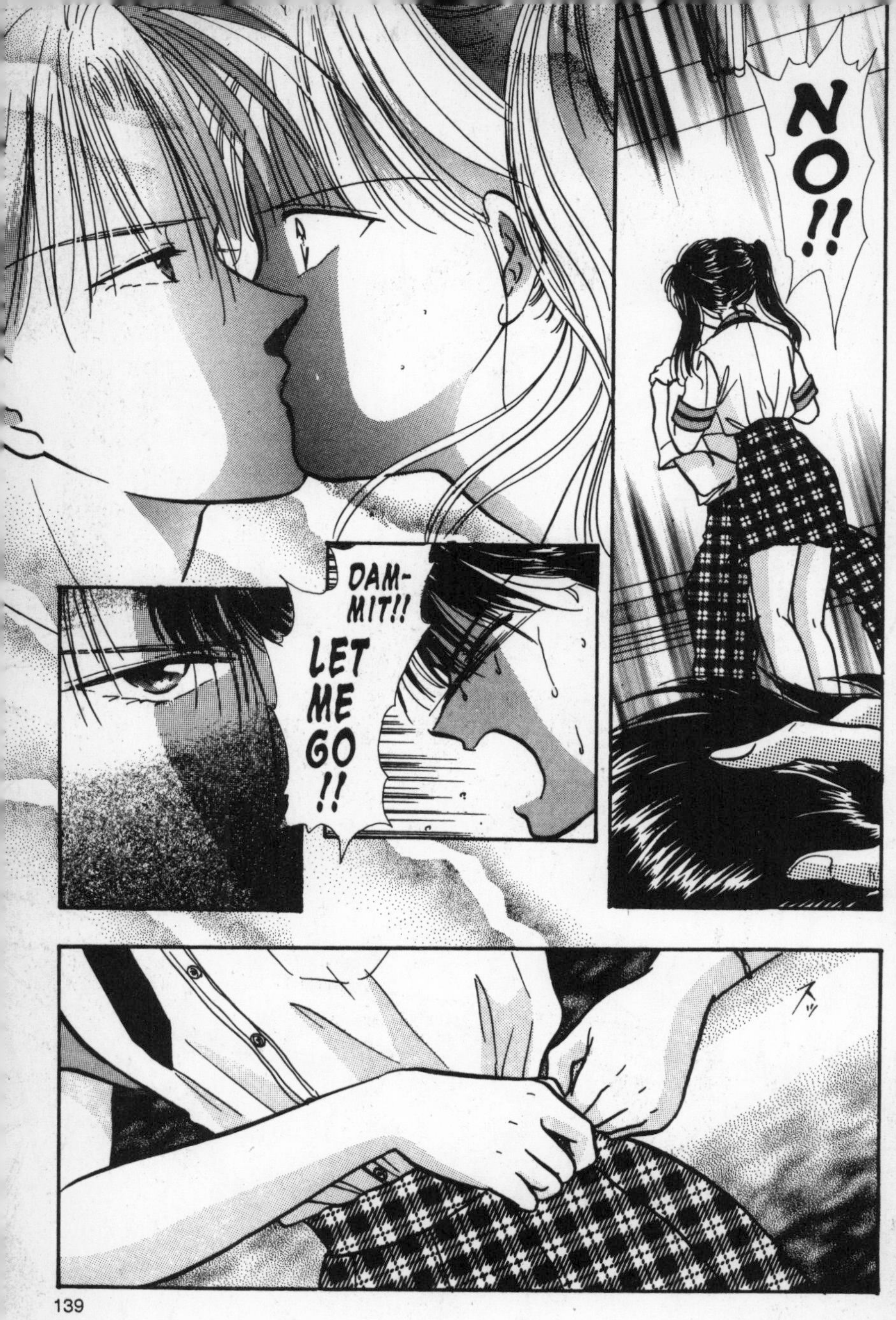
NO!!
DAM-MIT!!
LET ME GO!!
スッ

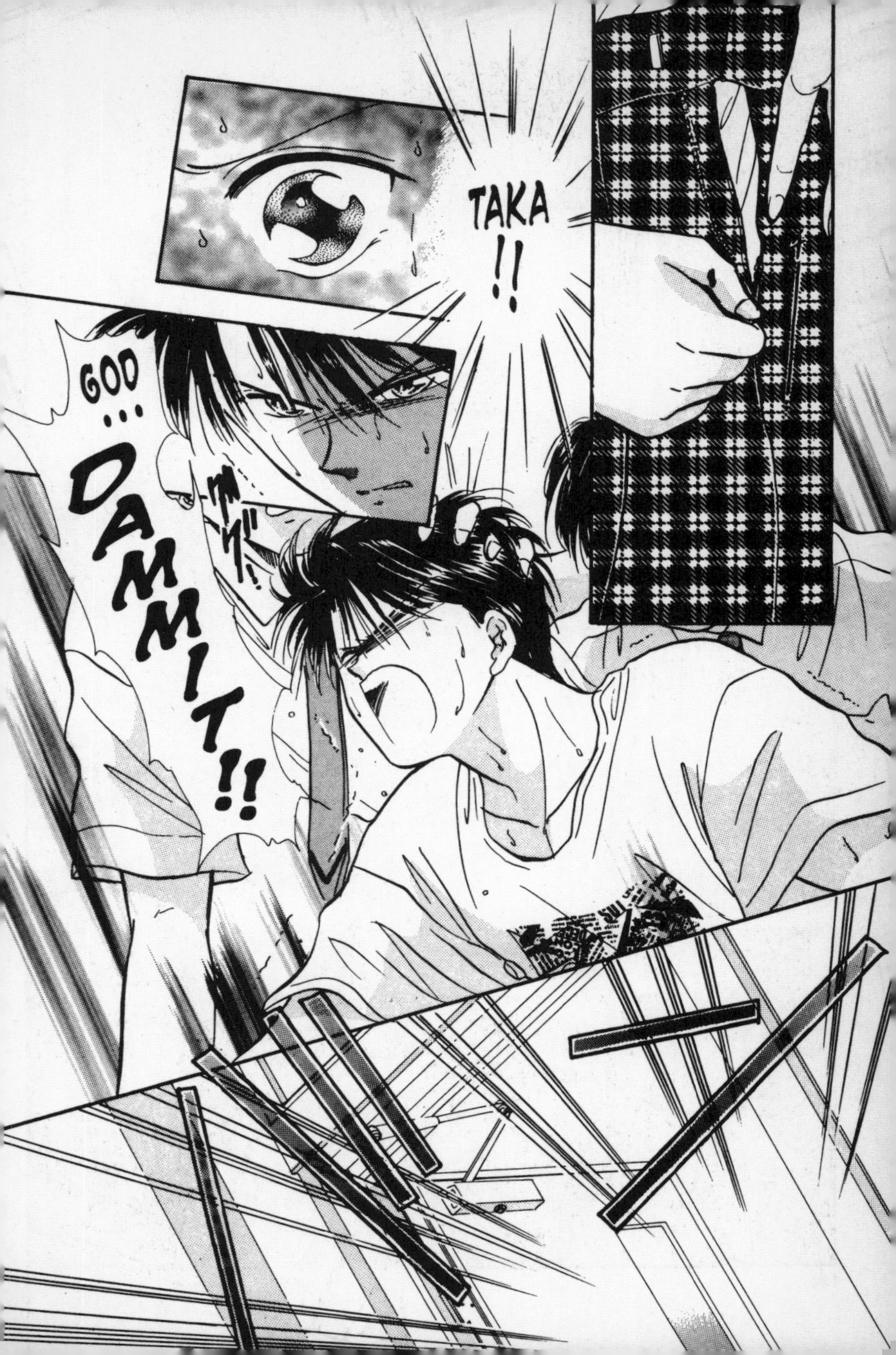
TAKA
!!
GOD... DAMMIT!!

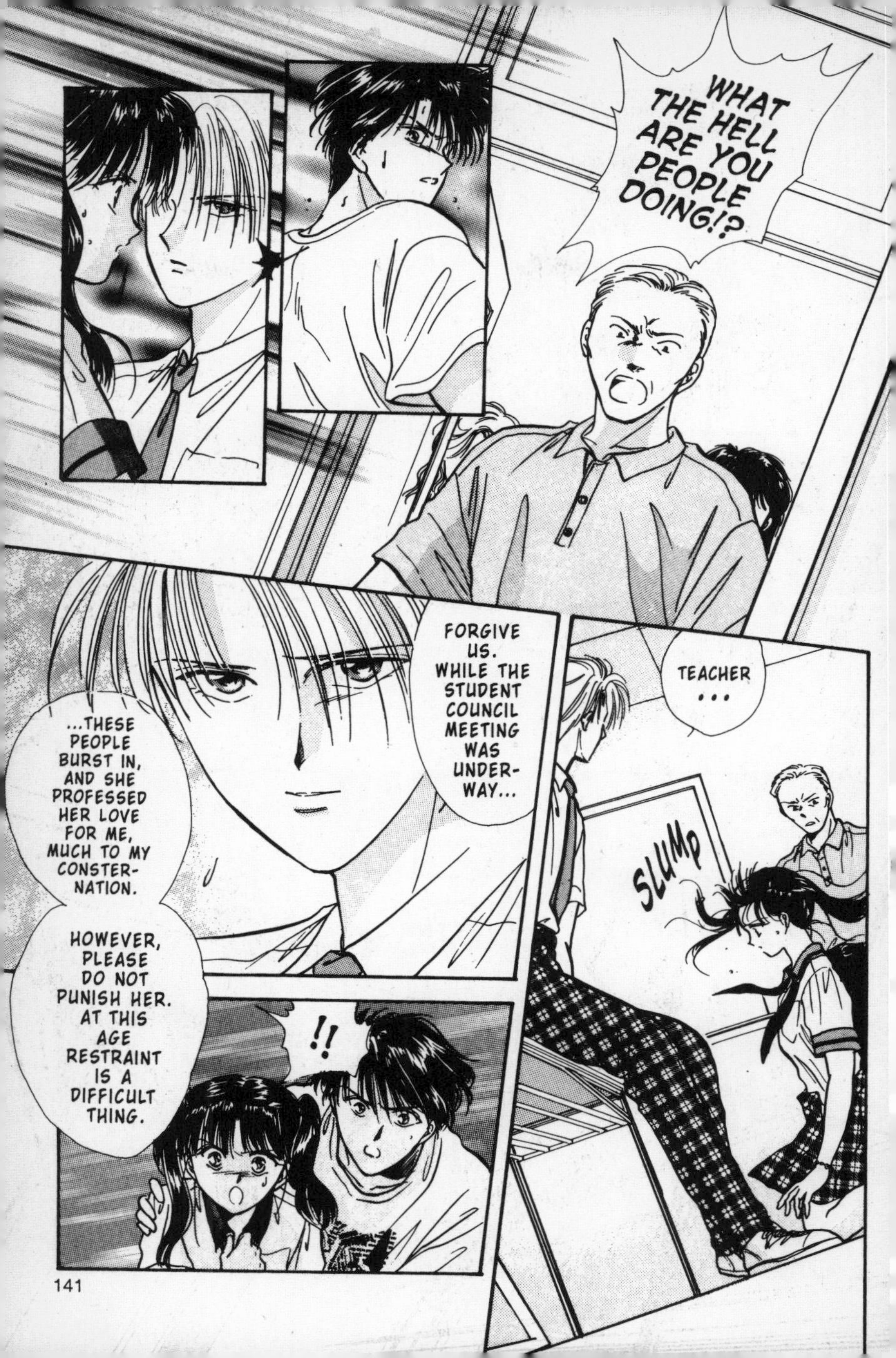
WHAT THE HELL ARE YOU PEOPLE DOING!?
TEACHER...
SLUMP
FORGIVE US. WHILE THE STUDENT COUNCIL MEETING WAS UNDER-WAY...
...THESE PEOPLE BURST IN, AND SHE PROFESSED HER LOVE FOR ME, MUCH TO MY CONSTER-NATION.
HOWEVER, PLEASE DO NOT PUNISH HER. AT THIS AGE RESTRAINT IS A DIFFICULT THING.
!!

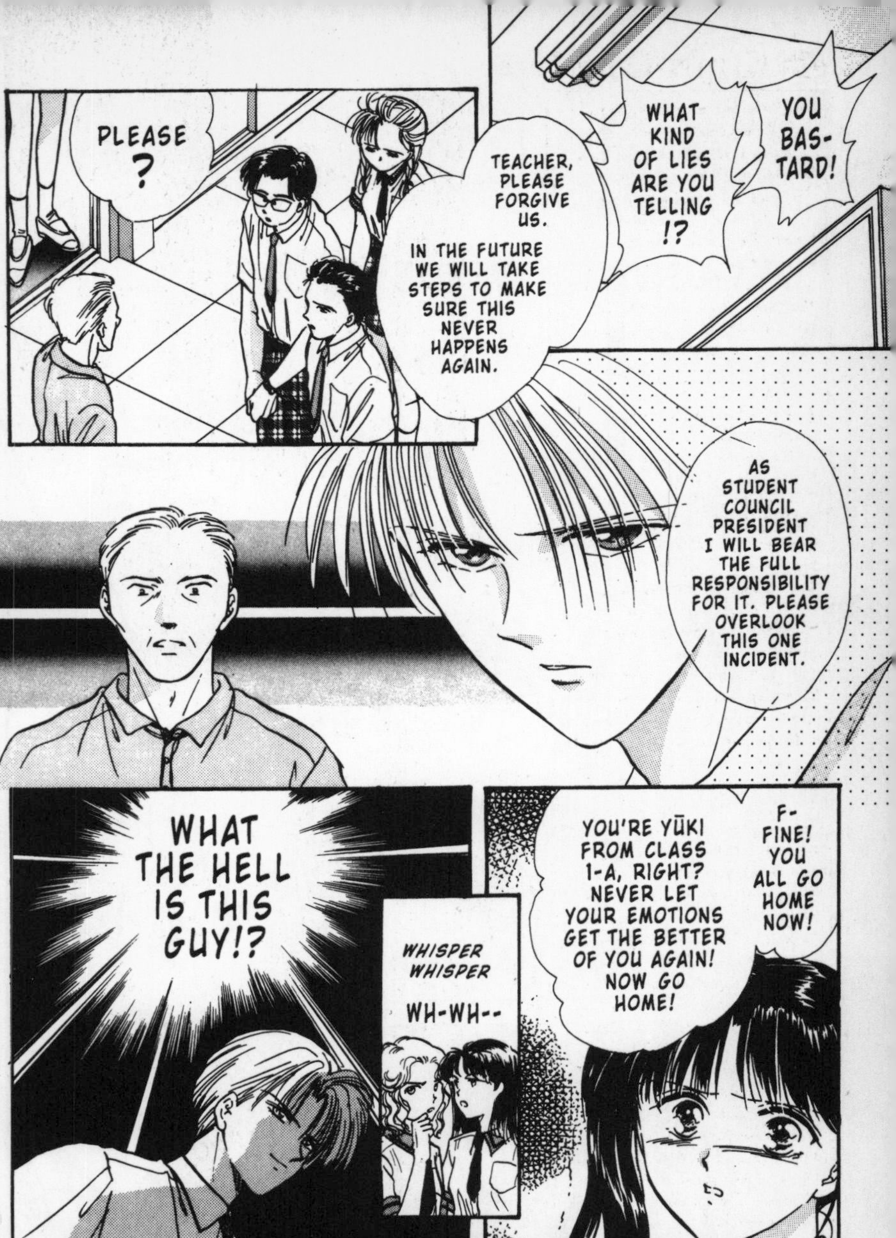

YOU BAS-TARD!
WHAT KIND OF LIES ARE YOU TELLING !?
PLEASE ?
TEACHER, PLEASE FORGIVE US.
IN THE FUTURE WE WILL TAKE STEPS TO MAKE SURE THIS NEVER HAPPENS AGAIN.
AS STUDENT COUNCIL PRESIDENT I WILL BEAR THE FULL RESPONSIBILITY FOR IT. PLEASE OVERLOOK THIS ONE INCIDENT.
F-FINE! YOU ALL GO HOME NOW!
YOU'RE YŪKI FROM CLASS 1-A, RIGHT? NEVER LET YOUR EMOTIONS GET THE BETTER OF YOU AGAIN! NOW GO HOME!
WHISPER WHISPER
WH-WH--
WHAT THE HELL IS THIS GUY!?

Guardian

The hotel was absolutely beautiful! ☺ And the car that came to pick us up was a Mercedes Benz! In addition, the plane trip was first class! I had a multi-course meal with wine! (Incidentally, when I flew to Hokkaido, I was given a free seat upgrade!) Quite seriously, I thank the happy fate that made me a manga artist! Now, about the signing... It was held in Mitsukoshi department store, and when I first heard that Taiwanese fans were really kind, I didn't really know what that meant, but now I fully understand! When someone told me that fans began lining up at the department store at closing time the night before (the Taiwanese stores don't close until 10 or 11 p.m.), I blurted out, "They don't even do that in Japan!!" ☺ The signing started at about 12:30 p.m., so I guess they stood in line almost 15 hours...? *(Just waiting?)* Before the signing, I shared a meal with a Taiwanese manga artist, and after the signing was over, a Korean artist joined us! It's pretty amazing for manga artists from three countries to be sitting at the same table! *Wooow!*
This was a joint event hosted by two large Taiwanese publishers, and they had artists who did manga for Japanese companies Shogakukan, Shueisha, and Kodansha (plus some Taiwanese artists, of course). It was really amazing! This would never ever happen in Japan! In the waiting room was this enormous illustration board, and I could not stop staring! Some of Japan's biggest manga artists had done illustrations and signed it... and so had the Taiwanese artists! If any huge manga fans had seen it, they would've just stood there and drooled! I left a drawing of Tamahome and Chichiri on it, but I was so nervous.
I hope Mitsukoshi stays in Taiwan forever! *Wow!*

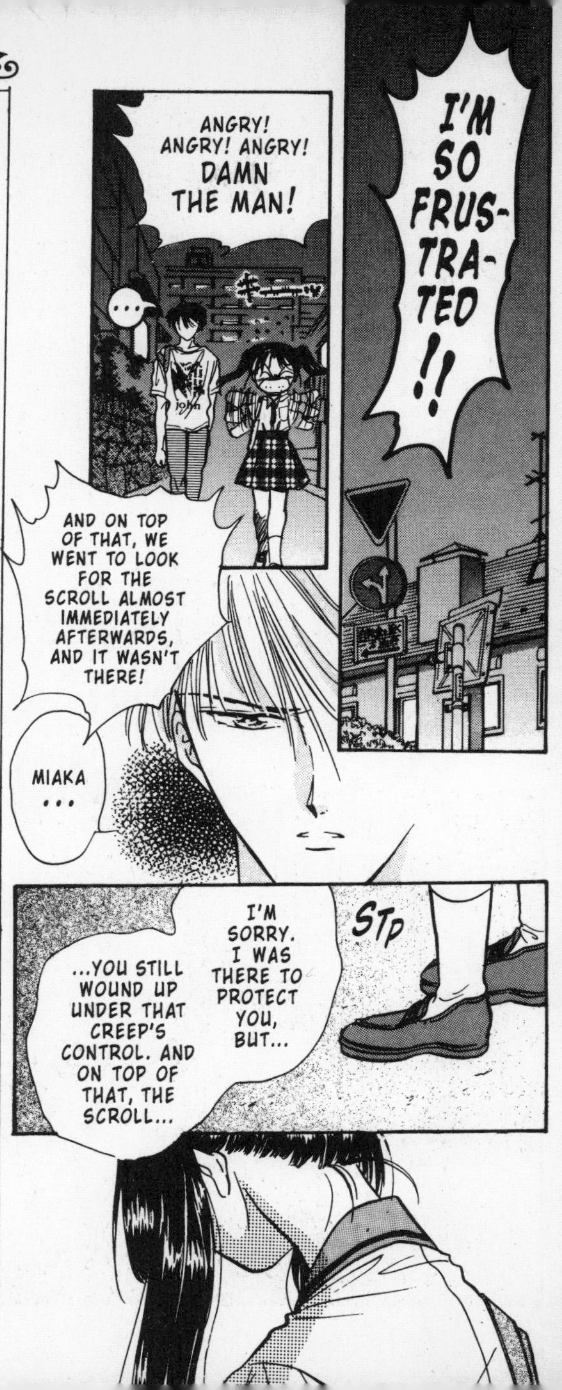
I'M SO FRUSTRATED!!
ANGRY! ANGRY! ANGRY! DAMN THE MAN!
AND ON TOP OF THAT, WE WENT TO LOOK FOR THE SCROLL ALMOST IMMEDIATELY AFTERWARDS, AND IT WASN'T THERE!
MIAKA...
STP
I'M SORRY. I WAS THERE TO PROTECT YOU, BUT...
...YOU STILL WOUND UP UNDER THAT CREEP'S CONTROL. AND ON TOP OF THAT, THE SCROLL...

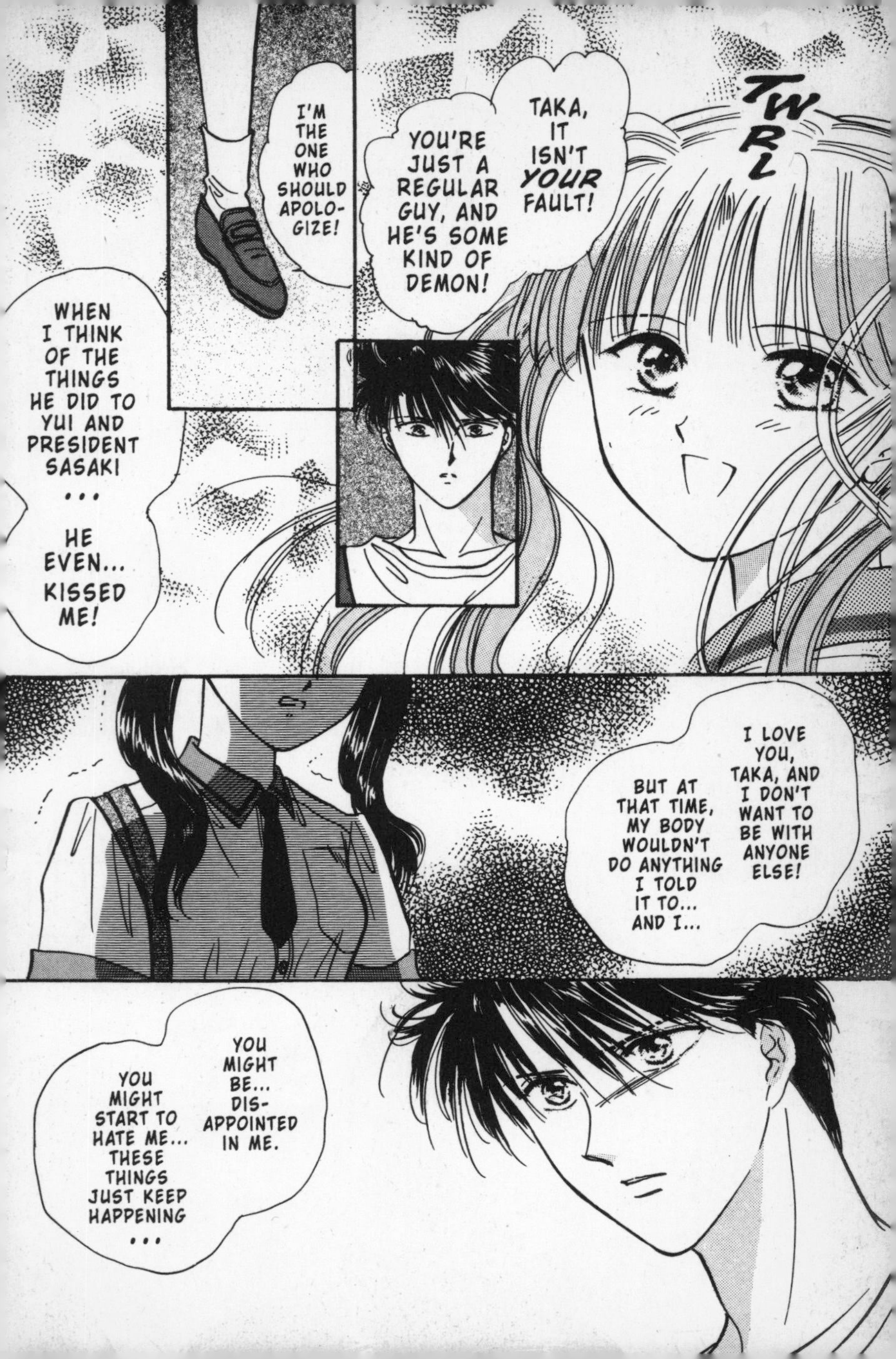
TWRL
TAKA, IT ISN'T *YOUR* FAULT!
YOU'RE JUST A REGULAR GUY, AND HE'S SOME KIND OF DEMON!
I'M THE ONE WHO SHOULD APOLO-GIZE!
WHEN I THINK OF THE THINGS HE DID TO YUI AND PRESIDENT SASAKI ...
HE EVEN... KISSED ME!
I LOVE YOU, TAKA, AND I DON'T WANT TO BE WITH ANYONE ELSE!
BUT AT THAT TIME, MY BODY WOULDN'T DO ANYTHING I TOLD IT TO... AND I...
YOU MIGHT BE... DIS-APPOINTED IN ME.
YOU MIGHT START TO HATE ME... THESE THINGS JUST KEEP HAPPENING ...

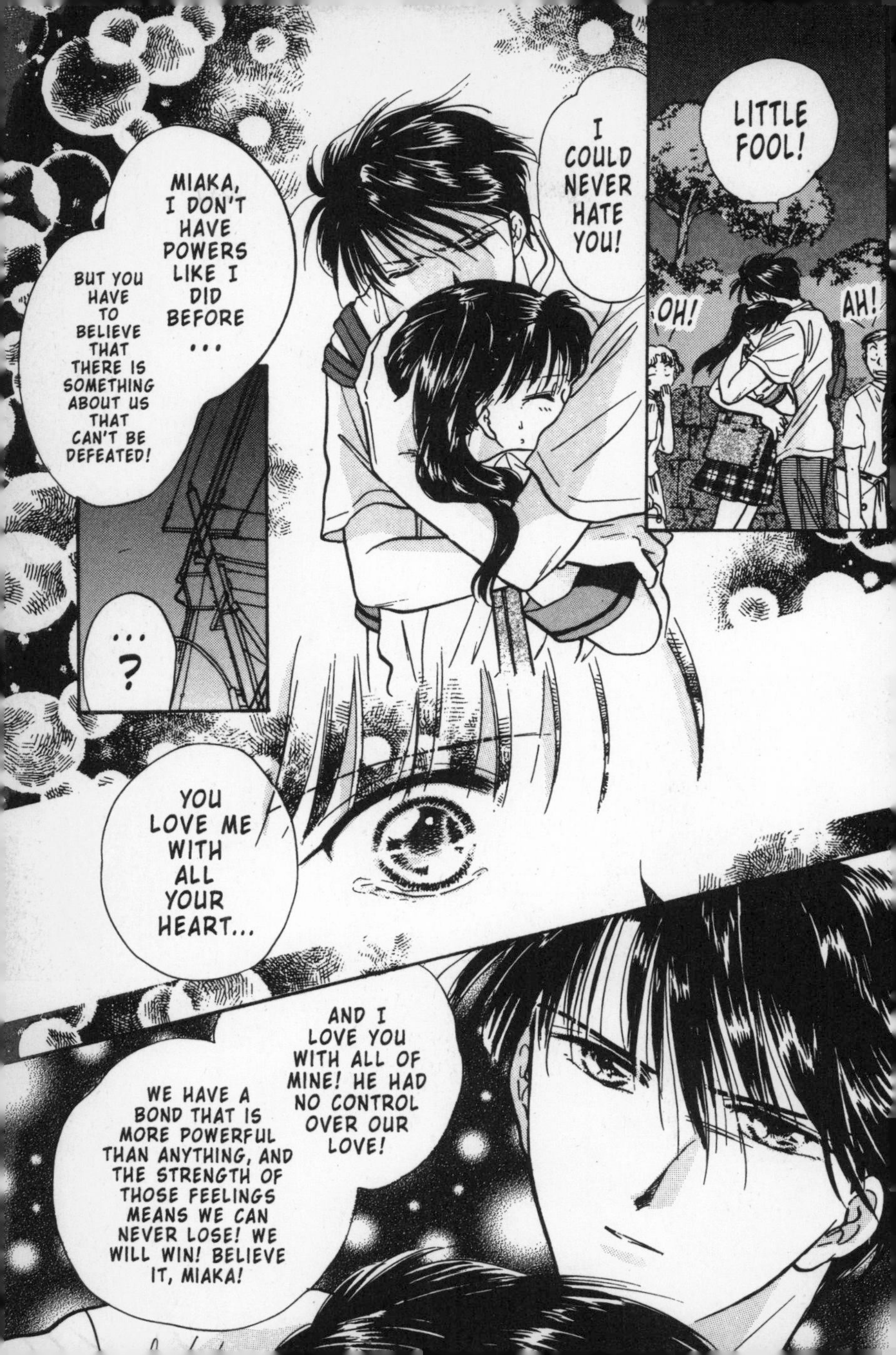
LITTLE FOOL!
AH!
OH!
I COULD NEVER HATE YOU!
MIAKA, I DON'T HAVE POWERS LIKE I DID BEFORE ...
BUT YOU HAVE TO BELIEVE THAT THERE IS SOMETHING ABOUT US THAT CAN'T BE DEFEATED!
...?
YOU LOVE ME WITH ALL YOUR HEART...
AND I LOVE YOU WITH ALL OF MINE! HE HAD NO CONTROL OVER OUR LOVE!
WE HAVE A BOND THAT IS MORE POWERFUL THAN ANYTHING, AND THE STRENGTH OF THOSE FEELINGS MEANS WE CAN NEVER LOSE! WE WILL WIN! BELIEVE IT, MIAKA!

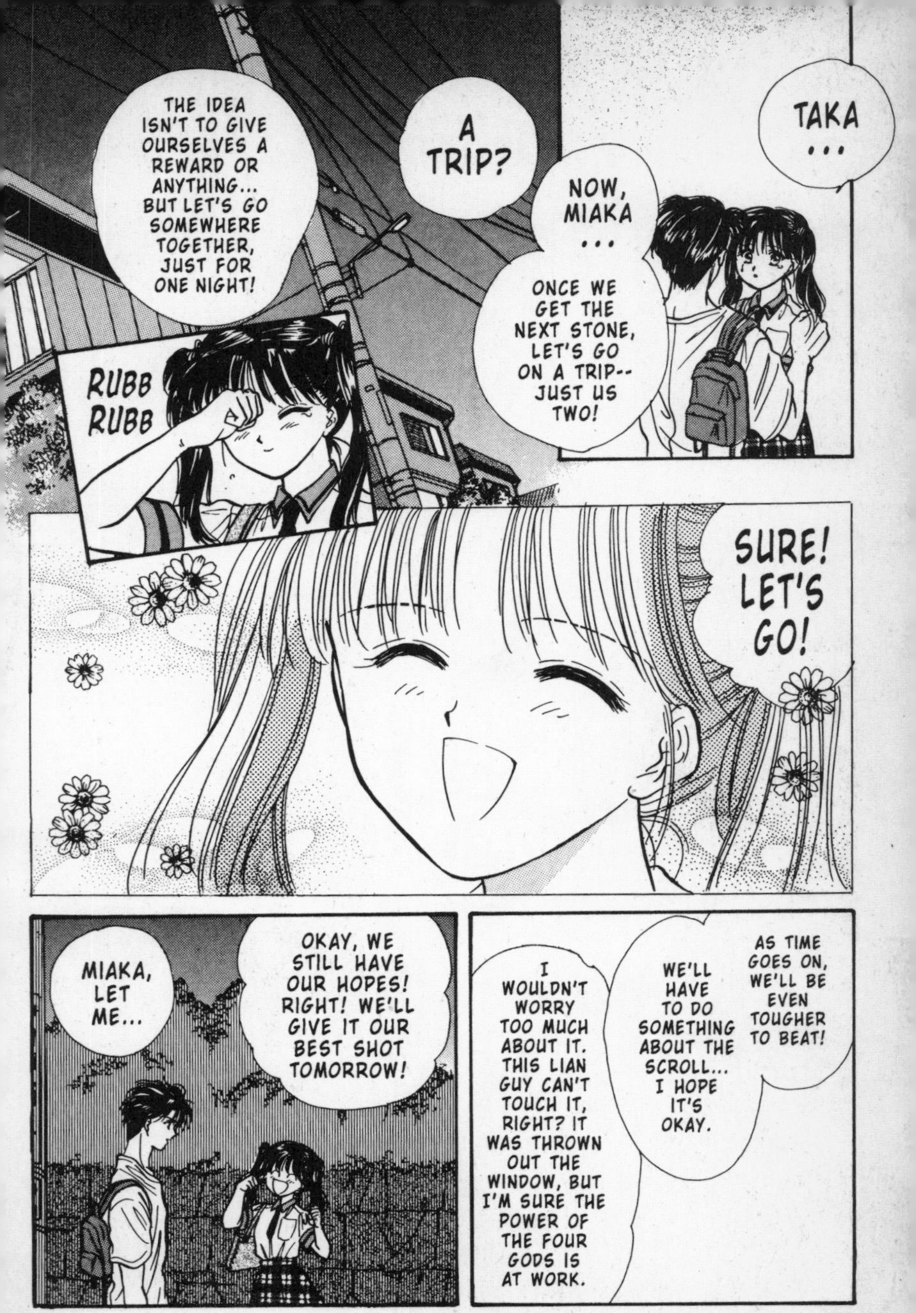
TAKA...
NOW, MIAKA...
ONCE WE GET THE NEXT STONE, LET'S GO ON A TRIP--JUST US TWO!
A TRIP?
THE IDEA ISN'T TO GIVE OURSELVES A REWARD OR ANYTHING... BUT LET'S GO SOMEWHERE TOGETHER, JUST FOR ONE NIGHT!
RUBB RUBB
SURE! LET'S GO!
AS TIME GOES ON, WE'LL BE EVEN TOUGHER TO BEAT!
WE'LL HAVE TO DO SOMETHING ABOUT THE SCROLL... I HOPE IT'S OKAY.
I WOULDN'T WORRY TOO MUCH ABOUT IT. THIS LIAN GUY CAN'T TOUCH IT, RIGHT? IT WAS THROWN OUT THE WINDOW, BUT I'M SURE THE POWER OF THE FOUR GODS IS AT WORK.
OKAY, WE STILL HAVE OUR HOPES! RIGHT! WE'LL GIVE IT OUR BEST SHOT TOMORROW!
MIAKA, LET ME...

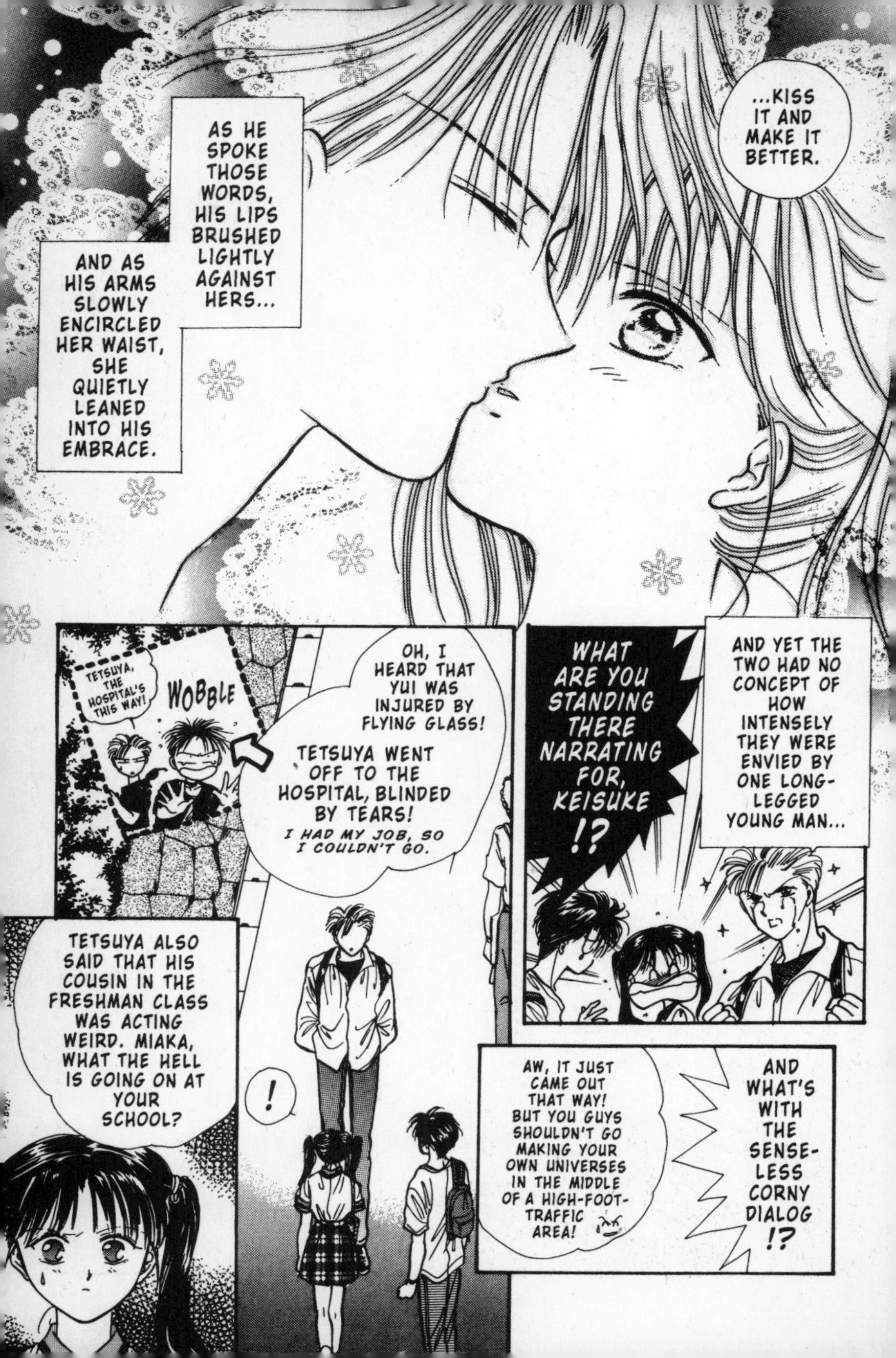
...KISS IT AND MAKE IT BETTER.
AS HE SPOKE THOSE WORDS, HIS LIPS BRUSHED LIGHTLY AGAINST HERS...
AND AS HIS ARMS SLOWLY ENCIRCLED HER WAIST, SHE QUIETLY LEANED INTO HIS EMBRACE.
AND YET THE TWO HAD NO CONCEPT OF HOW INTENSELY THEY WERE ENVIED BY ONE LONG-LEGGED YOUNG MAN...
WHAT ARE YOU STANDING THERE NARRATING FOR, KEISUKE !?
AND WHAT'S WITH THE SENSE-LESS CORNY DIALOG !?
AW, IT JUST CAME OUT THAT WAY! BUT YOU GUYS SHOULDN'T GO MAKING YOUR OWN UNIVERSES IN THE MIDDLE OF A HIGH-FOOT-TRAFFIC AREA!
OH, I HEARD THAT YUI WAS INJURED BY FLYING GLASS!
TETSUYA WENT OFF TO THE HOSPITAL, BLINDED BY TEARS!
I HAD MY JOB, SO I COULDN'T GO.
TETSUYA, THE HOSPITAL'S THIS WAY!
WOBBLE
!
TETSUYA ALSO SAID THAT HIS COUSIN IN THE FRESHMAN CLASS WAS ACTING WEIRD. MIAKA, WHAT THE HELL IS GOING ON AT YOUR SCHOOL?

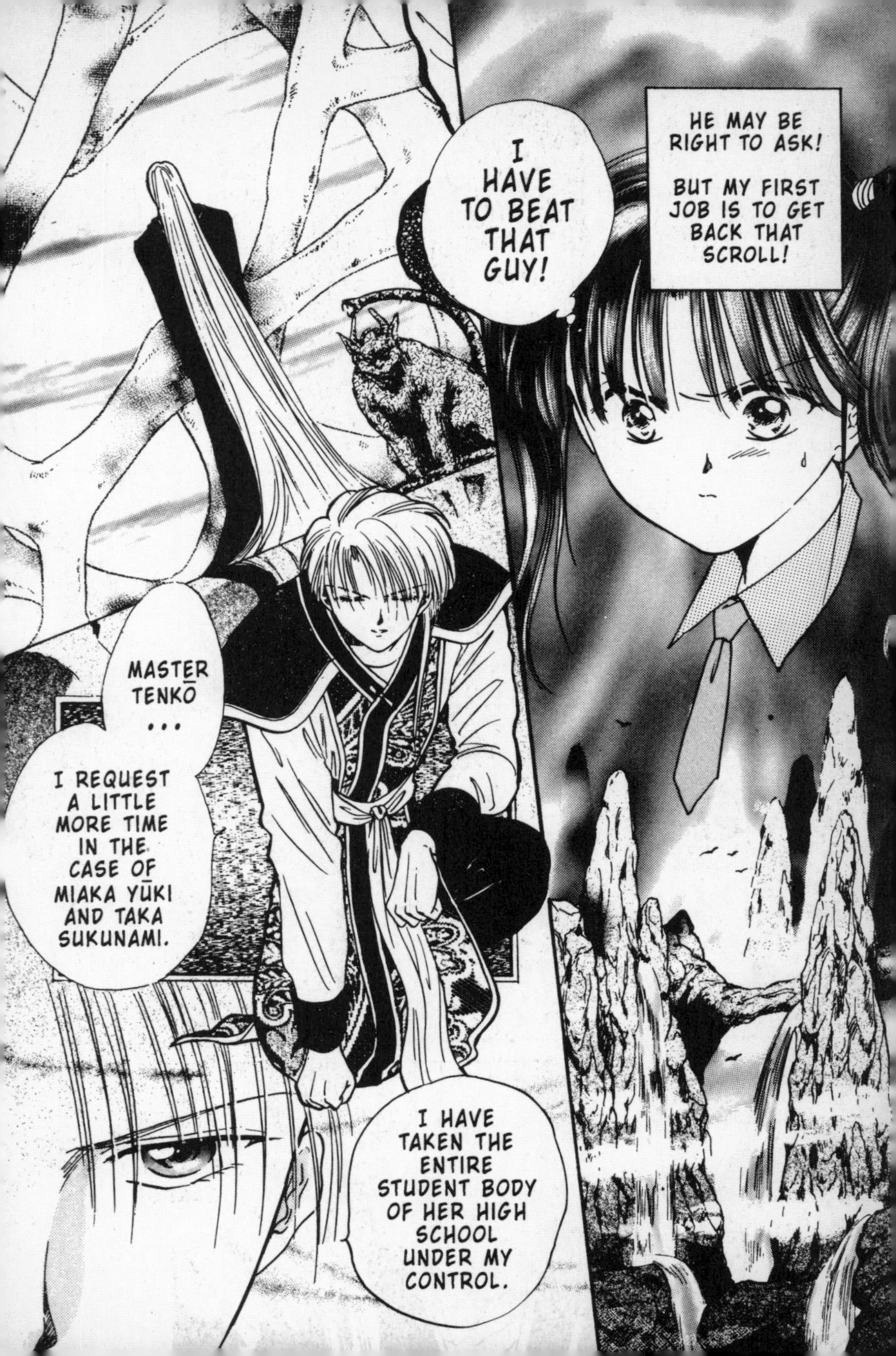
HE MAY BE RIGHT TO ASK!
BUT MY FIRST JOB IS TO GET BACK THAT SCROLL!
I HAVE TO BEAT THAT GUY!
MASTER TENKŌ ...
I REQUEST A LITTLE MORE TIME IN THE CASE OF MIAKA YŪKI AND TAKA SUKUNAMI.
I HAVE TAKEN THE ENTIRE STUDENT BODY OF HER HIGH SCHOOL UNDER MY CONTROL.

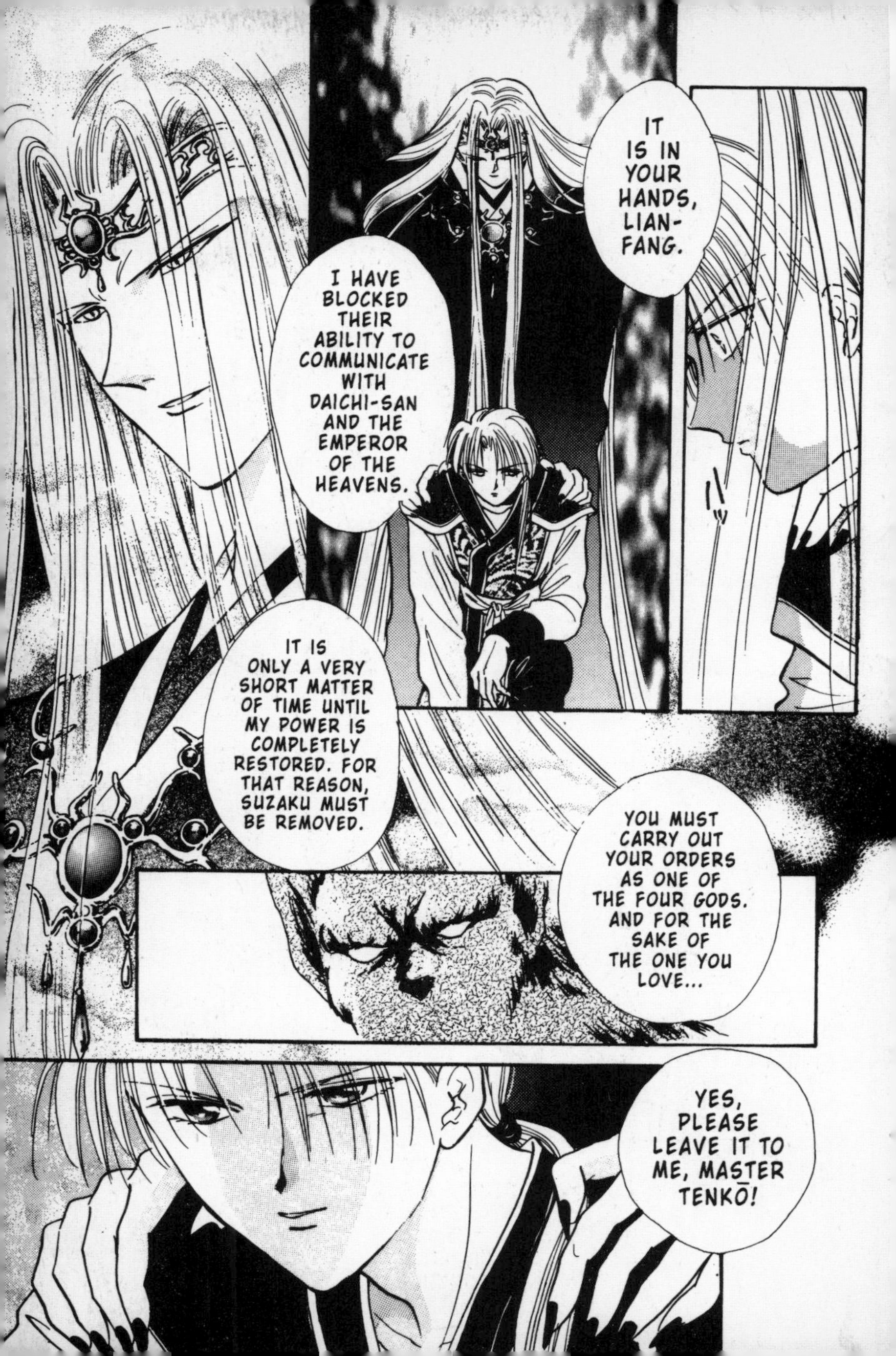
IT IS IN YOUR HANDS, LIAN-FANG.
I HAVE BLOCKED THEIR ABILITY TO COMMUNICATE WITH DAICHI-SAN AND THE EMPEROR OF THE HEAVENS.
IT IS ONLY A VERY SHORT MATTER OF TIME UNTIL MY POWER IS COMPLETELY RESTORED. FOR THAT REASON, SUZAKU MUST BE REMOVED.
YOU MUST CARRY OUT YOUR ORDERS AS ONE OF THE FOUR GODS. AND FOR THE SAKE OF THE ONE YOU LOVE...
YES, PLEASE LEAVE IT TO ME, MASTER TENKŌ!

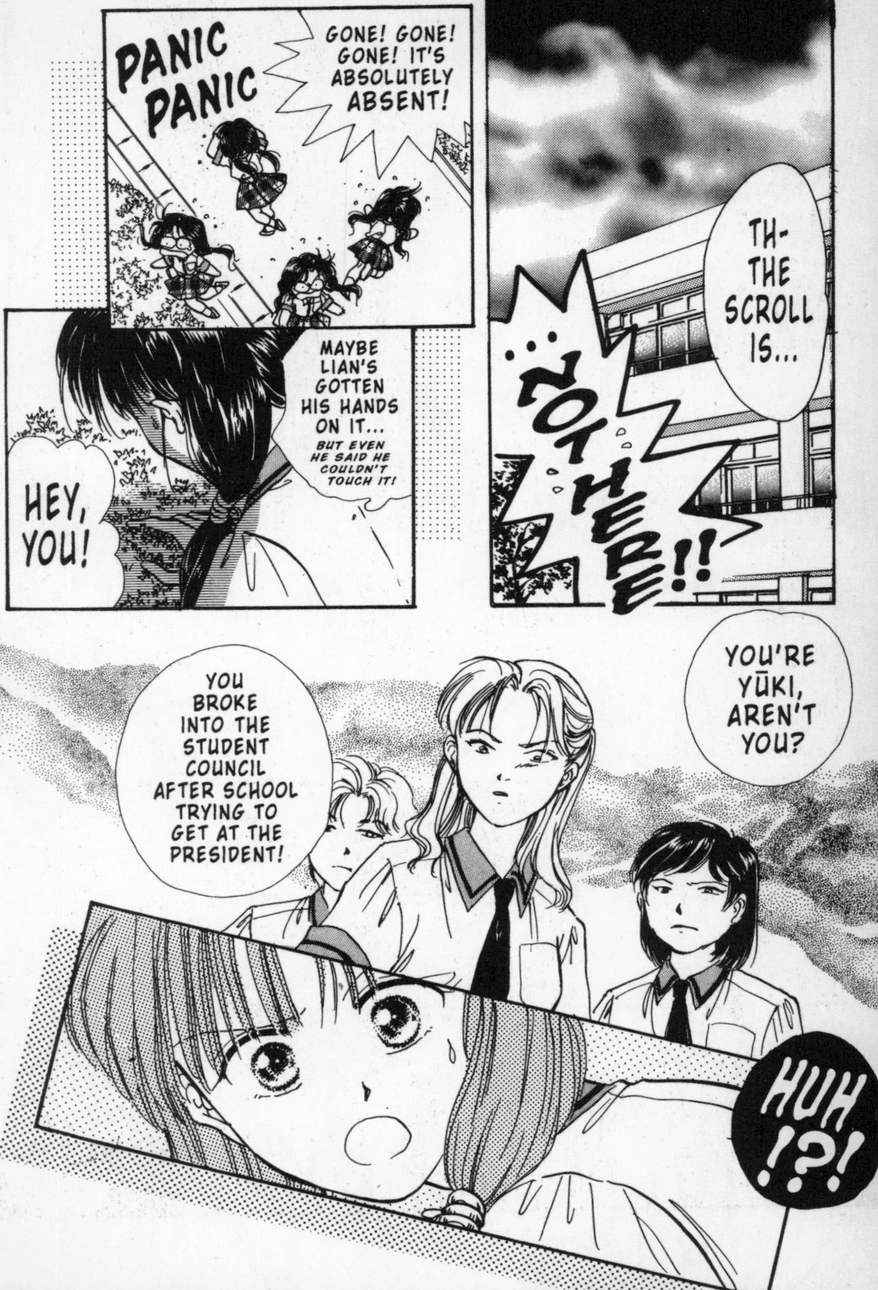
TH-THE SCROLL IS...
...NOT HERE!!
GONE! GONE! GONE! IT'S ABSOLUTELY ABSENT!
PANIC PANIC
MAYBE LIAN'S GOTTEN HIS HANDS ON IT...
BUT EVEN HE SAID HE COULDN'T TOUCH IT!
HEY, YOU!
YOU'RE YŪKI, AREN'T YOU?
YOU BROKE INTO THE STUDENT COUNCIL AFTER SCHOOL TRYING TO GET AT THE PRESIDENT!
HUH!?!

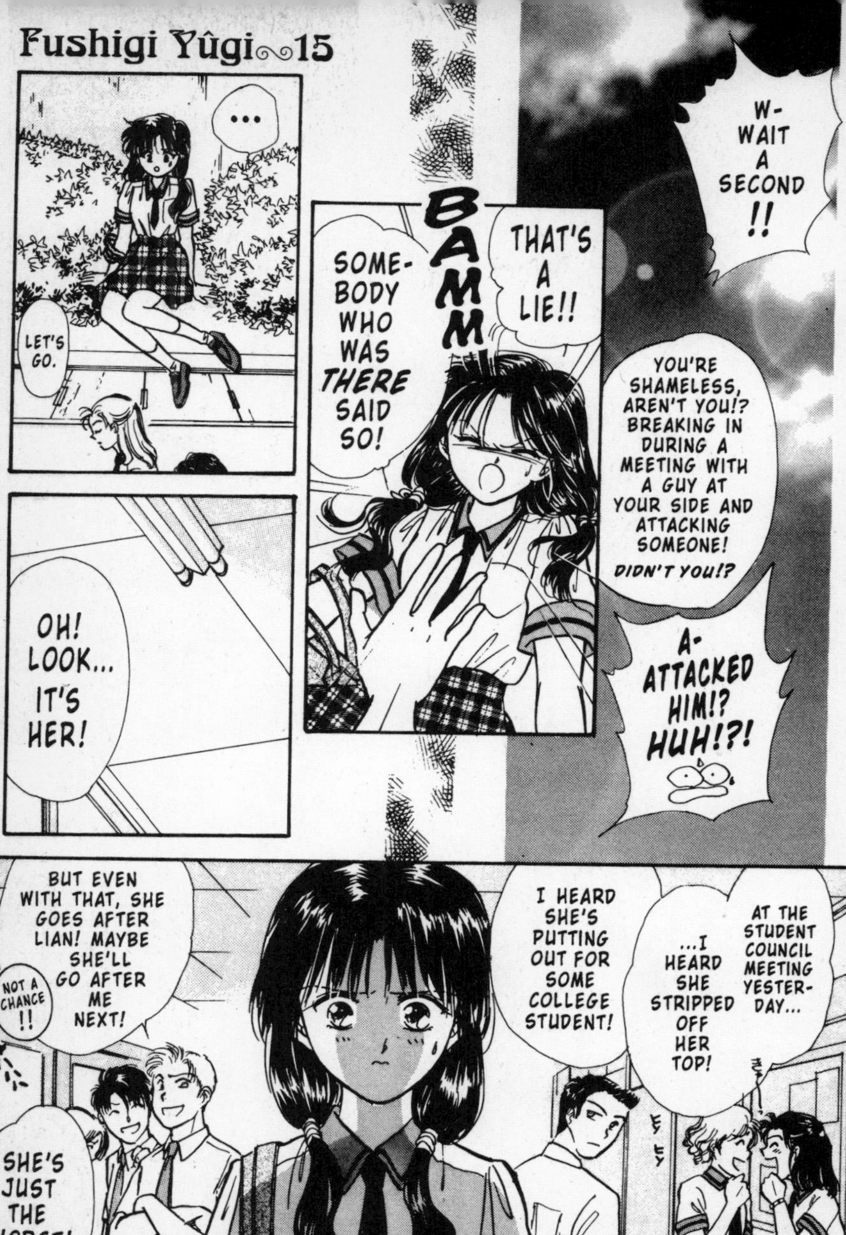
W-WAIT A SECOND!!
YOU'RE SHAMELESS, AREN'T YOU!? BREAKING IN DURING A MEETING WITH A GUY AT YOUR SIDE AND ATTACKING SOMEONE! DIDN'T YOU!?
A-ATTACKED HIM!? HUH!?!
BAMM
THAT'S A LIE!!
SOMEBODY WHO WAS THERE SAID SO!
...
LET'S GO.
OH! LOOK... IT'S HER!
AT THE STUDENT COUNCIL MEETING YESTERDAY...
...I HEARD SHE STRIPPED OFF HER TOP!
I HEARD SHE'S PUTTING OUT FOR SOME COLLEGE STUDENT!
BUT EVEN WITH THAT, SHE GOES AFTER LIAN! MAYBE SHE'LL GO AFTER ME NEXT!
NOT A CHANCE!!
SHE'S JUST THE WORST!

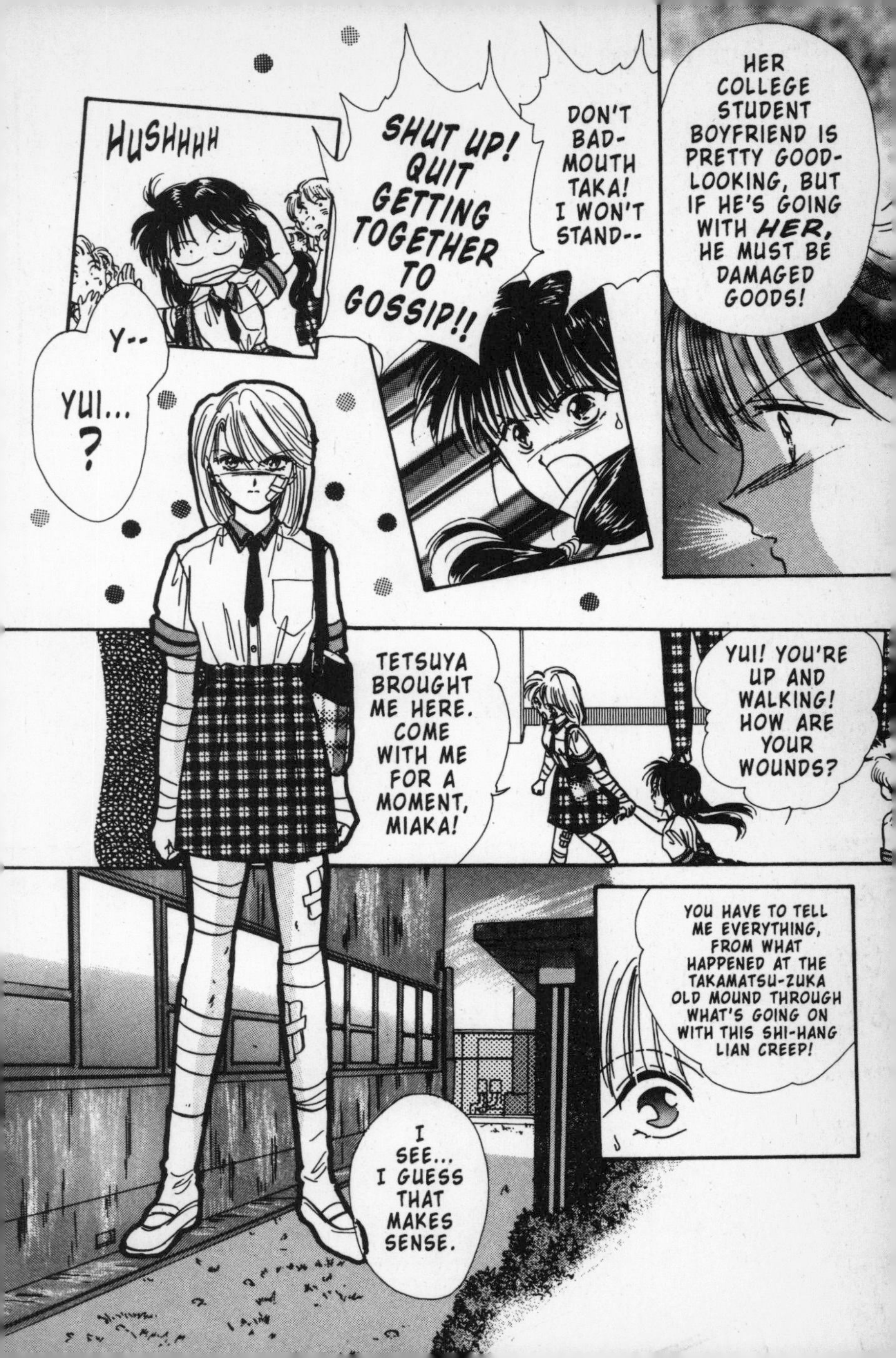
HER COLLEGE STUDENT BOYFRIEND IS PRETTY GOOD-LOOKING, BUT IF HE'S GOING WITH *HER,* HE MUST BE DAMAGED GOODS!
DON'T BAD-MOUTH TAKA! I WON'T STAND--
SHUT UP! QUIT GETTING TOGETHER TO GOSSIP!!
HUSHHHH
Y-- YUI... ?
YUI! YOU'RE UP AND WALKING! HOW ARE YOUR WOUNDS?
TETSUYA BROUGHT ME HERE. COME WITH ME FOR A MOMENT, MIAKA!
YOU HAVE TO TELL ME EVERYTHING, FROM WHAT HAPPENED AT THE TAKAMATSU-ZUKA OLD MOUND THROUGH WHAT'S GOING ON WITH THIS SHI-HANG LIAN CREEP!
I SEE... I GUESS THAT MAKES SENSE.

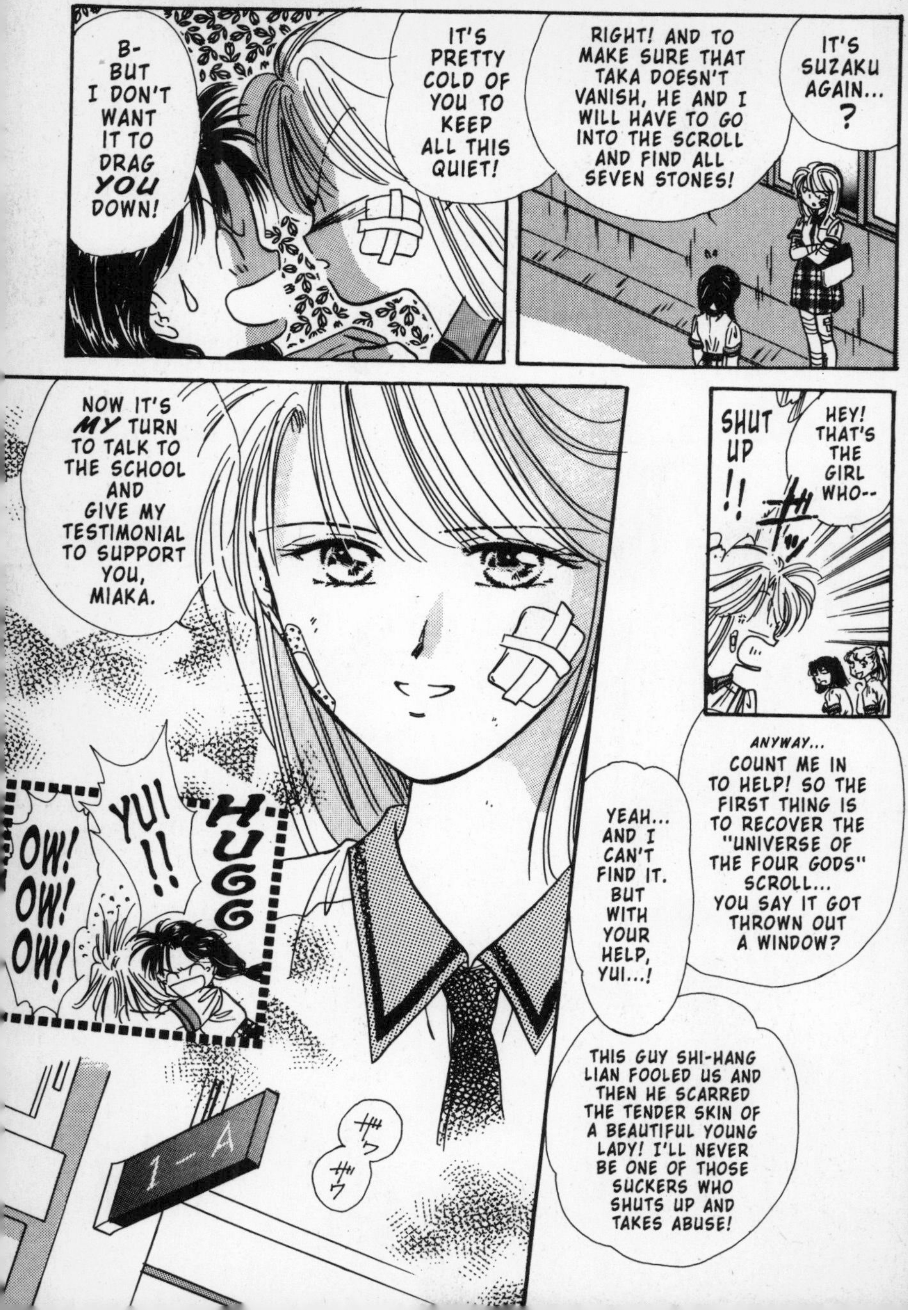
IT'S SUZAKU AGAIN... ?
RIGHT! AND TO MAKE SURE THAT TAKA DOESN'T VANISH, HE AND I WILL HAVE TO GO INTO THE SCROLL AND FIND ALL SEVEN STONES!
IT'S PRETTY COLD OF YOU TO KEEP ALL THIS QUIET!
B-BUT I DON'T WANT IT TO DRAG *YOU* DOWN!
HEY! THAT'S THE GIRL WHO--
SHUT UP!!
ANYWAY... COUNT ME IN TO HELP! SO THE FIRST THING IS TO RECOVER THE "UNIVERSE OF THE FOUR GODS" SCROLL... YOU SAY IT GOT THROWN OUT A WINDOW?
YEAH... AND I CAN'T FIND IT. BUT WITH YOUR HELP, YUI...!
THIS GUY SHI-HANG LIAN FOOLED US AND THEN HE SCARRED THE TENDER SKIN OF A BEAUTIFUL YOUNG LADY! I'LL NEVER BE ONE OF THOSE SUCKERS WHO SHUTS UP AND TAKES ABUSE!
NOW IT'S *MY* TURN TO TALK TO THE SCHOOL AND GIVE MY TESTIMONIAL TO SUPPORT YOU, MIAKA.
HUGG
YUI!!
OW! OW! OW!
1-A

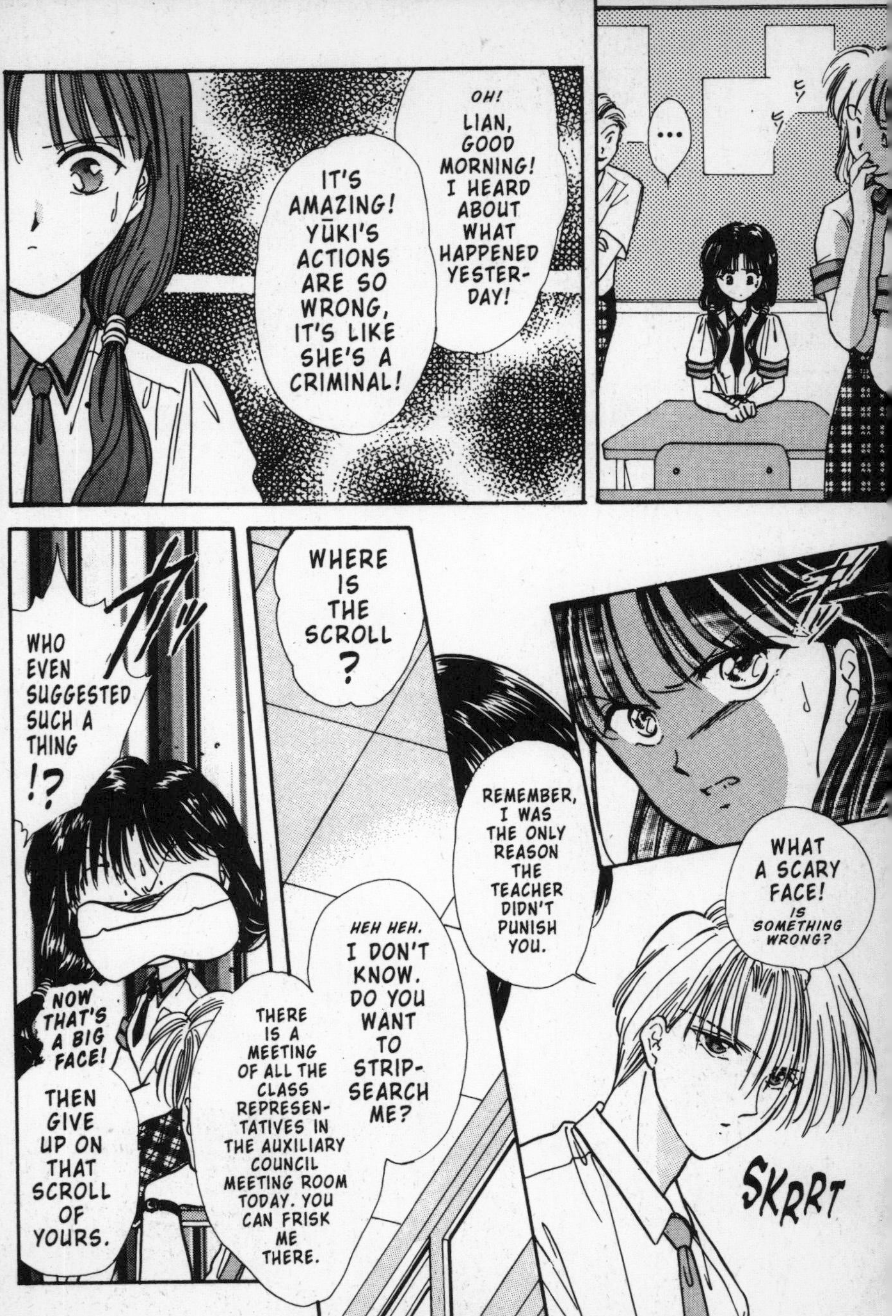
...
ヒソ ヒソ
OH! LIAN, GOOD MORNING! I HEARD ABOUT WHAT HAPPENED YESTER-DAY!
IT'S AMAZING! YŪKI'S ACTIONS ARE SO WRONG, IT'S LIKE SHE'S A CRIMINAL!
WHAT A SCARY FACE! IS SOMETHING WRONG?
REMEMBER, I WAS THE ONLY REASON THE TEACHER DIDN'T PUNISH YOU.
WHERE IS THE SCROLL?
HEH HEH. I DON'T KNOW. DO YOU WANT TO STRIP-SEARCH ME?
THERE IS A MEETING OF ALL THE CLASS REPRESEN-TATIVES IN THE AUXILIARY COUNCIL MEETING ROOM TODAY. YOU CAN FRISK ME THERE.
SKRRT
WHO EVEN SUGGESTED SUCH A THING!?
NOW THAT'S A BIG FACE!
THEN GIVE UP ON THAT SCROLL OF YOURS.

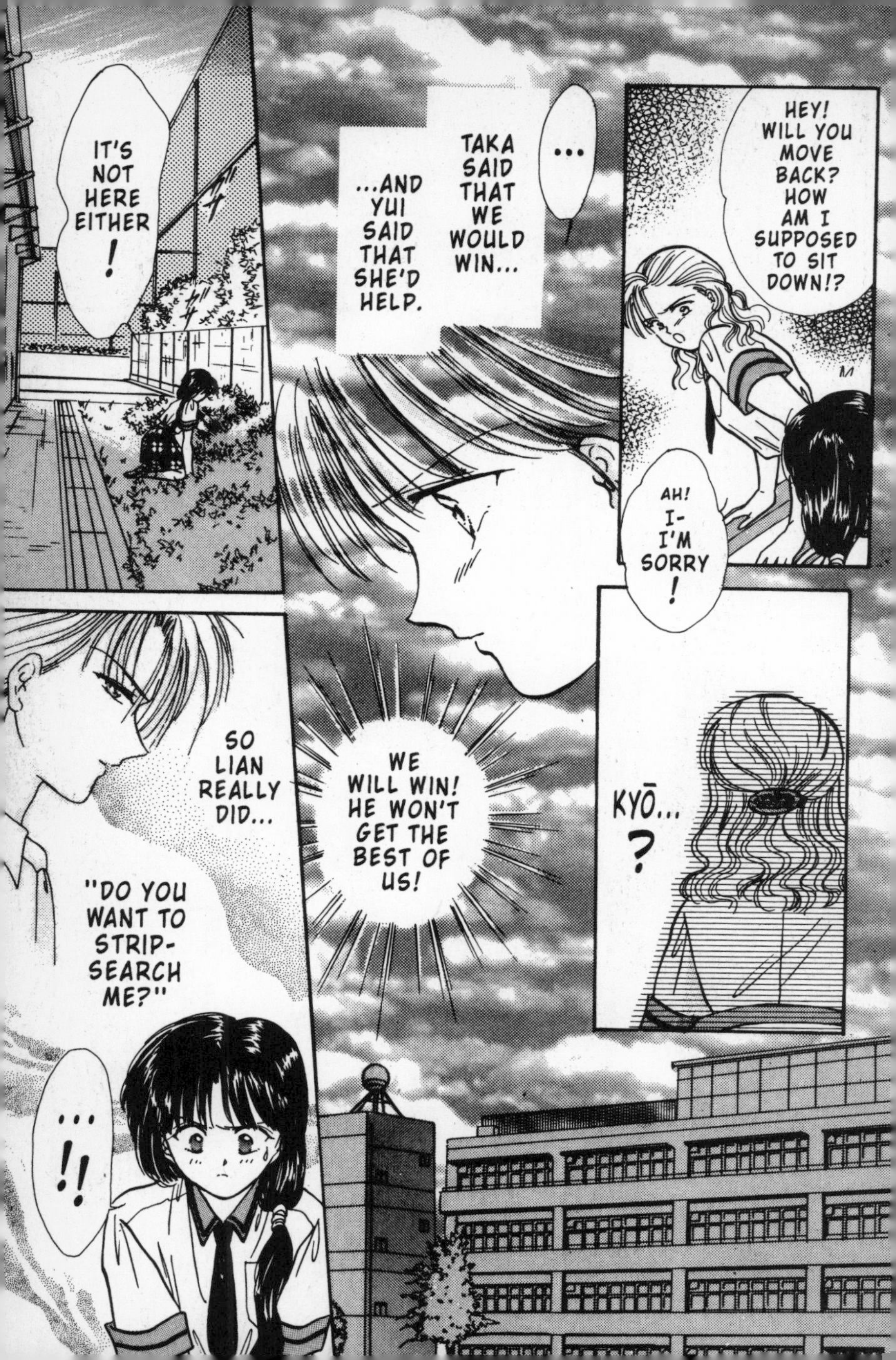
HEY! WILL YOU MOVE BACK? HOW AM I SUPPOSED TO SIT DOWN!?
AH! I- I'M SORRY!
...
TAKA SAID THAT WE WOULD WIN...
...AND YUI SAID THAT SHE'D HELP.
IT'S NOT HERE EITHER!
KYŌ...?
WE WILL WIN! HE WON'T GET THE BEST OF US!
SO LIAN REALLY DID...
"DO YOU WANT TO STRIP-SEARCH ME?"
...!!

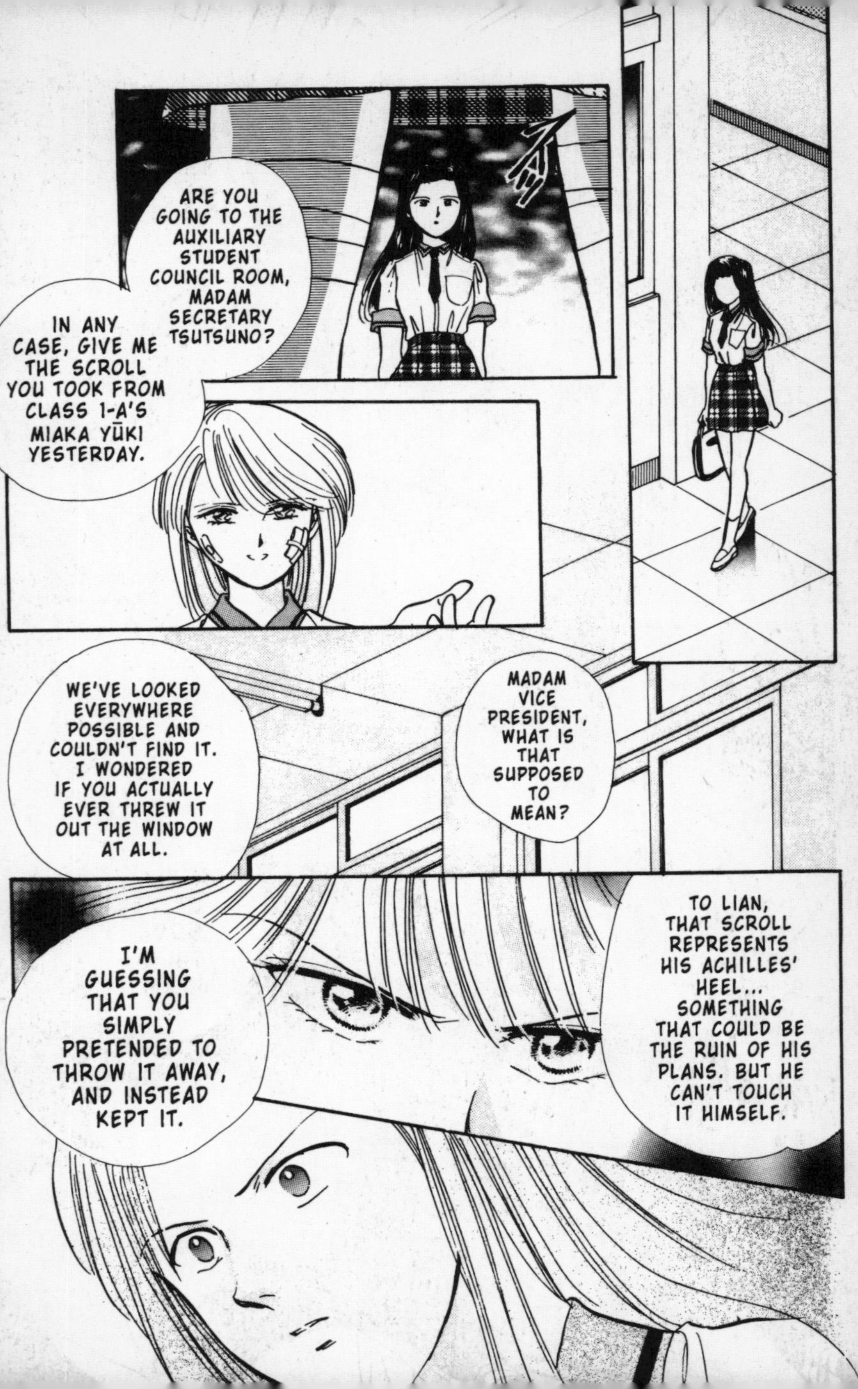

ARE YOU GOING TO THE AUXILIARY STUDENT COUNCIL ROOM, MADAM SECRETARY TSUTSUNO?
IN ANY CASE, GIVE ME THE SCROLL YOU TOOK FROM CLASS 1-A'S MIAKA YŪKI YESTERDAY.
MADAM VICE PRESIDENT, WHAT IS THAT SUPPOSED TO MEAN?
WE'VE LOOKED EVERYWHERE POSSIBLE AND COULDN'T FIND IT. I WONDERED IF YOU ACTUALLY EVER THREW IT OUT THE WINDOW AT ALL.
TO LIAN, THAT SCROLL REPRESENTS HIS ACHILLES' HEEL... SOMETHING THAT COULD BE THE RUIN OF HIS PLANS. BUT HE CAN'T TOUCH IT HIMSELF.
I'M GUESSING THAT YOU SIMPLY PRETENDED TO THROW IT AWAY, AND INSTEAD KEPT IT.

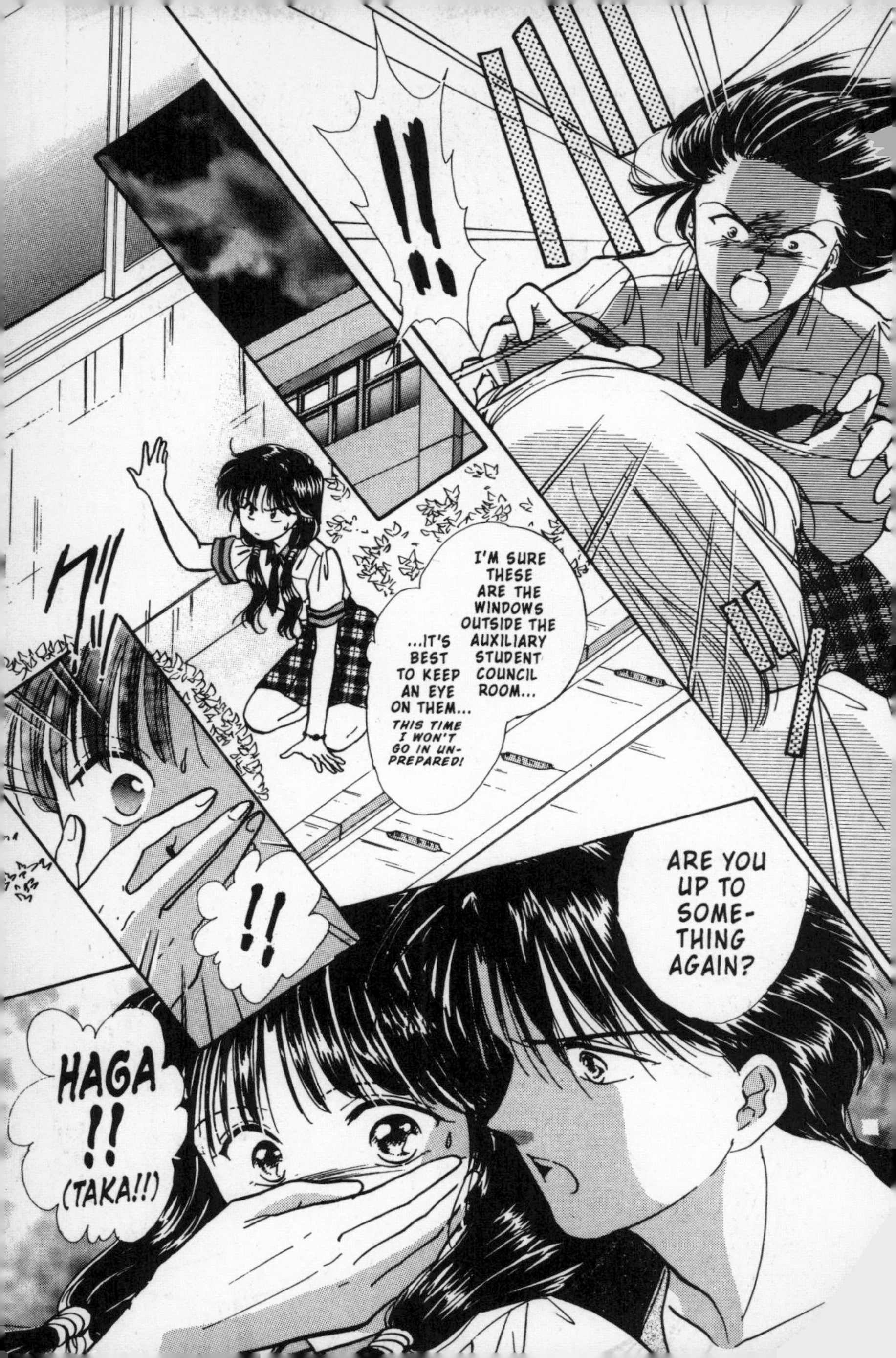
!!
I'M SURE THESE ARE THE WINDOWS OUTSIDE THE AUXILIARY STUDENT COUNCIL ROOM...
...IT'S BEST TO KEEP AN EYE ON THEM...
THIS TIME I WON'T GO IN UN-PREPARED!
!!
ARE YOU UP TO SOME-THING AGAIN?
HAGA !! (TAKA!!)

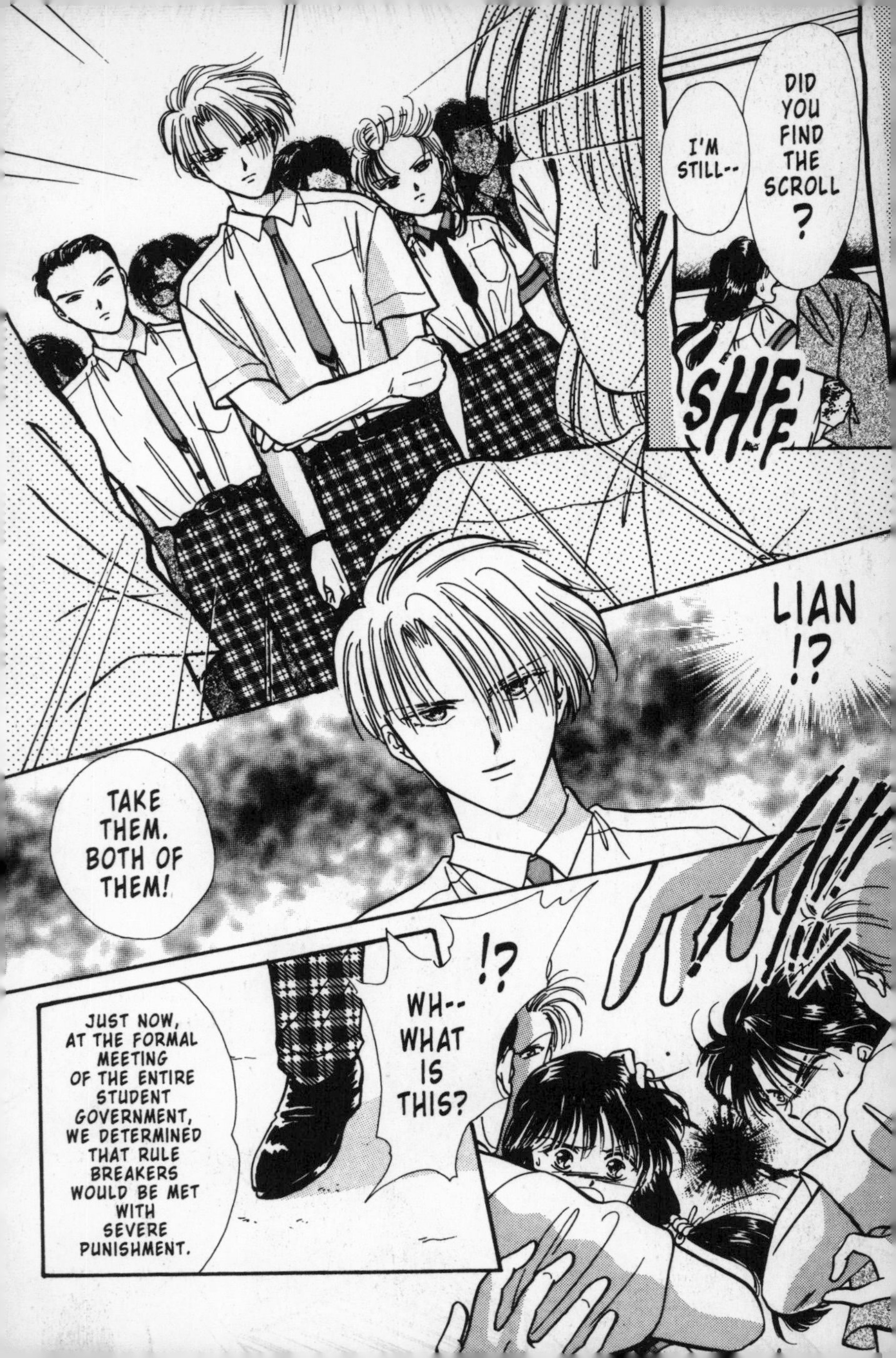
DID YOU FIND THE SCROLL?
I'M STILL--
SHFF
LIAN!?
TAKE THEM. BOTH OF THEM!
!?
WH-- WHAT IS THIS?
JUST NOW, AT THE FORMAL MEETING OF THE ENTIRE STUDENT GOVERNMENT, WE DETERMINED THAT RULE BREAKERS WOULD BE MET WITH SEVERE PUNISHMENT.

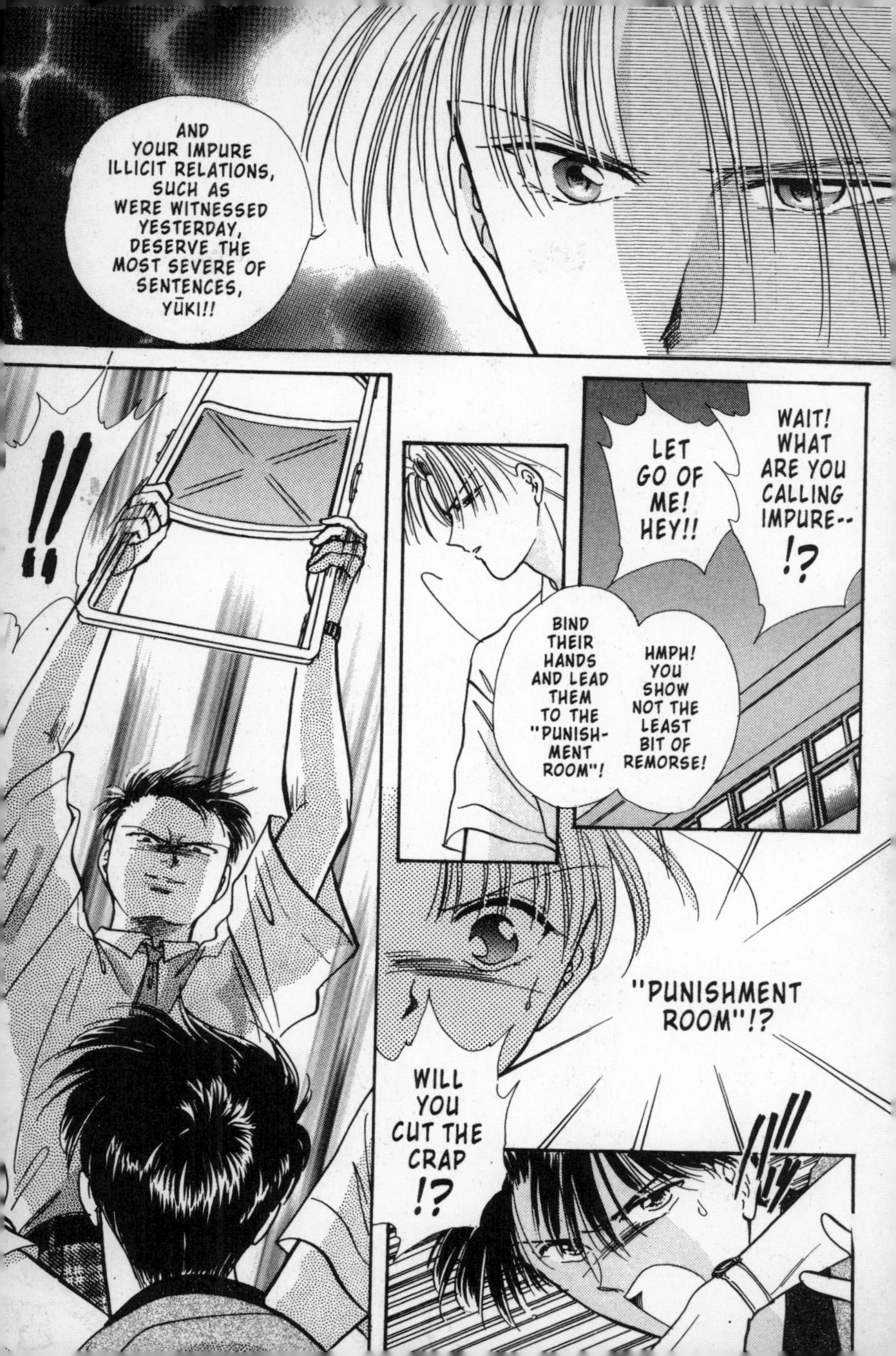
AND YOUR IMPURE ILLICIT RELATIONS, SUCH AS WERE WITNESSED YESTERDAY, DESERVE THE MOST SEVERE OF SENTENCES, YŪKI!!
WAIT! WHAT ARE YOU CALLING IMPURE--!?
LET GO OF ME! HEY!!
HMPH! YOU SHOW NOT THE LEAST BIT OF REMORSE!
BIND THEIR HANDS AND LEAD THEM TO THE "PUNISHMENT ROOM"!
"PUNISHMENT ROOM"!?
WILL YOU CUT THE CRAP !?
!!

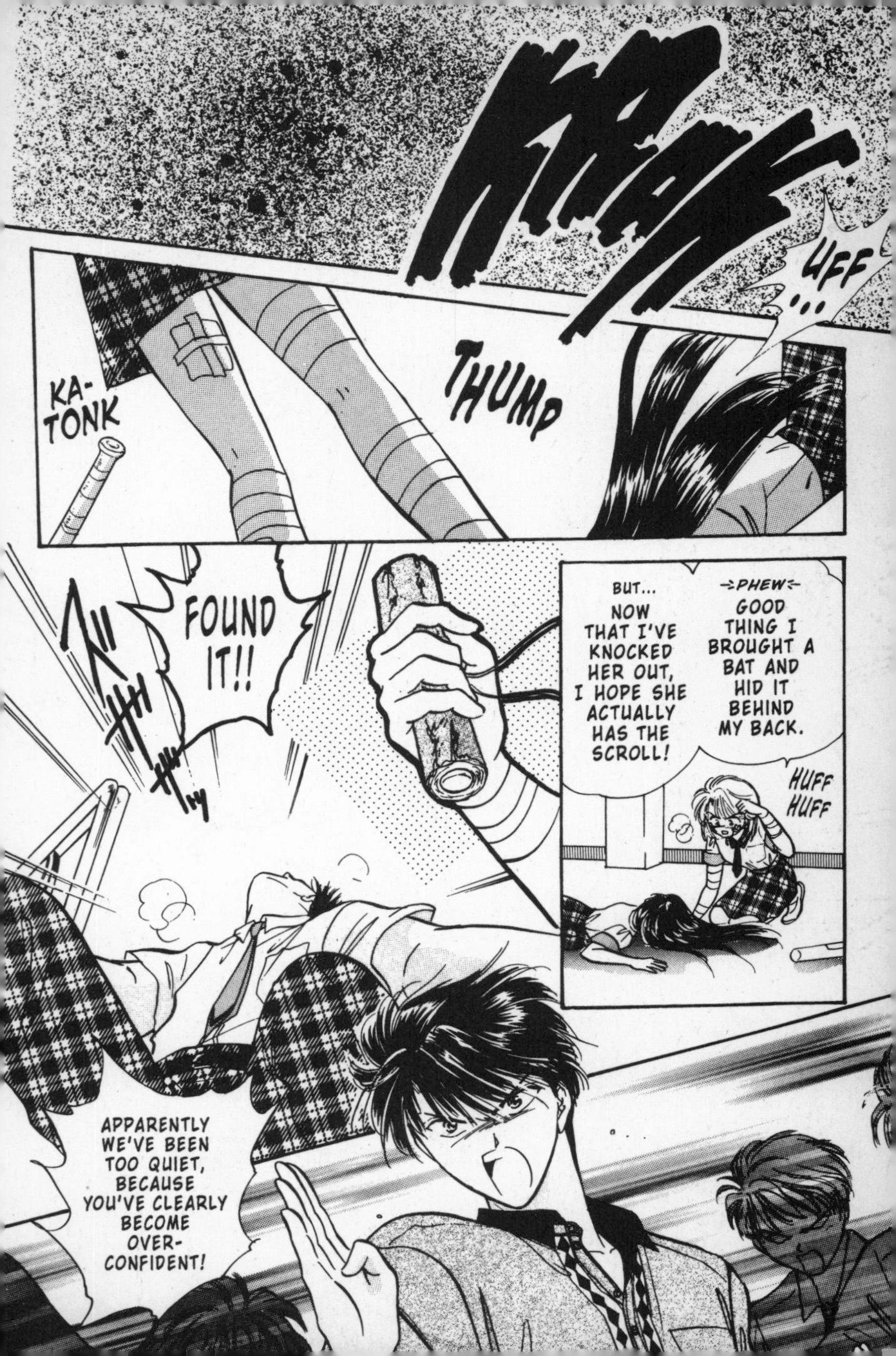

UFF...
THUMP
KA-TONK
-PHEW-
GOOD THING I BROUGHT A BAT AND HID IT BEHIND MY BACK.
BUT... NOW THAT I'VE KNOCKED HER OUT, I HOPE SHE ACTUALLY HAS THE SCROLL!
HUFF HUFF
FOUND IT!!
APPARENTLY WE'VE BEEN TOO QUIET, BECAUSE YOU'VE CLEARLY BECOME OVER-CONFIDENT!

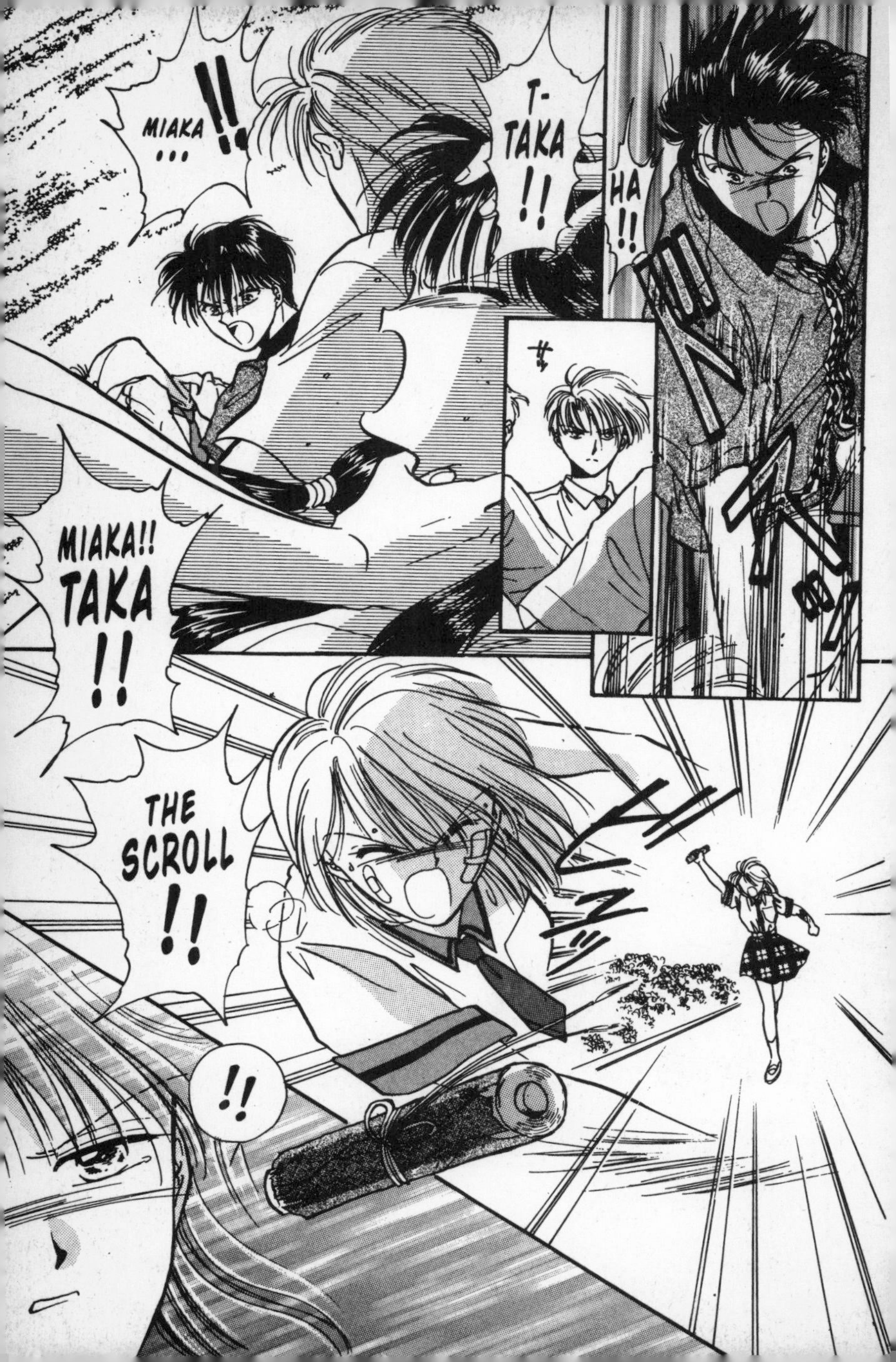
HA!!
T-TAKA!!
MIAKA... !!
MIAKA!! TAKA!!
THE SCROLL!!
!!

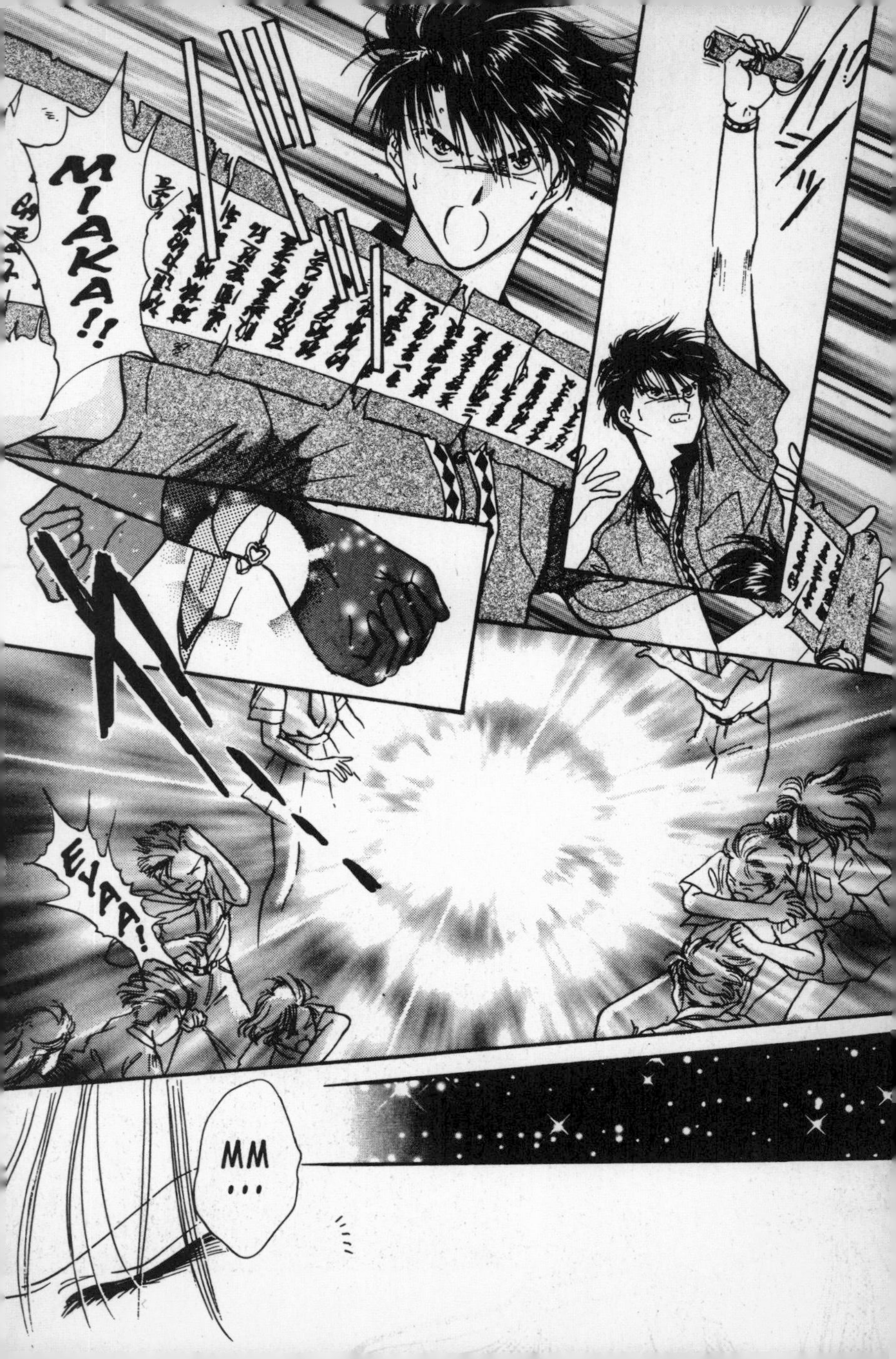
MIAKA!!
EYAA!
MM ...

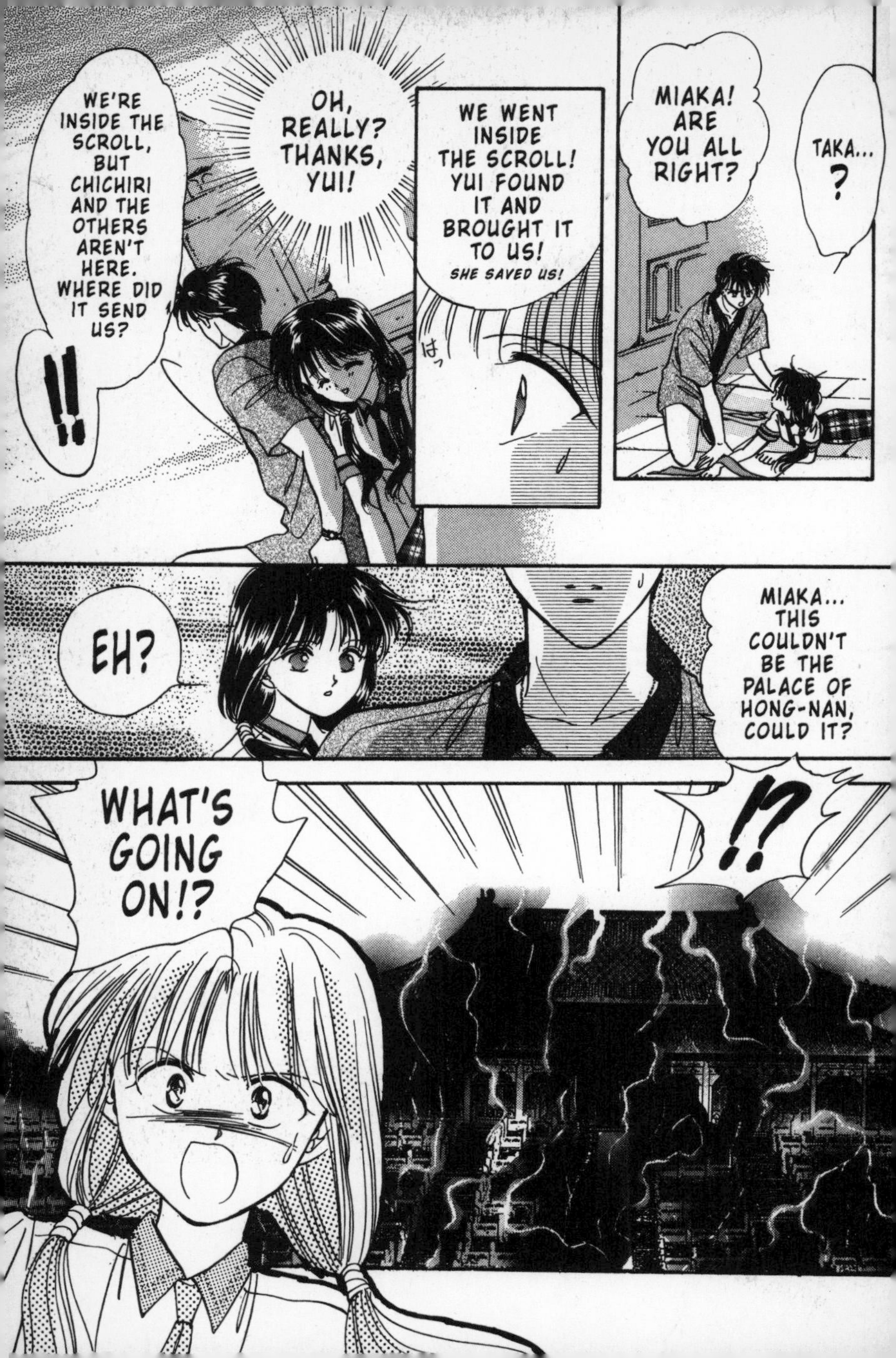
TAKA... ?
MIAKA! ARE YOU ALL RIGHT?
WE WENT INSIDE THE SCROLL! YUI FOUND IT AND BROUGHT IT TO US! SHE SAVED US!
はっ
OH, REALLY? THANKS, YUI!
WE'RE INSIDE THE SCROLL, BUT CHICHIRI AND THE OTHERS AREN'T HERE. WHERE DID IT SEND US?
!!
MIAKA... THIS COULDN'T BE THE PALACE OF HONG-NAN, COULD IT?
EH?
!?
WHAT'S GOING ON!?

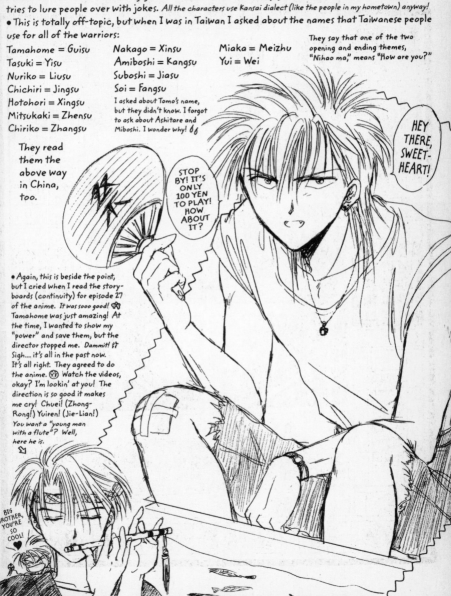

*There is no "Fushigi Akugi" for this volume! I'm back at my family home in the country, and I don't have copies to do the parody from!

• I just went to a local festival, and this image floated into my mind... ⇩ It's Tasuki as a booth worker at one of those "fishing game" stands... he looks really good! He'd be the kind of guy who tries to lure people over with jokes. *All the characters use Kansai dialect (like the people in my hometown) anyway!*

• This is totally off-topic, but when I was in Taiwan I asked about the names that Taiwanese people use for all of the warriors:

Tamahome = Guisu
Tasuki = Yisu
Nuriko = Liusu
Chichiri = Jingsu
Hotohori = Xingsu
Mitsukaki = Zhensu
Chiriko = Zhangsu

Nakago = Xinsu
Amiboshi = Kangsu
Suboshi = Jiasu
Soi = Fangsu

I asked about Tomo's name, but they didn't know. I forgot to ask about Ashitare and Miboshi. I wonder why!

Miaka = Meizhu
Yui = Wei

They say that one of the two opening and ending themes, "Nihao ma," means "How are you?"

They read them the above way in China, too.

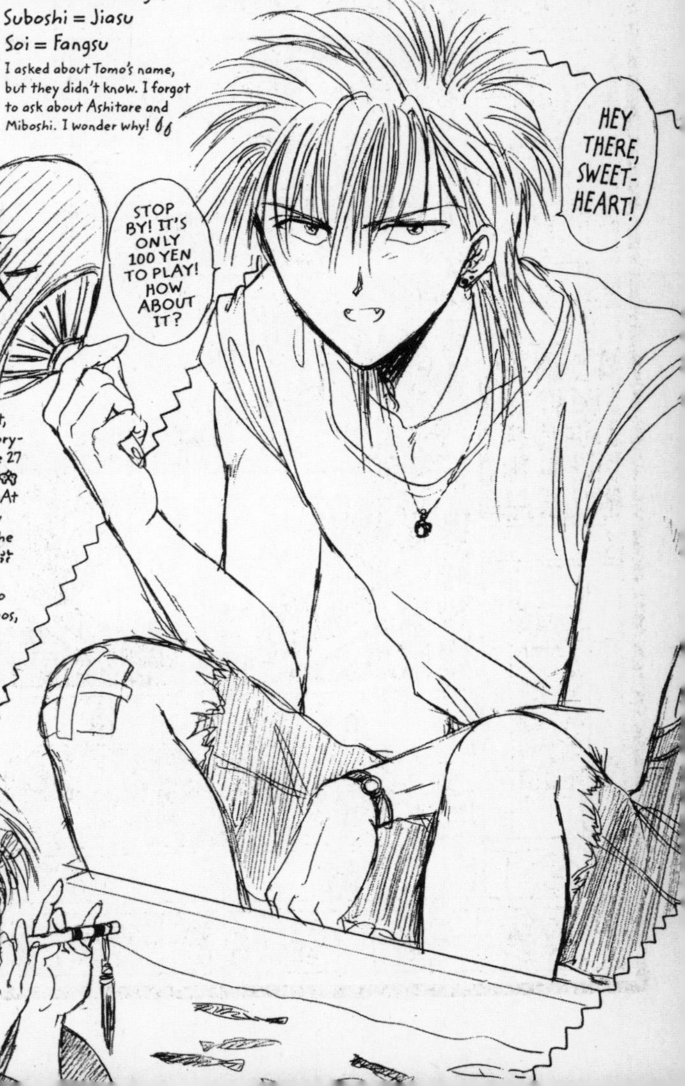
HEY THERE, SWEET-HEART!
STOP BY! IT'S ONLY 100 YEN TO PLAY! HOW ABOUT IT?

• Again, this is beside the point, but I cried when I read the story-boards (continuity) for episode 27 of the anime. *It was sooo good!* Tamahome was just amazing! At the time, I wanted to show my "power" and save them, but the director stopped me. *Dammit!* Sigh... it's all in the past now. It's all right. They agreed to do the anime. Watch the videos, okay? I'm lookin' at you! The direction is so good it makes me cry! Chuei! (Zhong-Rong!) Yuiren! (Jie-Lian!) *You want a "young man with a flute"? Well, here he is.* ⇩

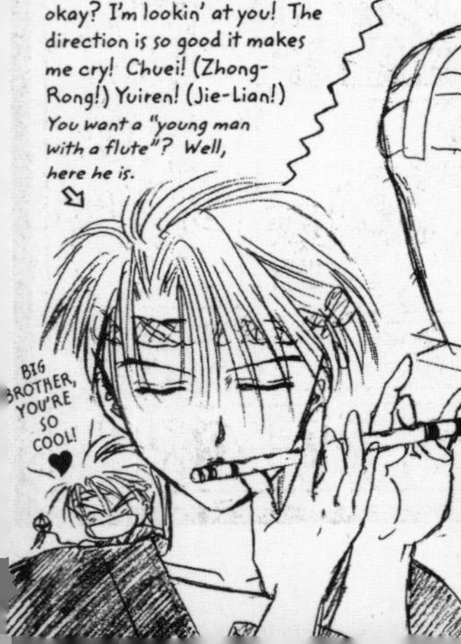
BIG BROTHER, YOU'RE SO COOL! ♥

CHAPTER EIGHTY-EIGHT

SENTIMENTAL TEARS

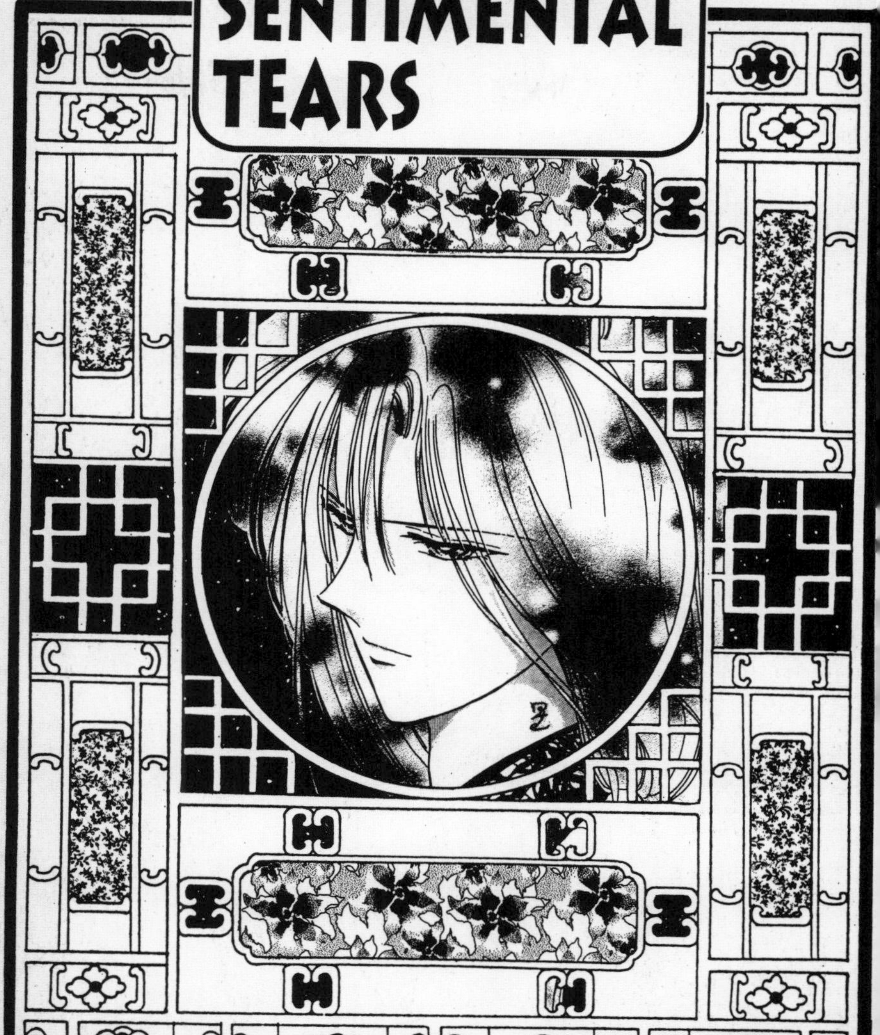

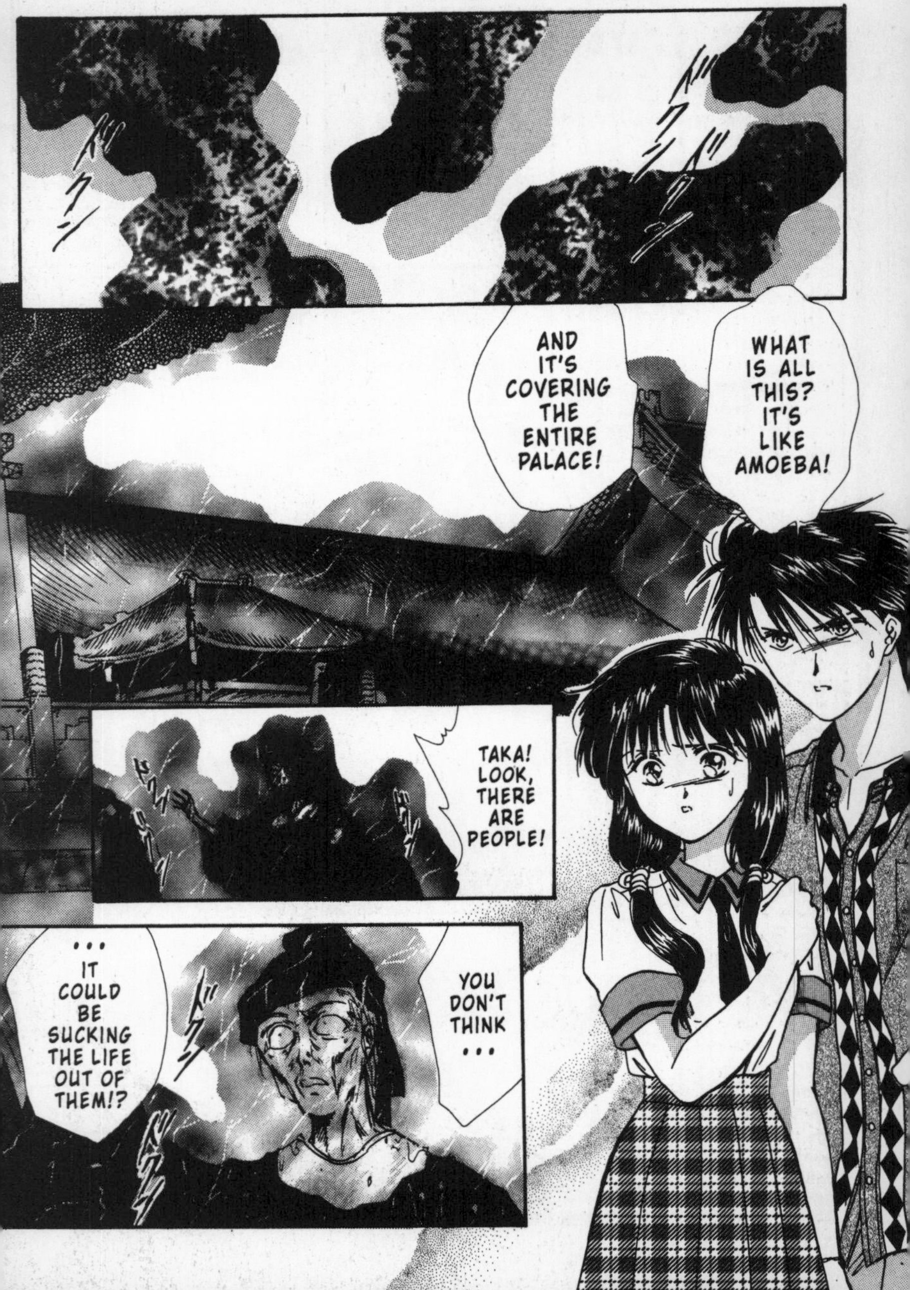
WHAT IS ALL THIS? IT'S LIKE AMOEBA!
AND IT'S COVERING THE ENTIRE PALACE!
TAKA! LOOK, THERE ARE PEOPLE!
YOU DON'T THINK ...
... IT COULD BE SUCKING THE LIFE OUT OF THEM!?

Fushigi Yûgi∾15

So as for the signing itself, I just want to tell you, Japan, that when it comes to crazy fannishness, you've been surpassed! ♪ It was incredible! The Taiwanese fans did their best to say in Japanese, "I love your manga and bought all of the books!" And more than just a few! A whole lot talked to me! At Japanese signings, I'm the one to thank the fans, but in Taiwan, there were a whole lot of people who smiled and said, "Arigatō Gozaimasu!" ("Thank you" in Japanese.) There were even some fans who were in tears when I gave them my signature. Also, there were a whole lot of guys. From the very first person in line, and all the way down, I had to wonder, "Are guys my only fans in Taiwan?" They cut the number off at 300, but nearly 1/3 of them were guys (there were a lot of kids, too). I still have a lot to say, but I'm running out of space, so I'll save it for next time.

Now, we'll be putting out a calendar this year, too. But as I mentioned earlier, there was so much to do this summer, there will only be four new art pieces in the calendar. *Same as usual, huh?* But I put my best effort into those! And there's going to be a calendar of anime images, too. I wonder what kind of images they will use! ♥♥ Whichever one you buy will make me happy.
The new CD book will be coming out in November (1995). Once again, there's new material from 135 and from Junko Ueno! *Yaaay!!* The God Suzaku theme is so cool! (I've only heard a demo version of it.) *I wanted them to use it for the anime, but they say that they can't.* Now, when I'm finished here, I'm going to head back to the country! *It's all decided!* I plan to have my first fun vacation in a while! Until next time...
BGM: Macross Plus "Information High"

Ms. Kanno's music is so good! 9/11

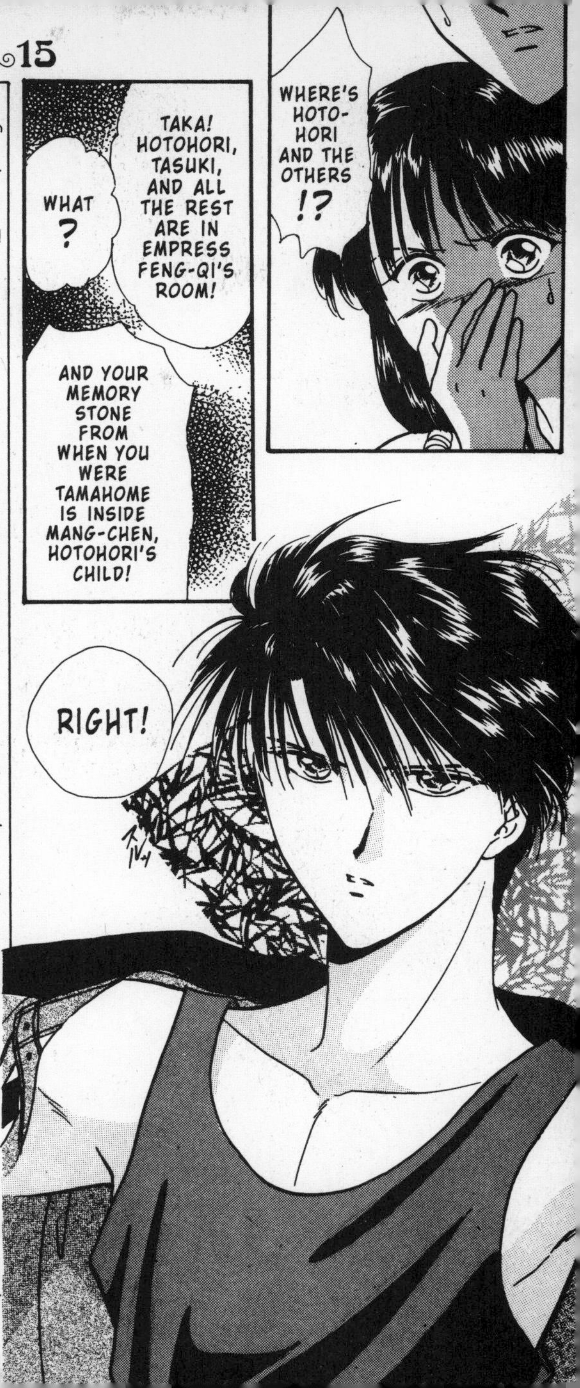
WHERE'S HOTOHORI AND THE OTHERS !?
TAKA! HOTOHORI, TASUKI, AND ALL THE REST ARE IN EMPRESS FENG-QI'S ROOM!
WHAT ?
AND YOUR MEMORY STONE FROM WHEN YOU WERE TAMAHOME IS INSIDE MANG-CHEN, HOTOHORI'S CHILD!
RIGHT!

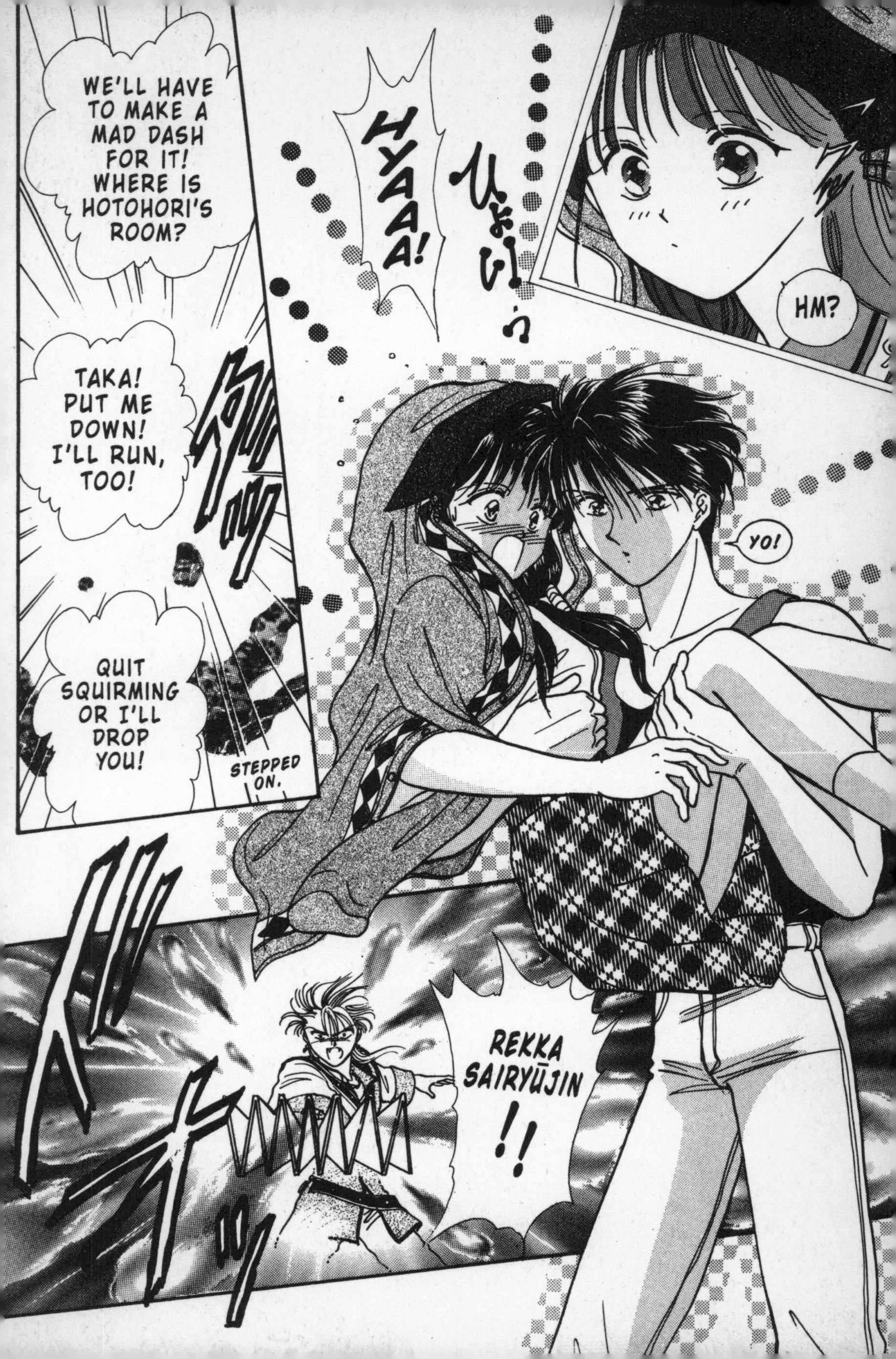

HM?
YO!
HYAAA!
ひょい
WE'LL HAVE TO MAKE A MAD DASH FOR IT! WHERE IS HOTOHORI'S ROOM?
TAKA! PUT ME DOWN! I'LL RUN, TOO!
QUIT SQUIRMING OR I'LL DROP YOU!
STEPPED ON.
REKKA SAIRYŪJIN !!

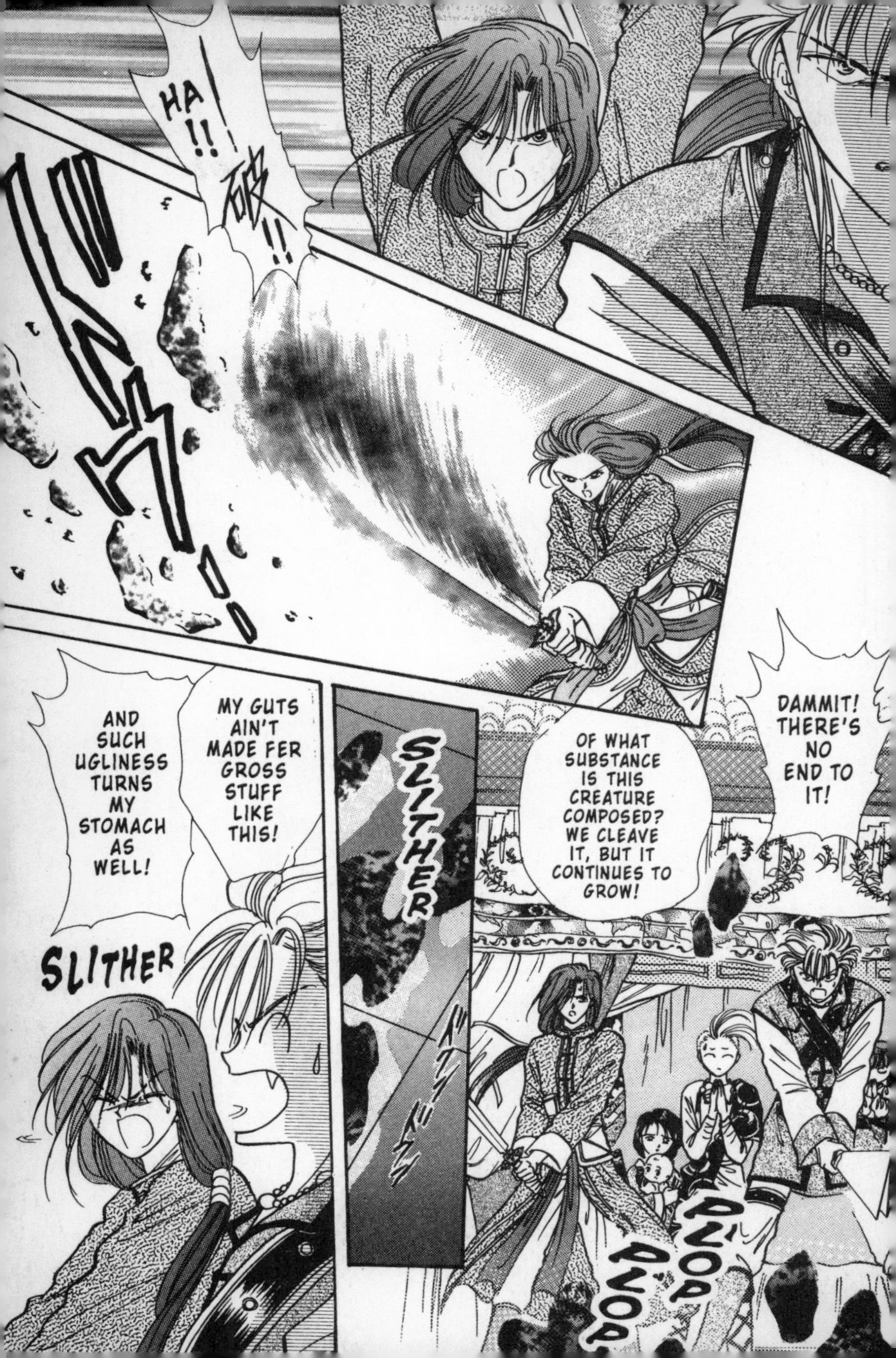
HA!! 破!!
DAMMIT! THERE'S NO END TO IT!
OF WHAT SUBSTANCE IS THIS CREATURE COMPOSED? WE CLEAVE IT, BUT IT CONTINUES TO GROW!
PLOP PLOP PLOP
SLITHER
MY GUTS AIN'T MADE FER GROSS STUFF LIKE THIS!
AND SUCH UGLINESS TURNS MY STOMACH AS WELL!
SLITHER

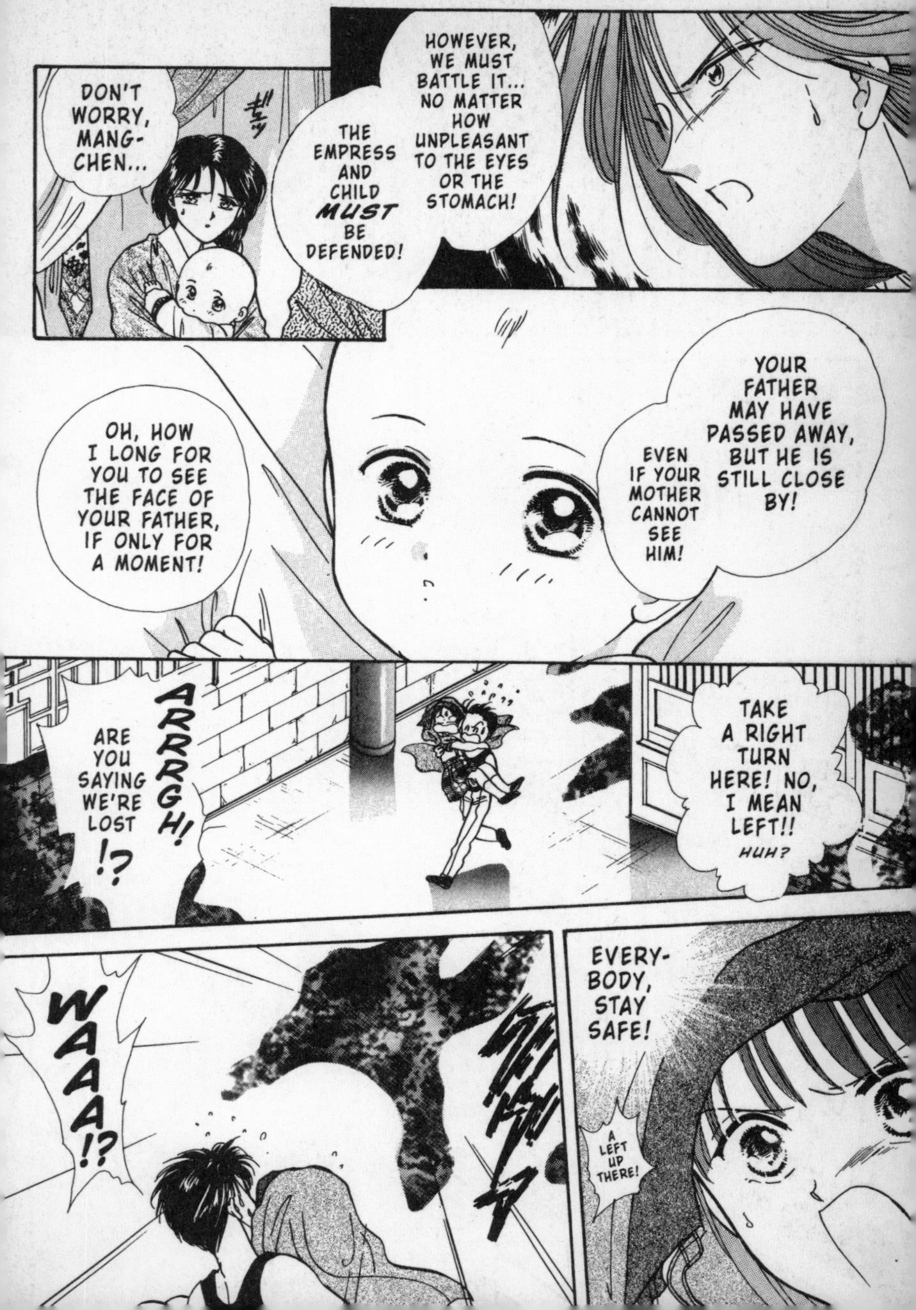
HOWEVER, WE MUST BATTLE IT... NO MATTER HOW UNPLEASANT TO THE EYES OR THE STOMACH!
THE EMPRESS AND CHILD MUST BE DEFENDED!
DON'T WORRY, MANG-CHEN...
YOUR FATHER MAY HAVE PASSED AWAY, BUT HE IS STILL CLOSE BY!
EVEN IF YOUR MOTHER CANNOT SEE HIM!
OH, HOW I LONG FOR YOU TO SEE THE FACE OF YOUR FATHER, IF ONLY FOR A MOMENT!
TAKE A RIGHT TURN HERE! NO, I MEAN LEFT!!
HUH?
ARRRGH!
ARE YOU SAYING WE'RE LOST !?
EVERY-BODY, STAY SAFE!
A LEFT UP THERE!
WAAAA!?

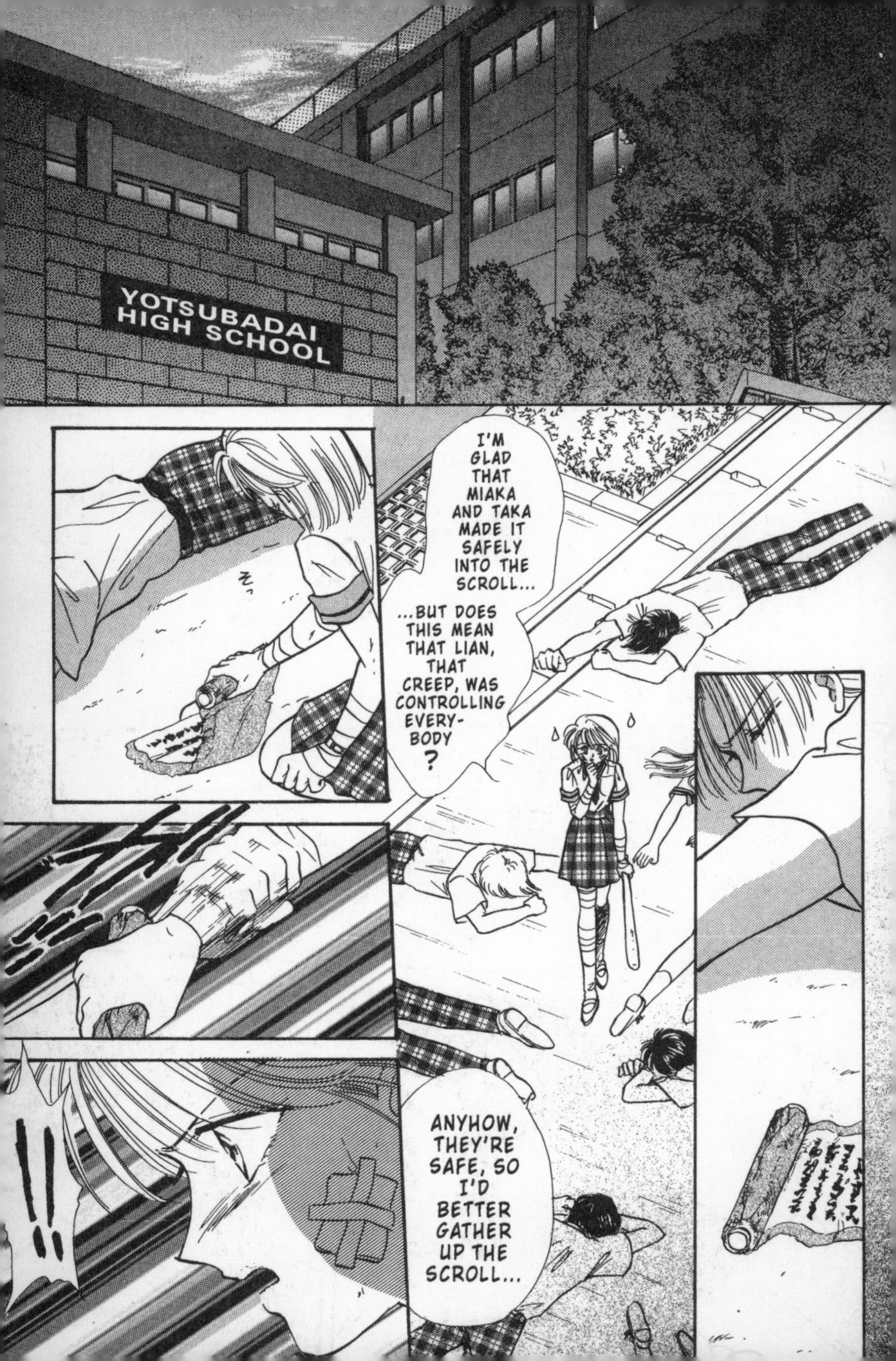
YOTSUBADAI HIGH SCHOOL
I'M GLAD THAT MIAKA AND TAKA MADE IT SAFELY INTO THE SCROLL...
...BUT DOES THIS MEAN THAT LIAN, THAT CREEP, WAS CONTROLLING EVERY-BODY?
ANYHOW, THEY'RE SAFE, SO I'D BETTER GATHER UP THE SCROLL...
!!

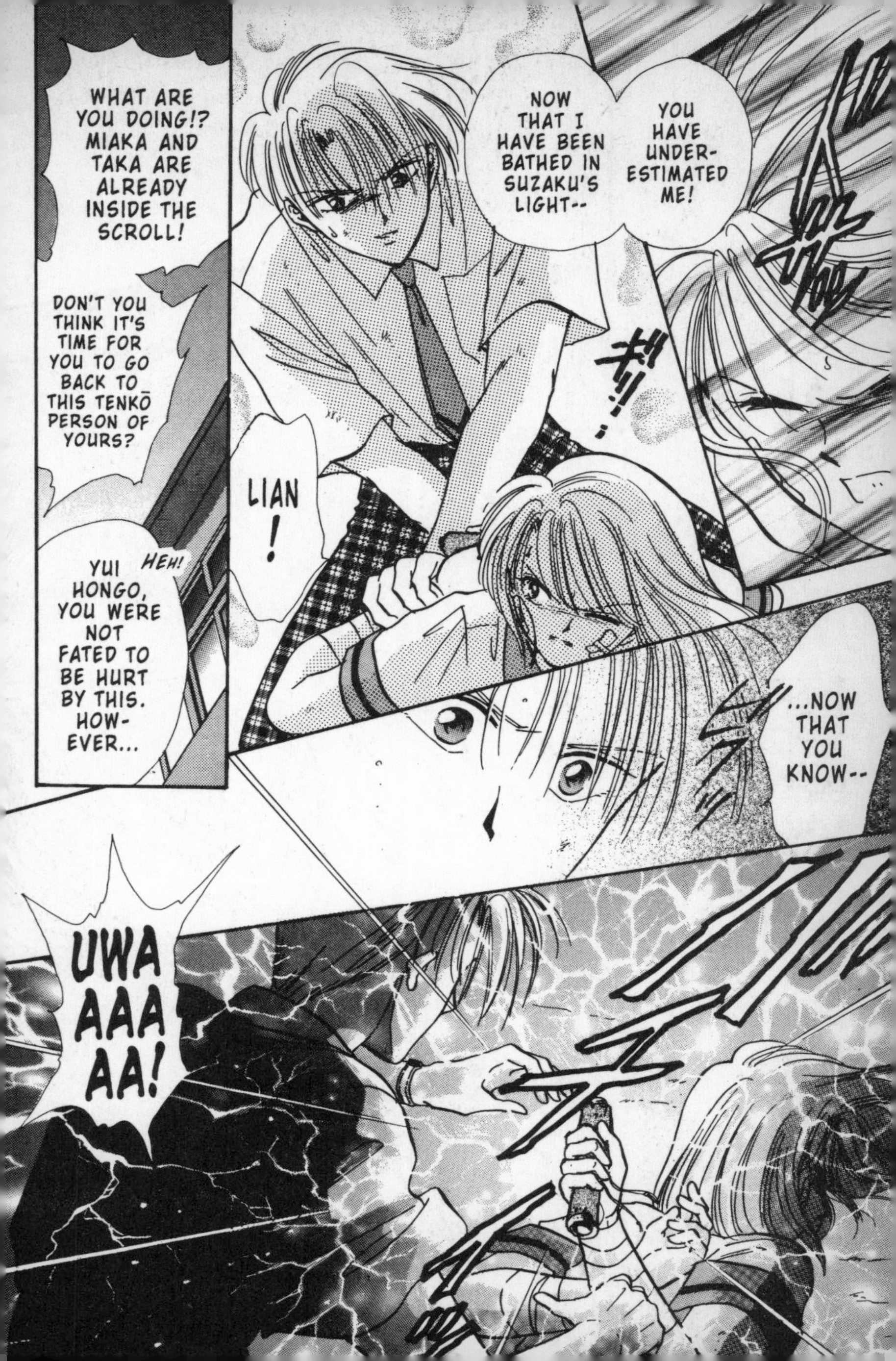
...
YOU HAVE UNDER-ESTIMATED ME!
NOW THAT I HAVE BEEN BATHED IN SUZAKU'S LIGHT--
LIAN!
WHAT ARE YOU DOING!? MIAKA AND TAKA ARE ALREADY INSIDE THE SCROLL!
DON'T YOU THINK IT'S TIME FOR YOU TO GO BACK TO THIS TENKŌ PERSON OF YOURS?
HEH!
YUI HONGO, YOU WERE NOT FATED TO BE HURT BY THIS. HOW-EVER...
...NOW THAT YOU KNOW--
UWA AAA AA!

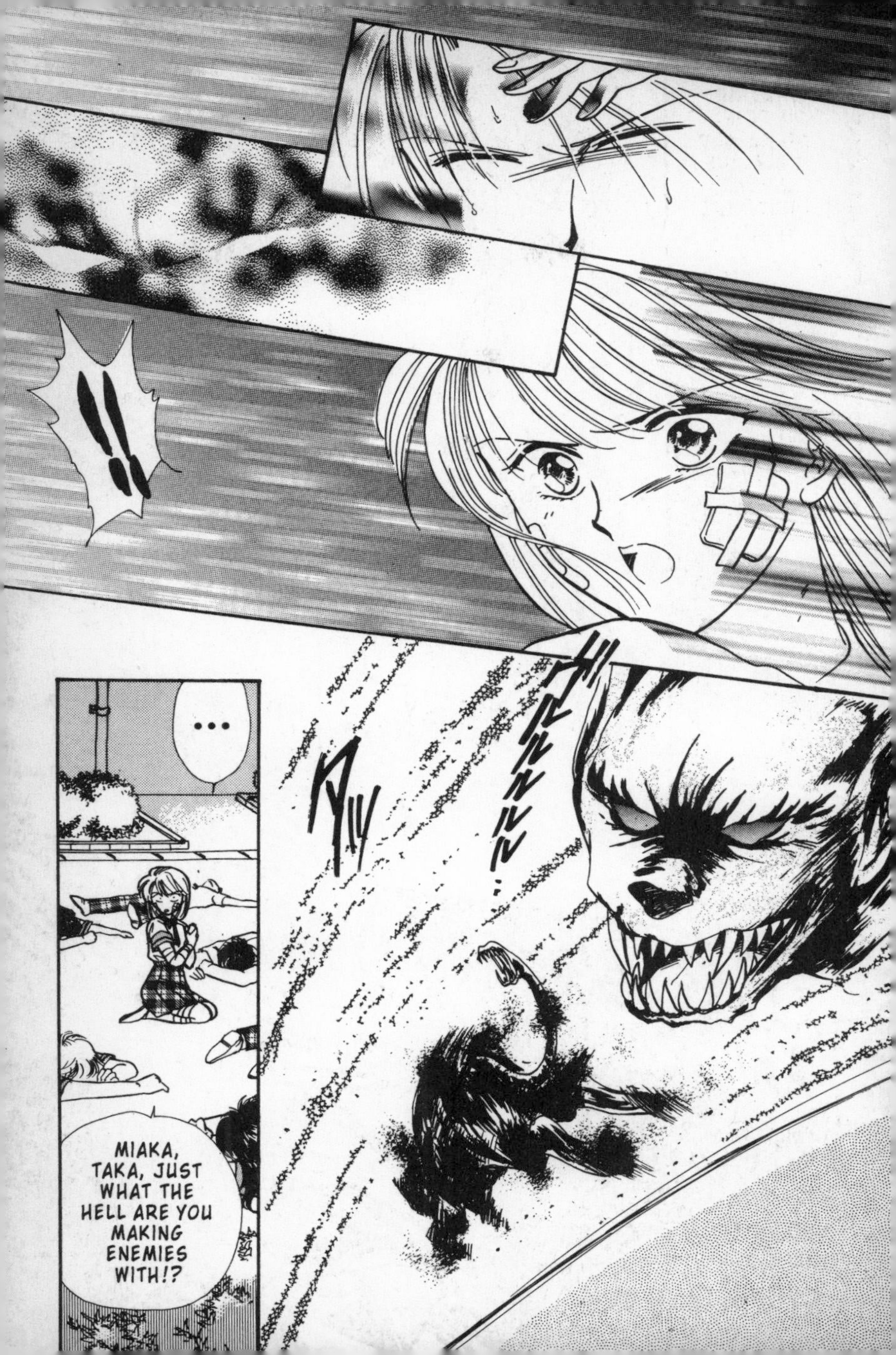
!!
...
MIAKA, TAKA, JUST WHAT THE HELL ARE YOU MAKING ENEMIES WITH!?

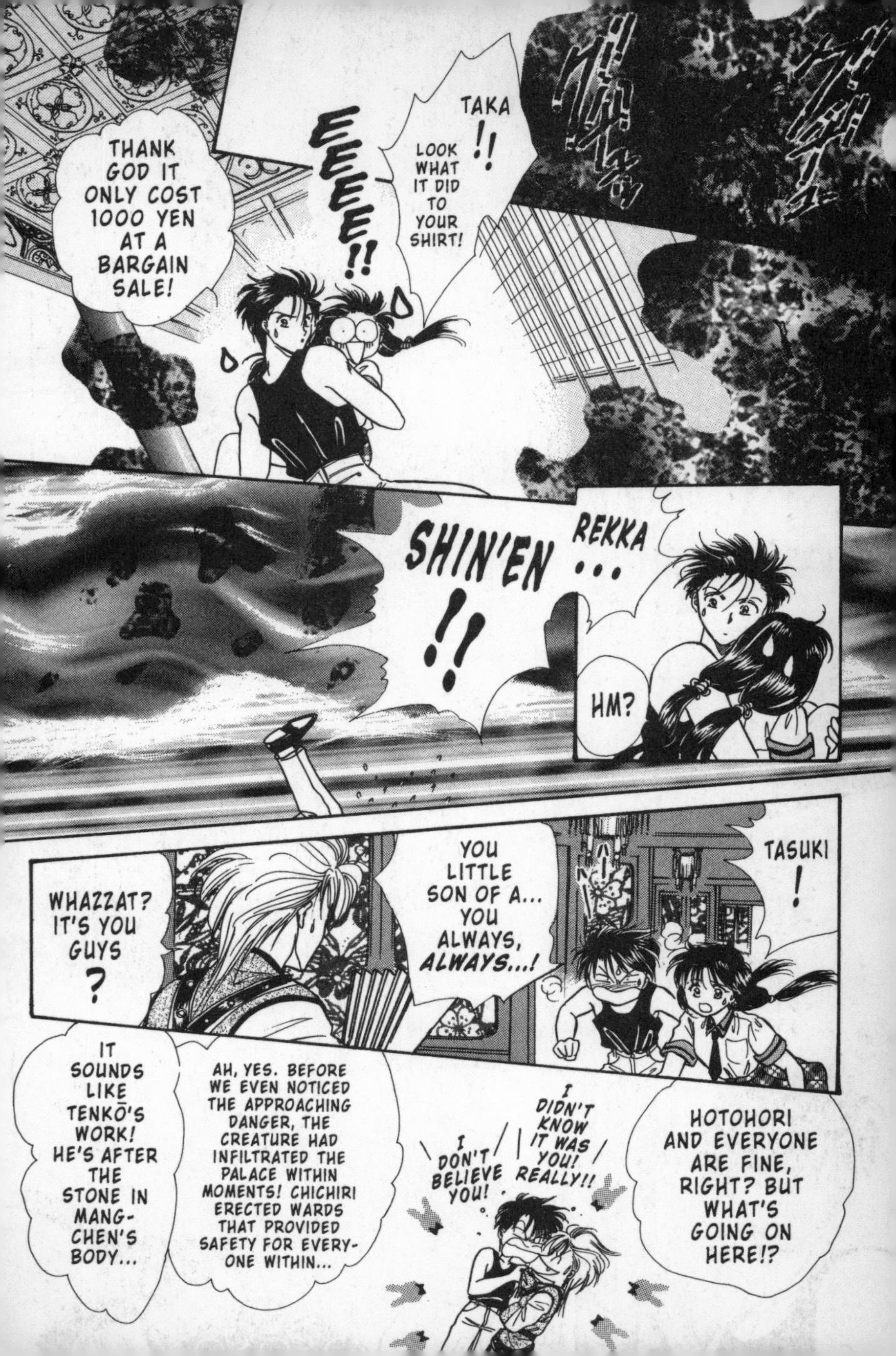

TAKA!!
LOOK WHAT IT DID TO YOUR SHIRT!
EEEE!!
THANK GOD IT ONLY COST 1000 YEN AT A BARGAIN SALE!
REKKA...
SHIN'EN!!
HM?
TASUKI!
YOU LITTLE SON OF A... YOU ALWAYS, *ALWAYS...!*
WHAZZAT? IT'S YOU GUYS?
HOTOHORI AND EVERYONE ARE FINE, RIGHT? BUT WHAT'S GOING ON HERE!?
I DIDN'T KNOW IT WAS YOU! REALLY!!
I DON'T BELIEVE YOU!
AH, YES. BEFORE WE EVEN NOTICED THE APPROACHING DANGER, THE CREATURE HAD INFILTRATED THE PALACE WITHIN MOMENTS! CHICHIRI ERECTED WARDS THAT PROVIDED SAFETY FOR EVERYONE WITHIN...
IT SOUNDS LIKE TENKŌ'S WORK! HE'S AFTER THE STONE IN MANG-CHEN'S BODY...

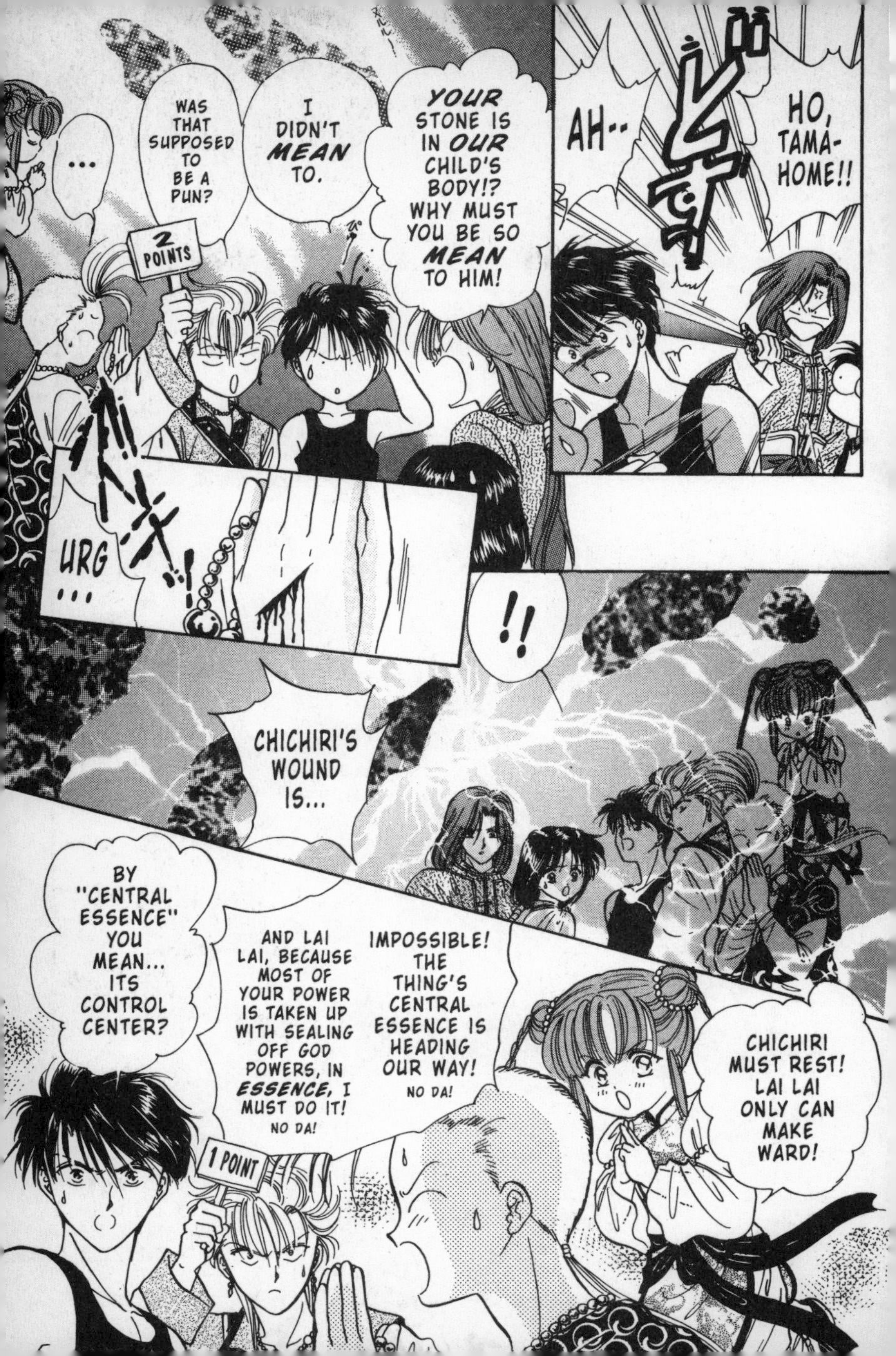
HO, TAMA-HOME!!
AH..
YOUR STONE IS IN OUR CHILD'S BODY!? WHY MUST YOU BE SO MEAN TO HIM!
I DIDN'T MEAN TO.
WAS THAT SUPPOSED TO BE A PUN?
...
2 POINTS
URG...
!!
CHICHIRI'S WOUND IS...
CHICHIRI MUST REST! LAI LAI ONLY CAN MAKE WARD!
IMPOSSIBLE! THE THING'S CENTRAL ESSENCE IS HEADING OUR WAY! NO DA!
AND LAI LAI, BECAUSE MOST OF YOUR POWER IS TAKEN UP WITH SEALING OFF GOD POWERS, IN ESSENCE, I MUST DO IT! NO DA!
BY "CENTRAL ESSENCE" YOU MEAN... ITS CONTROL CENTER?
1 POINT

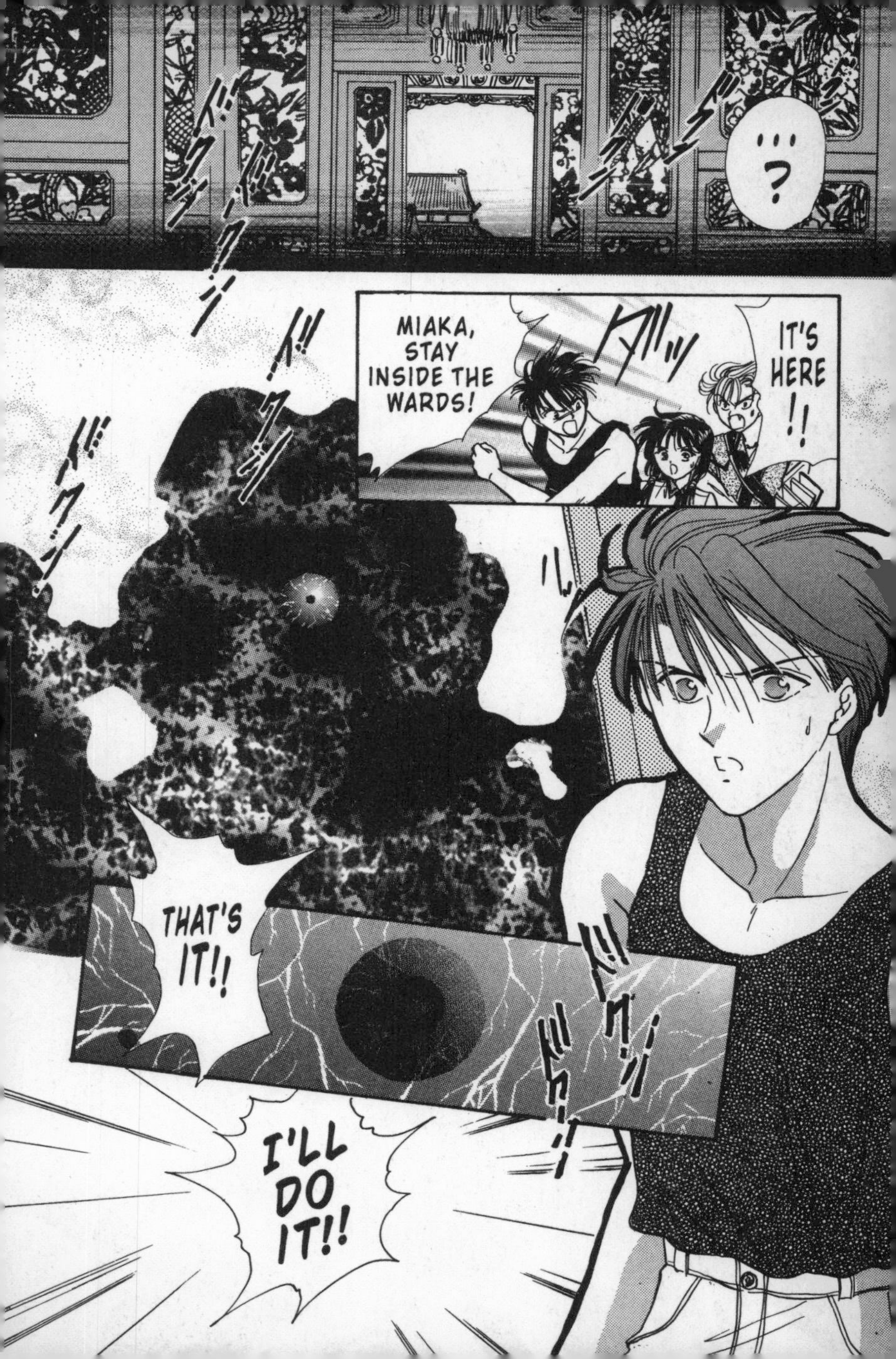
…?
IT'S HERE!!
MIAKA, STAY INSIDE THE WARDS!
THAT'S IT!!
I'LL DO IT!!

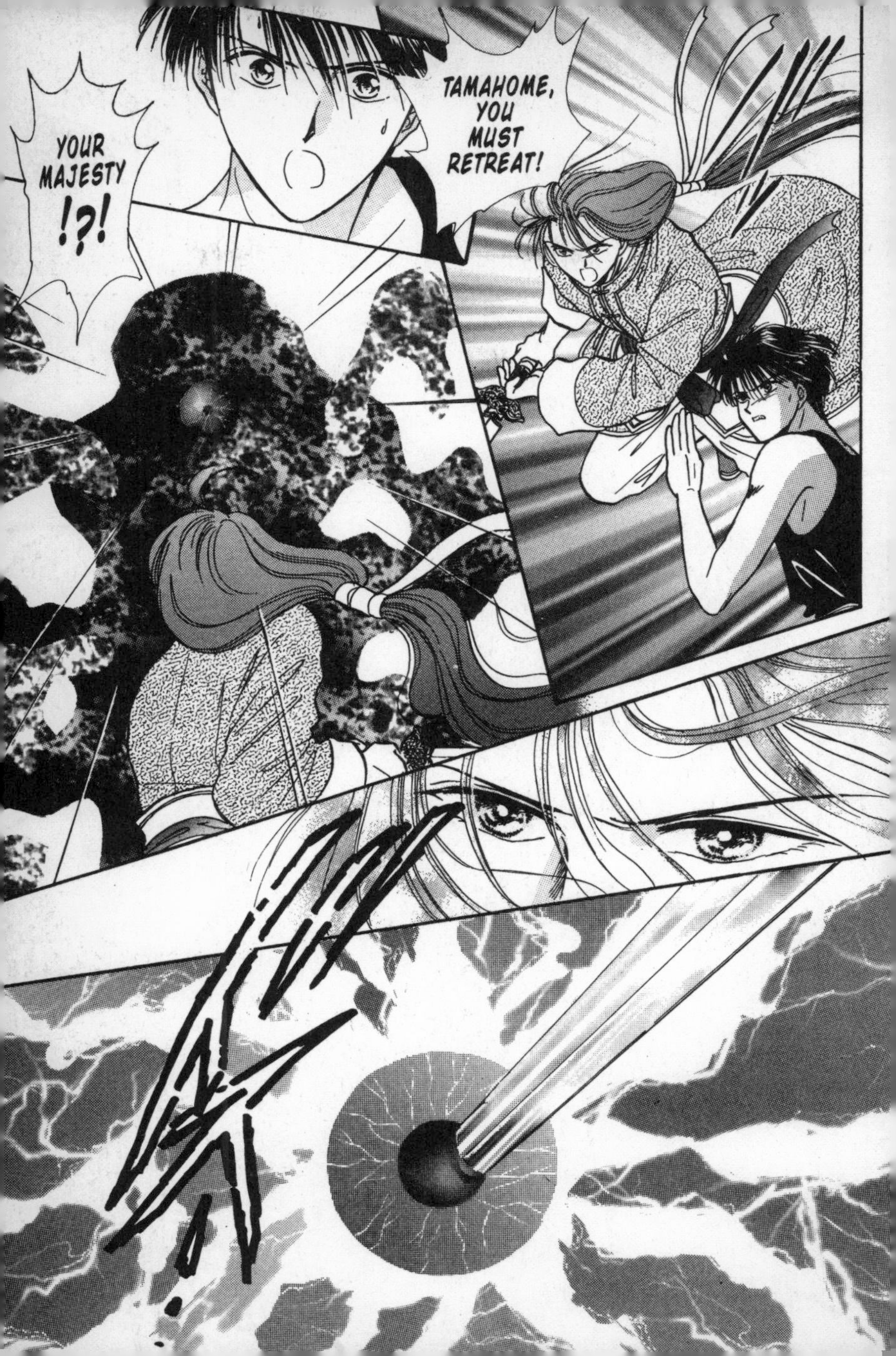
TAMAHOME, YOU MUST RETREAT!
YOUR MAJESTY !?!

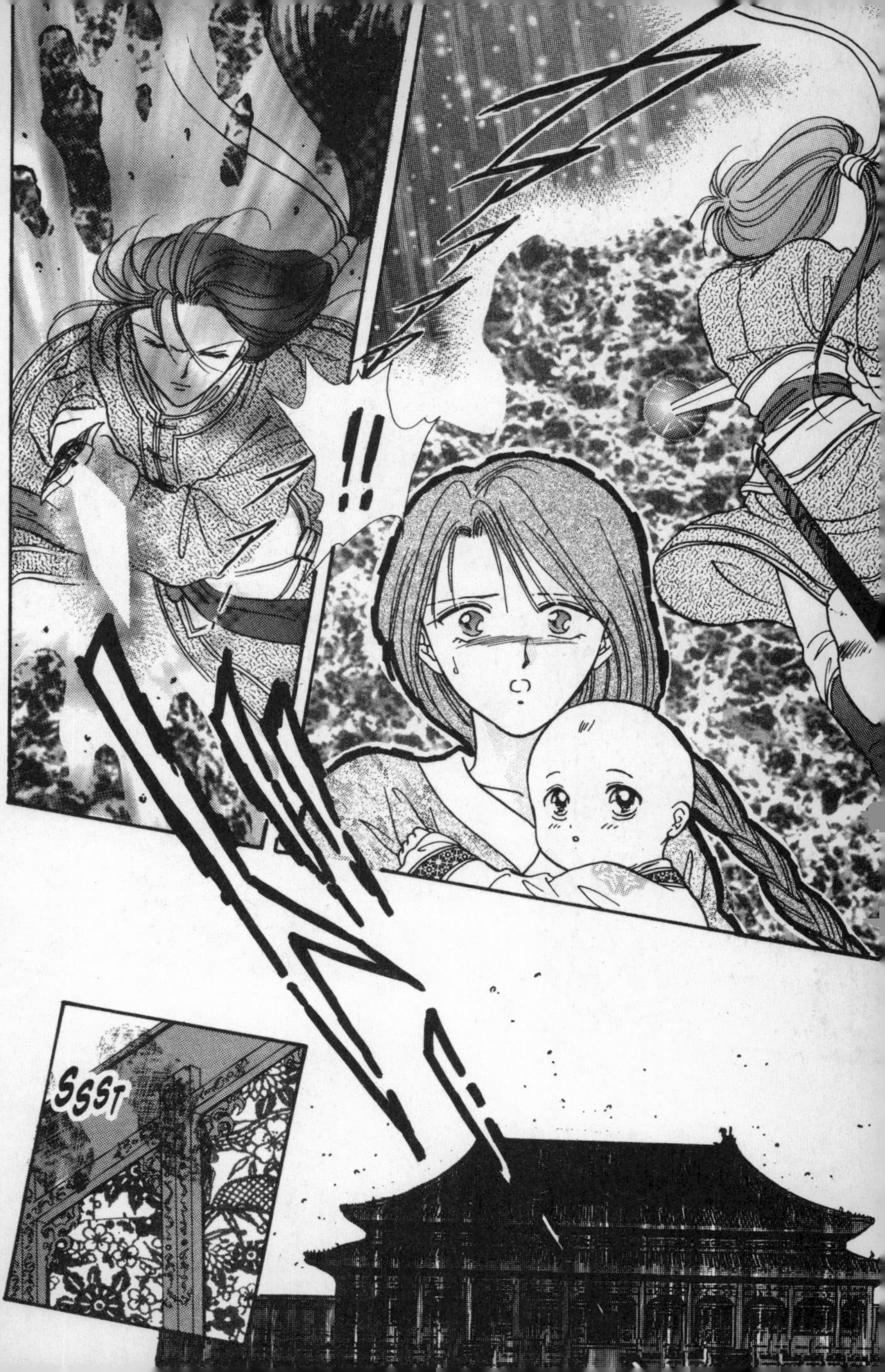

!!
SSST

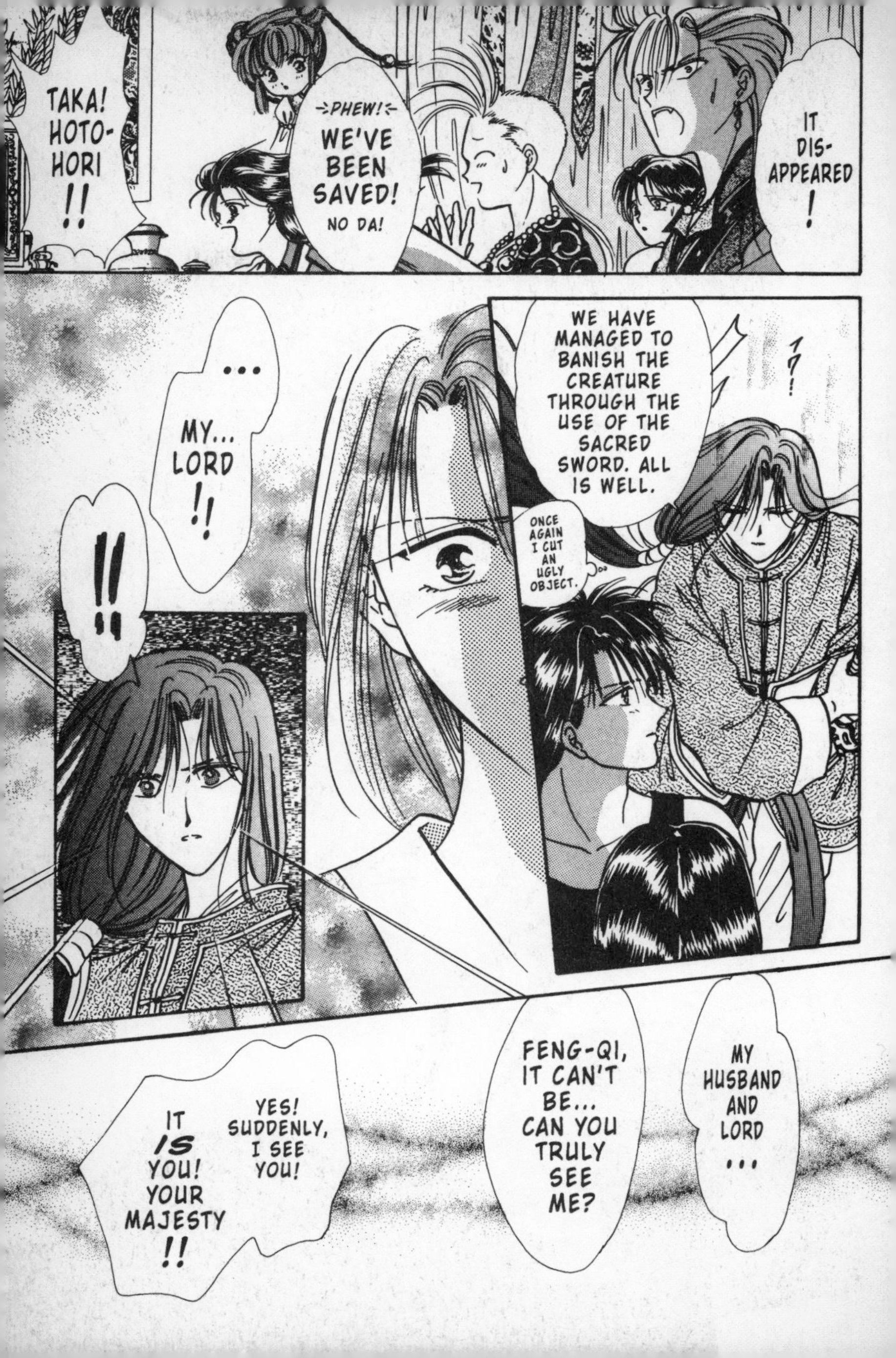
IT DIS-APPEARED!
-PHEW!- WE'VE BEEN SAVED! NO DA!
TAKA! HOTO-HORI!!
WE HAVE MANAGED TO BANISH THE CREATURE THROUGH THE USE OF THE SACRED SWORD. ALL IS WELL.
ONCE AGAIN I CUT AN UGLY OBJECT.
... MY... LORD !!
!!
MY HUSBAND AND LORD ...
FENG-QI, IT CAN'T BE... CAN YOU TRULY SEE ME?
YES! SUDDENLY, I SEE YOU!
IT IS YOU! YOUR MAJESTY !!

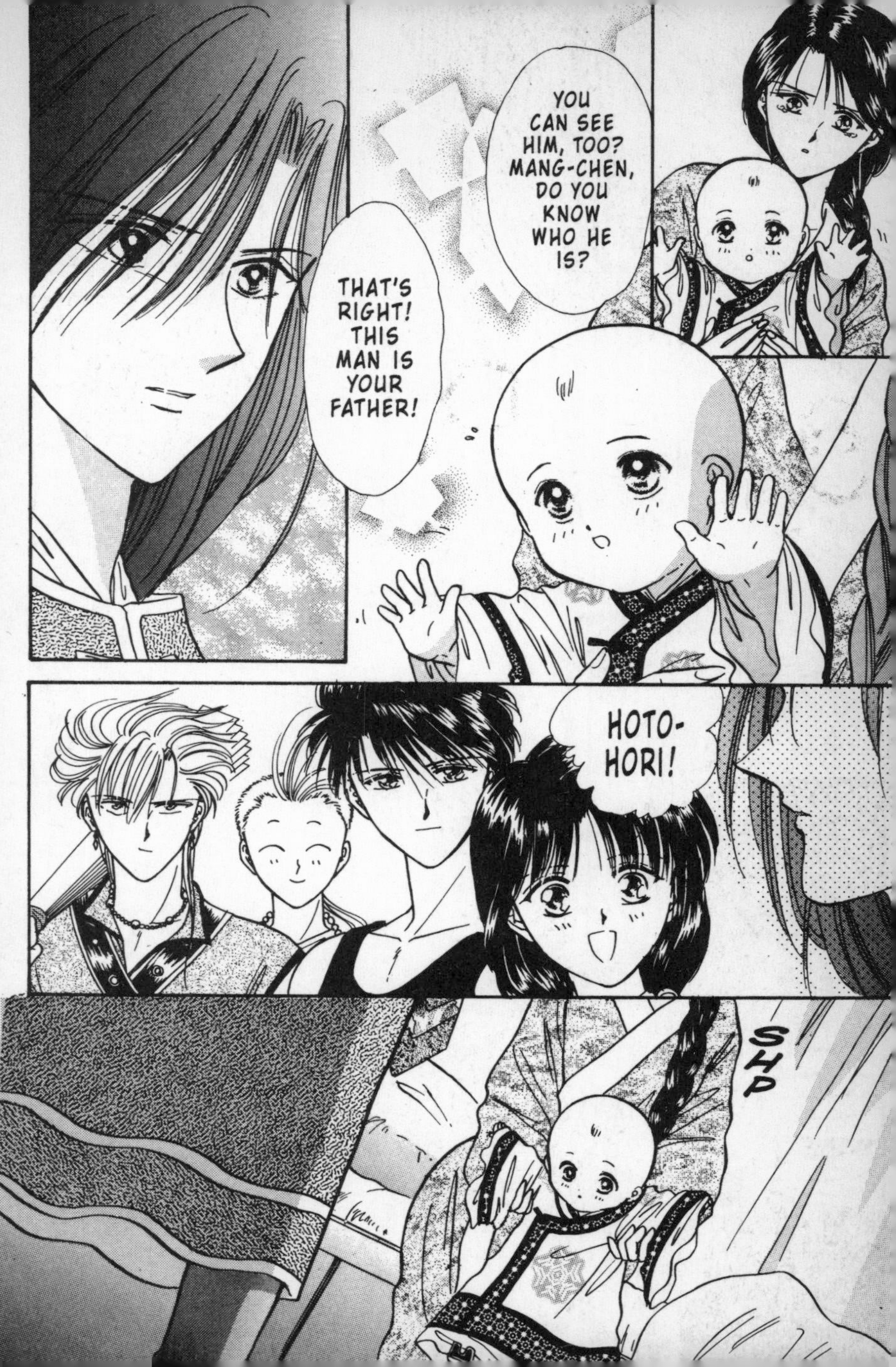
YOU CAN SEE HIM, TOO? MANG-CHEN, DO YOU KNOW WHO HE IS?
THAT'S RIGHT! THIS MAN IS YOUR FATHER!
HOTO-HORI!
SHP

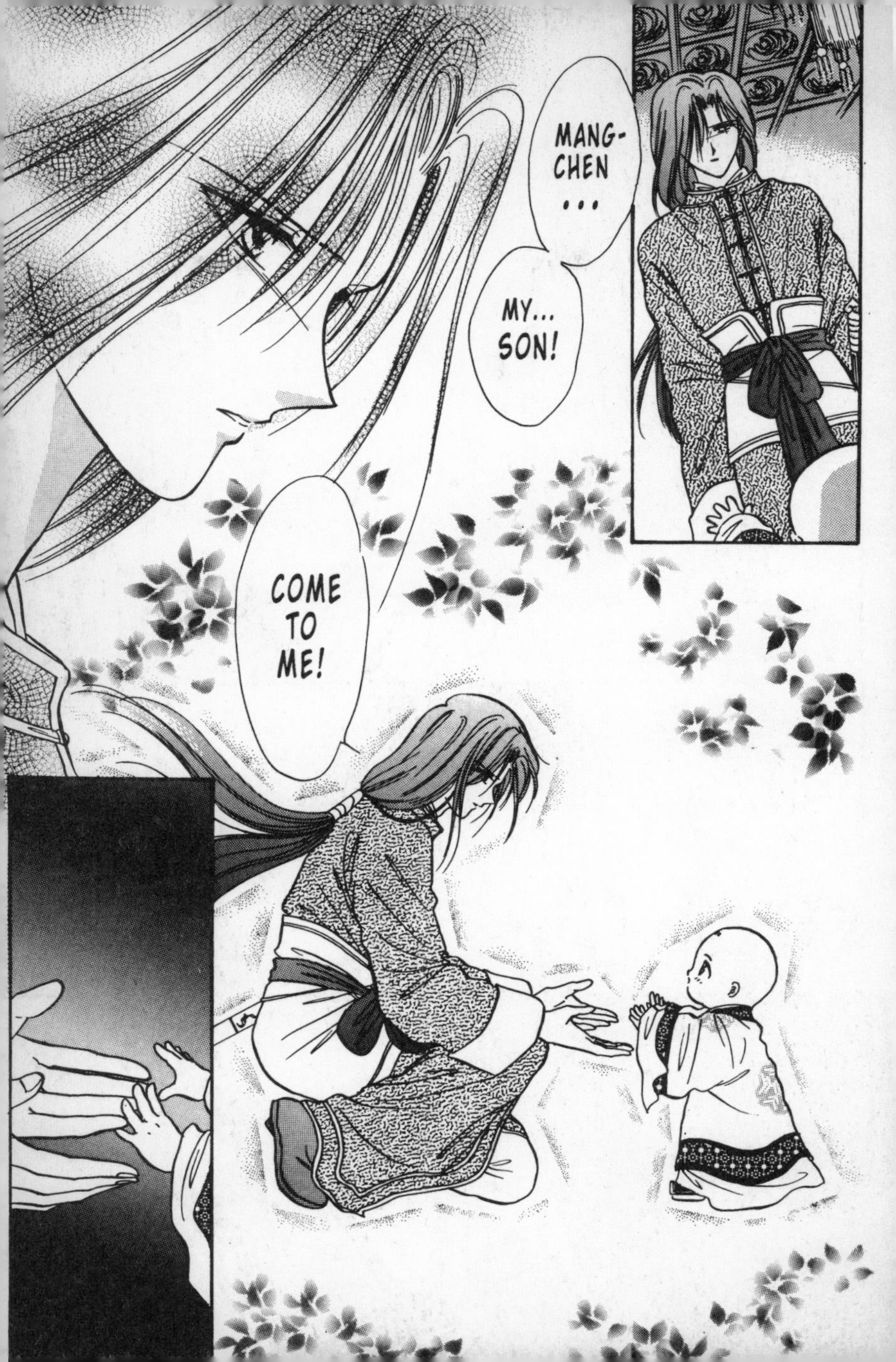
MANG-CHEN ...
MY... SON!
COME TO ME!

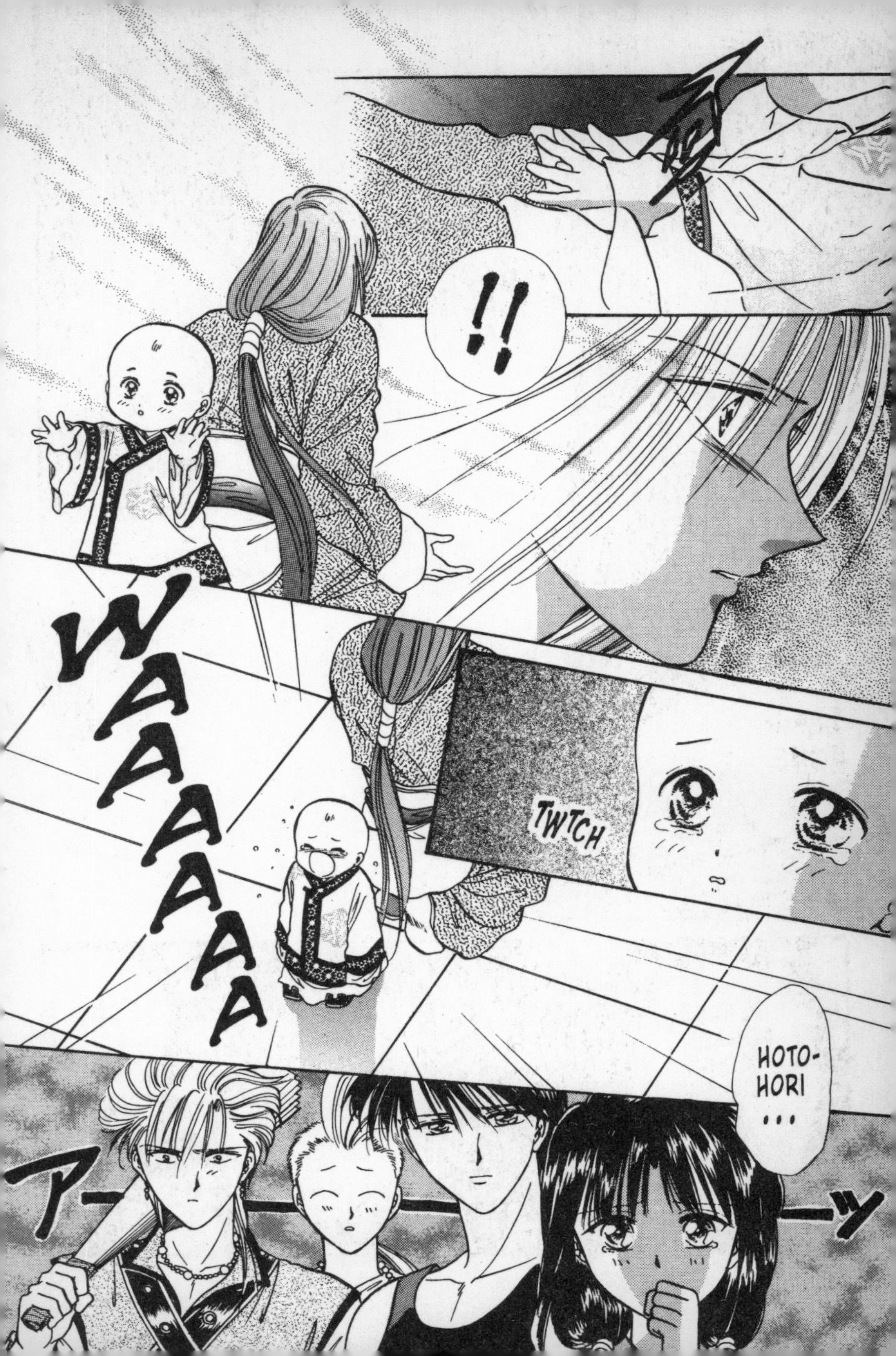
!!
TWITCH
WAAAAAA
HOTO-HORI...
アーーッ

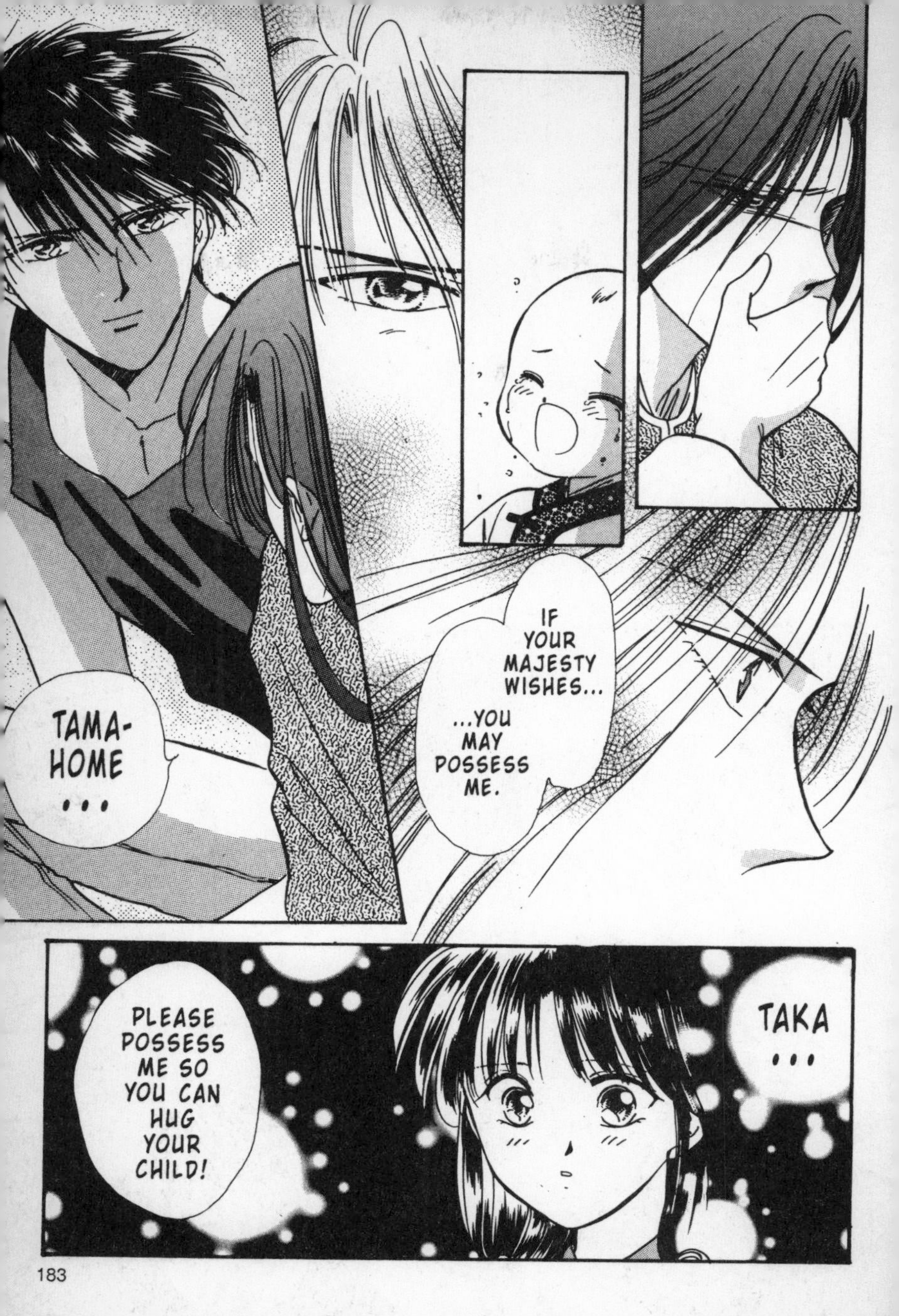
IF YOUR MAJESTY WISHES...
...YOU MAY POSSESS ME.
TAMA-HOME...
TAKA...
PLEASE POSSESS ME SO YOU CAN HUG YOUR CHILD!

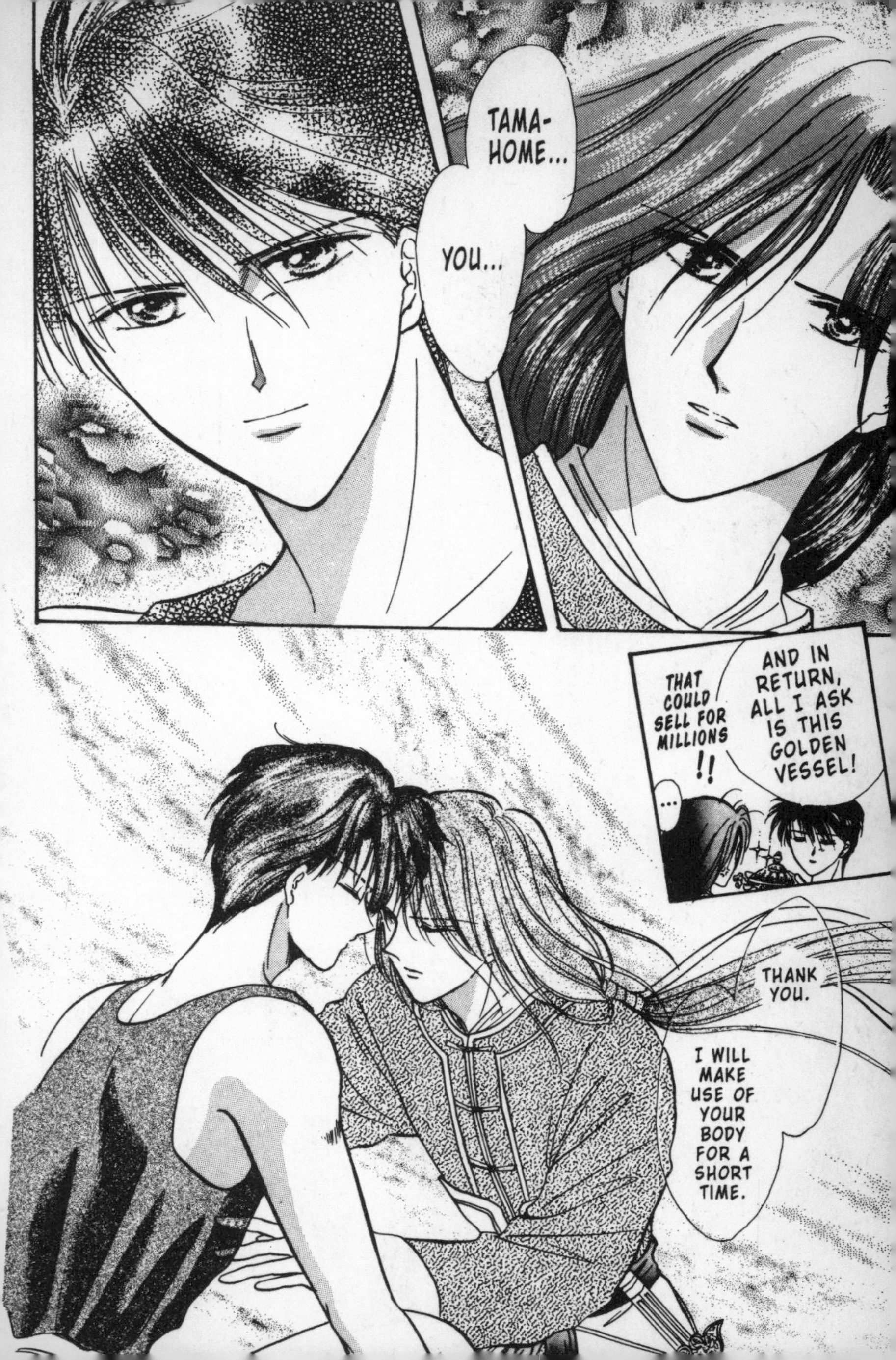
TAMA-HOME...
YOU...
AND IN RETURN, ALL I ASK IS THIS GOLDEN VESSEL!
THAT COULD SELL FOR MILLIONS !!
...
THANK YOU.
I WILL MAKE USE OF YOUR BODY FOR A SHORT TIME.

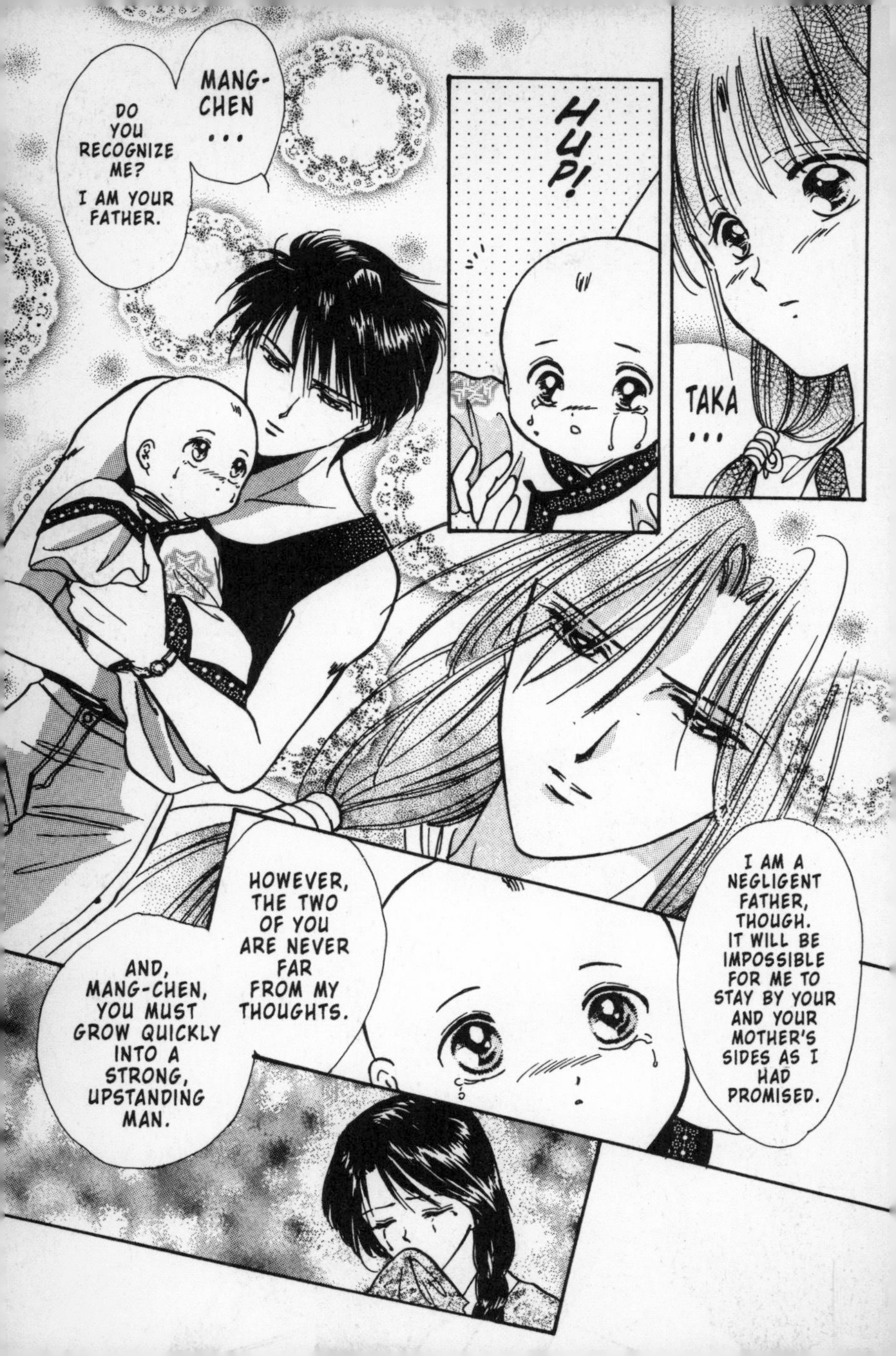

TAKA ...
HUP!
MANG-CHEN ...
DO YOU RECOGNIZE ME? I AM YOUR FATHER.
I AM A NEGLIGENT FATHER, THOUGH. IT WILL BE IMPOSSIBLE FOR ME TO STAY BY YOUR AND YOUR MOTHER'S SIDES AS I HAD PROMISED.
HOWEVER, THE TWO OF YOU ARE NEVER FAR FROM MY THOUGHTS.
AND, MANG-CHEN, YOU MUST GROW QUICKLY INTO A STRONG, UPSTANDING MAN.

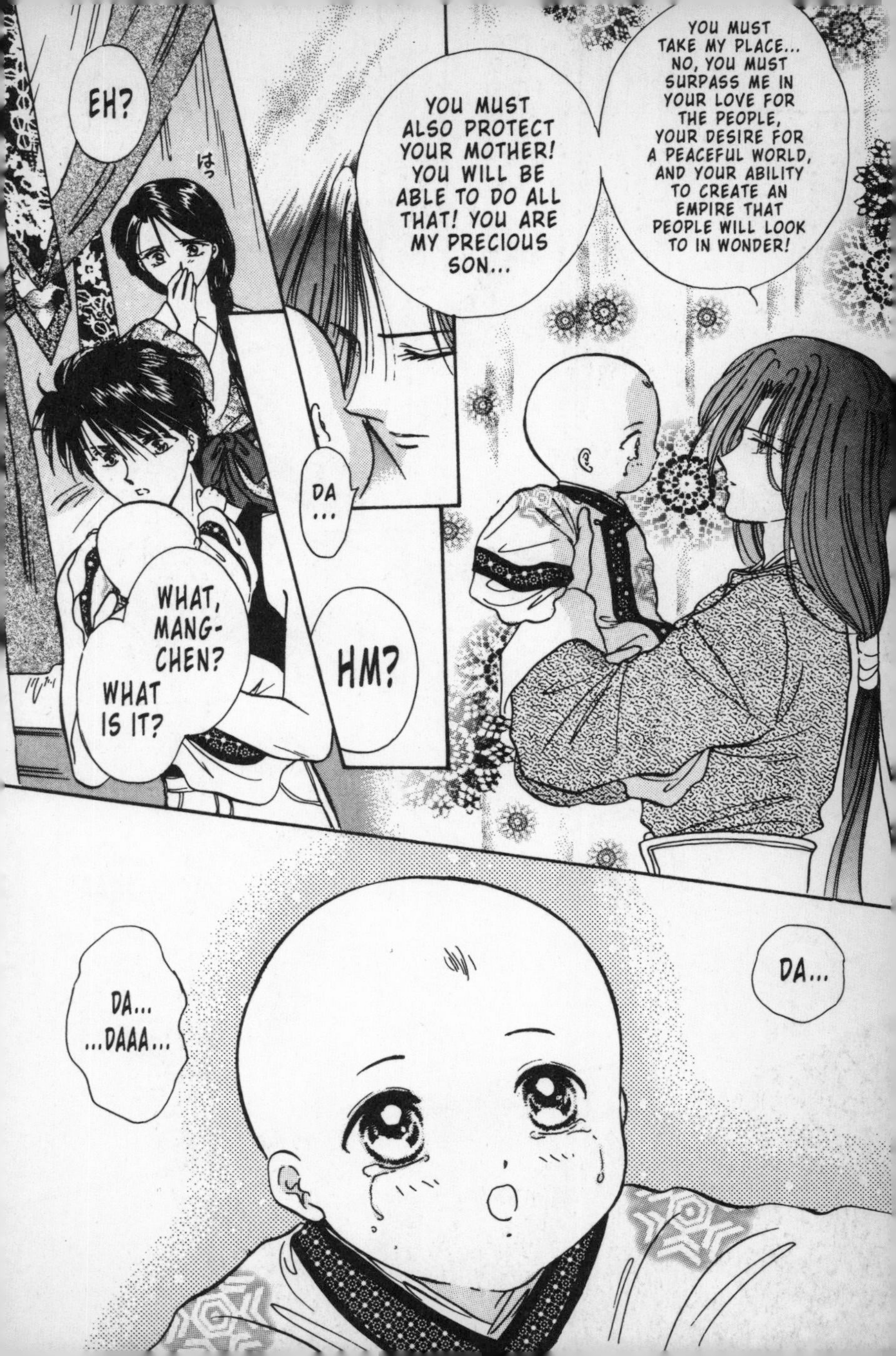
YOU MUST TAKE MY PLACE... NO, YOU MUST SURPASS ME IN YOUR LOVE FOR THE PEOPLE, YOUR DESIRE FOR A PEACEFUL WORLD, AND YOUR ABILITY TO CREATE AN EMPIRE THAT PEOPLE WILL LOOK TO IN WONDER!
YOU MUST ALSO PROTECT YOUR MOTHER! YOU WILL BE ABLE TO DO ALL THAT! YOU ARE MY PRECIOUS SON...
DA ...
HM?
EH?
はっ
WHAT, MANG-CHEN? WHAT IS IT?
DA...
DA... ...DAAA...

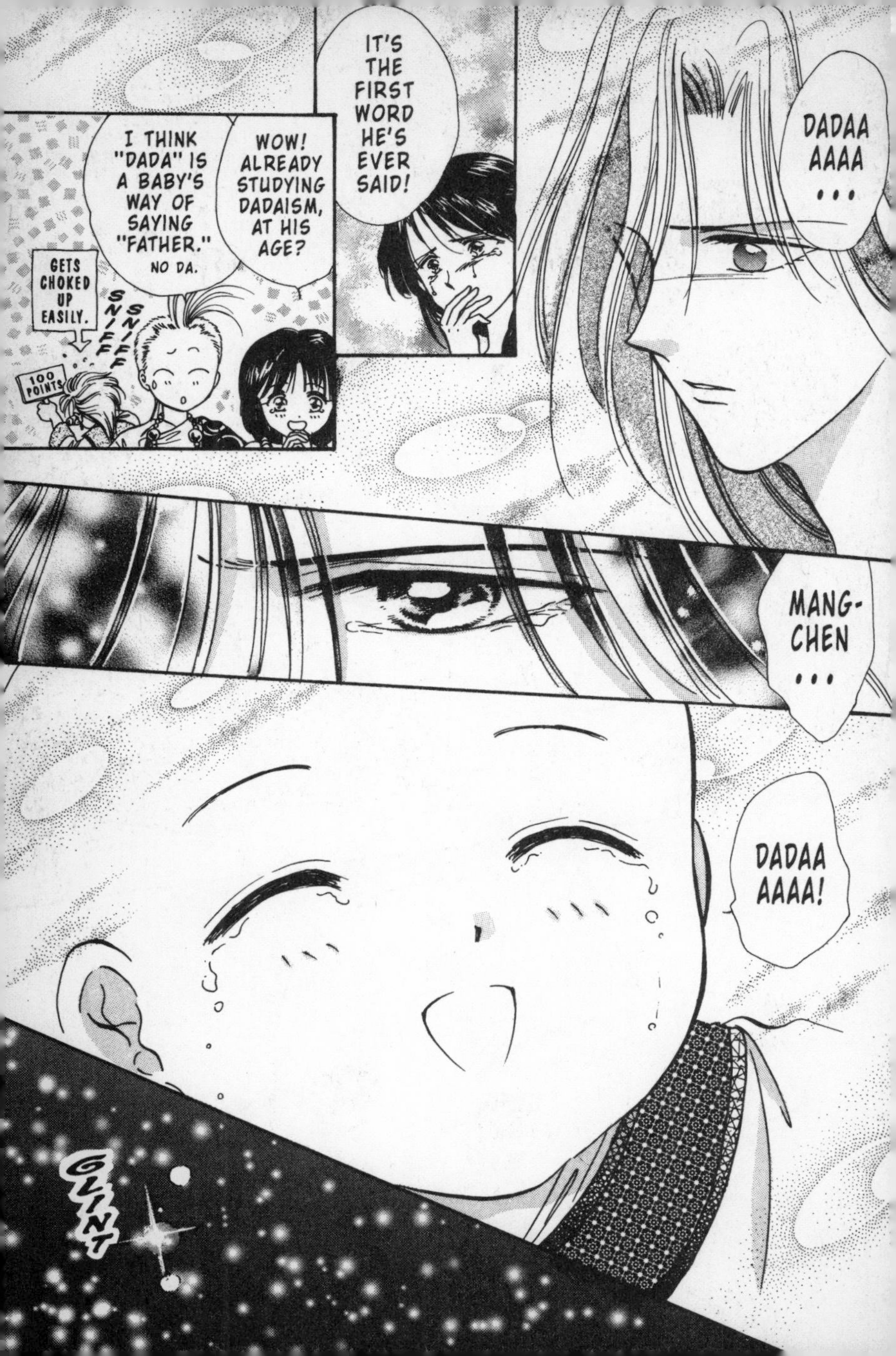
DADAA AAAA ...
IT'S THE FIRST WORD HE'S EVER SAID!
WOW! ALREADY STUDYING DADAISM, AT HIS AGE?
I THINK "DADA" IS A BABY'S WAY OF SAYING "FATHER."
NO DA.
SNIFF SNIFF
GETS CHOKED UP EASILY.
100 POINTS
MANG-CHEN ...
DADAA AAAA!
GLINT

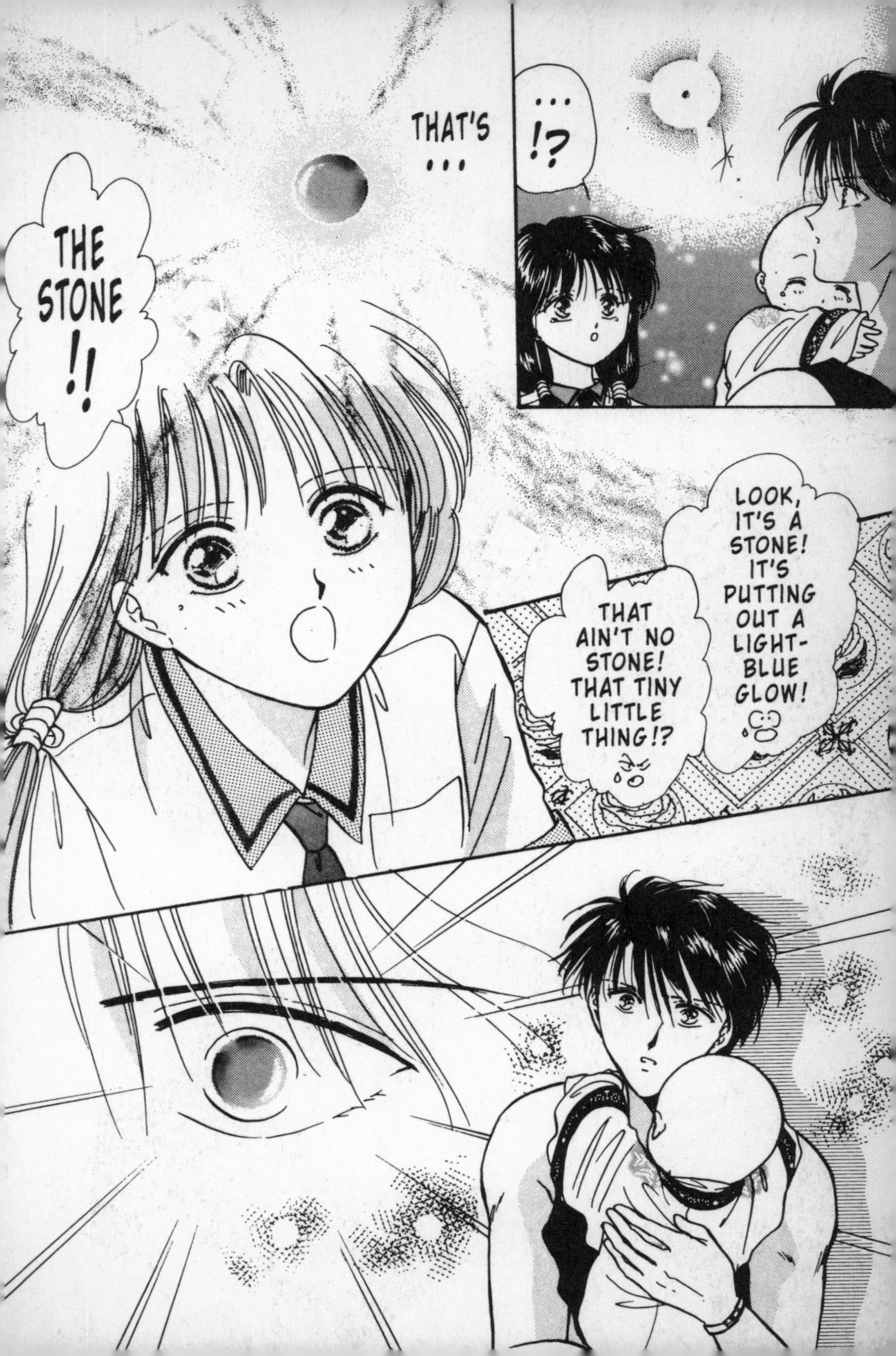
...!?
LOOK, IT'S A STONE! IT'S PUTTING OUT A LIGHT-BLUE GLOW!
THAT AIN'T NO STONE! THAT TINY LITTLE THING!?
THAT'S ...
THE STONE!!

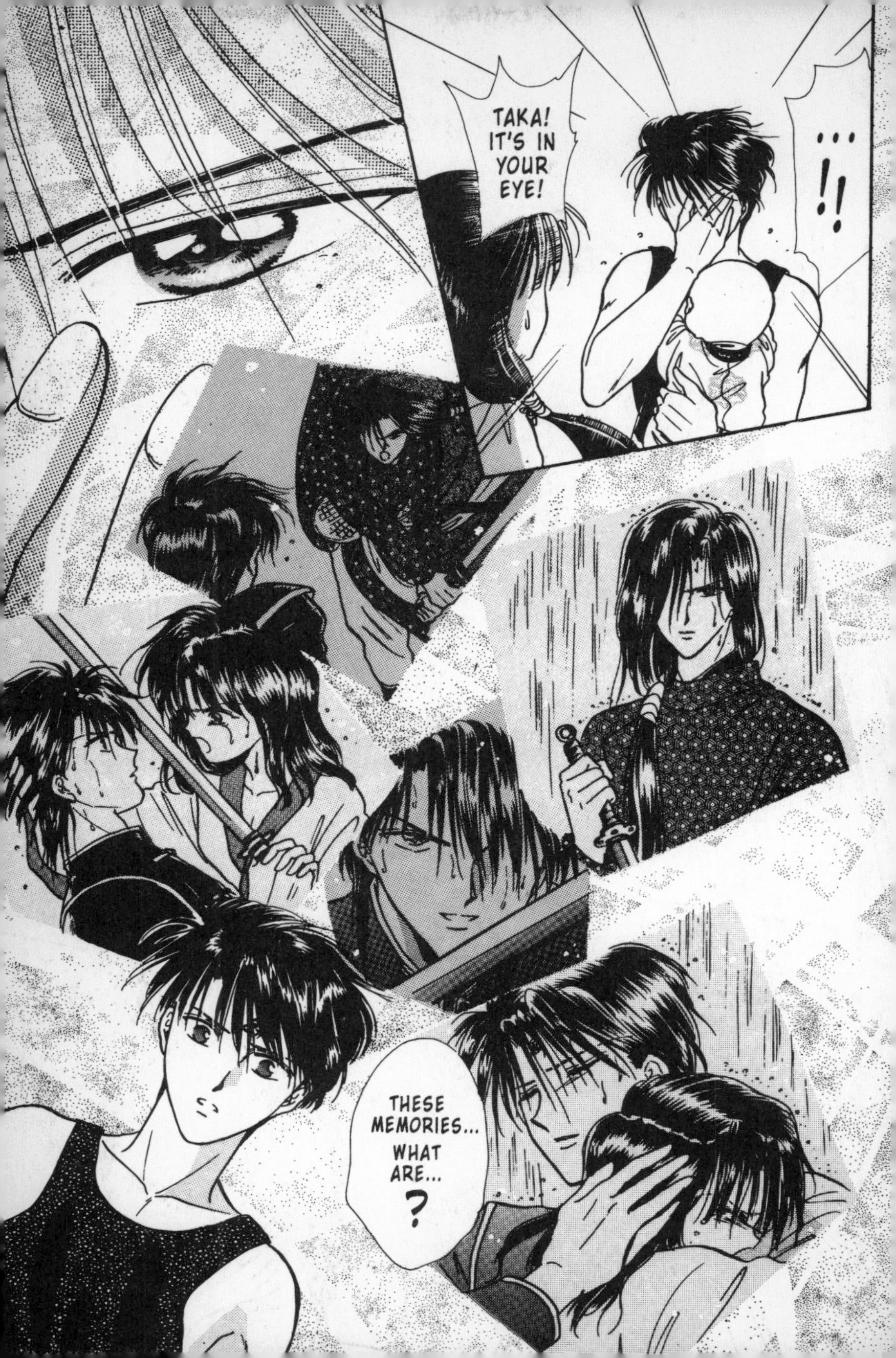
...!!
TAKA! IT'S IN YOUR EYE!
THESE MEMORIES... WHAT ARE...?

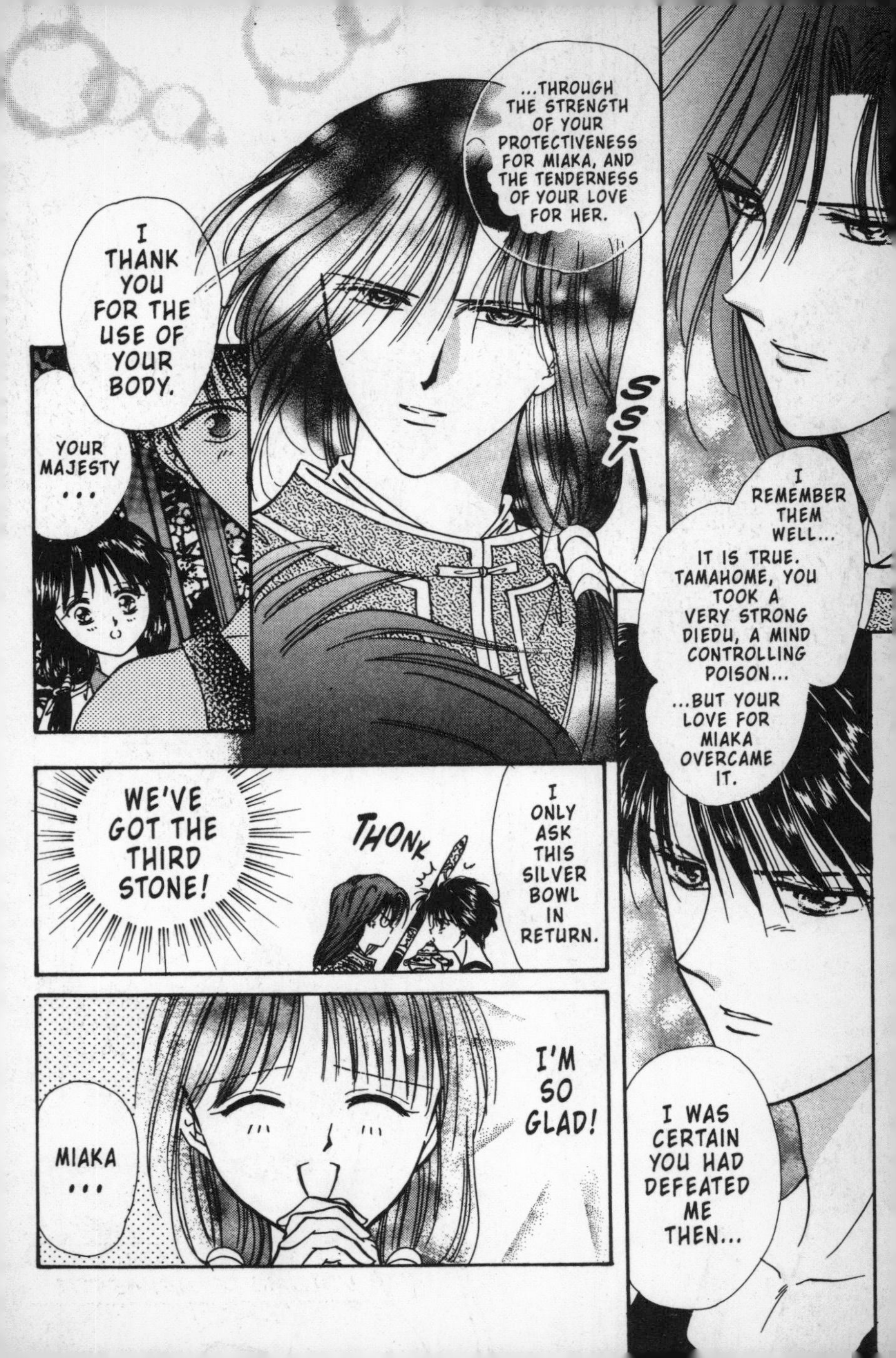

I REMEMBER THEM WELL...
IT IS TRUE. TAMAHOME, YOU TOOK A VERY STRONG DIEDU, A MIND CONTROLLING POISON...
...BUT YOUR LOVE FOR MIAKA OVERCAME IT.
I WAS CERTAIN YOU HAD DEFEATED ME THEN...
...THROUGH THE STRENGTH OF YOUR PROTECTIVENESS FOR MIAKA, AND THE TENDERNESS OF YOUR LOVE FOR HER.
SST
I THANK YOU FOR THE USE OF YOUR BODY.
YOUR MAJESTY...
I ONLY ASK THIS SILVER BOWL IN RETURN.
THONK
WE'VE GOT THE THIRD STONE!
I'M SO GLAD!
MIAKA...

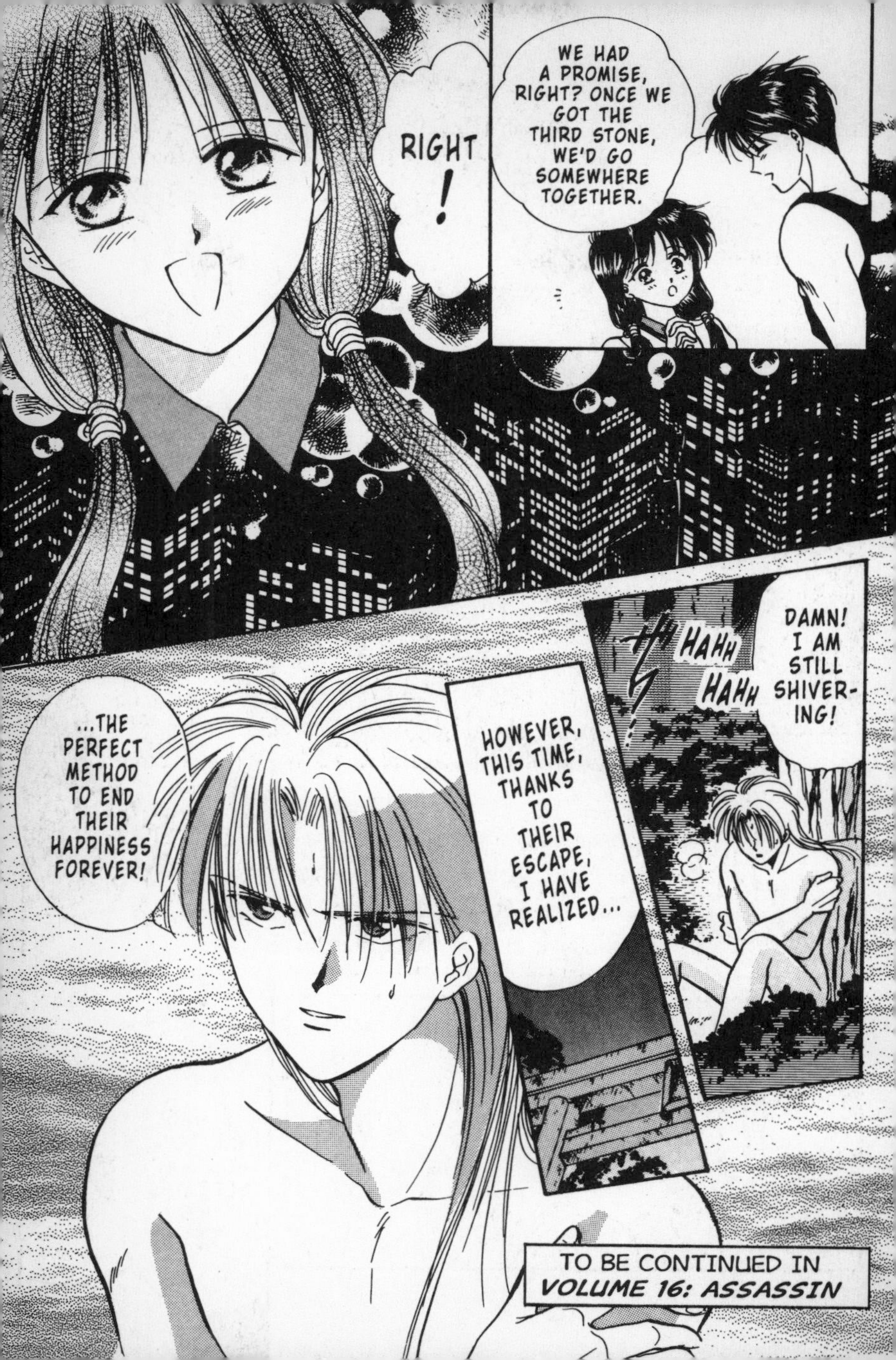
WE HAD A PROMISE, RIGHT? ONCE WE GOT THE THIRD STONE, WE'D GO SOMEWHERE TOGETHER.
RIGHT!
HAHH HAHH
DAMN! I AM STILL SHIVER-ING!
HOWEVER, THIS TIME, THANKS TO THEIR ESCAPE, I HAVE REALIZED...
...THE PERFECT METHOD TO END THEIR HAPPINESS FOREVER!
TO BE CONTINUED IN VOLUME 16: ASSASSIN

ABOUT THE AUTHOR

Yuu Watase was born on March 5 in a town near Osaka, Japan, and she was raised there before moving to Tokyo to follow her dream of creating manga. In the decade since her debut short story, *PAJAMA DE OJAMA* ("An Intrusion in Pajamas"), she has produced more than 50 compiled volumes of short stories and continuing series. Her latest work, *ZETTAI KARESHI* ("Absolute Boyfriend"), has recently completed its run in Japan in the anthology magazine *SHŌJO COMIC*. Watase's other beloved series *CERES: CELESTIAL LEGEND*, *IMADOKI! (NOWADAYS)*, and *ALICE 19TH* are now available in North America in English editions published by VIZ.

The Fushigi Yûgi Guide to Sound Effects

Most of the sound effects in FUSHIGI YÛGI are the way Yuu Watase created them, in their original Japanese.

We created this glossary for a page-by-page, panel-by-panel explanation of the action and background noises. By using this guide, you may even learn some Japanese.

The glossary lists page and panel number. For example, page 1, panel 3, would be listed as 1.3.

31.4 FX: HA (surprise)
32.3 FX: BASA (sudden movement)
33.1 FX: BORO BORO BORO (tears falling)
33.1 FX: KYU (jerking)
33.2 FX: SAWA (rustle)
33.5 FX: PISHA (a tear falling)
33.6 FX: HA (surprise)

CHAPTER EIGHTY-FOUR: THE YOUNG SORCERER

36.1 FX: GURURURURU (growling)
37.2 FX: BAN (door opening)
38.1 FX: GURURURURU (growling)
39.1 FX: HYOOOOOO (wind)
39.1 FX: GURURURURU (growling)
39.2 FX: VOOOOOO (roaring)
41.1 FX: DOKUN DOKUN (heavy heartbeats)
41.3 FX: DOKA (falling)
44.6 FX: PIII-POOO PIII-POOO PIII-POOO (sirens)
45.2 FX: PON (light tap)
48.5 FX: KAAAAN KOOOON (bell ringing)

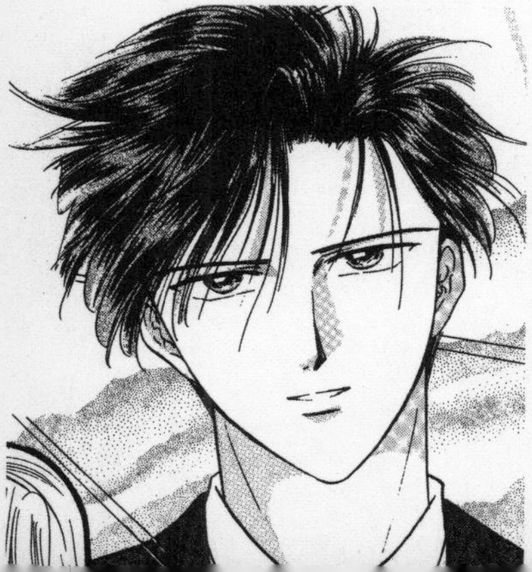

CHAPTER EIGHTY-THREE: THE GATHERING GLOOM

6.1 FX: KAAAN KOOON (dinng donng)
6.2 FX: WATA WATA (bustle bustle)
6.2 FX: WATA WATA (bustle bustle)
6.5 FX: NIKO (smile)
7.1 FX: GUI (grab)
7.3 FX: PERA PERA (speaking fluently)
7.4 FX: KAKI KAKI (quick writing)
8.1 FX: UIIIIIIIIIIN (high-pitched whine)
8.2 NOTE:In Japanese, her pun was "ankô," a sea toad.
8.4 FX: KACHA (latch opening)
9.2 FX: HA (sudden realization)
9.4 FX: GUOOOOO (roar)
10.2 FX: BA (throw)
10.5 FX: SHIN (silence)
11.5 FX: RRRRRR... (phone ringing)
12.2 FX: KYUN (chest tightening)
13.2 FX: KACHA (hanging up)
13.3 FX: GYU (hugging)
14.2 FX: DOTA (slump)
14.5 FX: DON (colliding)
16.5 FX: BYU (rushing air)
17.1 FX: BASHI (hitting)
17.4 FX: ZAWA (crowd noises)
18.3 FX: GU (surprise)
18.5 FX: KYAAA (happy screaming)
20.3 FX: DON (zooming in)
25.4 FX: GARA (rattle of a door)
30.1 FX: DOSA (hitting)
30.2 FX: BAN (banging)
30.3 FX: ZURU (sliding)
31.1 FX: FUUUU FUUUU (panting)
31.3 FX: BA (dramatic movement)

60.5 FX: DOKUN DOKUN DOKUN (heartbeats)
61.2 FX: DOKUN (heartbeat)
63.5 FX: PAKU PAKU (lips flapping)
64.2 FX: GA (grabbing)
64.5 FX: HYOOOOOO (wind)
65.1 FX: FUWA (weightlessness)
66.5-67.1 FX: BISHUN (flash)
67.2 FX: PASA (paper flapping)
68.1 FX: GON (bonk)
69.2 FX: HA (realization)
69.3 FX: BISHI BISHI BISHI (cracking sounds)
69.3-69.5 FX: ZUZUZUZUZU (rumbling)
69.4 FX: BISHI BISHI BISHI (cracking rocks)
71.2 FX: BISHI BISHI (rock cracking)
71.3 FX: DOON (shooting out)
72.1 FX: DOO (explosion)

CHAPTER EIGHTY-FIVE: THE SILENT CHILD

74.3 FX: DOBON (explosion)
75.1 FX: PASHAA (splashing)
75.1 FX: BATA (landing)
77.2 FX: NU (sudden appearance)
79.1 FX: SU (movement)
79.3 FX: IRA IRA (annoyance)
80.1 FX: SHAN (jingling)
81.4 FX: BAN (door noise)
82.2 FX: PI (awakening)
83.1 FX: ZA (weapons coming ready)
83.3 FX: JIIIIII (stare)
83.4 FX: ZAZAAAAAA (shocked movement)
85.5 FX: DOTA DOTA DOTA (running footfalls)
85.6 FX: DOKA (colliding)
86.1 FX: JIIIITO (sharp stabbing pain)
87.3 FX: SU (sudden appearance)
87.4 FX: DOKI DOKI DOKI (heartbeats)
87.4 FX: SUKA (hug)
87.6 FX: HA (sudden realization)
88.1 FX: DOO (explosion)
88.5 FX: SU (appearing)
89.3 FX: SU (disappearing)
89.4 FX: BACHI (electric-style shock)
90.1 FX: HA (realization)
90.2 FX: PAN (hitting the wall)
90.3 FX: PON PON (bouncing)

49.3 FX: NIKO (smile)
49.3 FX: NIKO (smile)
49.4 NOTE:Kyômoto's headband says "Shi-Hang Lian For President."
49.4 FX: HA (gasp)
50.2 FX: KYU (tightening)
50.3 FX: PARA PARA (trumpet)
50.3 FX: DON DOOON (drum)
50.5 FX: PYOKO (popping out)
50.6 FX: DO (stare)
51.4 NOTE:In Japanese, instead of "kiyoki" ("honest"), Miaka used the word "shioki" ("punishing").
51.4 FX: GON (hitting)
51.4 FX: BUHAAAA (going flat)
52.2 FX: SU (appearance)
52.3 FX: KYAAA (happy screaming)
52.3 FX: PACHI PACHI PACHI (clapping)
52.5 FX: PITA (sudden silence)
53.4 FX: SHIIN (silence)
53.5 FX: KATAN (chair rattling)
54.4 FX: WAA (roaring applause)
54.5 FX: PEKO (bow)
56.2 FX: JUUUUU (cooking noises)
56.4 FX: PAKU (gulp)
57.1 FX: GATAN (slapping her mouth)
57.3 FX: ZAWA (crowd noises)
57.4 FX: HA (surprise)
58.2 FX: PASHA PASHA (splashing)
58.3 FX: PASA (shaking wet hair)
59.1 FX: ZAWA (rustle)
59.2 FX: KACHA (hanging up)
59.5 FX: ZAWA ZAWA (rustling)
60.3 FX: GIKU (surprise)

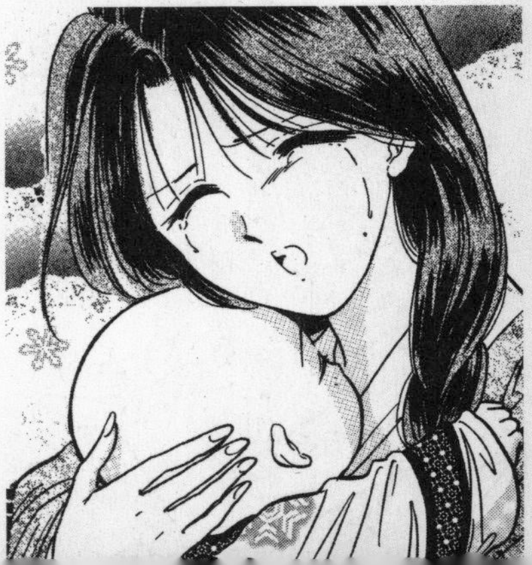

91.2 FX: HA (realization)
91.5 FX: GOO (wind roaring)
92.1 FX: ZA (slicing)
92.2 FX: HYUUUU (wind blowing)
93.1 FX: DOKUN DOKUN DOKUN (throbbing)
93.3 FX: DOKUN (throbbing)
93.5 FX: GUVAA (roaring)
94.2 FX: KA (flash of light)
94.3 FX: DON (internal explosion)
94.4 FX: BA (movement)
95.1 FX: KAAAAA (drawing sword)
95.2 FX: DOU (explosion)
95.2 FX: SU (smooth movement)
96.2 FX: DOSA (landing with a thud)
96.3 FX: GABA (getting up)
97.4 FX: BA (throwing open the door)
99.1 FX: GYU (hugging)
99.2 FX: JIIIN (stare)
101.2 FX: BASA BASA BASA BASA (wings flapping)
101.3 FX: SU (appearing)

CHAPTER EIGHTY-SIX: LAUGHTER FROM THE DARKNESS

103.1 FX: BASA BASA BASA (wings flapping)
103.2 FX: SHIIIIIN (silence)
103.5 FX: KATAAN (chair rattling)
104.1 FX: GA (grabbing)
105.3 FX: SU (appearance)
106.4 FX: SU (slight movement)
106.5 FX: BYUU (stabbing movement)
107.3 FX: BA (dramatic movement)
108.4 FX: SHU (quick movement)
109.4 FX: DOO (fiery explosion)
109.5 FX: FUWA (wafting on air)
109.6 FX: SUTA (a step)
110.1 FX: VOOOOOO (growling)
111.2-3 FX: KAAAAA (bright light)
112.1 FX: HA (sudden realization)
112.3 FX: FU (sudden disappearance)
112.5 FX: KA (flash of light)
114.4 FX: MUKU (looking up)
116.1 FX: ZAWA (rustling)
116.2 FX: VURURURURU (growling)
116.6 FX: GASA (rustle)
116.6 FX: VURURURU (growling)
117.2 FX: GORO GORO (purring)
117.5 FX: ZAWA ZAWA (crowd sounds)
120.4 FX: PACHI PACHI PACHI (clapping)
120.6 FX: SU (quietly opening)
122.5 FX: SU (movement)
124.1 FX: KA (blush)
124.2 FX: PASHI (hit)
125.5 FX: BYUUUUUU (approaching energy)
126.1 FX: PAN (explosion)
128.2 FX: SU (movement)
128.4 FX: DA (running)
130.2 FX: HA (realization)
131.2 FX: GU GU (pressing down)

CHAPTER EIGHTY-SEVEN: A FEAST FOR PUPPETS

137.3 FX: SU (movement)
137.6 FX: SHU (throwing)
138.1 FX: SU (movement)
139.5 FX: SU (clothing sound)
140.1 FX: CHIIIIII (zipper sound)
140.4 FX: GU GU (struggling)
140.5 FX: BAN (explosive entry)
143.2 FX: KIIIIII (anger)
149.1 FX: HA (sudden realization)
151.4 FX: KYAAA (happy screaming)
151.4 FX: HISO HISO (whispering)
151.4 FX: KYA HA HA HA (laughter)
153.3 FX: GI (anger)
153.7 FX: ZAWA ZAWA (crowd noises)
154.1 FX: HISO HISO (whispering)
154.3 FX: GI (anger)

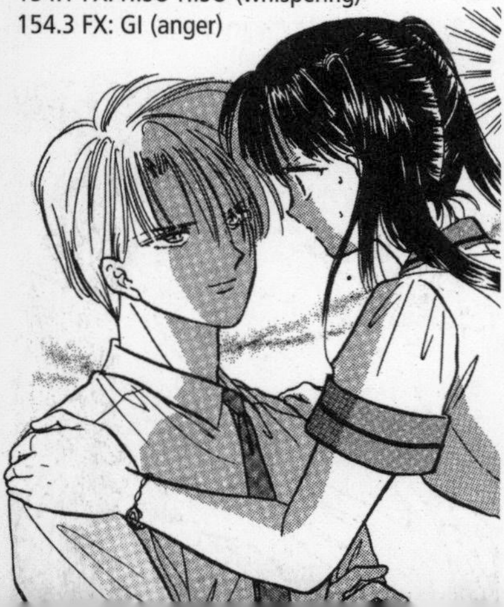

171.4 FX: SU (quiet movement)
171.5 FX: GA (grabbing)
172.1 FX: DOSA (hitting the ground)
172.2 FX: GII (pressing)
172.4 FX: BIKU (shock)
172.5 FX: BACHII (electric-style shock)
173.4 FX: VURURURURU (growling)
173.4 FX: TA (running off)
174.1 FX: GUCHU GUCHU (scrunching sounds)
174.5 FX: HAA HAA (heavy breathing)
175.1 FX: DOSU (thwack)
175.2 FX: PYUUU (blood spurting)
175.2 NOTE: This was a classic pun. Hotohori asks why Taka is so mean as to put a "stone" ("ishi") in his child's body. Taka answers that it wasn't by his "free will" ("ishi"). Tasuki's sign rates puns. Two points is a good score.
175.3 FX: ZUKI (pain)
176.1 FX: DOKUN DOKUN DOKUN (throbbing)
176.1 FX: DOKUN DOKUN (throbbing)
176.2 FX: DA (running)
176.3 FX: DOKUN DOKUN (throbbing)
176.3 FX: HA (surprise)
176.4 FX: DOKUN DOKUN (throbbing)
177.1 FX: BA (wind rushing)
177.5 FX: DOSU (stabbing)
178.1 FX: KAAAAAA (light)
178.3 FX: DO (explosion)
179.2 FX: FUWA (wafting)
179.2 NOTE: For those who don't know, Hotohori is using the famous words of Goemon from Lupin III, "Once again I cut a worthless object," and fashioning it more for his own personality.
182.1 FX: SU (passing through)
182.6 FX: AAAAAAA (crying)
186.4 FX: HA (emotional breath)
187.3 NOTE: In Japanese, Mang-Chen said "Chi...chi...e" which everyone but Miaka took as a child's version of "Chichi-ue," the word for Father. But because "Chichi" means breast and "e" means picture, Miaka took it to mean that he was talking about a picture of his mother's breast.
191.3 FX: ZAWA (rustling)

154.6 FX: KA (sudden embarrassment)
155.4 FX: GASA (rustling)
156.2 FX: SU (sudden appearance)
157.1 FX: BA (dramatic movement)
157.4 FX: GU (gulp)
158.3 FX: BA (dramatic movement)
159.4 FX: BA (dramatic movement)
160.5 FX: ZUZAZA (fighting sounds)
161.1 FX: DOSU (slam down)
161.2 FX: SA (moving in front)
161.4 FX: BYU (throwing)
162.1 FX: PASHI (catching)
162.2 FX: BA (dramatic movement)
162.3 FX: KA (flash of light)
163.2 FX: HA (surprise)

CHAPTER EIGHTY-EIGHT: SENTIMENTAL TEARS

166.1 FX: DOKUN DOKUN DOKUN (throbbing)
166.3 FX: DOKUN DOKUN DOKUN (throbbing)
166.4 FX: DOKUN DOKUN (throbbing)
168.1 FX: FUWA (light landing)
168.2 FX: HYOI (lifting)
168.3 FX: DA (running)
168.4 NOTE: The attack name translates to "Burning Fire: Crushing Dragon Attack!"
168.4 FX: DOO (flaming attack)
169.2 FX: DOO (explosive hit)
169.4 FX: DOKUN DOKUN (throbbing)
170.2 FX: GYU (hug)
170.6 FX: GUUU (blobbing out)

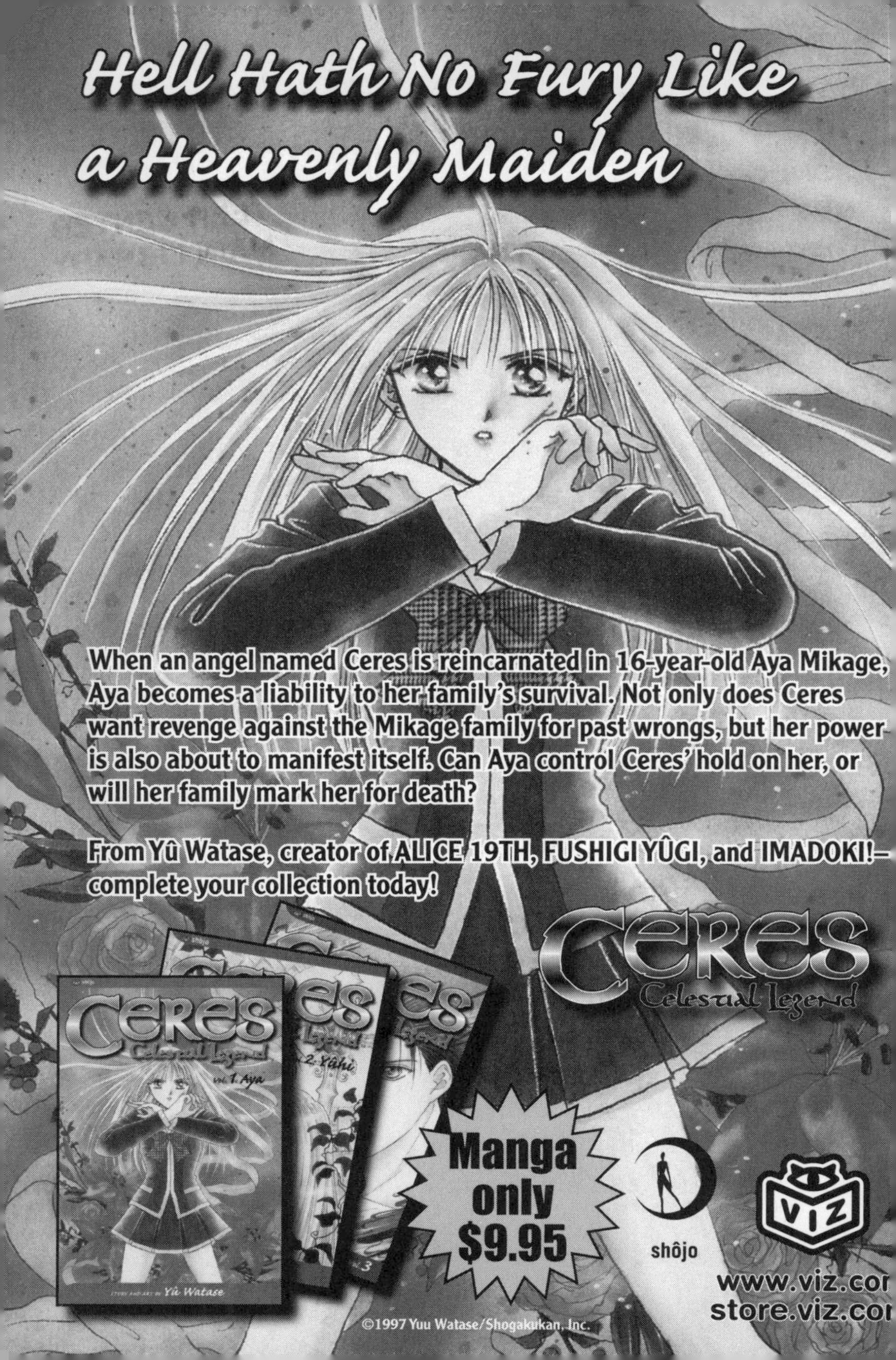
Hell Hath No Fury Like a Heavenly Maiden
When an angel named Ceres is reincarnated in 16-year-old Aya Mikage, Aya becomes a liability to her family's survival. Not only does Ceres want revenge against the Mikage family for past wrongs, but her power is also about to manifest itself. Can Aya control Ceres' hold on her, or will her family mark her for death?
From Yû Watase, creator of ALICE 19TH, FUSHIGI YÛGI, and IMADOKI!—complete your collection today!
Ceres
Celestial Legend
Ceres
Celestial Legend
vol. 1 Aya
Yû Watase
2 Yûhi
3
Manga only $9.95
shôjo
VIZ
www.viz.com
store.viz.com
©1997 Yuu Watase/Shogakukan, Inc.